A CONCISE HISTORY OF
EUROPEAN MONETARY
INTEGRATION

A CONCISE HISTORY OF EUROPEAN MONETARY INTEGRATION

From EPU to EMU

Horst Ungerer

Q

QUORUM BOOKS
Westport, Connecticut • London

Library of Congress Cataloging-in-Publication Data

Ungerer, Horst.
    A concise history of European monetary integration : from EPU to
EMU / Horst Ungerer.
        p.   cm.
    Includes bibliographical references and index.
    ISBN 0–89930–981–X (alk. paper)
    1. Monetary policy—European Economic Community countries.
2. Monetary policy—European Union countries. 3. Money—European
Economic Community countries. 4. Money—European Union countries.
I. Title.
HG930.5.U47   1997
332.4'94—dc21   96–50079

British Library Cataloguing in Publication Data is available.

Library of Congress Catalog Card Number: 96–50079
ISBN: 0–89930–981–X

First published in 1997

Quorum Books, 88 Post Road West, Westport, CT 06881
An imprint of Greenwood Publishing Group, Inc.

Printed in the United States of America

The paper used in this book complies with the
Permanent Paper Standard issued by the National
Information Standards Organization (Z39.48–1984).

10 9 8 7 6 5 4 3 2 1

Contents

Preface

This book grew out of lectures on the history of European monetary integration that I presented at universities and other academic institutions in the United States and in Europe over the past few years. When it came to making reading suggestions, I realized that there was hardly a single book covering developments from the end of World War II to the present in a comprehensive, yet concise and accessible, way. With this book, I try to close that gap.

More than 30 years of service in the Deutsche Bundesbank and the International Monetary Fund allowed me to witness and to become involved in many phases of European monetary integration and accorded me the privilege of meeting many of the principal actors. While I have been "pro-European" since my days in school and at university — no doubt strongly affected by my own war experience — my attitude on European monetary integration has been influenced greatly by working for those financially conservative institutions.

In addition to the many highly informative, and often groundbreaking, official reports and documents, there exists a plethora of excellent books, articles, and conference papers on European monetary integration, and I feel deeply indebted to their authors, many of whom I got to know personally over the years. In this book, I attempt to provide a concise history of European monetary integration that focuses on policy and institutional developments over the past 50 years — from the European Payments Union to the present efforts to turn the Maastricht blueprint for an economic and monetary union in Europe into reality. Moreover, the book

examines key economic-analytical issues and, when necessary, casts its
net beyond Europe, putting European monetary matters in an international context. In a way, it is also a history of concepts and ideas that provided the intellectual foundations for European monetary integration,
arguably one of the most interesting, yet technically complex, subjects in
modern economic history. On a limited scale, it may serve as a compendium on European monetary integration.

My book is directed at students and scholars of economics, political sci-
ences, international law, business administration, and history in the academic world as well as people in government, international business and
finance, and the press who want or need to know more about the main
issues and facts of European monetary integration. In the selection of
style and sources, a deliberate attempt has been made to be user-friendly.
Many of the cited sources have extensive bibliographies, inviting the
reader who is interested in a certain phase or a particular issue of European monetary integration to explore the more specialized literature, with
the prospect of a frequently fascinating journey.

Charles Kindleberger, in the foreword to the first edition of his seminal
book *A Financial History of Western Europe* (1984), wrote: "Some years ago
I reviewed a book with a broad overview of economic history and concluded that the author was superficial on everything I knew well but very
good on what I did not. This finally struck me as a compliment, and I
hope to do as well." And so do I.

I owe thanks to many people, mostly former colleagues and many of
them friends. I am particularly grateful to Karl F. Habermeier, Stephen
Overturf, and Hari Vittas, who went through the whole draft, and Wolfgang Rieke, who read several of the key chapters; they provided numerous and invaluable comments. For many helpful suggestions on individual chapters, I am indebted to Tamim Bayoumi, Margaret Garritsen de
Vries, Hans W. Gerhard, Julius Rosenblatt, Robert Solomon, and Werner
Ungerer (who happens to be my brother). For further assistance, I thank
Susan Becker, Peter Bekx, Patrick de Fontenay, and Bernd Goos. Many
more in the International Monetary Fund, in national central banks and
finance ministries, in the European Commission, and at the universities I
visited cannot be listed individually. In discussions and by working
together on specific projects, they helped me to develop my own views
and insights. Needless to say, all remaining errors are mine. I also want to
express my appreciation to Eric Valentine of Quorum Books, who guided
this book from the beginning to its publication.

I owe a particular debt of gratitude to Günther Schleiminger for sur-
veying important sections of the book. More importantly, after having
met in 1957 at the German delegation to the Organization for European
Economic Cooperation in Paris, he persuaded me, following my four-
month postdoctorate "sabbatical" in Aix-en-Provence and Cannes in the

summer of 1959, to join the Bundesbank and initiated me into the mysteries as well as the real-life experiences of European and international monetary affairs.

Finally, special thanks to my stepson, Daniel Kolak, and particularly warm thanks to my wife, Rajka, to whom this book is dedicated. Both encouraged me to start and keep writing this book, when at times I would have preferred to play "European masters" on the keyboards of my piano and harpsichord.

Acronyms

BIS	Bank for International Settlements
BWS	Bretton Woods system
CAP	Common Agricultural Policy
CLM	Community Loan Mechanism
COREPER	Comité des représentants permanents (Committee of Permanent Representatives)
CPI	consumer price index
CRU	collective reserve unit
DM	Deutsche mark
EAEC	European Atomic Energy Community
EC	European Community
ECB	European Central Bank
ECOFIN	economics and finance ministers
ECSC	European Coal and Steel Community
ECU	European Currency Unit
EEA	European Economic Area
EEC	European Economic Community
EFTA	European Free Trade Association
EMA	European Monetary Agreement
EMCF	European Monetary Cooperation Fund
EMF	European Monetary Fund
EMI	European Monetary Institute
EMS	European Monetary System
EMU	economic and monetary union

EMUA	European Monetary Unit of Account
EPU	European Payments Union
ERM	exchange rate mechanism
	exchange rate and intervention mechanism
ERP	European Recovery Program
ESCB	European System of Central Banks
EU	European Union
EUA	European Unit of Account
Euratom	European Atomic Energy Community
FECOM	Fonds européen de coopération monétaire (European Monetary Cooperation Fund)
G-10	Group of 10
GAB	General Arrangements to Borrow
GATT	General Agreement on Tariffs and Trade
GDP	gross domestic product
IBRD	International Bank for Reconstruction and Development
IDA	International Development Association
IFC	International Finance Corporation
IGC	Intergovernmental Conference
IMF	International Monetary Fund
ITO	International Trade Organization
MCA	monetary compensatory amount
MIGA	Multilateral Investment Guarantee Agency
MTFA	Medium-Term Financial Assistance
OCA	optimum currency area
OECD	Organization for Economic Cooperation and Development
OEEC	Organization for European Economic Cooperation
SDR	Special Drawing Rights
STMS	Short-Term Monetary Support
TARGET	Trans-European Automated Real-Time Gross Settlement Express Transfer System
UK	United Kingdom
UN	United Nations
VAT	value-added tax
VSTF	very short-term financing facility

Introduction

The quest for monetary integration has been one of the main political dramas played out on the European stage since the end of World War II: from the European Payments Union (EPU) to the goal of an economic and monetary union (EMU), expected to become a reality by the end of this century. Yet, the basic challenges have remained the same: to make a regime of stable and ultimately irrevocably fixed exchange rates compatible with economic policies that remain, to a large extent, under the sovereignty of individual countries and to create a framework for a common monetary policy so as to promote monetary and financial stability.

The history of European monetary integration is a sequence of actions and events as well as the unfolding of concepts and ideas. From the start, there never could be any doubt that monetary integration was an issue of great political importance, involving the merging of sovereignty in a vital area of modern political life. Indeed, it has been seen by many as an important step to, if not a promotor of, political unification. At the same time, the institutional and operational aspects of European monetary integration have been issues of such complexity and significance that they have attracted not only close scrutiny in many official documents and meetings of experts but also wide attention in a large body of academic literature.

Often, this analytical work has been conducted without regard to political issues and historical developments. Yet, European monetary integration — problems as well as solutions — cannot be fully understood without looking at the political forces behind it and placing it in its historical context. The building blocks of monetary union did not emerge out of the blue; they have been assembled over long periods of trial and error — sometimes at the cost of painful experiences — and as the fruits of intense (and, more often than not, inspired) debates. Well-known documents (including the Werner Report, the European Council resolution on the European Monetary System [EMS], and the Delors Report) and also lesser known contributions (such as the Barre Memorandum, the Schiller Plan, the Fourcade and Duisenberg proposals, and the various treaty drafts in preparation for the Intergovernmental Conference of 1990–91) as well as the writings of eminent policy practitioners and academics have shaped the debates and developments that culminated in the Maastricht blueprint for EMU.

European unification has been one of the principal political concerns in Western Europe since the end of World War II. Its objective has been to end centuries of political rivalry and strife between countries with a shared culture and tradition, to enable them to build and maintain democratic societies, to reconstruct their war-torn economies, and to foster economic growth and the wealth of their people. The main goal as well as the most important means of European unification has been to further economic integration. Monetary integration always has been an integral part of these efforts, and a single European currency has been viewed as indispensable for full economic integration.[1]

On the question of how to best promote monetary integration, an ideological debate developed — alive to this very day — between the "economists" and the "monetarists." The economists argued that a European currency could come only at the end as a crowning achievement of the integration process, once a high degree of economic convergence had been achieved. By contrast, the monetarists (not to be confused with Milton Friedman's brand of monetarism) held that, by setting up institutional arrangements in the monetary sphere (e.g., mutual credit facilities or a common exchange rate system), convergence would follow and the integration process would receive vital impulses, thus, gaining the necessary momentum for its ultimate success. At different times, the two strategies greatly influenced intermediate goals and methods of monetary integration. In hindsight, one could say that progress would hardly have been made without the monetarist approach and would not have been sustained without the economist approach.

The backdrop for developments in Europe were the plans for a new global economic and monetary order as put forward in the final years of World War II and embodied in the International Monetary Fund, the World Bank, and the General Agreement on Tariffs and Trade. It soon was recognized, however, that the task of rebuilding the economies of Europe had to be tackled on a regional basis. It was the Marshall Plan of the United States, providing financial support to Europe, that spearheaded economic and monetary integration in Europe after World War II.[2] The newly established Organization for European Economic Cooperation and the EPU, encompassing all European countries outside the sphere of Soviet domination, were instrumental in the liberalization of trade and payments in Europe, the prerequisite for the economic recovery of Europe. The accomplishments of the Organization for European Economic Cooperation and EPU paved the way to further advances in economic and monetary integration.

The European integration process acquired a strong political dimension when the six countries in the heart of "free" Europe (Belgium, France, Germany,[3] Italy, Luxembourg, and the Netherlands) founded in the 1950s the European Communities (later to be called the European Community [EC]). It began with the European Coal and Steel Community of 1951 in a confined but economically and politically important sector. The European Coal and Steel Community was supposed to be followed by a European Defense Community and a European Political Community, but concerns about a loss of national sovereignty — most strongly raised in France — led to the abandonment of those plans. After this setback, the six countries focused on the economic aspects of European integration. The result were the Treaties of Rome of 1957, creating the European Economic Community and the European Atomic Energy Community (Euratom). Nevertheless, the idea of political unification was inherent in the objectives and design of the European Communities.[4]

After the establishment of the customs union and the implementation of a Common Agricultural Policy by the end of the 1960s, the EC concentrated on expanding membership — Denmark, Ireland, and the United Kingdom joined in 1973 — and achieving closer economic and monetary policy cooperation in an effort to underpin the achieved degree of "market integration" with "policy integration."[5] The Werner Report of 1970 proposed the gradual realization of an EMU over a ten-year period, encompassing a single currency and a single monetary policy as well as intensified cooperation in other areas of economic policy. However, the plans to create an EMU went off the track in the face of the breakdown of the Bretton Woods system of fixed, although adjustable, exchange rates and the impact of the oil crisis of 1973 but also because of the EC's failure to find a common policy response to these outside events. The common exchange rate system, the "snake" — an attempt to insulate the EC from the world-wide trend toward flexible exchange rates — although still valuable to its participants, soon lost its EC character as it shrank to a few countries.

In the 1970s, the international climate of high inflation and economic stagnation and the threat of retrogression in the already accomplished degree of integration within the EC led to a search for ways to further monetary integration. In 1979, the EMS — a cooperative arrangement that centered on the stabilization of intra-EC exchange rates — was set up. The achievements of the EMS in its first decade of operation encouraged efforts to complete the common market for goods, capital, and services as envisaged in the Single European Act of 1986, the first substantial revision of the European Economic Community Treaty. Yet, doubts emerged about whether the EMS could meet the economic and political challenges of a more integrated EC. Renewed initiatives for the creation of EMU led to the proposals of the Delors Committee and the convening of the Intergovernmental Conferences on EMU and political union at the end of 1990.

In December 1991, the European Council, composed of the Heads of State or Government of the EC countries, agreed in Maastricht on the Treaty on European Union, known also as the Maastricht Treaty. At its center is the commitment to realize EMU in three stages, to establish an independent European System of Central Banks, and to introduce a single European currency (now named "euro") by, at the latest, January 1, 1999. It also provides for closer cooperation in foreign and security policies. The severe crises of the EMS in 1992 and 1993, triggered by huge speculative international capital movements, cast a heavy shadow on those intentions. Yet, the will to move on with the realization of EMU persisted. As an important step, the European Monetary Institute was set up in 1994. It became the focus of preparations for the third and final stage of EMU.

Over the years, membership in the EC has grown from the original 6 to 15 countries with the accession, as noted, of Denmark, Ireland, and the United Kingdom in 1973; Greece in 1981; Portugal and Spain in 1986; and Austria, Finland, and Sweden in 1995. In the process, the EC became more "European," but at the same time, its diversity in economic structure and political background increased. More countries in the Mediterranean and in Central and Eastern Europe have applied for membership. As a consequence, the task to come to unified positions on economic as well as political issues has become increasingly difficult, a point that applies also to the area of monetary policy.

At this juncture, many uncertainties surround the future of the European Union (as the EC now is called). With regard to monetary integration, at issue is how many member states will succeed in achieving in time the degree of economic convergence that is judged necessary for first-round participation in the new currency area. Will EMU indeed be launched in 1999, or will economic and political difficulties cause a delay? The way in which EMU will function and how the more general issues of strengthening the EC's organizational structure and expanding its membership are resolved will determine the shape and the international role of the European Union in the next century.

From the start, the history of European monetary integration has been characterized by underlying and recurrent issues and themes that have flown from and influenced actual events. They have determined the debates and decisions on monetary integration. The controversy between the advocates of the monetarist and economist strategies already has been mentioned; we shall add a few more of the most important themes.

The nature of the exchange rate regime has been at the heart of international trade and financial relations at least since the time of the classical gold standard. In the 1960s, the prevailing thinking moved from the "naive" doctrine of fixed exchange rates (which, at the time, were considered the precondition for stable international economic relations and taken more or less for granted) to the doctrine of flexible rates. They were assumed to serve as a license for autonomous national policies while allowing the effects of national policy disparities on international economic relations to be neutralized. Yet, economic integration within the EC was seen as requiring highly stable exchange rates. With the EMS, an "enlightened" doctrine of fixed rates emerged that emphasized convergence of economic policies and developments and domestic adjustment as the means to achieve exchange rate stability, although the possibility of exchange rate adjustments was not discarded. However, in the early 1990s, stable exchange rates became ossified and were not sufficiently supported by lasting convergence. The notion of a seamless (and perhaps even painless) path to EMU became prevalent — a new doctrine, as it were — only to be shattered during the EMS crises of 1992 and 1993. Related to the question of the function of exchange rates in the integration process has been the issue of "asymmetry," that is, a perceived lack of balance in the burden of operating a common exchange rate system and the role of the anchor currency of the system.

Another recurrent theme has been the issue of national sovereignty and how it could be safeguarded in the face of European integration as well as global interdependence. To what degree does national sovereignty need to be transferred or surrendered in favor of joined or merged responsibilities for the sake of the optimal realization of a single European market and the smooth functioning of a single European currency? Of great importance in this context is the role of national economic (in particular, budgetary) policies and the move from voluntary and frequently ineffective to binding and effective coordination.

An important issue has been the role and structure of a European central monetary policy institution and its relations to other decision-making institutions on the national and the European level. What should be its primary objective, and how independent should it be in carrying out its tasks?

Another recurring issue has been the role the United Kingdom was willing to play in the process of monetary integration and its ability to influence the course.

A last major theme worth mentioning has been the place and influence of a European monetary entity in the global context. For a long time, the EC was compelled more to react to developments than to exercise influence or leadership. This was in part a result of the nature and magnitude of events that swept the international system, in part a consequence of its lack of cohesion. With a single European currency, this may change — that is, at least, the hope.

NOTES

1.   It may be helpful to try to delineate economic integration and monetary integration. Economic integration deals with various aspects of "real" economic activity, such as production, investment, employment, wage formation, and trade. In a wider sense, it often is understood to include the integration of financial markets, although, here, the borderline with monetary integration becomes somewhat blurred, and the term "financial integration" is used sometimes. On occasion (at some places also in this book), monetary integration is included in more general references to economic integration. More specifically, however, monetary integration can be defined as being concerned with domestic monetary developments, such as credit, interest rates, banking activities, and the like, as well as external issues, such as exchange rate regimes and policies, international payments arrangements, balance of payments financing, and international reserves. Also included are the organization of central banks and the availability of various policy instruments to them.

      The delineation of economic and monetary integration also helps to define the domains of economic policy on the one side and monetary policy on the other. It only needs to be added that the important area of fiscal and budgetary policies is often regarded as a part of economic policies. Some aspects of budgetary policies, however (in particular, the methods of deficit financing), are directly linked to monetary policy. Although monetary policy is primarily the domain of central banks, in a number of countries, and to a degree that differs from country to country, monetary policy decisions have been in the hands of governments.

2.   Generally, the term "Europe" refers to Western Europe, that is, the countries west of the former Iron Curtain.

3.   For most of this book, "Germany" refers to the Federal Republic of Germany as established in 1949, that is, before German unification in October 1990.

4.   For surveys of monetary integration since the establishment of the European Economic Community, see Lelart (1994) and Overturf (in press).

5.   An important distinction has been made between "market integration," such as trade liberalization, the convertibility of currencies, and the freedom of capital movements, and "policy integration," relating to various aspects of economic and monetary policies with which to underpin and guide market integration. In the integration process, there is always an intense interaction between market and policy integration. Policy integration has promoted market integration but also has been challenged by market integration, as most visibly demonstrated by various crises in international financial markets.

1

The Background: Gold Standard and Interwar Period

Before World War I, there existed a functioning world economic order with free trade and an international payments system without controls and restrictions.[1] Under the classical international gold standard, which operated from about 1880 to 1914, the main currencies were tied to each other at fixed exchange rates and were freely exchangeable. This system, although not quite as perfect as frequently described but, nevertheless, working reasonably well, came to an end in 1914 with the beginning of World War I and perished for good in the political turmoil and the disintegration of the world economy in the aftermath of the war. What followed was a period of economic nationalism, characterized by protectionism in trade and well-nigh chaotic international monetary relations. Attempts to reestablish an international system of free trade and to restore the gold standard were unsuccessful.

Without understanding the events before World War I and during the interwar period, one cannot fully comprehend and evaluate international economic and monetary developments after World War II, including the history of European monetary integration. This chapter, therefore, provides a summary description and analysis of the international gold standard and of the interwar period.

THE PRINCIPLES OF THE GOLD STANDARD

Based on the traditional view as presented in many textbooks, the model of the classical gold standard and the "rules of the game" can be described as follows:

In each country that adopted the gold standard, a unit of its currency was tied to a specific weight of gold. Gold coins were permitted to circulate within its economy, and bank notes were fully convertible into gold at a fixed price. As countries allowed the free export and import of gold and permitted residents of other countries to exchange holdings of their currencies into gold or another convertible currency, an *international* gold standard was established. The price of gold expressed in national currencies defined the exchange rates between countries. They could fluctuate only within very small margins of less than 1 percent, which derived from the so-called gold points resulting from the costs of the physical movement of gold. The money supply in a country was determined by the national authorities' reserve requirements for note-issuing banks (which were not necessarily only central banks), that is, by a fixed ratio between the foreign reserves of a bank (normally gold but also, to a lesser degree, foreign exchange convertible into gold in the issuing country) and domestic liabilities, that is, notes and deposits denominated in national currency. In this way, the supply of money was linked to national gold and gold-related reserves and responded quickly to changes in the external economic situation, bringing about the changes in the domestic economy necessary for the restoration of external equilibrium. To safeguard the gold convertibility of a currency — the glue that linked currencies together — was considered the supreme objective of national monetary policy.

In case of a deficit in the current account of the balance of payments, there would be an outflow of gold, resulting in a corresponding fall in money supply. This, in turn, would cause interest rates to rise; economic activity and income would fall, and domestic prices would decline until external balance was restored. Higher interest rates also could attract short-term foreign funds, and such an import of capital could smooth the required domestic adjustment. Conversely, in the case of a current account surplus, there would be an inflow of gold, an expansion in money supply, and a rise in economic activity and domestic prices. To put it differently, the gold standard was assumed to provide for symmetrical adjustment, that is, external imbalances would lead to corrective changes in the domestic economic situations of deficit as well as surplus countries. Ideally, there was no conflict between external and domestic policy objectives; the requirements of external balance would, over time, restore internal balance.

THE REALITY OF THE GOLD STANDARD

The gold standard provided something akin to a global money supply, which, in the main, was not determined by the policies of central banks but by the availability of gold. It established for the participating countries a de facto monetary union with fully convertible currencies and fixed exchange rates in which adherence to the "rules of the game" rendered international coordination or harmonization of monetary policies superfluous. The period during which the gold standard flourished was a time of vigorously rising international trade, rapid industrialization, and generally strong growth in North America and many European countries.

In reality, the gold standard was much more complex but also more flexible than the idealized model described above suggests, and the process of domestic economic adjustment did not necessarily work as smoothly as assumed.[2] In the first place, the gold standard was not an international system in the sense that it was the outcome of an international agreement. Rather, it was a regime that resulted from policies and procedures chosen by individual countries who considered them as being in their national interest but also because they were in line with prevailing economic thinking. The durability of the system in an international context was, therefore, not derived from internationally agreed obligations but from unilateral commitments that reflected chiefly the desire of individual countries to generate and maintain international monetary credibility as a key to free trade and economic expansion.

Furthermore, the gold standard was not a truly global system. Only a limited number of economically more advanced countries were on the gold standard or some variant of it. Panic (1992, pp. 34–35) lists a dozen countries as "permanent members" of the gold standard "club," all of them industrialized countries, among them being the United Kingdom, France, Germany, Belgium, Denmark, Netherlands, Switzerland, United States, and Canada. The two latter were the only non-European countries and, at that time, did not have a central bank. Other countries adhered only to some aspects of the gold standard or adopted the standard only for a limited time or at a later stage. Several countries never adopted the gold standard. These included mainly less industrialized and primary-producing countries. Only a very few countries, such as the United Kingdom, Germany, and the United States, were on a "full" gold standard. Some were on a "limping" gold standard (e.g., France and Belgium) under which the authorities legally had the option of converting notes into gold or silver coins. A number of countries were on some form of gold-exchange standard, holding a large part of their reserves in foreign exchange (e.g., the Netherlands and most of the Scandinavian countries) (Bloomfield, 1959, p. 14).

The extent to which current account imbalances affected the domestic economy varied significantly depending on the size and openness of the economy and whether it was an industrial or primary-producing country (Ford, 1985, pp. 143–44). It was more difficult for a country that was an international debtor to attract compensatory capital imports than it was for an international creditor. Also, if a deficit country owned large gold reserves, it could afford to enact domestic adjustment less stringently. Surplus countries would not necessarily apply the "rule" of expanding their money supply but would at times either try to export capital or simply absorb the inflow of gold, a policy akin to what is now called "sterilized intervention." This introduced an asymmetrical feature into the system, that is, the domestic economies in surplus countries would not undergo changes to the same degree as those in deficit countries. The cutting or loosening of the link between external performance and domestic money supply would break the supposedly closed international liquidity circuit.

The somewhat mythical view of a fully automatic and balanced international monetary system under the gold standard also needs corrections in other respects. Although maintaining gold convertibility was the primary objective of monetary policy, it was not carried out with complete indifference to domestic economic consequences (Hayes, 1959). Nevertheless, during the time in which the gold standard was operative, there were significant fluctuations in economic activity and prices and in unemployment and income. The subordination of monetary policies to external objectives, coupled with the absence of any anticyclical orientation of fiscal policies, led at times to serious social problems in a number of industrialized countries. The assumed flexibility of prices and wages was not always large or fast enough to avoid distortions and inequities in domestic economic adjustment.

The cyclical consequences of the working of the gold standard at times were aggravated by fluctuations in gold production, which depended mainly on new discoveries and on technical improvements in the mining and production processes. For example, the downward pressure on world price levels during the depression of 1873–96 has been attributed to insufficient growth in gold production (Bloomfield, 1959, p. 21). Such problems were the reason for Keynes' famous characterization of gold as a "barbarous relic" (1924, p. 187).

In hindsight, it appears that the time of the gold standard — although it was largely a time of peace — was not the unequivocally "golden era" sometimes depicted. It was also the period of colonialism at its peak and a time of intensifying rivalries between the large European countries, which culminated in World War I.

The reality and the myth of the gold standard left behind a legacy of economic ideas and concepts that had a great influence after World War II and that are still being felt today on global as well as European monetary matters. In addition to the attempt after World War I to revive the gold standard, various proposals to base the international monetary system, in one form or another, more firmly on gold were presented after World War II. Gold was (and still is) widely seen as the ultimate form of international liquidity. The notion of a self-equilibrating global international economy — some sort of a prestabilized system — can be discerned in the original Articles of Agreement of the International Monetary Fund worked out in 1944 but also in the economic policy provisions of the treaty of 1957 that established the European Economic Community. Such notions were closely related to the long-held beliefs of many academic and practicing monetary policy experts that fixed exchange rates were a quasi-natural and highly desirable, even indispensable, element of any well-functioning international monetary system and that exchange rate adjustments were basically an aberration that should be resorted to only under exceptional circumstances. This view — which was reinforced by the negative experiences with exchange rate policy during the interwar period — was also to some extent responsible for considering the maintenance of stable exchange rates not only as an economic imperative but also as a matter of national prestige. Such a view exerted a powerful influence as recently as during the crises of the European Monetary System in 1992 and 1993.

THE INTERWAR PERIOD

World War I and the concomitant political, economic, and social upheavals brought about the breakdown of the pre-1914 order of free international trade and unrestricted payments. In the 1920s, a number of countries, led by the United Kingdom, tried to reestablish the gold standard in a modified form, only to be forced to abandon it during the Great Depression. In its aftermath, economic policies in the 1930s were characterized by mercantilistic thinking and an attitude of "everybody for himself." The following provides a summary of events in the main industrialized countries.

In the first few years after 1918, the major currencies were floating, that is, exchange rates were determined by market forces. However, even before the end of the war in November 1918, the British government formed a Committee on Currency and Foreign Exchange after the War, chaired by Lord Cunliffe, then Governor of the Bank of England. It recommended that the United Kingdom adopt a modified gold standard under which international debts would be settled in gold but the use of gold for domestic transactions would be restricted. This would have restored external gold convertibility for the pound sterling.

In 1922, at the invitation of the United Kingdom and France, 34 countries, including Germany and Russia but excluding the United States, attended a conference in Genoa, intended as a follow-up to an unsuccessful conference under the aegis of the League of Nations in Brussels in 1920. The United Kingdom submitted proposals for the adoption of an international gold standard in which major countries would hold their reserves entirely in gold and others would hold gold as well as foreign exchange reserves. Countries were encouraged to declare gold parities for their currencies. The conference, like the Brussels conference, was not successful (Kindleberger, 1993, pp. 323–25).

However, the issue of a return to some form of gold standard did not die down. In the United Kingdom, a debate ensued that involved, among others, John Maynard Keynes, Montagu Norman (the Governor of the Bank of England), and Winston Churchill (who in 1924 had become Chancellor of the Exchequer). Eventually, on April 28, 1925, the British Gold Standard Act was adopted, which provided for a return of the pound to the gold standard at its prewar parity of $4.86. Other countries followed the British lead in returning to the gold standard, including Belgium, France, Luxembourg, Netherlands, and Portugal. As a result, by 1928, a new, modified international gold standard was in place, limited, however, to external convertibility and resembling more a gold-exchange standard than the pre-1914 system (Haberler, 1976, p. 208).

Just six years later, on September 21, 1931, the United Kingdom was forced to abandon the gold standard and take recourse to a floating exchange rate following heavy losses of reserves by the Bank of England. An important reason for the closing of the gold window of the Bank of England was the policy of the Bank of France and some other European central banks to convert their foreign exchange reserves into gold. The pound-dollar exchange rate fell sharply to $3.25 in December 1931. Other countries, among them the members of the British Commonwealth and the Scandinavian countries, left the gold standard and experienced similar depreciations of their currencies.

The French franc experienced a sharp decline against the U.S. dollar immediately after the war. In 1928, France fixed the franc-dollar exchange rate at one-fifth of its prewar level. This resulted in a significant undervaluation of the franc, allowing France to register large balance of payment surpluses and a corresponding rise in its reserves. When France later encountered balance of payments difficulties, it did not abandon the gold standard as such but applied increasingly more severe import restrictions and, finally, in October 1936, devalued the franc. Of the other countries of the so-called gold bloc, Belgium had already devalued in March 1935, and Switzerland and the Netherlands followed France in 1936.

After the closing of the gold window of the Bank of England in September 1931, a number of countries, in particular France, Belgium, the Netherlands, and Switzerland, turned to the United States for the conversion of their dollar holdings into gold. In response, and despite gold holdings still in excess of reserve requirements, the United States also gave up the gold standard in the spring of 1933. The U.S. authorities let the dollar float for a limited time and, on February 1, 1934, increased the price of gold from \$20.67 to \$35, implying a devaluation of the dollar of about 40 percent.

After the hyperinflation of the early 1920s, Germany stabilized its currency in November 1923 — at 4.2 trillion marks per dollar! Nevertheless, in subsequent years, it experienced large current account deficits. Capital imports allowed Germany not only to finance these deficits but even to substantially increase its foreign exchange reserves. However, in 1929, capital inflows decreased and eventually turned into an outflow, which reached its peak in spring and early summer 1931. This forced the German central bank, the Reichsbank, to discontinue gold payments and, thus, to renounce the gold standard. In its place, Germany introduced in July 1931 a system of foreign exchange controls.

The gold standard as reestablished in the 1920s bore only a limited resemblance to the pre-1914 system. It was by no means an automatic system but was a highly managed one. It had important features of a gold-exchange standard, because, in many countries, reserves did not consist of gold but of dollar and sterling holdings. Furthermore, countries adhered less and less to the rules of the classical gold standard. Surplus countries would sterilize the monetary impact of gold inflows to avoid price increases, and deficit countries were not ready to accept deflation as a result of gold losses. The resulting persistent balance of payments disequilibria were one of the main reasons for the gradual collapse of the resurrected gold standard.

In response to the Great Depression (which began in 1929 and reached its peak in 1933) and the ensuing high unemployment rate but also as a consequence of increasingly nationalistic and isolationist ideologies, governments oriented their economic policies almost exclusively toward domestic objectives. They neglected the requirements of external equilibrium and paid little regard to international economic interdependence. Governments unabashedly adopted what has been called "beggar-thy-neighbor" policies. More and more countries abandoned the free trade ideals of the prewar period.

An international monetary and economic conference opened in London on June 12, 1933, with the aim of solving international financial problems and removing international trade barriers and ended without success (Kindleberger, 1993, p. 376). The Tripartite Monetary Agreement of September 1936 between the United States, the United Kingdom, and France had as its objective the stabilization of exchange rates but was not much more than a declaration of good intentions (Clarke, 1977). Protectionist custom tariffs, import quotas, bilateral trade agreements, competitive devaluations, and extensive exchange restrictions, many of them discriminatory in nature, were the order of the day. Even in the United States, which had emerged from the war as the world's strongest creditor country, and in the United Kingdom, the traditional stronghold of free trade philosophy, the support for free trade vanished, as demonstrated by the introduction of the "infamous" (Kaplan and Schleiminger, 1989, p. 9), highly protectionist Smoot-Hawley tariff in the United States in 1930 and the reinforcement of the Imperial trade preferences by the United Kingdom. World trade declined substantially, from 1929 to 1932 alone by 25 percent in volume terms. In her description of international economic developments of that period, Sima Lieberman (1992, p. 10) spoke of "economic warfare in the 1930s."

NOTES

Literature of general interest for this chapter: Bloomfield (1959, 1963); Clarke (1967); Deutsche Bundesbank (1976b); Eichengreen (1985); Haberler (1976); Hawtrey (1947); Kindleberger (1993); League of Nations (1944); Panic (1992).

1. How does one define "a functioning world economic order"? Ideally, it would facilitate and support mutually beneficial trade and financial relations among countries and, thus, foster economic growth and financial and monetary stability in individual countries as well as globally.

2. See also Joseph Schumpeter (1965, p. 941, my translation): "Perhaps the gold standard was never 'automatic.' If it ever was, this was not the case anymore toward the end of the period. The reasons were more of a political than a purely economic nature: They are related to neo-mercantilistic attitudes and the ever stronger tensions in international relations which appeared around 1900."

2

The Establishment of a New International Economic Order after World War II

In addition to the tremendous loss of life, World War II brought with it large-scale destruction of production capacities and economic dislocation. Havoc was wrought on victorious and defeated countries alike. For the governments of the countries that were affected most seriously by the war, low levels of production and the requirement to reconvert their economies to their peoples' peacetime needs, frequently of the most basic nature, posed unprecedented challenges.

The lack of freely usable foreign exchange and the disruption of normal political and economic relations caused by the war forced the European countries to take recourse to extreme bilateralism in their international trade and payments arrangements. To a large extent, economic relations were reduced in effect to barter trade. The United States emerged politically and economically as the leading power in the world. However, it soon was to be challenged in political as well as military terms by the Soviet Union, which, in the aftermath of the war, was able to extend its sphere of influence and domination right into the center of Europe.

After World War I, the United States had been eager to get out of European affairs, and the victorious European countries did not have a sufficient understanding of the economic and political dangers inherent in the impoverishment of the defeated countries. In 1920, John Maynard Keynes had warned with foresight but in vain: "If we aim deliberately at the impoverishment of Central Europe, vengeance, I dare predict, will not limp" (1988, p. 268). By contrast, after World War II, it soon was recognized that it was imperative to build a new international economic order to overcome the disintegration of the world economy and to engage in a determined effort for the reconstruction of the war-devastated European countries, whether winners or losers. It was seen as particularly important to rebuild Europe in order to avoid large-scale poverty, which could generate severe social and political unrest, and to face the emerging Communist threat in political, military, and economic terms.

Already, during the war, the United States and the United Kingdom took the initiative in founding a new global economic order to be based on international cooperation and mutual obligations and assistance. The United States took the lead also in the efforts to rebuild the European economies, supported by the United Kingdom, while France remained somewhat hesitant, and the Soviet Union stayed on the sideline. The smaller European countries (including such one-time allies of Germany as Italy and Austria [as part of the German Reich]) and the defeated Germany placed their hopes on a new political and economic order for the world as well as for Europe.

The chief objectives for the new international economic order were to reconstruct and develop the world economy, to establish free trade, and to set up an international monetary system based on stable exchange rates and on payment arrangements free of restrictions and distortions. The three main pillars of this new world economic order were to be the International Bank for Reconstruction and Development (IBRD, the World Bank), the International Trade Organization/General Agreement on Tariffs and Trade (ITO/GATT), and — as the central institution from a monetary point of view — the International Monetary Fund (IMF).

THE INTERNATIONAL MONETARY FUND

The creation of the IMF and the World Bank was agreed to at a conference that took place in July 1944 at Bretton Woods at the foot of Mt. Washington, New Hampshire. Forty-five countries attended the conference, including the Soviet Union and some other countries in Eastern Europe.

The Articles of Agreement of the IMF entered into force on December 27, 1945, and the Fund got started in May 1946. It then had 39 members. However, the Soviet Union and its satellites did not join or — in the case of Poland and Czechoslovakia — left after the Communist takeover. Nationalist China became a member, but since 1980, the government of the People's Republic of China represents China in the IMF. By now, all countries that formerly were part of the Communist bloc, including the successor states of the Soviet Union, are members of the IMF (and the IBRD), with the exceptions of North Korea and Cuba (which had been a founding member but left in 1964). At the end of 1996, 181 countries were members of the IMF.

The main objectives of the IMF are "to facilitate the expansion and balanced growth of international trade, and to contribute thereby to the promotion and maintenance of high levels of employment and real income and to the development of the productive resources of all members" (Articles of Agreement, Art. I). To this end, the IMF undertook to establish a global monetary system based on stable exchange rates, the avoidance of competitive devaluations, and the elimination of restrictions on current payments and of discriminatory or multiple currency practices.

At the center of the Fund was a system of fixed but adjustable exchange rates, expressed in terms of gold or in terms of the U.S. dollar, valued at $35 per ounce of fine gold. It is frequently called the "Bretton Woods system." Member countries, with the exception of the United States, were obliged to maintain the stability of their exchange rates within fluctuation margins of ±1 percent by intervening in exchange markets. The United States, in turn, met its obligation to keep the value of its currency stable by standing ready to freely sell or buy gold at its fixed price. That meant that any other member country could convert its U.S. dollar holdings into gold if it so desired.

Following the immediate postwar years, which were characterized by dollar shortages, the United States increasingly experienced balance of payments deficits. Although this supplied the international liquidity needed for the expansion of world trade, it also undermined international confidence in the dollar and led to the eventual demise of the Bretton Woods system in 1973 (see Chapter 11). In comparison with the international gold standard, the Bretton Woods system has been characterized as a gold-foreign exchange standard or, for example, by Milton Gilbert (1968), as a gold-dollar system.

The U.S. dollar was the key currency of the Bretton Woods system and served (and, to a large extent, still serves) as the main reserve and intervention currency of the international monetary system The Bretton Woods system was asymmetric in nature because the obligations for maintaining exchange rate stability for the U.S. dollar were different from those for all other currencies. Also, the United States could finance its balance of payments deficits with its own currency, subject, however, to gold conversions of dollar holdings by other countries.

According to Art. IV of the original Articles of Agreement (amendments took effect in 1969, 1978, and 1992), the par value of a currency could be changed only to correct a "fundamental disequilibrium" and only if proposed by the member country concerned. A par value change required the "concurrence" of the Fund, which certainly is a much lesser term than "approval." It was also of importance that the original Articles provided no room for the Fund to approve a no-par value status nor did they allow for a temporary free floating of exchange rates (Southard, 1979, pp. 23–24). The subtlety of language in these provisions signaled the importance that the founding fathers of the IMF attached to the stability of exchange rates and the avoidance of competitive devaluations — reflecting the negative interwar experiences — while still intending to not interfere too much with the sovereignty of member countries.

Existing foreign exchange restrictions on current payments, that is, payments for merchandise trade, services, and other current transactions, were to be gradually abolished, and discriminatory currency arrangements or multiple exchange rates were to be avoided (Art. VIII). To the extent that such practices existed, they were subject to consultation and Fund approval.

The Fund's concentration on current transactions was reflected in the provisions of the IMF Agreement that "a member may not make net use of the Fund's resources to meet a large or sustained outflow of capital, and the Fund may request a member to exercise [capital] controls. . . . Members may exercise such controls as are necessary to regulate international capital movements, but no member may exercise these controls in a manner which will restrict payments for current transactions" (Art. VI).

If countries encountered balance of payments difficulties stemming from current transactions, the Fund could provide financial assistance "under adequate safeguards" (Art. I(v)), that is, subject to economic policy conditions. (The first amendment of the Articles of 1969 additionally inserted the word "temporarily" into the phrase "making the Fund's resources available.") Each member country had a quota, related to the size of its domestic and external economy, which determined the amount of financial assistance it could obtain as well as its contributions to financial assistance for other countries.

In later years, starting in the 1960s and related to the independence of former colonies, the IMF got engaged increasingly in technical assistance concerning fiscal policy, central banking, and statistical issues. It established a number of financing facilities that were designed mainly to meet the needs of developing countries and to deal with the consequences of the oil price increases of 1973 and 1979. In 1969, the IMF was empowered to create international liquidity in the form of Special Drawing Rights "to meet the need, as and when it arises, for a supplement to existing reserve assets" (Art. XXI of the Articles of Agreement as amended in 1969). However, for various reasons, until now, the Special Drawing Rights scheme did not play any significant role in the supply of international liquidity (see also Chapter 7).

Following the breakdown of the Bretton Woods system in 1973, many countries no longer maintained fixed exchange rates vis-à-vis the U.S. dollar and each other. The second amendment of the IMF Articles, which entered into force in April 1978, in effect permitted each country to choose the exchange rate system it considered most suitable to meet its own needs and the general objectives of the IMF, subject to a general obligation to assure orderly exchange arrangements. Each country is to notify the IMF of its exchange arrangements, and exchange rate policies are subject to IMF surveillance.

Today, the Fund is deeply involved in assisting developing countries in a variety of ways and in aiding countries in Central and Eastern Europe as well as the successor states of the Soviet Union in stabilizing and restructuring their economies. Correspondingly, its involvement in extending assistance to industrialized countries greatly diminished over time, and there has been no financial assistance to those countries since 1977. The IMF continues, however, to exercise surveillance over all member countries' exchange rate and monetary policies and to analyze and report on international economic developments.

The record of achievements of the IMF in the more immediate postwar period is somewhat mixed. On the one hand, the stability of exchange rates was hardly in danger, once the much needed devaluation of the British pound in 1949 and its repercussions on other currencies were out of the way and as long as the U.S. dollar was the undisputed key currency of the international monetary system. If anything, the main danger was that of currencies sticking for too long to a given par value. In this respect, the belief in the paramount importance of stable exchange rates (at any price, one is tempted to add) as well as reasons of national prestige were decisive factors.

On the other hand, the IMF in its early years had only limited success in freeing the international system of bilateralism and exchange restrictions. The degree of disintegration of the world economy at the end of the war and the imbalances resulting from the overwhelming economic strength of the United States and the simultaneous weakness of most other industrialized countries made any significant progress toward a multilateral and free international payments system difficult. The problem was compounded by the initial lack of an effective strategy for dealing with large external imbalances and the absence of a structured framework of mutual obligations for the dismantling of bilateralism in trade and payments, such as the one that emerged later for Europe. Ironically, the insistence on stable exchange rates and the limitation of exchange rate changes to cases of "fundamental disequilibrium" were important factors in the emergence and stickiness of balance of payments disequilibria, which, in turn, impeded the move from bilateralism to multilateralism in trade and payments (Lieberman, 1992, pp. 22–23).

It turned out that substantial progress toward the transferability and convertibility of currencies could be more easily achieved on a regional than a global scale (see Triffin, 1957; Carli, 1982, pp. 161–69). In Europe, progress in this field was stimulated by special financial assistance from the United States (the Marshall Plan; see Chapter 3) and synchronized with efforts to multilateralize trade. The liberalization of trade and payments was implemented in the institutional framework of the Organization for European Economic Cooperation (OEEC) and the European Payments Union, with clearly defined commitments and obligations between countries that, by and large, had similar economic structures and economic policy principles. Only after most Organization for European Economic Cooperation countries had achieved convertibility at the end of 1958, the vision of a wider system of free payments as embodied in the IMF Articles of Agreement came closer to realization.

THE WORLD BANK

The main task of the World Bank was to support the reconstruction of the European economies and to promote the development of less developed countries, primarily by providing funding for specific projects. After the start of the Marshall Plan in 1948, the IBRD directed its efforts increasingly to the countries of the Third World, many of which had become independent after World War II. More recently, after the collapse of the Soviet-dominated Communist system in Eastern Europe and the disintegration of the Soviet Union itself, this region became an important additional focus of the activities of the World Bank. .

The World Bank group of organizations include also the International Finance Corporation (IFC, established 1956), the International Development Association (IDA, 1960), and the Multilateral Investment Guarantee Agency (MIGA, 1988).

THE GENERAL AGREEMENT ON TARIFFS AND TRADE

The intended task for the ITO was the establishment of a system of free trade to foster economic growth and international economic integration. This was to be achieved by abolishing quantitative trade restrictions, reducing custom tariffs, and setting up an international "code of good behavior" for international trade relations.

However, a number of countries, among them the United States, failed to ratify the "Havanna Charta" of 1948, which would have led to the creation of ITO. Instead, the GATT — originally envisaged as an interim solution until the establishment of ITO — took over the main tasks of ITO. An attempt in 1955 to establish an Organization for Trade Cooperation also was unsuccessful because, again, a number of countries, including the United States, did not ratify the agreement. Legally, the GATT was not an international organization (as the ITO would have been) but an agreement between participating countries (the "contracting parties"). In effect, however, the GATT functioned very much like an international organization. At the end of 1994, 128 countries were members of GATT, and another 11 countries applied de facto its rules on a reciprocal basis.

The responsibility of GATT covered mainly trade in industrial goods. Special rules applied to agriculture and fishery. Several multilateral conferences — so-called "tariff rounds" — were aimed at simultaneous reductions of tariffs on industrial goods by all GATT participants. The last one — the "Uruguay round" — was concluded in May 1994, after years of difficult and sometimes acrimonious negotiations. In addition to a cut in industrial tariffs of up to 40 percent, agreement was also reached to reduce subsidies for agricultural exports and to set new rules for trade in services and agricultural goods and for the protection of intellectual property.

Furthermore, the agreement provided for the creation of the World Trade Organization, which was to absorb and broaden the responsibilities of GATT and to underpin the efforts to liberalize international trade with a common and strengthened organizational structure. At the end of 1994, a sufficient number of countries (this time including the United States) had ratified the agreement, and effective January 1, 1995, the World Trade Organization was established. As of January 1, 1997, it had 129 members.

NOTE

Literature of general interest for this chapter: Crockett (1977); de Vries (1976); de Vries (1985); de Vries (1987); Horsefield (1969); James (1996); Southard (1979).

3

The Reconstruction of Europe

After the war, it soon became apparent that, for the reconstruction of the European economies and the reestablishment of normal economic relations in Europe but also in order to wean Europe from the strong dependence on the United States, a special and more focused effort was needed. The International Monetary Fund (IMF) and General Agreement on Tariffs and Trade had been designed to establish a global framework for economic relations free of restrictions and distortions so as to promote economic growth and high levels of employment. To a certain degree, this presupposed that the participating countries would function more or less normally and would operate on a comparable economic footing; this was not the reality of postwar Europe.

Furthermore, the task of the IMF was to assist countries in restoring external balance and, by implication, domestic equilibrium. However, for the European countries in the immediate postwar period, anything resembling equilibrium simply did not exist. The challenge was to rebuild the European economies. Although the World Bank was to help in the reconstruction and development of the European economies, its possibilities were confined by its global responsibilities and its limited financial capacity. Robert Triffin (1957, p. 143) remarked: "The Bretton Woods conference had indulged in the luxury of drawing up blueprints for a far distant future. . . . In the meantime, European countries had to live and to find some basis on which to resume their international trade and payments in an inconvertible world."

There was another and very important aspect. The reconstruction effort in Europe needed to involve more closely the European countries themselves. The job hardly could be done by organizations that were world-wide in scope and by geography and experience somewhat removed from the problems that the European countries were facing.

It was recognized that the European countries required financial assistance on a substantial scale to meet their immediate needs and strong encouragement to mobilize their own resources and to cooperate with each other in an institutional framework. For the United States, humanitarian considerations were an important reason not to allow a large number of countries to remain in a desolate situation, but there was also a healthy element of self-interest; after all, if Europe would not get back on its feet, it would primarily fall to the United States to provide long-term support. Finally, the specter of a Europe embracing Communist ideology and being dominated by the Soviet Union was a frightening prospect.[1]

The answer to these problems was the Marshall Plan and the creation of the Organization for European Economic Cooperation (OEEC) and the European Payments Union (EPU).

THE MARSHALL PLAN

The United States took the initiative and developed a new strategy, specifically aimed at Europe. A return to political and economic isolationism in the mold of the time after World War I was not considered advisable or feasible. The efforts to assist Europe included, early on, Germany, still divided into four zones of occupation by the major allied powers, the United States, the United Kingdom (UK), France, and the Soviet Union. The Morgenthau Plan of 1944 — named after U.S. Treasury Secretary Henry Morgenthau, Jr. — which had envisaged reducing Germany to an essentially agrarian economy, was discarded.[2] War reparations played a much less significant role in the policy of the Western allies than after World War I, when they had a crippling effect on the countries concerned and on economic relations between countries (Cohen, 1968, pp. 275–79). The new U.S. policy on Europe was visionary and, at the same time, pragmatic.

It all began with the famous speech by U.S. Secretary of State George Marshall at Harvard University on June 5, 1947 (Weil, 1965, pp. 4–6). He said:

The truth of the matter is that Europe's requirements for the next three or four years of foreign food and other essential products — principally from America — are so much greater than her present ability to pay that she must have substantial additional help, or face economic, social and political deterioration of a very grave character. The remedy lies in breaking the vicious circle and resorting in the confidence of the European people in the economic future of their own countries and of Europe as a whole. . . . It is logical that the United States should be doing whatever it is able to do to assist in the return of normal economic health in the world, without which there can be no political stability and no assured peace. Our policy is not directed against any country or doctrine but against hunger, poverty, desperation and chaos.

With Marshall's speech, all European countries, including those in Eastern Europe and the Soviet Union, were invited to work together in rebuilding their economies. The Soviet Union, however, and the countries in its sphere of influence rejected the U.S. proposals.[3] Consequently, only the countries in Western Europe (with the exception of Franco-ruled Spain, which had not been invited) participated in a conference, held from July 12 to September 22, 1947, in Paris. A Committee of European Economic Cooperation was formed, which worked out the European Recovery program (ERP). On this basis, the U.S. Congress passed on April 3, 1948, the Foreign Assistance Act, providing for the first year of the program financial aid in the amount of $5.3 billion, most of it as grants.[4] Over the four years of the program, the United States provided more than $13 billion of assistance to be used for the import of raw materials, food supplies, and investment goods. This became known as the Marshall Plan.

For the administration of the ERP, the United States set up the Economic Cooperation Administration. Its head, Paul Hoffman, had cabinet rank. For the implementation of the ERP, the United States concluded bilateral agreements with all participating countries, leaving the detailed administration of the program to the countries concerned.

THE ORGANIZATION FOR EUROPEAN ECONOMIC COOPERATION

Marshall's speech acknowledged that financial assistance only could play a catalytic role in the reconstruction of the European economies by jump-starting the normalization of economic relations. Beyond that, it was essential to establish an economic order in Europe that was based on the free exchange of goods and services and on unrestricted payments. This task fell to the OEEC and the EPU.[5]

On April 16, 1948, the Convention for European Economic Co-operation was signed and the OEEC established, with its seat in Paris. Members were all European countries west of the Iron Curtain, with the exception of Spain, Finland, and Yugoslavia. The western part of Germany initially was represented by the military commanders of the Western occupation powers. It became a member in its own right after the foundation of the Federal Republic of Germany in September 1949, bringing the membership to 17.[6] Eastern Germany (the Soviet occupation zone) was not part of the OEEC. In June 1950, the United States and Canada joined the OEEC as associated members. Spain became an associated member in January 1955 and obtained full membership in July 1959. Yugoslavia and Finland were associated in February 1955 and May 1956, respectively.

The OEEC was an international organization without supranational powers, in contrast to the European Communities. It has been characterized as a "permanent intergovernmental conference" (Schleiminger, 1960, p. 386). A Council met twice a year at the ministerial level and more frequently at the level of permanent national representatives. Decisions required unanimity. Work was carried out mainly in several committees that brought together national experts in various fields; they were assisted by an international secretariat, headed by a secretary general.

Although the genesis of the OEEC was closely linked to the ERP, its final goals were to liberalize trade, services, and capital movements among the European countries and eventually also vis-à-vis other countries and to restore and maintain the stability of their economies and confidence in their currencies. After the war, trade relations between Western European countries were ruled by a maze of government regulations in the form of quantitative import restrictions (quotas) and foreign exchange restrictions. In the late 1940s, there were some 200 bilateral trade and payments agreements in force (Kaplan and Schleiminger, 1989, p. 7). They not only served to safeguard the balance of payments of the respective countries but also had the effect of protecting noncompetitive sectors of the respective economies. Frequently, they implied a discriminatory treatment of trading partners. As a result, intra-European trade remained on a low level, far below its prewar volume, and comparative cost advantages and economies of scale could not be realized.

The policy of the OEEC was to gradually reduce import restrictions on a multilateral basis. Initially, as of January 15, 1949, the target for the reduction of import quotas was set at 50 percent of total private imports. With the start of the EPU on July 1, 1950, the target was raised to 60 percent, as of February 1, 1951, to 75 percent, and, eventually, effective January 14, 1955, to 90 percent. At the beginning of 1959, on average, 90 percent of intra-European trade was effectively liberalized. Starting in 1953–54, the improvement in the balance of payments situation of the OEEC countries also allowed a step-by-step reduction of import restrictions against the United States and Canada. Although services were almost completely liberalized in 1960, progress in the liberalization of capital movements was much slower.[7]

THE EUROPEAN PAYMENTS UNION

The counterpart to the liberalization of trade was efforts to achieve the transferability and convertibility of European currencies. Trade liberalization could be sustained only if there was commensurate progress in the field of payments. The existing regimes of exchange restrictions and bilateral agreements and the lack of mutual credit facilities hampered decisive progress in trade liberalization. The scarcity of internationally usable reserves, that is, gold and dollar holdings, caused countries to worry that the abolition of trade barriers would imperil their precarious reserve positions.

The most noticeable manifestation of the lack of reserves was the "dollar gap," which mirrored the high demand for U.S. goods and the inability of European countries to pay for needed imports. The dollar gap also led to an early end of the attempt by the UK to restore the external convertibility of the pound in 1947 as other countries acquired sterling balances and converted them into dollars (Kaplan and Schleiminger, 1989, p. 13). Later, in September 1949, the pound was devalued by 30 percent. It was followed by devaluations of the currencies of the sterling area and of all Western European countries (see de Vries, 1969, pp. 96–100).

A first attempt to deal with those problems was the Intra-European Payments and Compensations Scheme, concluded in October 1948 and modified in 1949. It introduced a multilateral element into the network of bilateral payments arrangements. However, it soon became apparent that nothing short of a full-fledged multilateral payments system (which would ensure the full transferability of European currencies) would suffice to underpin the policy of trade liberalization.

This led to the creation of the EPU on September 19, 1950, within the framework of the OEEC. It entered into force retroactively on July 1, 1950. All OEEC members were also members of the EPU. It was administered by a managing board of seven independent experts, with final decisions resting with the OEEC Council. The Bank for International Settlements (BIS) in Basle acted as the financial agent for the EPU.[8]

The EPU was a clearing union that replaced the existing array of bilateral payment agreements by a multilateral settlement and credit mechanism. For each country, bilateral claims and liabilities were consolidated on a monthly basis in a single net position against the EPU (net deficit or net surplus positions), representing the balance of payments of a country vis-à-vis the rest of the EPU area (including the sterling area). Settlement of these net positions took place also on a monthly basis, in part by "cash" payment in gold or dollars, in part by the automatic granting of credit on the part of surplus countries. Quotas determined the cumulative amount of credit a country could receive or was obliged to provide. The quotas were based on countries' intra-European trade (15 percent of the sum of payments and receipts in 1949 for trade in goods and services). If a debtor country exhausted its quota, it had to settle its deficit entirely in gold; however, it could obtain a special, nonautomatic credit (see below). EPU transactions were expressed in a unit of account, defined by the same gold content as the U.S. dollar (0.88867088 gram of fine gold).[9]

The combination of "cash" and credit elements in the settlement provisions turned out to be a highly effective device, providing a "balance between the financing and adjustment of intra-European payments disequilibrium" (Lamfalussy, 1989, p. viii). The credit element protected countries against a rapid decline of their international reserves and, thus, bolstered their willingness to go ahead with trade liberalization. The cash element acted as a constraint on unsustainable economic policies and compelled countries to adopt adjustment measures in case of balance of payments deficits.

The EPU was intended as a transitional system — a "half-way house," as Jacob Kaplan and Günther Schleiminger called it (1989, p. 1) — on the way from bilateralism to full convertibility in Europe. At the start, the cash to credit ratio was set on average at 40 to 60, the actual ratio for an individual country depending on the use of its quota within tranches: the higher a country's liability toward the EPU, the larger was the cash requirement for settlement. The increase of international reserve holdings of the OEEC countries since 1953 allowed in 1954 a move to a flat ratio of 50 to 50 and in 1955 to a ratio of 75 to 25. This marked a substantial "hardening" of the settlement modalities (dubbed "three-quarter convertibility") which, as Peter Kenen (1991, p. 259) observed, "diminished the practical distinction between transferability and convertibility." Kaplan and Schleiminger (1989, p. 3) emphasized that the EPU "maintained a tight link between liberalizing trade and freeing payments from restrictions."

The EPU had at its disposal a "working capital" of $350 million (coming from Marshall Plan funds), allowing the granting of special ad hoc credits to countries in balance of payments difficulties who had exhausted their debtor quotas. Such credits were subject to economic policy conditions. One of the main activities of the EPU Managing Board was the discussion of such economic policy conditions (which formally were set by the OEEC Council) and the monitoring of the progress of debtor countries in stabilizing their economies. These procedures were the first comprehensive arrangement of "multilateral surveillance" of economic developments for a group of countries. The first credit of $120 million under this facility went to Germany during the balance of payments crisis of 1950–51 in connection with the Korean War. Among later recipients were France and the UK.

On December 27, 1958, a majority of EPU members accepted the obligations of Art. VIII of the IMF Articles of Agreement and introduced external convertibility for their currencies.[10] The assumption of convertibility also eliminated the still existing border lines between the EPU area and the dollar area. On the same day, the EPU entered into liquidation. Claims and liabilities toward the EPU (i.e., unsettled cumulative net positions) were consolidated in bilateral agreements among the countries concerned, covering $1.7 billion. Of this amount, $1.4 billion were repaid within three years.

Recently and related to the issue of closer economic integration of the states of the former Soviet Union, Barry Eichengreen (1993) raised the questions of whether the EPU had been necessary and whether current account convertibility would not have been a viable option. In his view, most preconditions for the viability of current account convertibility appeared to have been met in 1950 (p. 62). He pointed out, however, that, in the countries concerned, the EPU was part of a "social pact" aimed at protecting real income (according to his estimates, restoring convertibility would have required a devaluation of 15 percent, in addition to the 1949 devaluations [p. 87]) and avoiding an increase in unemployment. Internationally, the EPU lent credibility to the commitment to trade liberalization and European integration, which, in the longer run, was not only an economic but also a political objective. Eichengreen concluded that such considerations were decisive in opting for a payments union and against convertibility (p. 89). The view "that the *realistic* choice was not between EPU and convertibility, but between EPU and bilateralism" (italics added) had been clearly voiced at the time of the discussions leading to the creation of the EPU in early 1950 (Kaplan and Schleiminger, 1989, pp. 42–43; see also Coffey and Presley, 1971, p. 6).

THE EUROPEAN MONETARY AGREEMENT

Already, in 1955, the EPU members agreed to continue their monetary policy cooperation after the transition to convertibility and the termination of the EPU by signing the European Monetary Agreement (EMA) on August 5.[11] The main goal of the EMA was to enable all OEEC members, whether their currencies had become convertible or not, to maintain a high level of trade liberalization among themselves. A European Fund was to provide members with a potential source of nonautomatic credit in case of temporary balance of payments difficulties. A Multilateral System of Settlements was to facilitate the settlement of transactions in member currencies by offering interim financing between the monthly settlements and was to encourage settlements through foreign exchange markets. The unit of account for the multilateral system was the same as in the EPU. Like the EPU, the EMA had a managing board of independent experts.

The EMA entered into force on December 27, 1958, as the EPU was dissolved. At the end of 1972, the EMA was terminated and the European Fund liquidated.

Although the EMA resembled the EPU in a number of aspects, there were crucial differences. It was not so much a payments system but, rather, a "code of behavior" designed for an environment of convertibility. Member countries committed themselves to maintain their exchange rates against the common standard of the U.S. dollar within margins as moderate and stable as possible, if necessary by market intervention. Most countries voluntarily limited the fluctuations of their currencies against the dollar to 0.75 percent on either side of parity, compared with the ±1 percent mandated by the IMF Articles of Agreement. Most important, EMA members accorded each other limited exchange rate guarantees in case of exchange rate changes. Although participation in the multilateral system of settlements was voluntary, the system provided a kind of safety net, with the aim of forestalling any relapse in the liberalization of trade and payments. Its rules were put to use infrequently.

Apart from the limited provisions for interim financing and unlike the EPU, the EMA did not allow for any automatic credits. In case of temporary balance of payments difficulties, the European Fund of $600 million ($607.5 million after Spain joined the OEEC and the EMA in July 1959) allowed the granting of credits with a maturity of not more than two years on a case-by-case basis. Credits were subject to economic policy conditions, comparable with the special credits in the EPU.

As in the EPU, the managing board conducted regular consultations about member countries' balance of payments developments and exchange rate policies.

THE ORGANIZATION FOR ECONOMIC COOPERATION AND DEVELOPMENT

By the late 1950s, OEEC and EPU had largely achieved their objectives of liberalizing trade and payments within Western Europe and vis-à-vis other countries. Foreign trade expanded vigorously, and the European countries enjoyed strong growth and high employment, generally under conditions of external and domestic stability. The establishment of the European Economic Community in 1958 and of the European Free Trade Association in 1960, which, in the economic field, picked up where the OEEC left off, required another look at the OEEC. It was felt desirable to maintain a framework in which the two European trade blocs and the United States and Canada — roughly speaking, the Western industrialized countries — could pursue their cooperation in the areas of economic, monetary, and development assistance policies. These considerations led to the establishment of the Organization for Economic Cooperation and Development (OECD) on September 30, 1961, as the successor to the OEEC.[12] The initial members were the 18 OEEC countries and the United States and Canada. They later were joined by Finland, Japan, Australia, and New Zealand, thus, extending membership beyond the North Atlantic area. In April 1994, Mexico became a member. The Czech Republic joined in November 1995, Hungary in May 1996, Poland in October 1996, and South Korea in December 1996, bringing total membership to 29.

The OECD is similarly organized as the OEEC. However, it is mainly a consultative body that has been characterized as a think tank for its members. One of its main functions is to serve as a forum for consultation about monetary and exchange rate policies. In this, an important role is played by the so-called Working Party No. 3, a subgroup of the OECD's Economic Policy Committee (sometimes termed the "Monetary Committee of the OECD"). It consists of senior officials from finance ministries and central banks of the larger member countries.

The OECD performs an important bridging function between the European countries and other industrialized countries. Within the limits of its competences, it frequently is seen as a complement to (but sometimes also as a competitor with) the IMF. Questions also have been raised as to its raison d'être among regional — and expanding — groupings such as the European Union (as the European Community is now called), a specialized monetary institution like the BIS with a world-wide albeit limited membership and a global organization like the IMF. The answers may lie in the pool of nearly unique experience and knowledge the OECD can offer on a wide range of economic policy issues and its usefulness to an increasingly diverse membership as a marketplace for the exchange of information and ideas, not least in — but not limited to — the monetary and financial field.

NOTES

Literature of general interest for this chapter: European Payments Union (1951–59); Organisation for Economic Co-operation and Development (1949–61, 1978); Coffey and Presley (1971); de Vries (1969); Diebold (1952); Hogan (1987); Kaplan and Schleiminger (1989); Triffin (1957); Urwin (1995).

1. It was on March 4, 1946, that Churchill coined the term "Iron Curtain" in a speech at Westminster College, Fulton, Missouri, and called for the unity of the Western democracies.

2. John Foster Dulles commented: "As we studied the problem of Germany, we became more and more convinced that there is no economic solution along purely national lines. Increased economic unity is an absolute essential to the well-being of Europe" (quoted in Hogan, 1987, p. 38).

3. Charles Kindleberger (1993, p. 422) observed that "the exit of the Soviet Union was viewed with considerable relief by both Western Europeans and the United States." Derek Urwin (1995, p. 16) commented that "the United States

must have taken into account that the offer would be rejected by Moscow and its satellites."

4.   It was not by accident that Congressional passage followed closely the beginning of the Berlin blockade by the Soviet Union on March 24, 1948.

5.   The rejection by the Soviet Union and its satellites of the U.S. proposals outlined in Marshall's speech and the unfolding of the Cold War were among the reasons for which the implementation of the ERP was not entrusted to the newly established Economic Commission for Europe, a UN body, in which the countries of the Soviet bloc were members.

6.   Austria, Belgium, Denmark, France, Federal Republic of Germany, Greece, Iceland, Ireland, Italy, Luxembourg, Netherlands, Norway, Portugal, Sweden, Switzerland, Turkey, and UK.

7.   The reluctance to proceed decisively with capital liberalization was reflected also in the limited liberalization obligations of the European Economic Community Treaty and the lack of progress until the implementation of the Single Market Program of 1986 (see Chapter 5).

8.   The BIS was established in 1930, with its seat in Basle, in the context of German war reparation payments and to promote the cooperation of central banks. After World War II, it became an important forum for international monetary cooperation. The BIS has acted as an agent for the EPU, the EMA, and the European Monetary Cooperation Fund.

9.   For a detailed description of the mechanism of the EPU, see Kaplan and Schleiminger, 1989, pp. 91–96; European Payments Union, Managing Board, First Annual Report, 1951, pp. 11–16, and Third Annual Report, 1953, Annexes I and II.

10.   External convertibility has been defined as "the freedom of non-residents of a country to sell that country's currency for any other currency" (Coffey and Presley, 1971, p. 22).

11.   For a description of the EMA, see Schleiminger, 1960, pp. 393–94; Rees, 1963, pp. 167–83.

12.   For aims and structure of the OECD, see Organisation for Economic Co-operation and Development (1972).

4

The Creation of the European Communities and Their Institutions

The achievements of the Organization for European Economic Cooperation (OEEC) and the European Payments Union (EPU) had shown the benefits that could be derived from cooperation and mutual, institutionally secured commitments. The liberalization of trade and payments under the tutelage of the two organizations had paved the way for a rapid expansion of intra-European trade and an astonishing rise of production and employment in Western Europe in the 1950s. Politically, the success of OEEC and EPU had demonstrated that the pursuit of common interests could overcome the aftermath of a destructive war and help surmount national rivalries. The big question was how to proceed further.

There was no doubt that most European countries wanted to continue and intensify their cooperation in economic matters and to deepen the integration of their economies. At issue were the methods to be used and the ultimate objectives. Should there be a tight organizational structure or not? Was economic integration to be seen as an end in itself or also as a promise for, if not a commitment to, closer political cooperation?

For the six countries in the heart of non-Communist Europe — Belgium, France, Germany, Italy, Luxembourg, and the Netherlands — the answers were quite clear. Their desire was to move toward closer political cooperation and to reach for an even deeper integration of their economies. Five of them had been occupied during the war by Germany. Germany, in turn, ended up a divided country that only gradually and over many years regained its sovereignty, and it was not united until 1990. The aim was to promote prosperity and safeguard peace and to integrate Germany in a community of democratic European nations. To this end, the "Six" were ready to give up part of their national sovereignty and, in the process, gain in joint sovereignty.

The United Kingdom (UK) was not willing to commit itself to an ambitious and politically motivated integration process. Although interested in closer economic cooperation and further advances in liberalizing intra-European trade, its main political goal was to retain its political and economic position in the world on the basis of the British Commonwealth of Nations and a "special relationship" with the United States.[1]

Other countries that had suffered directly from the war had different reasons for not joining the efforts toward a closer integration with ultimately political objectives. Denmark and Norway maintained a strong sense of independence and treasured their Scandinavian and Nordic identity, which they shared with the other countries in Northern Europe. Among those countries, Sweden and Finland adhered to the principle of political neutrality, which for Sweden was based on a long and beneficial tradition and for Finland was mandated by its historically determined, complex political relationship with the Soviet Union. Austria had obtained its independence after the war in 1955 as a result of a treaty with the four occupation powers that committed it to political neutrality. Ireland also followed a policy of neutrality and, in the economic field, had particularly close ties to the UK. Switzerland, in turn, was determined to maintain its traditional neutrality and had no interest in forsaking any significant part of its sovereignty — an attitude that, until today, has conditioned its policies on European integration. Portugal and Spain were not considered candidates for European Community (EC) membership as long as they were ruled by right-wing dictators. Greece was handicapped by a substantial lag of economic development relative to most of Western Europe. It goes without further elaboration that the countries in Eastern Europe that were under the domination of the Soviet Union (including Eastern Germany, which in 1949 became the German Democratic Republic) could not participate in any grouping of Western countries aimed at closer economic, let alone political, cooperation. However, the German Democratic Republic became part of the EC when it was united with the Federal Republic of Germany in October 1990.[2]

THE BEGINNING OF THE EUROPEAN COMMUNITIES

In a famous speech in Zürich on September 19, 1946, Winston Churchill called for the creation of a united Europe (defined at the time as continental Europe) and expressed the view that the first step on this path had to be a partnership between France and Germany (Schwarz, 1980, pp. 51–52).[3]

In a declaration on May 9, 1950, the French Foreign Minister, Robert Schuman, presented on behalf of his government what has become known as the Schuman Plan, masterminded by Jean Monnet. Schuman emphasized that "the gathering of the nations of Europe requires the elimination of the age-old conflict between France and Germany." He proposed "to place Franco-German production of coal and steel under a common High Authority, within the framework of an organization open to the participation of the other countries of Europe" (Weil, 1965, p. 11). With this, Schuman addressed the political motives of the initiative and identified French-German cooperation as the major element for the successful European integration. Since then, the partnership between France and Germany has set the pace of European integration and determined, to a large degree, its achievements as well as its failures.

The UK declined to participate. However, the six countries that were ready to commit themselves to closer integration agreed on a treaty establishing the European Coal and Steel Community (ECSC), which entered into force on July 27, 1952. The ECSC created a common market for coal and steel. It was administered by a High Authority with important decision-making powers, composed of nine officials exercising their functions in complete independence. Monnet was its first president. The preamble to the ECSC Treaty made clear the political motivation of the founding fathers. It mentioned safeguarding peace, substituting for age-old rivalries the merging of essential interests, and creating "the basis for a broader and deeper community among peoples long divided by bloody conflicts." It was, therefore, no accident that the first area of integration was coal and steel, the availability of which was at that time the precondition for the possibility to wage war.[4]

Also in 1950, the French government put forward a plan for the creation of a European Defense Community, named after French Prime Minister René Pleven. The proposal was directed at all "free countries of Europe." It has to be seen against the background of the Korean War and the increasingly aggressive stance of the Soviet Union in Europe (e.g., blockade of West Berlin in 1948). It envisaged a European army that would include German units and a European defense minister who would be appointed by the governments of the participating countries. It was recognized that, in the longer run, a rearmament of Germany was inevitable. However, in a European Defense Community, German forces would be integrated into a European army, and an independent membership of Germany in the North Atlantic Treaty Organization, which, at that time, was considered undesirable, would be avoided. The plan did not receive an enthusiastic response. In particular, in France, there was strong opposition from the Gaullists as well as the Communists. On May 27, 1952, the Six signed a treaty, but in the end, the French parliament did not adopt the treaty.

How heavily considerations of national sovereignty weighed in dealing with issues of European unification was even more clearly demonstrated by the fate of various proposals for a political unification of Europe, such as for the creation of the United States of Europe (May 1951), a European Political Community (March 1953), or of a Union of European Peoples (Fouchet Plans I and II, 1961 and 1962). Such initiatives, however, advanced hardly beyond the drafting stage. The only politically oriented institution, which already had come into existence in May 1949, was the Council of Europe. It is strictly an international organization, without supranational features, with largely consultative functions, and with a special emphasis on human rights issues. Membership is open to all democratic European nations and amounted at the end of 1996 to 40 countries.

THE CREATION OF THE EUROPEAN ECONOMIC COMMUNITY AND THE EUROPEAN FREE TRADE ASSOCIATION

The efforts to come to closer economic cooperation and integration continued among the Six. Already in September 1944, well before the end of the war, the governments of Belgium and Luxembourg (which, since 1922, were joined in the Belgium-Luxembourg Economic Union) and the Netherlands had signed in London a convention on the elimination of custom duties among themselves and the establishment of common external custom tariffs, which went into effect in June 1948. It was on the initiative of these three countries that the foreign ministers of the Six met on June 1–2, 1955, in Messina. They agreed in principle on the creation of a "common market," without trade barriers among themselves and with a common external custom tariff, and of a common institution for the development and use of atomic energy for peaceful purposes. An Intergovernmental Committee on European Integration, the Spaak Committee (named after its chairman, Belgian Foreign Minister Paul-Henri Spaak) was set up.

The Spaak Report, completed in April 1956, formed the basis for the Treaty Establishing the European Economic Community (EEC) and the Treaty Establishing the European Atomic Energy Community (EAEC, Euratom). Both treaties were signed on March 25, 1957, in Rome, hence, the reference to the "Rome Treaties."[5] They became effective on January 1, 1958. The preamble to the EEC Treaty emphasized the determination "to lay the foundations of an ever closer union among the peoples of Europe," affirmed "as the essential objective . . . the constant improvement of the living and working conditions of their peoples," and the pooling of resources "to preserve and strengthen peace and liberty." It called on "the other peoples of Europe who share their ideal to join in their efforts."

The conception and the creation of the EEC would not have been possible without the achievements of the OEEC and the EPU, but there were still many hurdles on the way. In a number of European countries, the Korean War of 1950–51 led to economic difficulties, notably inflationary pressures and balance of payments deficits, which could have interrupted the process of economic normalization in Europe. A special EPU credit to Germany in this connection is mentioned in Chapter 3.

In the second half of the 1950s, France suffered from increasingly strong inflationary pressures and a marked deterioration in its balance of payments, partly because of the war in Algeria. A sharp decline in its foreign reserves forced France to draw on the International Monetary Fund, borrow from the EPU, and defer debt repayments to the United States. In the summer of 1957, the French government suspended the OEEC-inspired liberalization of imports and introduced a system of import levies and export subsidies of 20 percent each, amounting to a de facto devaluation.[6] After General Charles de Gaulle came to power in June 1958, the de facto devaluation was made official. In December of the same year, the franc was again devalued, trade with European partner countries was to 90 percent reliberalized, a strict domestic stabilization program was implemented under Finance Minister Antoine Pinay, and a "nouveau franc" was introduced, equal to 100 old francs (Kaplan and Schleiminger, 1989, pp. 270–86). With these measures, France entered the EEC with a competitive exchange rate, an important precondition for the smooth realization of the customs union as set out in the EEC Treaty.

Proposals in the 1950s for a synchronized reduction in custom tariffs within the OEEC did not come to fruition, chiefly because of objections on the part of the UK, which had a strong interest in the maintenance of trade preferences within the Commonwealth. However, there was also a more general concern about the discrimination of non-OEEC countries. As the Six moved ahead with their plan to establish the customs union among themselves, the UK proposed the creation of a large European free-trade area comprising all OEEC countries. A special committee, named after its British chairman Reginald Maudling, was formed in October 1957 to conduct negotiations. The creation of a large free-trade area could have blunted the momentum toward creation of the EEC or led to its absorption and neutralization in such a larger area. The British proposal was not realized, in some part because of the technical difficulties inherent in a free-trade arrangement without common external tariffs but certainly also because the Six were not willing to abandon their vision of a community that held out the promise for full economic union and closer political cooperation.[7]

Following the creation of the EEC and the collapse of the negotiations on a large European free-trade area in November 1958, eight of the remaining countries of the OEEC (Austria, Denmark, Iceland, Norway, Portugal, Sweden, Switzerland, and the UK) agreed to form the European Free Trade Association (EFTA). The EFTA Treaty, which entered into force on May 3, 1960, was limited to the elimination of trade barriers on industrialized goods among member countries, did not have provisions for common external tariffs, and was devoid of any commitment to a common approach in such sensitive areas as agriculture and fishery or with regard to economic and monetary policies. Finland became an associated member of EFTA in 1961.

THE INSTITUTIONS OF THE
EUROPEAN COMMUNITIES

Let us start with a note of definitional clarification. What is being commonly called the "European Community" actually consists of three communities: The ECSC, the EAEC (Euratom), and the EEC. We generally shall use the term "EC" unless there is a need to refer to the three communities or specifically to one of them. When the Maastricht Treaty entered into force on November 1, 1993, the EC became the European Union (EU).

In conceptual and actual terms, the European Communities have been, from the beginning, more than the usual international organization such as the International Monetary Fund or the OEEC. They had explicit political objectives and were endowed with tighter and more elaborate institutional structures. The Council of Ministers has been the main decision-making body. Powerful executive organs, named "Commission" in the case of the EEC and Euratom and High Authority for the ECSC, were assigned important responsibilities. The creation of a parliamentary assembly and of a court of justice emphasized the underlying political nature of the European Communities.[8]

The "Assembly" (later called the "European Parliament") and the "Court of Justice" have been serving all three communities since their establishment. In 1967, the policy-making and undoubtedly most important institutions of the communities, namely, the three councils of ministers and the executive organs (the EEC Commission, the Euratom Commission, and the High Authority of the ECSC) were merged.[9] However, this measure did not extend to the merger of the three communities themselves, a step that had been considered but was not undertaken. The three treaties continued to apply in their respective areas, and the differing rules with regard to the responsibilities of the various institutions, including voting requirements for the Council of Ministers, remained in place.

The Council of Ministers

The Council of Ministers (in the legal texts called simply "The Council") is the main decision-making institution of the EC, in which the ministers represent the member countries. This underlines the fact that decision-making power in the EC is resting essentially with the national governments, that is, the member countries. The Council can meet in different compositions (e.g., foreign ministers, also called "General Affairs Council"; economics and finance ministers, called "Ecofin Council"; agriculture ministers), depending on the matters to be decided. Decisions generally were to be made by majority (Art. 148), but the most important ones were subject to unanimity. However, majority voting largely had been avoided and became normal practice only after the Single European Act of 1987 (amending the treaties establishing the European Communities) and the Maastricht Treaty had significantly expanded the scope for majority decisions.

In mid-1965, President de Gaulle allowed the negotiations on the financing of the Common Agricultural Policy (CAP) to collapse and introduced a "policy of the empty chair" by withdrawing the French representatives from the EC institutions. The French move, for which the CAP was only the pretext, had the objective of reaffirming the principle of national sovereignty by eliminating majority decisions and weakening the "supranational" Commission that, under its President Walter Hallstein, had played an increasingly influential role. The crisis was resolved in January 1966 by the Luxembourg Compromise. It virtually required unanimity for decisions in which a member country's vital interests (in effect defined by the country concerned) were at stake and, thus, "reintroduced the national veto through the backdoor" (Tsoukalis, 1993, p. 33).

For decisions that require a qualified majority, the votes of member countries are weighted. In its design, the requirement of a qualified majority was a finely tuned instrument that ensured, on the one hand, that the larger member countries could not be outvoted by the smaller ones (which, in terms of population, are overrepresented) and, on the other hand, that the smaller countries could not be overruled by just a few of the larger ones. It also meant that, in the original Community of the Six, no single large country could block a majority decision. In the Community of Twelve, not even two large member countries had a blocking minority. With a membership of 15, a blocking minority needs at least two large and two small member states or four medium-sized states plus two small ones.[10]

The presidency in the Council rotates on a half-yearly basis. The day-to-day work is carried out by the Committee of Permanent Representatives of the member countries, in the rank of ambassadors. (This committee is frequently referred to as "Coreper," derived from the French term "Comité des représentants permanents.")[11] The work of the committee is assisted by various working groups, composed of national experts. The Council has its own secretariat.

If matters pertaining to the EC that go beyond the scope of the treaties are to be discussed or decided, ministers of the member states also meet under the heading of a "conference of representatives of member states." Any decision then requires unanimity as a matter of course. It was in such conferences (where the economics and finance ministers are often joined by the central bank governors in so-called informal meetings) that decisions concerning the European Monetary System, which is outside the legal framework of the EEC Treaty, were made.

The European Council

The regular, at least bi-annual, EC summit conference of the Heads of State or Government has become known as the "European Council." It often is confused with the Council of Ministers or (even more misleading) with the Council of Europe (previously discussed in this chapter). The European Council was not mentioned in the EC treaties and had no formal decision-making power. The Single European Act (Art. 2) brought the European Council into the legal framework of the EC. The Maastricht Treaty stated in Article D that the European Council "shall provide the Union with the necessary impetus for its development and shall define the general political guidelines thereof."

By reaching a political consensus on important issues, the European Council on various occasions paved the way for formal decisions of the Council of Ministers. The agreements and views of the European Council usually are made public in the form of resolutions, communiqués, or conclusions of the presidency. It was the European Council that took the decisive step, with its resolution of December 5, 1978, toward the creation of the European Monetary System and, at its conference on December 9 and 10, 1991, in Maastricht, concluded the intergovernmental negotiations on the formation of a European Union and its centerpiece, the economic and monetary union, by reaching agreement on a number of unresolved issues. The European Council is to play an important role in the framework of the Maastricht Treaty but, interestingly, not under its own name but under the disguise of the "Council, meeting in the composition of Heads of State or Government" (Art. 109j, 3. and 4. of the Maastricht Treaty; see Chapter 20).

The Commission

The Commission is the executive organ of the EC and has been frequently called "the guardian of the treaties." It has two main functions: to implement the decisions of the Council of Ministers and to propose new measures and directions for the EC. This "right of initiative" is a powerful instrument that, on many occasions, has shaped EC policies. (It is, therefore, not surprising that voices in the UK who would like to slow if not reverse the process of European integration favor limiting the right of initiative of the Commission.) In a number of fields, for example, in the CAP, implementing EC policies implied for the Commission the right and responsibility for legislative action.

The influence of the Commission rests, in large part, on the fact that its members are formally not committed to any national policies or preferences. The commissioners are independent in the performance of their duties (Art. 157 of the original EEC Treaty and Art. 10 of the Treaty Establishing a Single Council and a Single Commission of the European Communities, 1967). They are appointed by "common accord of the Governments of the Member States." In practice, the individual member countries nominate candidates who then are formally appointed for a period of five (originally four) years. The candidates usually have been politicians or well-known personalities with special expertise and close links to national governments and political parties. In the Community of Twelve, there were 17 commissioners, two for each of the five large countries and one for each of the smaller countries. The three countries that joined the EC in 1995 have one commissioner each, bringing the total to 20. The president and the vice-presidents (presently two) of the Commission are to be appointed from among its members for a term of two years; their appointments may be renewed. (In practice, the European Council decides first on the choice of president.)

The Commission in the wider sense is a staff recruited from all member countries. Although governments frequently nominate their nationals for higher positions, the majority of people in senior positions have risen through the ranks. The staff of the Commission numbers about 15,000 people, of which roughly 10 percent are translators and interpreters. All languages of member countries — a total of 12 — are official languages of the EC; French and English are the main working languages.

The European Parliament

The European Parliament represents the peoples of member states. Early on, its members were designated by national parliaments; since 1979, they are directly elected every five years. The 370 million citizens of the Community of Fifteen are represented by 626 members. Originally, the Parliament had only a consultative role. Subsequent treaties have extended its powers to amending and even adopting legislation. As a consequence, Parliament and Council of Ministers now share the decision-making power in a number of areas. Of particular importance is the power of the Parliament to approve the EC budget. Also, the Parliament can pass a motion of censure on the Commission and force it (but not individual commissioners) to resign. The Committee for Economic and Monetary Affairs and Industrial Policy (one of several committees) conducts hearings, issues reports, and drafts resolutions for the Parliament as a whole.

The European Court of Justice

The European Court of Justice originally consisted of seven independent judges. The number of judges was increased as additional countries joined the EC and amounts now to 15. They are assisted by 9 advocates general. The Court decides on the interpretation and implementation of EC law. The Court has played an important role in shaping the EC as it is functioning today. Traditionally, it has upheld the community interest over national interests. Court decisions are directly binding for the parties concerned. They ranged initially from important policy issues to issues of personnel policy of the European institutions. In 1989, the Court of First Instance, also with 15 judges, was established to deal with actions brought against EC decisions by companies and individuals.

NOTES

Literature of general interest for this chapter: Borchardt (1995); Friend (1991); Noël (1979); Sbragia (1992); Urwin (1995); Serving the European Union (1996).

1. Helmut Schmidt, the former German chancellor, once observed somewhat sarcastically that "Britain is notorious for governments, Labour or Conservative, that think the Atlantic is narrower than the channel" (quoted in Urwin, 1995, p. 176).

2. Denmark, Ireland, and the UK joined the EC in 1973. Norway attempted twice to join, once together with Denmark, Ireland, and the UK, the second time in the 1990s together with other Nordic countries; however, in both instances, the results of popular referenda were negative. Greece became a member on January 1, 1981, and Portugal and Spain on January 1, 1986. After the collapse of the Soviet empire, Austria, Finland, and Sweden joined the EC as of January 1, 1995.

3. At the time of his speech, Churchill was out of office.

4. On the day Foreign Minister Schuman announced his plan, German Chancellor Konrad Adenauer declared that merging the production of coal and steel would create a precondition for the elimination of conflict between France and Germany.

5. Frequently, the term "Treaty of Rome" is applied solely to the EEC Treaty.

6. I was, at that time, an intern at the German delegation to the OEEC and remember a meeting during which the French delegate declared that the

measures were not a devaluation but a "nouveau régime des changes." "Devaluation," then and later, was not a popular term.

7. See also Urwin (1995, pp. 90–96).

8. For a discussion of the supranational elements of the European Communities, see W. Ungerer (1993, pp. 26–28).

9. Treaty Establishing a Single Council and a Single Commission of the European Communities, *Official Journal of the European Communities*, No. 152, July 13, 1967.

10. The definitions of a qualified majority are as follows:

In the Community of Six, there was a total of 17 votes: France, Germany, and Italy had 4 votes each; Belgium and Netherlands, 2 each; and Luxembourg, 1. Decisions on Commission proposals required 12 votes; all other decisions required 12 votes plus at least 4 member states. Blocking minority was 6 votes.

In the Community of Twelve, the total was 76 votes: France, Germany, Italy, and the UK had 10 votes each; Spain, 8; Belgium, Greece, Netherlands, and Portugal, 5 each; Denmark and Ireland, 3 each; Luxembourg, 2. Majority requirements were 54 votes and 54 votes plus at least 6 member states, respectively. Blocking minority was 23 votes.

In the Community of Fifteen, the total is 87 votes: for both Austria and Sweden, 4 votes were added; for Finland, 3 votes. Majority requirements are 62 votes and 62 votes plus at least 8 member states, respectively. Blocking minority is 26 votes.

11. For the work of Coreper, see Lionel Barber (1995).

5

Economic and Monetary Policies in the Treaty Establishing the European Economic Community

The European Economic Community (EEC) Treaty concentrated on the creation of a customs union for industrial goods, a common trade policy vis-à-vis third countries, and a common policy for the agricultural sector. The treaty provisions on economic and monetary policies were limited in number and fairly general in nature. Nevertheless, it is of interest to examine them in some detail. They not only reflected the thinking at the time about the role of those policies in achieving the objectives of the treaty but also offer some explanation for the actual course of monetary integration over a number of years. Comparing them with the comprehensive policy provisions of the Maastricht Treaty (see Chapter 20) makes for instructive study.

The realization of the customs union and the common trade policy involved the gradual elimination of all customs duties and quantitative trade restrictions between member countries and the setting up of a common customs tariff vis-à-vis third countries during a transitional period of 12 years. It also aimed at the elimination of administrative barriers that would directly affect the establishment and functioning of the common market. Furthermore, the treaty stipulated the establishment of a Common Agricultural Policy (CAP) and a common organization of agricultural markets. As discussed in Chapter 7, the design of the CAP, as implemented, was greatly influenced by the prevailing views on the durability of stable exchange rates and had consequences for the actual conduct of exchange rate policies.

Although the treaty's emphasis was on the creation of the customs union, it contained important elements of an economic union. It envisaged the freedom of movement for workers and the abolition of restrictions on the freedom of establishment, on the freedom to provide services within the EEC, and on the free movement of capital (the "four freedoms"). Furthermore, the treaty called for common rules on cross-border transports and set rules for competition. However, all these provisions were tied closely to the creation of the customs union and, in the longer run, of an integrated "common" or "single" market but did not amount to the establishment of a full-fledged economic union.

THE SCOPE OF THE ECONOMIC AND MONETARY POLICY PROVISIONS

The provisions of the treaty on economic and monetary policies dealt more with policy principles (considered important for the creation, functioning, and protection of the common market and its heart, the customs union) than with setting out specific rules and obligations. The treaty did not provide for common policies in these areas, in contrast to the common trade policy and the CAP. It relied, instead, on the coordination of the policies of individual member states and on provisions to guard on a case-by-case basis against crises that could endanger the common market.

Apart from general references to the coordination of economic policies and to the internal and external financial stability of the member states in Part One (entitled "Principles") of the EEC Treaty (Art. 2, Art. 3 (g), and Art. 6), only 7 of the 240 articles of the treaty dealt exclusively with economic, monetary, and exchange rate policies (Art. 103–9). For comparison, there were 29 articles dealing with the establishment of the customs union alone. In fact, the term "monetary policy" did not appear in any of the headings of the respective chapters of the treaty. It was explicitly mentioned only once, in Art. 105. The treaty contained also seven articles on the free movement of capital (Art. 67–73).

A number of reasons account for this rather surprising lack of precision and detail in a treaty that was seen as an important milestone toward closer economic integration and policy cooperation and that, after all, was the instrument for the creation of a European *economic* community.

In the mid-1950s, when the negotiations on the EEC Treaty started, there existed a global monetary framework under the auspices of the International Monetary Fund (IMF) that did not seem to require, on a regional basis, specific obligations for the coordination of monetary and exchange rate policies. (Consequently, the European Payments Union agreement did not contain such obligations.) The Bretton Woods system of fixed but adjustable exchange rates was functioning, and the U.S. dollar met its responsibilities as the key currency of the international monetary system. Furthermore, the European countries were aiming at (and achieved in 1958) the convertibility of their currencies in the context of the European Payments Union.

The widely held view was that exchange rates would remain stable, providing the basis for the successful establishment and working of the customs union. Parity changes generally were seen as a last resort. Possible disturbances could be dealt with by the coordination of economic and monetary policies. Should more serious balance of payments difficulties arise, ad hoc mutual assistance — financial and otherwise — and recourse to escape clauses for the temporary suspension of treaty obligations would restore equilibrium within and between member countries.

Furthermore, economic and monetary policies were considered an integral part of national sovereignty and identity. The founding fathers were, therefore, reluctant to encroach on the sovereignty of member states. Also, there were no simple and automatic mechanisms by which economic and monetary policies could be harmonized, in contrast to the establishment of the customs union, where custom duties and quantitative trade restrictions could be abolished and an external custom tariff be built up in a predetermined and phased way. There was the feeling that the coordination of policies should be developed step by step as needed for the realization of the common market. It was, of course, recognized that a harmonization of policies and, in the long run, common policies and even a common currency would be required if the vision of fully integrated economies and the desired progress toward political unification was to be achieved. D. C. Kruse (1980, pp. 14–16) observed that "the goal of creating economic and monetary union was implicit in the Treaty of Rome, [but] it was certainly not one of its most immediate objects."

THE TREATY ARTICLES ON ECONOMIC AND MONETARY POLICIES

The preamble of the EEC Treaty set out the broad objectives of the EEC, including "to strengthen the unity of [Member States'] economies and to ensure their harmonious development." In Part One of the treaty ("Principles"), Art. 2 spoke of "progressively approximating the economic policies of Member States," and Art. 3, which described the main activities of the EEC, referred to "procedures by which the economic policies of Member States can be coordinated and disequilibria in their balances of payments remedied." In Art. 145, the task of the Council of Ministers "to ensure coordination of the general economic policies of the Member States" was laid down.[1]

The following is a short discussion of the provisions for economic, monetary, and exchange rate policies in the original EEC Treaty of 1957.

It should be noted that they were extensively modified by the Maastricht Treaty of 1992.

Article 6

In the section on "Principles," Art. 6 was somewhat more detailed than the already mentioned broad guidelines contained in the same section. It reads:

1.   Member States shall, in close cooperation with the institutions of the Community, coordinate their respective economic policies to the extent necessary to attain the objectives of this Treaty.
2.   The institutions of the Community shall take care not to prejudice the internal and external financial stability of the Member States.

Of particular interest is that the obligation to coordinate economic policies was circumscribed by the phrase "to the extent necessary to attain the objectives of this Treaty." If one identifies the creation of the customs union, the realization of the four freedoms, and the development of common policies for agriculture and foreign trade as the main objectives of the EEC Treaty, then the obligations under this article appear quite unambitious, even more in view of the use of the relatively weak term "coordinate" instead of, say, "harmonize" or "unify."

Furthermore, the lack of an explicit reference to the maintenance of stable exchange rates in this or any other article of the treaty seems peculiar, because stable nominal exchange rates generally have been considered an important feature of, if not precondition for, a common market. As already indicated, this omission can be explained by the somewhat naive trust in the stability of existing exchange rates in the framework of the Bretton Woods system and by the recognition of the politically highly sensitive nature of exchange rates as important policy instruments and as symbols of national sovereignty. Art. 6 referred, instead, somewhat vaguely to "internal and external stability," foreshadowing the use of similar words in the resolution of the European Council of December 5, 1978, on the creation of the European Monetary System (EMS). These words came to be interpreted as references to price and exchange rate stability, respectively. Also, neither here nor in the later articles on economic policies (see the discussion of Art. 104) was there any attempt to address the possible conflict between internal and external policy objectives, a problem that has vexed international and European monetary cooperation since the disappearance of the pre-1914 gold standard and all the way up to the severe EMS crises in 1992–93.

Article 103

Economic, monetary, and exchange rate policies were specifically dealt with in Part Three ("Policy of the Community"), Title II ("Economic Policy") of the treaty, in Chapters 1 ("Conjunctural Policy") and 2 ("Balance of Payments").

Art. 103 stated as a broad guideline that "Member States shall regard their conjunctural policies as a matter of common concern. They shall consult each other and the Commission on the measures to be taken in the light of the prevailing circumstances." The choice of the term "conjunctural policies" for the English language version of the treaty, a literal translation from the original four languages of the treaty ("Konjunkturpolitik," "politique de conjoncture," and so on) was somewhat unfortunate; it should be read as referring to "short-term economic policies," that is, the policies that are oriented toward the maintenance of economic equilibrium on the path to longer-term objectives, such as sustained growth.

The relatively weak obligation for consultation, not even coordination, left the economic policy autonomy of member states basically untouched. This and the requirement of unanimity for the adoption of any measures under this article made decisive common policy action somewhat unlikely. In practice, Council action under this article generally was limited to recommendations or resolutions. Also, the treaty remained silent as to what areas of short-term economic policy could be subject to Council action. The provision that "the Council may . . . decide upon the measures appropriate to the situation" indicated that the power of the Council was more of an ad hoc nature and did not necessarily extend to the establishment of an institutional framework and the setting of priorities for short-term policies.

Another point of interest is whether the term "conjunctural policies" should be interpreted more widely to cover also monetary policy (more precisely, central bank policy) or more narrowly to cover only *other* short-term policy areas. This question was of importance in view of the fact that, in some member states (Germany, Netherlands, less so Belgium), central banks enjoyed a high degree of independence while in others (mainly France but also Italy, and among the countries that joined the European Community (EC) later, in particular the United Kingdom, Spain, and Portugal), governments had an important say in monetary policy. The issue did not lead to serious conflicts because, as already mentioned, economic policy remained basically in the domain of member states and, thus, was subject to national demarcations of responsibility. Furthermore, the requirement of unanimity gave each country a veto right that could be used to protect national institutional arrangements. When the Council addressed monetary policies — which, after all, are an

important aspect of short-term policies — it was done in the form of recommendations, for example, in the recommendation for the reestablishment of the internal and external equilibrium of April 15, 1964, which
dealt with inflationary pressures (*Official Journal of the European Communities*, April 22, 1964, pp. 1029–31).

Article 104

This article set out a kind of basic law for the economic policy objectives of member states: "Each Member State shall pursue the economic
policy needed to ensure the equilibrium of its overall balance of payments
and to maintain confidence in its currency while taking care to ensure a
high level of employment and a stable level of prices."

This is the classical definition of the "magic triangle" of economic policy. (In view of its somewhat illusory nature, it sometimes has been called
the "uneasy triangle.") If one can discern in the wording of the article a
slightly stronger emphasis on the equilibrium of the balance of payments
than on the other objectives, this would appear justified, considering the
importance of the balance of payments of each member state for creating
and safeguarding the common market.

Again, the stability of exchange rates was not explicitly mentioned but
only hinted at with the obligation "to maintain confidence in its currency," which has an internal as well as an external dimension. Theory has
explained and experience has shown that the simultaneous pursuit of
internal and external monetary stability can cause tremendous difficulties
for economic policy. The only way out frequently has been a change in the
exchange rate, which, however, was considered incompatible with the
maintenance of a common market. The other solution, more in line with
the notion of a "community," would have been to agree on common priorities of policy objectives that then would guide the policy actions of the
individual member states. This has been successfully undertaken in the
1980s in the framework of the EMS, following the negative experiences of
the 1970s.

Article 105

Art. 105 was concerned with the implementation of the policy objectives laid down in Art. 104: "In order to facilitate attainment of the objectives set out in Article 104, Member States shall coordinate their economic
policies. They shall for this purpose provide for cooperation between
their appropriate administrative departments and between their central
banks."

It also stipulated: "In order to promote coordination of the policies
of Member States in the monetary field to the full extent needed for the

functioning of the common market, a Monetary Committee with advisory status is hereby set up." The committee was charged with the task "to keep under review the monetary and financial situation of the Member States and of the Community and the general payments system of the Member States." The Monetary Committee was established in early 1958, soon after the EEC came into existence. Member states and the Commission each appointed two members (and their alternates) to the committee — in the case of member states, one each from the central bank and the government, usually the finance ministry. Although the status of the committee was described as "advisory," it acquired over the years an important policy role. This has applied not only to national and intra-EC economic problems but also, following a Council decision of May 8, 1964, to the international monetary policies of the EC, for example, in the context of the negotiations on the reform of the international monetary system in the second half of the 1960s that led to the establishment of the Special Drawing Rights facility of the IMF (see Chapter 7) or in connection with the breakdown of the Bretton Woods system in the period from 1971 to 1973 (see Chapter 10). A very significant role has been played by the committee with regard to operations of the EMS; decisions by the ministers of EMS countries have been prepared and frequently determined by discussions within the committee.

In later years, in order to give the efforts to coordinate economic and monetary policies a stronger institutional framework, additional committees were set up, among them, in 1964, the Committee of the Governors of the Central Banks (see Chapter 8).

Article 106

This article dealt with the liberalization of payments "connected with the movement of goods, services or capital, and any transfers of capital and earnings, to the extent that the movement of goods, services, capital and persons between Member States has been liberalised." At the time this article was drafted, full transferability and convertibility of currencies had not yet been achieved. When at the end of 1958 the major European countries, including all EC member states, declared the convertibility of their currencies, this article became redundant, except as a safety net in case of unforeseen difficulties.

Article 107

Art. 107 required that each member state "shall treat its policy with regard to rates of exchange as a matter of common concern." Subdivision 2 dealt with exchange rate changes "which [are] inconsistent with the objectives set out in Article 104 and which seriously distort . . . conditions of competition." In such a case, the Commission was empowered, after consulting the Monetary Committee, to authorize other member states to take temporary countermeasures.

Also in Art. 107, there was no explicit reference to any obligation to maintain stable exchange rates, for the reasons discussed earlier, although it was recognized that exchange rate policies were of great importance for the realization of the common market. Subdivision 2 did not contain any general rule for allowing exchange rate changes, such as the notion of "fundamental disequilibrium" in the IMF Articles of Agreement, but, reflecting in particular the experiences of the interwar period, was concerned with possible competitive devaluations, that is, devaluations that were designed not only to restore competitiveness but also to gain a competitive advantage over other countries.

After World War II, competitive devaluations have not been a serious problem for the EC area or for the industrialized world as a whole. Rather, it has been the stickiness of exchange rates that were significantly out of line and created serious balance of payments difficulties, triggering heavy speculative capital flows and severe international financial crises, particularly in the late 1960s and the early 1970s and again in 1992 and 1993 within the EMS. However, it was also in the framework of the EMS that commitments to maintain stable exchange rates have been used as a disciplinary device in the pursuit of "hard currency" policies, oriented toward the achievement of domestic monetary and price stability. This provided the basis for the sustained stability of exchange rates from the mid-1980s to the early 1990s.

In reviewing EMS developments after the 1992 crisis, however, it has been asked whether the strong depreciations of the Italian lira and the British pound did not result in significant undervaluations of these currencies. Yet, whether this amounted to "competitive devaluations," as sometimes claimed, is difficult to judge, because both currencies have been floating.

Articles 108 and 109

These two articles were devoted to the management of balance of payments difficulties.

Art. 108 addressed situations in which balance of payments difficulties "are liable in particular to jeopardise the functioning of the common market or the progressive implementation of the common commercial [i.e., trade] policy." It set out procedures, involving the Commission, the Monetary Committee, and the Council, for recommending, as a first step, measures to a country concerned and — if that proved insufficient — for the granting of mutual assistance, to be decided by the Council with a qualified majority. Such assistance could include but was not limited to the granting of credits by other member states. Should the Council not grant the recommended assistance, then the Commission could authorize the country in difficulties to take specified protective measures, which, in turn, could be revoked or changed by the Council acting by qualified majority. The provisions for mutual assistance were activated in favor of France following the crisis of May 1968, although no financial assistance from within the EC was granted.

Art. 109 dealt with a sudden balance of payments crisis. The country concerned could take the necessary protective measures, which "must cause the least possible disturbance in the functioning of the common market." They were subject to EC examination, and the Council could, on the advice of the Commission and the Monetary Committee, decide (with qualified majority) on the amendment, suspension, or abolition of these measures.

The rather complex procedures outlined in these two articles were to ensure that a country with balance of payments difficulties would obtain the necessary assistance while the functioning of the common market would not be put at risk. Of special interest is the envisaged interplay between the "supranational" Commission, the "advisory" Monetary Committee, and the Council representing the member states. The articles were designed to operate on an ad hoc basis. In later years, the financial aspect of mutual assistance was institutionalized by the creation of a number of credit facilities: the Short-Term Monetary Support (1970), the Medium-Term Financial Assistance (1971), and the Community Loan Mechanism (1975). (For details on these facilities, see Chapters 8 and 12.)

FREE MOVEMENT OF CAPITAL

Chapter 4 in Title III ("Free Movement of Persons, Services and Capital") of Part Two ("Foundations of the Community") of the treaty deals in Art. 67–73 with the liberalization of capital movements, listed in Art. 3 among the activities of the EC.

Article 67 was the most important one. It reads:

1. During the transitional period and to the extent necessary to ensure the proper functioning of the common market, Member States shall progressively abolish between themselves all restrictions on the movement of capital belonging to persons resident in Member States.

2. Current payments connected with the movement of capital between Member States shall be freed from all restrictions by the end of the first stage at the latest.

Special attention needs to be given to the qualification "to the extent necessary." Policymakers interpreted this provision rather narrowly, as shown by the "First Directive for the Implementation of Article 67 of the Treaty," which was adopted by the Council of Ministers on May 11, 1960 (a minor amendment followed on December 18, 1962) (*Official Journal of the European Communities,* July 12, 1960, pp. 919–32; January 23, 1963, pp. 62–74). The directive essentially consolidated and codified the degree of liberalization that the EC countries had reached in the framework of the Organization for European Economic Cooperation. Some countries, in particular Germany, which had already gone substantially beyond the requirements of the directive, undertook not to introduce any new exchange restrictions on transactions they had liberalized.

The directive called for the freedom of those capital movements that are closely related to the other freedoms — the free movement of goods and services, of workers, and the right of establishment. The directive divided capital transactions into four categories. Only for the first two categories was complete liberalization required, mainly affecting direct investments; investments in real estate; capital movements of a personal nature, such as gifts, dowries, or inheritances; short-term and medium-term credits in respect of commercial transactions; and operations in securities quoted on stock exchanges. A third category of capital transactions also was to be liberalized, but a member state could maintain or reintroduce restrictions when their abolition "might form an obstacle to the achievement of the economic policy objectives of a Member State." This category included mainly operations in securities not quoted on stock exchanges, long-term credits related to commercial transactions, and medium-term credits not related to commercial transactions. For the last category, mainly short-term investments in treasury bills and other short-term money market instruments and short-term credits not related to commercial transactions, there was no obligation to liberalize.

The directive also laid down rules for the operation by the Belgium-Luxembourg Economic Union of the dual (or two-tier) foreign exchange market, which had been introduced in 1954. Under this system, capital transactions were carried out on a separate, "free" market for which no commitment to observe intervention margins existed; most current transactions had to be conducted on the "official" market within the fixed intervention limits. The purpose of the rules was to limit the extent and duration of exchange rate fluctuations on the free market (*IMF Survey,* January 8, 1973).

As part of the Single Market Program of 1986, a directive of June 1988 stipulated in principle the complete liberalization of capital movements by July 1, 1990, while allowing some member states with structurally weaker economies temporary exemptions (for details, see Chapter 15).

Art. 73 was the other important article in this section of the treaty. It provided an escape clause should "movements of capital lead to disturbances in the functioning of the capital market in any Member State." In such a case, following certain procedures, a country could take protective measures in the field of capital movements.

During the monetary crises of the late 1960s and the 1970s, nearly all member states made use of this provision, and some countries maintained such restrictions well into the 1980s. Since about 1983, there was a general trend toward more liberalization, related to the efforts to complete the common market and facilitated by the progress in achieving more convergence in economic performance. This culminated in the already mentioned directive of June 1988.

The remaining articles on capital movements called for policies that are "as liberal as possible" and "non-discriminatory" (Art. 68); called for "the progressive coordination of exchange policies" and "the highest possible degree of liberalization" relating to capital movements between member states and third countries (Art. 70); and requested member states "to avoid introducing . . . any new exchange restrictions on the movement of capital and current payments connected with such movements" and to be ready "to go beyond the degree of liberalisation of capital movements provided for in the preceding Articles in so far as their economic situation, in particular the situation of their balance of payments, so permits" (Art. 71).

EVALUATION

An examination of the treaty provisions on economic and monetary policies and on the liberalization of capital movements shows that safeguarding the common market was the main concern of the drafters of the treaty. To this end, the treaty relied basically on the coordination of policies, although procedural details were not spelled out; on a number of escape clauses for countries in balance of payments or other difficulties (including an escape clause with regard to the common trade policy in Art. 115); and on the assurance of solidarity in the form of financial and other forms of ad hoc mutual assistance. The balance of payments situation of member states and their exchange rate policies were accorded explicit importance. However, clear reference to objectives for the latter was avoided.

The wording of the treaty strongly suggests that the stability of "nominal" exchange rates was taken more or less for granted. The "real" exchange rate (i.e., the nominal exchange rate adjusted for changes in costs or prices) as a theoretical concept and an analytical tool was not yet familiar. Although changes in nominal exchange rates were not excluded, the basic problem of exchange rate policy — divergent trends in economic policies and developments and the resulting changes in relative real exchange rates — was not recognized. Similarly, the essential requirement for exchange rate stability — the convergence of economic performance among EC members, based on a consensus on economic policy objectives — was not openly addressed, given the concern to preserve national sovereignty.

In later years, the inability to define common economic policy objectives would frustrate efforts to intensify monetary policy integration in line with progress in economic market integration and led to the abandonment of the project for an economic and monetary union in the EC, as embodied in the Werner Report of 1970. The emphasis on the convergence of economic policies and developments in the framework of the EMS in the years 1983 to 1990 paved the way for the resumption of the economic and monetary union project with the Delors Report of 1989 and the Maastricht Treaty of 1992.

NOTE

1.   I cannot agree with Tommaso Padoa-Schioppa (1994, p. 54), who saw in Art. 145 an explicit commitment to let the autonomy of national policies yield to the needs of coordination, but I certainly agree that this has not been done.

6

Important Monetary Events in the European Community in the 1960s

In the first decade of the implementation of the European Economic Community (EEC) Treaty, the political energy of the member states and of the Commission was directed mainly toward the realization of the customs union, the centerpiece of the common market, and the creation of the Common Agricultural Policy (CAP). Both had far-reaching implications for the economies of member states and for their political and social developments.

During a transitional period of 12 years, customs duties and quantitative trade restrictions for industrial goods between European Community (EC) members had to be gradually abolished and a common external customs tariff vis-à-vis third countries set up, both difficult tasks in view of differing economic structures of member states and varying patterns of foreign trade in terms of geography and composition. A perhaps even more daunting challenge was the design and implementation of the CAP. Not only did the size and the structure of the agricultural sector differ from country to country, but also there existed widely disparate systems of support for producers and consumers of agricultural goods.

The job of establishing the customs union and the CAP was made easier by generally harmonious economic developments in the EC during the first half of the 1960s. Economic growth was healthy, and unemployment and inflation remained generally low. Nevertheless, the 1960s were, by no means, free of problems. As time went on, economic disparities between EC countries appeared, and the emergence of monetary crises within as well as outside the EC tested and increasingly put into question two of the basic assumptions on which the economic and monetary policy provisions of the EEC Treaty were built: that exchange rates would on the whole remain stable, and that difficulties could satisfactorily be dealt with by the coordination of policies and by ad hoc mutual assistance.

THE GERMAN REVALUATION OF 1961

In reaction to the devastating experiences of the big inflations after the two world wars, Germany pursued strict anti-inflationary policies after the radical currency reform of June 1948, which introduced the Deutsche mark. They were based on a firm consensus between the people and the economic policymakers in government and the central bank and provided framework and foundation for the much praised "economic miracle."

In 1959 and 1960, the economic situation in Germany increasingly was characterized by the simultaneous appearance of domestic overheating and inflationary pressure on the one hand and a significant balance of payments surplus on the other. This created a dilemma for monetary policy. Although the inflationary pressures accompanying the boom called for restrictive demand management, a tightening of monetary policy would have caused further inflows of funds from abroad. A debate ensued whether the mark should be revalued or not. The Deutsche Bundesbank, Germany's central bank, was against a revaluation out of principle, while representatives of the German banking sector and industry were concerned mainly about exports.[1] Within the German government, the Federal Ministry for Economics was the strongest advocate of a revaluation; the Chancellor, Konrad Adenauer, was initially against it. The academic community, realizing the existence of an underlying disequilibrium, was, in large part, in favor of a revaluation. Other options that were discussed included an increase in official capital exports, restrictions on capital imports, and a multilateral exchange rate realignment, at that time a somewhat unrealistic option.

In any event, the Deutsche mark was revalued by 5 percent on March 6, 1961. In view of the close links between the German and the Dutch economies, the Netherlands authorities, while criticizing the lack of prior consultation, followed suit two days later and revalued the guilder by the same magnitude. Internationally, the revaluation of the mark generally met with understanding, although the managing director of the International Monetary Fund (IMF), Per Jacobsson, as the "guardian" of stable exchange rates, did not hide his disappointment about the German decision (Emminger, 1986, p. 126).

The revaluation of the mark was, by today's standards, relatively small. It brought to the fore a near-ideological controversy. On the one side, the stability of exchange rates still was widely regarded as a sacrosanct principle of international economic relations and as prerequisite for international financial stability. The Bundesbank (1960, p. 49) spoke for many when it emphasized that the revaluation was a "non-recurrent and final measure" and that parity changes were not a normal monetary policy instrument but an expedient of last resort, to be used only when all other means failed. A number of policymakers and a large part of the academic community, however, recognized the potential conflicts between domestic and external policy objectives and regarded the exchange rate as an important instrument to help resolve such conflicts. In any event, the 1961 revaluation turned out to be a first breakthrough in exchange rate philosophy that opened the way to the more radical approaches adopted in the monetary crises of 1968–69 and, in particular, in connection with the breakdown of the Bretton Woods system during the period 1971–73.

THE ITALIAN BALANCE OF PAYMENTS CRISIS OF 1964

Italy experienced in 1962 and 1963 large wage increases, which soon resulted in excess demand, inflationary pressure, and, ultimately, serious balance of payments difficulties. In March 1964, the Italian lira was exposed to a strong speculative attack. To be able to defend the lira exchange rate, Italy secured international credit lines amounting to $1,050 million from the IMF, the U.S. monetary authorities, and several European central banks. Italy was not forced to devalue and, in the end, needed to make only limited use of these credit lines. Italy's international reserve position recovered quickly, and its repayment obligations were met with ease within a short time.

Apart from the avoidance of a devaluation, from an EC point of view, it was of interest that the provisions for mutual assistance of Art. 108 and 109 of the EEC Treaty were not activated. This would have involved EC institutions, in particular, the Commission and the Council of Ministers. Charles A. Coombs, the long-time senior vice-president of the Federal Reserve Bank of New York for foreign exchange and gold operations, wrote in his memoirs (1976, p. 84) that "efforts by the Italian government to round up additional credits from its Common Market partners had broken down as the political negotiators on both sides became involved in some ill-tempered bargaining." Instead, Italy obtained the needed financial assistance outside the EC framework, as mentioned above. By comparison, when Italy was in need of financial assistance in 1974, it took recourse to the by-then-established credit facilities of the EC.

THE MONETARY CRISES OF 1968 AND 1969

In May 1968, large-scale student demonstrations and a general strike erupted in Paris. After some time, the French government under

President Charles de Gaulle restored order but at the price of significant economic concessions, in particular, wage increases of more than 10 percent. They impaired the international competitiveness of French industry and spurred a surge of imports. More important, however, than the deterioration of the trade balance was the impact on the international reserve position of France of large speculative capital outflows that immediately followed the "May events" (as the period of social unrest came to be called).

In October, the speculation against the French franc was exacerbated by a world-wide speculation on a revaluation of the Deutsche mark. It was triggered not by the German overall balance of payments (which, in the first ten months of 1968, showed even a moderate deficit) but by the very high surplus on current transactions. This seemed to indicate a significant undervaluation of the mark. Speculation reached a peak in the first three weeks of November, when the Bundesbank was swamped with an inflow of DM 9.5 billion (at the then-prevailing exchange rate equivalent to about $2.4 billion) while the Bank of France lost large amounts of reserves. The speculative pressure also spread to the British pound.

On November 20–22, 1968, the finance ministers and central bank governors of the countries of the G-10 (Group of Ten, i.e., the ten most important industrial countries participating in the General Arrangements to Borrow affiliated with the IMF) met in Bonn to discuss ways to end the crisis. At the same time, the foreign exchange markets in France, Germany, and the United Kingdom were closed. Initially, the hope was to reach agreement on a combined revaluation of the Deutsche mark and devaluation of the French franc. The conference — described as a frustrating experience by participants (Coombs, 1976, p. 183; Emminger, 1986, p. 146) — did not come to an agreement. Already, before the start of the conference, Germany rejected a revaluation of its currency. During the conference, France appeared ready to devalue.

However, on the evening of Saturday, November 23, the day following the conclusion of the conference, President de Gaulle, in a surprise television appearance, declared unequivocally: "La France ne dévalue pas" [France is not going to devalue].[2] Once again, considerations of a basically political nature prevailed over economic reasoning.

Several countries showed understanding for the French position, in particular, the United States, which may have feared that a large French devaluation could further undermine the already weakened position of the dollar (Solomon, 1982, p. 161). However, the crisis brought some relief to the United States because France, the country most likely to present its dollar holdings for conversion into gold (a move that would have further drained U.S. gold reserves), was itself in trouble.

Nevertheless, the situation required measures to defuse the crisis. Germany, although rejecting a revaluation, went ahead with the introduction of a special border tax on exports and tax relief on imports of nonagricultural goods of generally 4 percent, both of which had been announced before the ill-fated conference. This measure amounted to a partial revaluation and was promptly dubbed an "ersatz revaluation." Additionally, the German authorities imposed restrictions on certain short-term capital inflows and raised to 100 percent the reserve requirements on foreign deposits in German banks. France, in turn, tightened exchange controls and took measures to cut the budget deficit for 1969 in half, while partner central banks provided credit lines of $2 billion. The United Kingdom also took restrictive actions to protect the pound's exchange rate, which had been under persistent pressure for some time.

In the context of the conference, EC Commission Vice-President Raymond Barre, a French economics professor who later became French prime minister and a presidential candidate, took the position (1968, p. 16) that a revaluation of the Deutsche mark was "politically undesirable"; instead, the difficulties related to Germany's persistent current account surplus could be solved only "by energetic measures for speedier growth and the stimulation of imports and by special action to inhibit the flow of speculative capital into Germany." In turn, the French franc "should not be devalued, since there was no technical justification for such a step in the state of the French economy."

For a while, foreign exchange markets remained calm, but unrest flared up again in March 1969 in connection with a referendum in France on a constitutional reform. On April 10, President de Gaulle announced that he would resign if the proposed reform was rejected, and on April 28, after the negative outcome of the referendum, he left office. He was succeeded by Georges Pompidou. Now, the pace of speculation became frantic, and Germany had to absorb an inflow of capital of nearly DM 17 billion (equivalent to more than $4 billion), at that time an unheard-of amount. Again, on May 9, the German coalition government under Christian-Democratic Chancellor Kurt Georg Kiesinger rejected a revaluation, against the advice of Economics Minister Karl Schiller from the Social-Democratic Party and the Bundesbank.

France was strongly affected by the turmoil surrounding the Deutsche mark, but following an election success by President Pompidou, the crisis subsided. It came, then, as a complete surprise when, "in a cleanly executed maneuver" (Coombs, 1976, p. 187) and without much prior consultation with its EC partners, France devalued the franc by 11.1 percent effective August 10, 1969.[3] At the same time, the French government introduced a temporary price freeze and a package of restrictive fiscal and monetary measures and concluded a stand-by agreement with the IMF for $985 million in September 1969. Coombs (1976, p. 187) wryly observed: "The defense of the franc over the preceding 15 months had cost France reserve losses of roughly $5 billion."

In Germany, the quarrel about the revaluation became one of the main issues in the campaign for the election of a new parliament on September 28, 1969, with both sides claiming to defend the "stability" of the Deutsche mark — a nice mix-up of the concepts of "external" and "internal" monetary stability. Not surprisingly, in the weeks before the election, there was a new wave of speculation. Immediately after the election, the acting German government, on the recommendation of the Bundesbank, permitted the Deutsche mark to float temporarily — a first for a major European currency after World War II.[4] The IMF was notified of the German action and recognized its urgency.[5] The new coalition government of Social Democrats and Free Democrats, under Willy Brandt as chancellor and with Schiller as economics minister, decided on October 24 to revalue the Deutsche mark by 9.3 percent. The border taxes and the special reserve requirement for foreign deposits in German banks were eliminated. However — as Otmar Emminger (at the time, in charge of international affairs at the Bundesbank and from 1977 to 1979 its president) observed with hindsight — it was too late to curb domestic inflation (1977, p. 26).

Thus, the until-then biggest monetary crisis in the EC came to an end. Within a period of two years, the three most important European currencies — pound sterling (in November 1967; see Chapter 7), French franc, and Deutsche mark — had changed their parities. Yet, the difficulties of the most important currency of the international monetary system, the dollar, had not come any closer to a solution (see Chapter 7). Before the exchange rate adjustments of August and October 1969 had taken place, the Bundesbank, in its 1968 Annual Report (p. 30), observed: "A system of basically fixed exchange rates can only be maintained without the risk of heavy disturbances and crises if at least the major countries agree on their economic policy objectives and march in step in their realisation. . . . The experience made over recent years demonstrates, however, that there does not yet exist complete harmony among the leading industrial countries as far as the aims of economic policy are concerned."

EXCHANGE RATE CHANGES AND THE COMMON AGRICULTURAL POLICY

The changes in the parities of the French franc and the Deutsche mark created problems for the CAP of the EC. Also, in future years, conflicts emerged between the need to adjust exchange rates and the exigencies of the CAP.

The CAP as implemented from 1962 on was based on a system of common prices for most agricultural goods, expressed in a unit of account with a gold content (0.88867088 gram) equal to the U.S. dollar before the 1971 devaluation. Prices in national currencies were obtained by converting the prices expressed in units of account at official parities.[6] The underlying assumption was that either a sufficient degree of economic convergence would occur more or less by itself to make exchange rate changes redundant or the choice of a regime of common prices for agricultural goods would induce a degree of policy coordination consistent with fixed exchange rates.[7] Both assumptions proved to be illusory, revealing a high degree of naivety regarding the risk of divergent economic developments under conditions of national economic policy autonomy.[8]

The important point is that a smooth functioning of the agricultural price system required a virtually complete stability of exchange rates. Any change in parity implied, if the uniformity of prices across borders was to be preserved, that a devaluation would result in an instantaneous rise in agricultural prices in the country concerned and a revaluation in an instantaneous fall. The consequences — an increase of consumer prices or a decline in agricultural incomes, respectively — were neither economically nor politically acceptable to the countries concerned. However, to abandon the principle of uniform prices would have led inevitably to major trade distortions.

In connection with the exchange rate changes in 1969, the possibility of changing the agricultural unit of account as a means to mitigate the consequences of exchange rate changes, as foreseen in an EC regulation of May 30, 1968, was examined but not recommended by the Monetary Committee.[9] Instead, as a way out, the Council of Ministers agreed on a set of measures that were meant to be transitional. Their aim was to keep prices in national currencies at previous levels and to preserve agricultural incomes. The ad hoc nature of these measures made it evident that the parity changes of 1969 were considered (at least in agricultural policy circles) as exceptions in a world of otherwise stable exchange rates.

When EC currencies were allowed to float in May and August 1971, and with the large adjustments of exchange rate parities in the framework of the Smithsonian Agreement of December 1971 (see Chapter 11), the notion of permanently stable exchange rates had to be abandoned. In May 1971, the ad hoc arrangements of 1969 were replaced by a general system of border compensation. The objective was to neutralize or mitigate the impact of exchange rate changes on domestic agricultural prices while maintaining common prices (or, rather, the illusion of common prices). For purposes of the CAP, the old parities continued to be applied as "green parities." The gaps between green parities and actually existing exchange rates (and, thus, the differences between national price levels of agricultural goods) that resulted either from central rate changes or (in the case of floating currencies) from changes in market rates were bridged by "monetary compensatory amounts" (MCAs). They took the form of export levies and import subsidies for countries with devalued currencies and of import levies and export subsidies for countries with revalued currencies, designed to keep prices unchanged in national currencies. Green exchange rates and MCAs were supposed to be phased out eventually in order to provide equal conditions between the agricultural and nonagricultural sectors within a given country and between farmers in different EC countries. In practice, the dismantling of MCAs encountered great difficulties and led, at times, to acrimonious discussions among EC countries, which, in early 1979, even delayed the start of the European Monetary System (EMS).

In March 1984, the system of MCAs was modified so as to facilitate the return to price unity. The common price level was tied to the exchange rate of the strongest EC currency. Thus, price unity was restored after EMS realignments by raising prices in individual member states by the same percentage as their currency's depreciation against the strongest currency in the system.[10] This arrangement had to be abandoned when recurrent realignments raised the common price level, which not only increased the cost of the CAP but also caused friction with the EC's trade partners on account of rising subsidies. Moreover, with the widening of the EMS fluctuation margins from normally ±2.25 percent to ±15 percent in August 1993 (see Chapter 22), the arrangement became impractical, because there could be significant exchange rate movements without realignments. Currently, member states keep agricultural support prices unchanged as long as exchange rate movements are small enough not to disrupt trade, but beyond that, they follow the original rules by raising prices in the event of a depreciation and lowering them when their currency appreciates.

Although the principle of uniform prices for agricultural goods and the technical complexity of MCAs made decisions about exchange rate adjustments more difficult and, at times, may have tended to delay them, it cannot be said that they seriously impaired them. Rather, the at-least-temporary sheltering of the agricultural sectors of EC countries from the impact of exchange rate changes by virtue of the MCAs actually may have facilitated agreement on needed exchange rate adjustments. Any resistance to exchange rate adjustments, as, for instance, in September 1992, was primarily related to general economic concerns such as inflation and competitiveness or to considerations of political credibility, prestige, and sovereignty.

NOTES

Literature of general interest for this chapter: Coombs (1976); Emminger (1977, 1986); Solomon (1982); Deutsche Bundesbank, Annual Reports.

1.   From today's perspective, this concern can be fully understood only if one recognizes the adverse impact of external financial problems on the German economy during the interwar period and the reliance on exports as the "engine of growth" and a guarantor of social stability after World War II.

2.   The Bundesbank had sent me to Paris for a meeting of the EC Monetary Committee on Sunday, November 24, at which the expected French devaluation was to be discussed. The evening before, I was stunned to watch on French television de Gaulle's announcement. I immediately called my boss, Otmar Emminger, at that time the Bundesbank board member in charge of international affairs, who had attended the Bonn conference; he also was taken completely by surprise. However, IMF Managing Director Pierre-Paul Schweitzer reported to the IMF Executive Board immediately after the Bonn meeting "that at no time had the French authorities at the meeting announced an intention to devalue: it was always perfectly clear that they reserved for their Government the choice between no devaluation or a devaluation of a very limited amount" (de Vries, 1976, Vol. I, p. 453). For a detailed account of the November 1968 events, see Harold James (1996, pp. 193–97).

3.   There are conflicting views on whether a *prior* consultation had taken place. In fact, it was not until Saturday, August 9, that a meeting of the Monetary Committee in Brussels was called for the morning of Sunday, August 10 (which I attended as representative of the Bundesbank), although the devaluation became effective on Sunday at 8 P.M., Paris time. Therefore, although one could argue that, formally, a prior consultation had taken place, it was certainly not in time to allow France's EC partners to consider any action of their own in response to the French move. This, of course, was the purpose of the obligation to enter into prior consultations.

4.   The Belgian franc was allowed to float for a short time in September 1949. In September 1950, the Canadian government decided to let their currency float in response to capital inflows from the United States.

5.   The Bundesbank (1969, p. 32) observed that the excellent technical functioning of this "interim float" found internationally keen interest, with a view to the possible legalization of "interim floats" within the IMF.

6.   Since 1979, common agricultural prices have been expressed in ECU.

7.   The EEC Treaty, Art. 40, did not mandate a "European market organisation" with common prices but offered also the options of "common rules on competition" and "compulsory coordination of the various national market organisations." The choice of a system with common prices could be called one of the most glaring examples of the "monetarist" integration strategy (described in more detail in Chapter 8) if monetary integration would have been the immediate objective. Yet, the system of common prices was conceptualized and implemented solely from an agricultural policy point of view, with, at best, scant regard to its monetary policy implications.

8.   Quite appropriately, Loukas Tsoukalis (1977, p. 59) called the respective section of his book "The Agricultural Mythology."

9.   *Official Journal of the European Communities*, May 31, 1968. Such a measure would not have allowed preservation of prices expressed in national currencies but resulted only in a shift in the level of the common prices. Depending on the direction and the extent of the change in the unit of account, this would have

resulted in unchanged prices for a revaluing country and correspondingly higher prices for all other countries, unchanged prices for a devaluing country and correspondingly lower prices for the other countries, or anything in-between. Obviously, neither would have solved the economic and political problems of rising or falling agricultural prices.

10.   For details of the monetary aspects of the CAP, see Deutsche Bundesbank (1984, pp. 37–43) and Julius Rosenblatt et al. (1988, pp. 46–48).

7

International Monetary Developments in the 1960s

Monetary events in the 1960s outside the European Community (EC) had a strong impact on developments in the EC. Most important were the difficulties of the pound sterling and the persistent and growing balance of payments problems of the United States. Because of the central role of the dollar in the international monetary system as key and reserve currency, a growing lack of confidence in the stability of the dollar inevitably generated doubts about the stability of the international monetary system as mapped out in the International Monetary Fund (IMF) Articles of Agreement and as it had evolved in the years after the war. The international monetary developments of the 1960s eventually resulted in a far-reaching reshaping of the international monetary system and greatly influenced the global monetary role of the EC. They also stimulated and influenced the thinking, strategies, and decisions within the EC regarding its own monetary organization.

THE DIFFICULTIES OF THE POUND STERLING

The difficulties surrounding the British pound after World War II were, in large part, a result and echo of the pound's overriding importance as an international currency before World War I and — albeit much less so — during the interwar period. They stemmed on the one hand from the desire of the United Kingdom (UK) to maintain its international political role and to safeguard the role of the pound as an international reserve currency, in particular for the sterling area, and on the other hand from the diminishing weight and strength of the British economy. The sterling area comprised mainly the former parts of the British Empire that, in a long process after World War II, had achieved independence and most of which remained associated with the UK in the Commonwealth and other countries such as those in the Middle East whose history was closely tied to the UK.

It should be recalled that the UK was not a founding member of the European Communities. After having decided in 1956 not to participate in the discussions on the creation of the European Economic Community, the UK applied in August 1961 for membership but was rejected in January 1963 by President Charles de Gaulle, who doubted the European credentials of the UK. It reapplied in May 1967 but was again turned down by de Gaulle. It finally joined the EC in 1973, together with Ireland and Denmark. For a long time — and one could even argue, still today — the UK has not considered itself part of Europe; Europe was the "continent," the countries across the channel. Instead, not least in economic and monetary affairs, the UK tried to follow its own, separate policies, to muster its own resources, and to rely on its "special relationship" with the United States. This was so with regard to the European Payments Union (Kaplan and Schleiminger, 1989, pp. 164–84), at the start and during the earlier phases of the integration process of the European Communities, later with respect to the European Monetary System, and finally in the context of the efforts to form an economic and monetary union. To be sure, there were valid economic reasons for the UK to try to follow its distinct policies (in particular, the close economic ties within the Commonwealth), but in essence, the British attitude of reserve was politically motivated.

The basic issue for the pound in the postwar years was whether it was able to perform its traditional role as a reserve currency — even if on a reduced scale — in view of the difficulties the UK had to face after the war and the narrowed base of the British economy. These problems were interrelated but also need to be seen separately. The problems of the British balance of payments proper had, in the final analysis, to be solved by the UK itself. A sudden collapse of the reserve system of the pound, however, would have inflicted great damage on the international monetary system and the world economy. It was, therefore, a matter of common international concern.

Already, early in the life of the European Payments Union, in 1951 and 1952, the UK faced balance of payments difficulties. Later on, in 1957, speculative attacks on the pound as well as on the French franc took place as concern about the balance of payments positions of the two countries mounted. At the same time, the large balance of payments surplus of Germany gave rise to speculation about a possible revaluation. France decided to devalue its currency (in 1957 and 1958; see Chapter 4), while

Germany and the UK were determined to maintain their parities. The British authorities responded with restrictive budgetary policies and an increase of the discount rate to 7 percent, the highest rate since 1920. Simultaneously, the German authorities lowered the discount rate from 4.5 to 3 percent. The British actions can be seen as the beginning of the "stop and go" cycles — periods of domestic adjustment followed by unsustainable expansion — that were a hallmark of British economic policies for many years.

During the 1960s, the UK experienced a series of increasingly serious balance of payments crises that required large-scale international support operations and culminated in the 1967 devaluation of the pound. In 1961, a substantial balance of payments deficit emerged when, in the first months of the year, short-term capital flows changed direction and gave rise to doubts about the exchange rate of the pound. European central banks provided short-term assistance of nearly $1 billion. A stabilization program, presented in July, was supported by a $1.5 billion drawing on the IMF and an additional stand-by facility of $500 million.

An even more serious situation developed in 1964 when a sustained and vigorous upswing in the British economy resulted in a sharp deterioration of the trade balance. Through August, this was concealed by rising sterling holdings of sterling area countries and short-term capital inflows. In September, mistrust in the parity of the pound asserted itself strongly and required several support operations. Partner central banks supplied $1 billion in credit lines. The new Labour government of Prime Minister Harold Wilson, which had come into office on October 16, 1964, ruled out any change in parity. When on November 19 — a Thursday, the traditional day for any discount rate action — the rate was not raised, sterling came under heavy pressure. On Monday, November 23, the authorities did raise the rate, from 5 to 7 percent, but to no avail. The severe attack on the pound resumed, requiring unprecedentedly large international assistance to stave off a devaluation. European central banks, the Bank for International Settlements (BIS), and the U.S. Export-Import Bank mobilized a total of $3 billion, and a $1 billion drawing on the IMF in December was used to repay the central bank credits obtained in September. (The December drawing involved the first activation of the General Arrangements to Borrow [GAB]; see section on the U.S. dollar.)

The size of the support for sterling gave rise to some discussion about the role of short-term central bank credit in the international monetary system and the implied "moral hazard" (i.e., the temptation to forego one's own efforts and to rely instead on the assistance of others), which could weaken the working of the international adjustment process. In a speech on February 15, 1965, Lord Cromer, the governor of the Bank of England, addressed this problem when he pointed out that "in this system of mutual support and assistance the counterpart of taking assistance is a responsibility to the other members, assumed by him who takes it, to put his house in order at the earliest reasonable moment" (quoted in Deutsche Bundesbank, Annual Report 1964, p. 29). These observations pointed to the underlying problem facing the pound as well as other currencies, the exchange rates of which have come under pressure: that, in order to safeguard the stability of the exchange rate, economic developments and policies had to be in line with those of partner countries or — to put in the terms of the ongoing debate about participation in the economic and monetary union — that economic convergence needed to be ensured.

The recovery of the pound following the support operations in late 1964 was not a lasting one, and in the course of 1965, the pound showed renewed signs of weakness. In May, the UK drew another $1.4 billion from the IMF, exhausting its drawing possibilities and again invoking the GAB. In September, partner central banks (this time without the Bank of France) provided another large pool of short-term credits. The sheer size of the assistance sufficed to calm speculation, and the Bank of England did not need to use these facilities.

However, the saga of the pound continued. In the summer of 1966, restrictive measures triggered an improvement in the balance of current and long-term capital transactions. Yet, reserve losses by far exceeded the remaining deficit of the basic balance. This led to two support operations. The first one addressed the international role of sterling and was concluded in June 1966 at the BIS in Basle. It was a "group arrangement" between the Bank of England and a number of European central banks, initially for a period of nine months and later extended by one year, under which the Bank of England obtained a credit line of $1 billion for the compensation of reserve losses caused by fluctuations in the sterling balances held by other countries. Large reserve losses during the summer necessitated the second operation in September 1966, mainly financed by the Federal Reserve System.

The year 1967 finally brought the travails of sterling to its peak. Signs of improvement in spring 1967 soon gave room to renewed pressure on the pound. The Six-Day Arab-Israeli War in June 1967, the closing of the Suez Canal, and shifts of Arab-held sterling balances into other currencies and gold thrust a heavy burden on sterling. Doubts about the pound parity also arose in connection with the renewed British application for EC membership and its rejection by President de Gaulle in May 1967. Last, a strengthening of the restrictive policies initiated in summer 1966 ran into domestic economic and political obstacles, in particular, a dock strike. Despite last-minute increases in the discount rate, action on the exchange rate proved inevitable.

The devaluation of 14.3 percent, announced on November 18, 1967, shook international confidence in the existing international exchange rate structure and seriously undermined the generally held assumption of a lasting stability of exchange rates. Yet, in contrast to the 1949 devaluation, when most European and many other countries followed the British lead in a widespread realignment of par values, only Spain and a limited number of smaller countries with close economic ties to the UK — among them Cyprus, Denmark, Iceland, and Ireland — also devalued. In addition, the UK initiated parity changes for most of the currencies of its non-metropolitan territories in the Caribbean and other parts of the world.

Following the devaluation, in an exercise of confidence building, credit facilities from various sources totaling $4 billion, including a new IMF stand-by credit of $1.4 billion, were put at the disposal of the UK authorities. Throughout 1968 and 1969, in part related to the unrest surrounding the French franc and the Deutsche mark, sterling remained vulnerable to speculative pressure, and the Bank of England had to draw on its available credit facilities.

A number of observers felt — with the benefit of hindsight, to be sure — that the pound should have been devalued much earlier, although some would have preferred a floating of the pound. At the time, both ideas went against prevailing exchange rate philosophy but, as Robert Solomon observed (1982, p. 86), "the resolution of the crisis of sterling contributed to a change of thinking in official circles on the virtues of fixed exchange rates."

THE RESERVE CURRENCY ROLE OF STERLING

As already mentioned, one of the big problems for the external situation of the UK was the obligations from the reserve currency role of the pound. The sterling balances were the liquid reserves of governments, central banks, and private entities of sterling area countries. They were built up when the external accounts of those countries were in surplus and drawn down and, as needed, converted into other currencies to finance their external deficits. This feature disconnected the actual balance of payments performance of the UK from its reserve position, frequently (as we have seen) undermining confidence in the parity of the pound.

The Basle "group arrangement" of June 1966 was a first effort to address this problem. A second group arrangement between the Bank of England and 12 central banks and the BIS was agreed on in September 1968. It provided, initially for three years, a credit line of $2 billion to compensate for fluctuations in sterling balances. At the same time, bilateral agreements were concluded with over 60 sterling area countries under which the British government gave a dollar guarantee for the bulk of their sterling balances provided that they held a minimum proportion of their reserves in sterling (H. M. Treasury, 1968). A third Basle facility was announced in January 1977, designed to allow a rundown of official sterling balances rather than stabilizing them at an earlier level. In the words of the Chancellor of the Exchequer at the time, the purpose of the agreement was "to ensure that sterling and the exchange markets ceased to be affected by pressures associated with any rundown of the official sterling holdings . . . [and] to enable the British government to achieve an orderly reduction in the role of sterling as a reserve currency" (quoted in McMahon, 1982, p. 48). In June 1971, in connection with the future accession of the UK to the EC, the British authorities had declared that they were "prepared to envisage an orderly and gradual rundown of official sterling balances after our accession" (Act concerning the Conditions of Accession and the Adjustment of the Treaties, Exchange of Letters on Monetary Questions, *Official Journal of the European Communities*, Special edition, March 27, 1972). Following the first oil price shock of October 1973, there was a large inflow of funds from oil-producing countries into sterling. As Christopher McMahon, deputy governor of the Bank of England, noted (1982, p. 47), sterling balances were "again serving to conceal the extent of disequilibrium in the economy, and thereby . . . delaying the necessary adjustment measures." The near-halving of official sterling balances from their peak in March 1975 to September 1976 "[was] a major component of the sterling crisis of that year, and greatly strengthened the feeling that the maintenance of a residual reserve currency role for sterling was anachronistic." In 1960 sterling had still accounted for 38 percent of international currency reserves; by 1980, this proportion had fallen to 2 percent.[1]

THE U.S. DOLLAR PROBLEM

Even more momentous for the international monetary system and for monetary developments in the EC than the difficulties of pound sterling were the problems of the U.S. dollar. When, in the first decade after the war and in part as a consequence of the economic rebirth of Europe, the "dollar gap" was gradually replaced by a deficit in the U.S. balance of payments, this nourished the recovery and growth of the European economies. Over time, however, the deficits led to a saturation with dollars, and concerns emerged about "imported inflation" and the stability of the international monetary system. The worry was not that inflation in the United States, which was low, would have spilled over to Europe. Rather, a number of European countries were worried that, as a result of the inflow of dollars, excessive creation of domestic liquidity would undermine the stability of their economies. To be sure, there were European as well as many non-European countries that were keen on boosting their international reserves while, in one or the other of the complaining countries, political sensitivities about the hegemony of the United States were as strong as economic concerns. France, in particular, was in such a position. It was highly critical of the "privileged" position of the United States that enabled it to finance balance of payments deficits with its own currency without being subject to the same kind of domestic adjustment pressure as other countries. A logical outgrowth of this view was the French policy of converting dollar holdings into gold and its calls for a comprehensive reform of the international monetary system, even for a return to some form of gold standard.

Perhaps even more important than the stability concerns of individual countries was another problem. An adequate supply of international liquidity for the growing world economy depended, in view of the insufficient and unreliable world gold production, on deficits in the U.S. balance of payments. Yet, over time, the continuation of U.S. deficits tended to undermine international confidence in the stability of the dollar as the anchor of the international monetary system and, thus, of the system as such. This had important implications for European integration, because the monetary policy provisions of the European Economic Community (EEC) Treaty were, in part, based on the implicit assumption of the durability of the Bretton Woods system. It also eroded the trust in the ability of the United States to honor its commitment to convert official dollar holdings of other countries into gold. On the other hand, the elimination of the U.S. deficit would have cut off this source of international liquidity (the "Triffin dilemma"; Triffin 1960). The troubles of the other large reserve currency — the pound sterling — were seen as putting an additional burden on the dollar and heightened apprehension about reserve currencies in general.

By the end of the 1950s, it became clear that something had to be done about the U.S. balance of payments. President John F. Kennedy introduced in February 1961 a program for the improvement of the balance of payments and, at the same time, confirmed the U.S. commitment to convert official dollar holdings into gold at the fixed price of $35 per ounce. This is not the place to describe in detail the development of the U.S. balance of payments or specific measures of the United States to strengthen its external position, such as the "Roosa bonds" of 1962, the interest equalization tax of 1963, the comprehensive balance of payments program of President Lyndon Johnson of January 1968, or special arrangements with other countries, such as the offset agreements with Germany. Instead, the international efforts to shore up the position of the dollar, in which EC countries played an important role, will be briefly discussed.

In the 1960s, the United States experienced persistent overall balance of payments deficits, although the balance on current transactions showed healthy surpluses. The deficits were, in part, the result of military expenditures abroad and foreign aid but also reflected large private capital outflows. At the same time, countries such as France, Belgium, and the Netherlands, which traditionally held a large portion of their international reserves in gold, converted newly acquired dollars into gold. Other countries were reluctant to pursue a similar strategy, mainly out of concern over the stability of the international monetary system.

In March 1954, the London gold market was reopened. It served as the main sales outlet for the gold production of South Africa and the Soviet Union, and it met the demand of private parties for industrial and other uses but also for central banks that were reluctant to approach the gold window of the U.S. Treasury. To avoid potentially destabilizing fluctuations of the free market price for gold, in November 1961 the central banks of the United States and seven European countries (Belgium, France, Germany, Italy, Netherlands, Switzerland, and the UK) agreed on the establishment of a "gold pool" for the sale or purchase of gold close to the official price of $35.

The gold pool worked well until rising international monetary tensions started to generate doubts about the viability of the international monetary system in its then-existing form. In the wake of the pound devaluation in November 1967, private speculative purchases in international gold markets intensified and became a veritable "gold rush." From November 1967 until the gold market was closed on March 15, 1968, the gold pool sold $3 billion worth of gold, close to one-eighth of the gold reserves of participating countries. The governors of the seven central banks of the gold pool (France had dropped out in summer 1967) met for an emergency session in Washington on March 16 and 17, 1968. The communiqué of the conference stated:

[The Governors] noted that the U.S. Government will continue to buy and sell gold at the existing price of $35 an ounce in transactions with monetary authorities. . . . The Governors believe that henceforth officially-held gold should be used only to effect transfers among monetary authorities and, therefore, they decided no longer to supply gold to the London gold market or any other gold market. Moreover, as the existing stock of monetary gold is sufficient in view of the prospective establishment of the facility for Special Drawing Rights, they no longer feel it necessary to buy gold from the market. (Solomon, 1982, pp. 121–22)

This meant the establishment of a two-tier gold market in which the free market price for gold would be divorced from the official price and would freely respond to supply and demand. Subsequently, only very few central bank purchases took place in the free market. In a related development, a few days before the conference, the U.S. Congress decided to remove the gold cover for dollar notes. A number of observers interpreted the decision to end the gold pool, together with the pending agreement on the creation of the IMF Special Drawing Rights (SDR) facility, "as constituting a demonetization of gold at the margin"

(Solomon, 1982, p. 123). Future events took a somewhat different path than envisaged at the time, but the process of removing gold from the center of the international monetary system had begun. The two-tier gold market was terminated in November 1973 by agreement of the participating countries.

As a "first line of defense" for the U.S. dollar, but also for currencies such as the pound and the Canadian dollar and any other currency in need, the Federal Reserve System and the leading central banks of Europe, the Bank of Canada, and the BIS agreed in the course of 1962 to establish "reciprocal currency arrangements" in the form of bilateral short-term swap agreements. At the end of 1963, this network of credit lines amounted to more than $2 billion. By their very nature, such mutual credit lines were intended mainly to cope with capital flows that were expected to reverse themselves within a relatively short period.

As a "second line of defense," the ten main industrial countries (subsequently labeled the "Group of Ten" [G-10]) concluded in 1962 with the IMF the GAB. Switzerland, which at that time was not yet a member of the IMF, later concluded a parallel agreement with the Fund. The purpose of the GAB was to provide the IMF with supplementary resources of up to $6 billion with a maturity of up to five years for lending to participating countries. As mentioned earlier in this chapter, the GAB was first activated in connection with the December 1964 drawing of the UK.

These arrangements were based on the implicit assumption that the imbalances affecting the dollar (and, up to a point, also those of the pound) would, over time, revert themselves and that a devaluation of the dollar would create more problems than it would solve. More radical solutions, in particular, a transition to a regime of freely floating exchange rates (as we shall discuss later) were not yet seriously considered. The story of the U.S. dollar and its role in the international monetary system will be taken up again and its impact on European monetary integration discussed in Chapter 11.

THE REFORM OF THE INTERNATIONAL MONETARY SYSTEM

The decrease in the reserve role of the pound and the unresolved balance of payments problems of the United States led, since the 1950s, to a number of people, mainly in the academic world, to express concern over the sustainability of the existing international monetary system and to reflect on its reform. The issue was, of course, also of great relevance for the EC, although, at the time, this was only gradually realized. It was still seen as a problem that related mainly to the countries concerned — the UK and the United States — and their financial relations to individual European countries. Moreover, in the 1960s, the EC was very much occupied with realizing its chief goal, namely, to establish a common market for industrial as well as agricultural goods. The following summary of the international reform efforts could, nevertheless, assist in bringing the more specific challenges to European monetary integration into sharper focus.

The debate about the reform of the international monetary system concentrated primarily on the overall framework of the system and not so much on how its various elements interacted. Thus, the main issues were whether the world economy was adequately furnished with international liquidity and how the traditional sources of liquidity — gold and dollars — could be supplemented or replaced. The supply of gold was dependent on the vagaries of production and the marketing strategies of the main producer countries, South Africa and the Soviet Union. For an increase in dollar reserves, one had to rely on deficits in the U.S. balance of payments, which, in the longer run, eroded the stability of the dollar. Proposals for creating a "synthetic" international reserve asset were presented by such well-known authors as Robert Triffin (one of the earliest critics of the dollar-exchange standard), Maxwell Stamp, Friedrich A. Lutz, and Edward M. Bernstein (see Hawkins, 1965; de Vries, 1976, Vol. I, pp. 17–24). By the early 1960s, international organizations and groups, such as the IMF, the Organization for Economic Cooperation and Development, and the G-10, and national officials had joined the debate about a reform of the international system. In addition to the issue of international liquidity, the international role of gold, the improvement of the international adjustment process, and the role of exchange rates were discussed.

The Role of Gold

A number of economists, among them Jacques Rueff, Sir Roy Harrod, Michael Heilperin, and Milton Gilbert, argued that a sharp increase, possibly a doubling, of the price of gold would provide the needed international liquidity.[2] Others held that such a sudden increase in international liquidity would entail great inflationary risks for the world economy and discriminate in favor of countries with large gold stocks. An even more radical proposal was to return to some form of gold reserve standard, under which gold would be the only form of international reserves. This would have made the international monetary system completely dependent on the supply of gold from producing countries — not an endearing prospect. Others proposed to phase out gold altogether. This was equally unrealistic in view of the near-mythical attachment of many countries to gold and the importance of gold in the international reserves of many countries. Ironically, this strong attachment to gold and the reluctance to part with it led over time to an increasing demobilization of gold and, thus, to its de facto demonetization

In any event, the official gold price remained fixed until the devaluations of the dollar in December 1971 and February 1973. It was abolished when the second amendment of the IMF Articles of Agreement entered into force in 1978. However, gold remained an important part of countries' monetary reserves. In the private markets, after the abandonment of the gold pool in 1968 and especially in connection with the wide exchange rate swings following the breakdown of the Bretton Woods system in 1971–73, the price of gold rose strongly, mainly driven by private hoarding.

The International Adjustment Process

At issue was how the international adjustment process could be improved, that is, how the emergence of imbalances could be avoided, how existing imbalances could be more quickly reduced or eliminated, and what individual countries could do to correct imbalances in their external accounts by appropriate domestic adjustment policies.[3] In this way, the need for monetary reserves could be lowered on the national and the international levels.

One important aspect of the international debate was the call for "burden sharing" or more "symmetry" in the adjustment process, terms that we shall encounter again later in the context of the European Monetary System. The underlying notion was that deficit as well as surplus countries suffered from imbalances basically of their own making. The "asymmetry" issue arose because deficit countries were perceived as carrying more of a burden, because they could run out of reserves while surplus countries would continue to accumulate reserves, although admittedly with inflationary risks. National policies should be oriented toward the correction of payment imbalances. Deficit countries should follow more restrictive policies to reduce their deficits, and surplus countries should initiate more expansionary policies to rein in their surpluses. An implicit assumption in the call for more symmetry, although not clearly spelled out, was that, on average, economic growth would be encouraged while inflation could be kept low. However, the stability-oriented surplus countries did not believe that rules and commitments to induce deficit countries to correct imprudent policies would be followed and feared that they would have to bear the inflationary consequences of such policies. In turn, deficit countries hardly were inclined to accept binding rules that would impinge on their sovereignty and limit their options in the pursuit of domestic policy objectives. At the heart of the dispute was that a more efficient adjustment process — whether achieved by rule or discretion — presupposed a basic consensus on the priorities of economic policies and on the best ways to achieve them. Such a consensus did not exist.

A special working group in the framework of the Organization for Economic Cooperation and Development presented a report with a number of fairly general recommendations on a better mix of national fiscal and monetary policies, on measures to influence capital imports and exports, and for an "early warning system" that would facilitate the coordination of economic policies.[4] Interestingly, in the discussions about an improvement of the adjustment process, the role of exchange rates (including a possible change in the international exchange rate *system*) received little attention.

Fixed Versus Flexible Exchange Rates

The question of whether fixed or flexible exchange rates would be better suited to safeguard international financial equilibrium and foster international trade while protecting the stability of individual countries had been a subject of discussion among academics for quite some time. Well-known advocates of flexible rates were Milton Friedman and Egon Sohmen. However, in official circles — national administrations as well as international organizations — there was a strong adherence to the principle (perhaps, one should say, the doctrine) of fixed exchange rates. This was understandable, because many officials had witnessed the havoc that flexible exchange rates and competitive devaluations brought to international trade and to economic and financial stability between the two wars. The supporters of flexible exchange rates considered the exchange rate as a price that would balance supply and demand for foreign exchange.[5] Flexible rates would tend to eliminate external imbalances and provide countries with the opportunity to follow their own brand of domestic policies without external constraints (and to "make their own mistakes," as the saying goes). Those in favor of fixed exchange rates argued that they were the indispensable basis for stability in international economic relations and a precondition for growth in international trade.[6] Flexible exchange rates, it was said, far from solving national economic problems, tended to bottle them up.

The issue of fixed versus flexible exchange rates, its relevance for the establishment of a common or single market, and its importance for the pursuit of policies oriented toward national objectives has continued to be a central point of debate within the EC ever since the early 1970s, when the Bretton Woods system of fixed but adjustable exchange rates broke down and the EC exchange rate system, the "snake," gradually disintegrated.

In the debate about the role of exchange rates, there emerged also concepts aiming at more flexibility without abandoning the principle of fixity. The discussion was in part about *more* flexible exchange rates, in particular, about wider fluctuation margins, and such exchange rate regimes as crawling or frequently adjusted pegs, whether of an automatic or discretionary nature.

At the time, the advocates of fixed exchange rates carried the day. However, the events of 1969 (Chapter 6) and even more of 1971 and 1973 (Chapter 11) showed that flexible rates were, indeed, an option for countries for shielding themselves, at least temporarily, from the consequences of monetary developments outside their control. It took, however, several more years and many reports to officially discard the global system of fixed but adjustable exchange rates as embodied in the original IMF Articles of Agreement and to give countries the freedom to choose their own exchange rate regimes. This happened with the agreement of the IMF Interim Committee (a top-level group of the IMF) in Jamaica in January 1976 and its formal enshrinement in the Articles of Agreement with the second amendment of April 1, 1978.

The experience with flexible exchange rates in the 1970s was mixed. It has often been stated (in my view, correctly) that the world economy could hardly have coped satisfactorily with the turmoil of the 1970s, in particular, the crisis of the dollar and the sharp increases of the oil price in 1973. However, wide fluctuations and overshooting of exchange rates, often unrelated to developments in the fundamentals such as prices, costs, or external current accounts, and serious misalignments caused economic difficulties in many countries. Therefore, there was widespread dissatisfaction with the way the international monetary system — some called it a "nonsystem" — worked. There were repeated calls for an international conference, a "new Bretton Woods," to discuss the international monetary system (see James, 1996, p. 428). Proposals were presented to achieve more stability in exchange rates, for example, by the introduction of "target zones" (sometimes also called "reference zones") and concomitant policy obligations (see Williamson, 1983; Frenkel and Goldstein, 1986; Bergsten, 1988). However, such proposals were met with skepticism because their successful realization on a global scale would require a reconciliation of national priorities in economic policies, which hardly could be expected among countries with widely differing economic conditions, needs, and philosophies. Among EC countries, France from time to time voiced its preference for a global system of stable exchange rates; other countries, like Germany and the Netherlands, saw little basis for such a system.

With regard to intra-EC exchange rate relations, it was evident that flexible exchange rates, whether fully free or partially managed, were not conducive to a process of economic and monetary integration. This explains why, after the breakdown of the Bretton Woods system in 1973, the EC kept on searching for a common exchange rate system that would provide a high degree of exchange rate stability but leave participating countries room for their own policies. As we shall see later in the discussions on exchange rate regimes for the EC, some of the generally discussed concepts such as target zones and wider fluctuation margins gained some significance.

A New Reserve Asset: The Special Drawing Rights

The discussions and negotiations about the establishment of a new, "synthetic" reserve asset were carried out mainly in the IMF and the G-10 in the mid-1960s. The main questions were:

Is there a need for a reserve asset, and how can such a need be determined?

What form should such a reserve asset take?

Who should be responsible for its creation?

There was soon a broad consensus that the establishment of a facility for the creation of reserves in addition to the traditional sources of international liquidity was called for, at least as a contingency measure. It should be a true reserve asset, not just another credit facility, although the final agreement contained certain credit elements. Its function should be to help finance payment imbalances, not capital needs. Its creation should, therefore, be geared toward the long-term global need for reserves, not toward the needs of special groups of countries. At the beginning, there was a debate whether a limited group of countries — that is, the G-10 — or the IMF as a world-wide organization should be in charge. Following the famous dictum of the IMF Managing Director, Pierre-Paul Schweitzer, that "international liquidity is the business of the Fund," the task fell to the IMF.

Among the industrialized countries, the United States and the UK were strongly in favor of the establishment of a reserve facility, whereas most EC countries were more cautious, in particular with regard to the conditions under which reserves should be created. France opposed a new reserve asset.[7] After intense negotiations, a basic agreement — the Outline of a Facility Based on Special Drawing Rights in the Fund — was approved by the Board of Governors of the IMF at its annual meeting in Rio de Janeiro in September 1967. Negotiations in the IMF Executive Board on a draft amendment of the IMF Articles of Agreement were completed in April 1968. France at first did not vote for the amendment but, in the end, ratified it in December 1969, five months after it had gone into effect.

A first allocation of SDRs took place on January 1, 1970, as part of an allocation over a period of three years of SDR 9.5 billion (equivalent to the same amount of dollars).[8] Another round of allocations, totaling SDR 12 billion, started in January 1979. The SDR did not meet the expectation that it would gradually replace other reserve elements. The continuation of the balance of payments deficits of the United States, the rapid growth of the Euro-currency markets, and, more generally, increased capital mobility led to the view in many quarters that, if anything, there existed rather too much international liquidity than too little. A new attempt to reach agreement on another allocation of SDRs, undertaken in 1994, failed.

The EC countries played an important role in the negotiations leading to the SDR facility, demonstrating their increased clout in international monetary matters. The Monetary Committee played an important role in coordinating the views of EC members, although, on a variety of issues, disagreements could not be resolved.[9] During the negotiations, the EC secured a special majority requirement of 85 percent in the IMF for decisions on the allocation of SDRs, giving the EC a veto.

By the end of the 1960s, the international monetary tensions increasingly threatened the international monetary system, and it became more and more obvious that cautious and gradual reform efforts probably could not salvage it. By that time, the chapter of the British pound as an important reserve currency was almost closed. It was the problem of the dollar, its relations to the other important currencies — the Japanese yen and the EC currencies — and the gradual breakdown of the Bretton Woods system of fixed but adjustable exchange rates that characterized the international monetary landscape. The redefinition of the international monetary system in the 1970s as a "mixed system" of pegged exchange rates and of free and managed floating — at times, more a somewhat chaotic process than a system — was closely related to the efforts of the EC to establish itself as not just a trade bloc but also a monetary entity. We shall return to these issues in later chapters.

NOTES

Literature of general interest for this chapter: Coombs (1976); de Vries (1976); James (1996); Solomon (1982); Bank for International Settlements, Annual Reports; Deutsche Bundesbank, Annual Reports.

1. For an assessment of British economic policies, see Roll (1995).
2. See also de Vries (1976, Vol. I, p. 21). The official price of gold had remained unchanged since March 1933, when the U.S. dollar was devalued by 41 percent by raising the price of gold to $35 per ounce from $20.67.
3. The adjustment process in an individual country was defined by Milton Gilbert (1966, p. 4) as follows: "By the adjustment process is meant the chain of

corrective changes in the domestic economy, and even directly in transactions of the balance of payments, whereby countries in deficit or surplus come back into equilibrium."

4. Working Party No. 3 (1966). The discussions in the working group (in which I participated) revealed early on that the views with regard to a more systematic approach were irreconcilable.

5. Flexible exchange rates frequently are also called "fluctuating" or "floating rates"; a distinction then is made between "free" and "managed" floating. In this context, the emphasis is on freely floating rates, because their advocates considered interference with the markets as counterproductive.

6. "Fixed" is not necessarily synonymous with "fixed but adjustable," because even occasional parity changes were strongly resisted on grounds of principle. Furthermore, the terms "fixed" and "stable" exchange rates, although often used interchangeably, do not always cover the same ground. Strictly speaking, "fixed" refers to an exchange rate *regime*, and "stable" characterizes exchange rate *behavior*.

7. In 1964, France had proposed a new reserve asset, the "collective reserve unit" (CRU), which was to be linked to gold and to be created and used by G-10 members outside the IMF.

8. Originally, 1 SDR was equivalent to 0.88867088 gram of fine gold, the same as for U.S. $1 at the time. Since 1974, the value of the SDR has been determined by a basket of currencies.

9. At the time of the SDR negotiations, I was the Alternate Executive Director for Germany in the IMF and in charge of the discussions in the IMF Executive Board. It was sometimes amusing, sometimes irritating to see how, after the Monetary Committee was to have agreed on a common EC position on specific issues, the executive directors from EC countries apparently received differing instructions or, at least, interpreted them differently.

8

Striving for Better Policy Coordination in the European Community in the 1960s

The 1960s were characterized in the monetary field by a number of problems within the European Community (EC) and on a global scale. The potential risks of autonomous and uncoordinated national economic and monetary policies for the emerging common market and the growing tensions between EC economies could no longer be disregarded. They underlined the need for improved cooperation on economic and monetary policies. The difficulties surrounding the pound sterling and, even more so, the persistent and growing problems of the dollar not only posed a serious threat to the functioning of the international monetary system but also had a strong impact on EC monetary developments. These risks and the unfolding discussions about a reform of the international monetary system made it imperative for the EC to establish a coordinated position and to assert its interests in regard to world-wide monetary developments. How did the EC respond to these challenges?

The European Economic Community (EEC) Treaty provided only for a modest degree of economic and monetary policy cooperation. It became increasingly evident that the realization of the common market and the rising international financial interdependence required decisive steps toward a more effective policy coordination. Yet, member countries appeared to be fully occupied with the tasks of realizing the customs union and implementing the Common Agricultural Policy and — in the monetary field — helping to keep the international monetary system afloat. Also, in the first half of the decade, the monetary problems within the EC were related to individual countries — Germany and Italy — and were still seen as largely isolated events. However, more important was that member states showed great reluctance to undertake any commitments that would have seriously impaired their sovereignty with regard to economic and monetary policies. They were not ready to go significantly beyond the existing arrangements for consultation and coordination.

In this context, "coordination" often proved to be a euphemism for what frequently was not much more than mutual information and — by no means always — consultation about policy matters.[1] Exceptions were the ad hoc central bank actions of financial support for ailing currencies. Nevertheless, the various measures discussed in this chapter undoubtedly strengthened the institutional framework for policy cooperation in the EC. This was a prerequisite and became the basis for future progress in policy coordination.

It was mainly the "supranational" institutions of the EC, the European Parliament, and, especially, the Commission that, time and again, stressed the need to improve the policy coordination machinery and presented many ideas and concrete proposals as to how this could be done.

"MONETARISTS" AND "ECONOMISTS"

Another aspect that did little to facilitate progress toward effective coordination procedures was the debate between the "monetarists" and the "economists" about the best way to proceed. Although this debate raised a number of issues on which one could reasonably differ, there was also a strong ideological element involved, which complicated matters. It can be traced to basic differences in economic policy philosophy between a more interventionist, institution-oriented, and more market-oriented approach in economic policies. The "monetarists" believed in the importance of building institutional arrangements and putting in place commitments in monetary policy matters, for example, the narrowing of exchange rate fluctuation margins or mutual credit lines. This would — so went the argument — induce common policies and the convergence of economic developments, thus, allowing the early introduction of a common currency. (Sometimes, this also is called the "institutionalist" approach.) The "economists" argued that the close coordination and compatibility of policies, not just in the monetary but also in other economic policy areas such as fiscal and wage policies, and a high degree of convergence had to come first. Then, in the end, a common monetary policy and a common currency could be aimed at as a "crowning" achievement ("coronation theory"). The monetarist strategy was advocated mainly by France, Belgium, Luxembourg, and, significantly, the EC Commission. Germany, the Netherlands, and, to a lesser degree, Italy and, later, also the United Kingdom (UK), adhered to the economist strategy. As we shall see, those seemingly contradictory views have continued to influence strongly the debate about European monetary integration. Yet, actual decisions and developments often were characterized by a middle position, by the notion that, in reality, the two strategies interacted and cross-fertilized each other.[2]

THE STRENGTHENING OF THE INSTITUTIONAL FRAMEWORK

The Short-Term Economic Policy Committee

Early on, on March 9, 1960, the Council of Ministers decided to set up a Short-Term Economic Policy Committee as a complement to the Monetary Committee. Its mandate was to "participate in the conduct of the consultations between Member States and the Commission provided for in Article 103 of the Treaty . . . [and to] provide guidance and assistance to the Commission in exercising the powers conferred on it by that Article." (Art. 103 deals with short-term economic policies "as a matter of common concern.") With the same decision, member countries undertook to "keep the Commission informed of the broad lines of any project which may affect the conjunctural situation of the Member States" (Monetary Committee, 1974, p. 93).

The Van Campen Report

The first comprehensive report on the coordination of monetary policies in the EC came from the European Parliament's Committee for Economic and Monetary Affairs and was published in April 1962. Named after its rapporteur, it became known as the Van Campen Report (European Parliament, 1962). The basic message of the report was that monetary policy could not be considered by itself but should be coordinated with measures in other areas of economic policy. Because of the consequences of EC monetary developments for the international monetary system, external monetary policies also should be coordinated. The report stressed that, for the realization of an economic union and in view of the underlying final political objective of the EEC Treaty, a mere coordination of monetary policies would not be enough; there was a need for a common institution for the organized cooperation of national central banks, modeled after federal central bank systems as in the United States and Germany. Such an institution should have an independent management, eschew the automatic granting of credit, and maintain monetary discipline, which meant, above all, the safeguarding of price stability. Based on this report, the European Parliament adopted on October 17, 1962, a resolution that called for the step-by-step establishment of a federal organization of EC central banks in a central institution for the conduct of a common monetary policy. It concluded that a common monetary policy was an essential precondition for the economic and political unification of Europe.

The 1962 Action Program of the Commission and the Council Decisions of 1964

In the same year, on October 24, 1962, the EC Commission issued an Action Program for the Second Stage, that is, for the time after the completion of the customs union. The chapter on monetary policy proclaimed that economic union would require fixed exchange rates between member states with very narrow fluctuation margins, at the latest after the end of the transitional stage, that is, after the completion of the customs union (Commission, 1962, Chap. 8). Each exchange rate change would upset the trade of countries and cause such sudden changes in agricultural prices and incomes that the common market itself could be imperiled.

The Commission proposed a council of central bank governors, joint meetings of finance or economics ministers and central bank governors, and prior discussion of important monetary policy decisions. In external policy matters, there should be consultations on the use of International Monetary Fund (IMF) credit facilities, central bank policies on reserve currencies should be harmonized, and a common position on the reform of the international monetary system should be worked out. An intergovernmental agreement should lay down the obligations with regard to mutual assistance according to Art. 108 of the EEC Treaty.

The establishment of the monetary union could be the objective of the third stage toward the common market. The council of central bank governors then would become the central organ of a federal central bank system. The EC finance and economics ministers would decide on the volume of national budgets and of the EC budget and on their financing.

As a follow-up, the Commission submitted to the Council of Ministers on June 19, 1963, several draft decisions for the establishment of additional committees and on cooperation in the field of international monetary relations. In explanatory notes, the Commission pointed out that monetary policy cooperation could not be limited to central bank action but also should include budgetary measures that had a similar, sometimes even more decisive bearing on monetary developments.

On the basis of the Commission recommendations, the Council of Ministers decided on May 8, 1964, the following (Monetary Committee, 1974, pp. 45–49, 53, 54, 96):

establishment of a Committee of Governors of the Central Banks of the Member
   States of the European Economic Community with the main task of holding

"consultations concerning the general principles and the broad lines of policy of Central Banks, in particular as regards credit and the money and foreign exchange markets";

prior consultations within the Monetary Committee with regard to decisions and positions in the field of international monetary relations, in particular, the working of the international monetary system, recourse by EC countries to international credits, and participation in monetary support operations in favor of third countries;

prior consultations before changes in exchange parities, in consideration of Art. 107 of the EEC Treaty, which proclaimed exchange rate policies "a matter of common concern";[3]

the establishment of a Budgetary Policy Committee with the task "to study and compare the broad lines of the budgetary policies of the Member States."

Earlier, on April 15, 1964, the Council had decided on the establishment of a Medium-Term Economic Policy Committee, which was to prepare "a preliminary draft of a medium-term economic policy programme outlining in broad terms the economic policies which the Member States and the institutions of the Community intend to follow" (Monetary Committee, 1974, pp. 94–95).

The Commission's Action Program had stressed the need to coordinate economic policies through a strengthening of the consultative process. It had a distinct monetarist flavor by asking for a formalization of mutual financial assistance and by implying the desirability of narrower fluctuation margins. There was not much discussion about the preconditions for a successful coordination of policies and any move toward a closer linkage of exchange rates, namely, the definition of common policy priorities, and the strategies for their realization. In its formal proposals of June 1963, the Commission concentrated on setting up a more comprehensive institutional framework for consultations. The member states followed this lead very closely, and the decisions of the Council in substance did not go very much beyond the design and commitments of the EEC Treaty. It is not unlikely that, initially, the Commission wanted to be more ambitious but that, in advance explorations, the Commission found member states reluctant to go beyond a strengthening of consultation procedures.

Looking at the decisions, one could get the impression of a saturation of the EC with committees. Later, in February 1974, the committees for short-term and medium-term economic policies and for budgetary policy were merged into one Economic Policy Committee. At the time, however, even if the committees did not fully meet the expectations for an effective coordination of policies, they served a very useful function. They allowed high officials of EC countries and the Commission to meet regularly, to get acquainted with each others' problems, and to understand the philosophy and implementation of national policies as well as differences in institutional arrangements.

The Dichgans Report

Another report of the European Parliament, issued on November 28, 1966, and named after its author, was bold and naive at the same time (European Parliament, 1966). It called for a harmonization of short-term economic, fiscal, and budgetary policies in order to render exchange rate changes superfluous. Cooperation could not be limited to the actions of central banks but should extend to budgetary policy, which often was more significant for monetary developments than central bank policies. The report accepted that a monetary union with a common currency could be only the final step in a longer-term development. As a transitional phase, there could be a currency union in which member states would commit themselves to accept each others' coins, and European coins would be issued. The corresponding resolution of the European Parliament of December 16, 1966, took up the idea of European coins. It also called for progress in the liberalization of capital movements in the EC and for a further approximation of views on international monetary issues, including the improvement of the international monetary system.

The idea of issuing European coins as an image-building action before the establishment of a monetary union has resurfaced from time to time. What its proponents consistently have been overlooking is the following: Any issue of European coins before the formation of a monetary union, or at least before the irrevocable fixing of exchange rates between EC currencies, would, in the end, lead only to disappointment, because exchange rates inevitably require adjustments, and it would discredit efforts to move ahead with monetary integration. There was no shortcut to the arduous and time-consuming process of creating a monetary union.

THE BARRE MEMORANDUM OF FEBRUARY 1969

The 1964 decisions did not lead to tangible results, and no significant further action to deepen monetary integration was taken. In the monetary field, member states were occupied with international issues (in particular, the problems of the pound and dollar) and the reform of the international monetary system. Another factor might have been that France, under President Charles de Gaulle, was in general not very receptive to a deepening of European integration, which inevitably would have led to some loss of national sovereignty. This was demonstrated by the French policy of the "empty chair" in 1965 and the insistence on a de facto national veto power as encapsuled in the Luxembourg Compromise of January 1966 (see Chapter 5). In this atmosphere of indecision and political maneuvering, the monetary disruptions of 1968 and 1969 and the eventual parity changes for the French franc and the Deutsche mark came as a shock.

Soon after the outbreak of the crisis of May 1968 in France, the Commission examined the economic situation and the measures taken by the French government and recommended to the Council the granting of "mutual assistance" under Art. 108 of the EEC Treaty. The communication did not include any proposals for financial assistance but was limited to general recommendations for the economic policies the member states other than France should pursue to support the stabilization efforts of France. On July 20, 1968, the Council adopted a directive along these lines (*Bulletin*, No. 8, 1968, pp. 25–26).

On February 12, 1969, the Commission (1969a) presented to the Council a comprehensive memorandum "on the Co-ordination of Economic Policies and Monetary Co-operation within the Community," the so-called Barre Memorandum (named after the commissioner in charge of economic and monetary matters). The memorandum repeated a number of earlier proposals that failed to trigger any action. It underlined the interdependence of economic developments in EC countries. Resulting problems could not be solved by a single economic policy, because the necessary preconditions did not yet exist, or by a mere juxtaposition of independent national policies. The Commission called for the compatibility of medium-term economic objectives but underlined that agreement on medium-term guidelines would not suffice unless member states pursued joint short-term economic policies consistent with these guidelines.

The memorandum deplored the failure to activate the mutual assistance provisions of Art. 108 when Italy experienced a balance of payments crisis in 1964 and the fact that, following the May events of 1968, mutual assistance was granted to France only after "clumsy and complex procedures" and excluded financial assistance, and that recourse to safeguard measures could not be prevented. The memorandum contained, therefore, proposals for setting up mechanisms for quasi-automatic short-term monetary support and for conditional medium-term financial assistance. The Commission also proposed to study the definition of a European Unit of Account (EUA) that could be used in all fields of EC action requiring a common denominator, in place of the array of existing units of account.

As an immediate follow-up to the Barre Memorandum, the Council adopted on July 17, 1969, a decision on the coordination of short-term economic policies, providing for prior consultations on important short-term policy measures within the Monetary Committee, the Short-Term Economic Policy Committee, and the Budgetary Policy Committee (Monetary Committee, 1974, p. 97).

THE ESTABLISHMENT AND
USE OF CREDIT FACILITIES

Action on the proposals for the short-term and medium-term assistance mechanisms took more time because some EC countries were reluctant to create new credit facilities.[4] During the discussions of the proposals, it was urged that the credit mechanisms should be linked to an effective coordination of policies. A consensus emerged that short-term monetary support could be justified only in case of reversible balance of payments deficits and should not be fully automatic. Medium-term financial assistance should not necessarily serve to consolidate unconditional short-term central bank credits and should be subject to economic policy conditions.

The Short-Term Monetary Support

On February 9, 1970, the five central banks of the EC countries (Luxembourg has no central bank of its own) concluded an Agreement Setting Up a System of Short-Term Monetary Support (STMS) (Monetary Committee, 1974, pp. 67–75). Art. 1 stated that the "implementation of the system shall be closely linked with the standing arrangements for consultation and coordination of economic policy among the Member States." Under the facility, the participating central banks agreed to provide each other with unconditional (also labeled "quasi-automatic") credits for a period of three months in case of temporary balance of payments deficits. A credit could be renewed for another three months. The granting of monetary support set in train consultations about the economic situation of the debtor country. Each central bank received a quota to determine the amount of support it could receive and the amount it agreed to finance. In addition, these amounts could be increased by "debtor" and "creditor rallonges." Total quotas (which initially were expressed in national currencies) were equivalent to $1 billion at then-existing parities. The STMS agreement provided for the mobilization of creditor claims if a creditor country itself experienced balance of payments problems.

The individual quotas and the total amounts of the STMS were changed several times. In 1973, when Denmark, Ireland, and the UK joined the EC, quotas for these countries were added, as were quotas in 1980 for Greece, in 1985 for Spain and Portugal, and in 1995 for Austria, Finland, and Sweden. Enlargements of quotas were decided in February 1974, in December 1977, and in connection with the creation of the European Monetary System (EMS) in March 1979.[5]

The STMS was activated for the first time in March 1974 when Italy took recourse to a credit line set up in June 1973. In May 1976, Italy received another credit line, which lapsed in June 1977 without being used.

The Medium-Term Financial Assistance

On March 22, 1971, the EC Council adopted the Decision Setting Up Machinery for Medium-Term Financial Assistance (MTFA), with explicit reference to Art. 108 of the EEC Treaty. It became effective as of January 1, 1972 (Monetary Committee, 1974, pp. 76–80). While STMS credits were granted by the central banks, the use of the MTFA was to be decided by the Council of Ministers, with qualified majority. Credits would be made available to member states with balance of payments difficulties. They had a maturity of two to five years and were subject to economic policy conditions to be laid down by the Council. For each member country, a ceiling limited its contribution. The total of creditor ceilings was initially set at 2 billion units of account, at the time equal to $42 billion. On the debtor side, there were no ceilings, but (as an amendment to the original decision in December 1977 specified) no country could normally draw more than 50 percent of the total credit ceilings. As with the STMS, the amounts of the MTFA were adjusted several times, in particular in connection with the accession of new members to the EC and the creation of the EMS. As did the STMS, the MTFA provided for the mobilization of creditor claims.

The MTFA was activated only once, in December 1974, when Italy obtained a credit of 1,159.2 million units of account. It was used to replace in part the STMS credit of 1,562.5 million units of account of March of the same year; the remaining amount of 403.3 million units of account was provided on a short-term, renewable basis by the UK, which was unable to participate in the MTFA operation because of its own balance of payments difficulties.

The Use of Credit Facilities

Both credit facilities have not been used since the establishment of the EMS in March 1979, which raises some interesting questions. Did the establishment of the two facilities come too late, were they unnecessary, or were they inadequate? Without doubt, the facilities would have come in very handy when the Italian lira was under pressure in 1964 and perhaps even more during the crisis of the French franc, triggered by the social unrest in May 1968. On both occasions, recourse had to be taken to ad hoc credit arrangements that reached beyond the confines of the EC. It hardly could be argued that the facilities were too small, especially taking into account the significant enlargements undertaken in 1977 and in connection with the creation of the EMS.

Generally, it turned out that other avenues were more convenient for debtor and creditor countries alike. As a consequence of the internationalization of credit markets, debtor countries found it comparatively easy to satisfy their needs on the international markets without going through the politically and procedurally cumbersome process of consultation and approval within the EC. In this respect, the existence of the EC credit facilities, however, may have acted as a "security umbrella," making it easier for the countries concerned to obtain loans on the markets. This role of the EC to act as a "guarantor of last resort" was formalized with the establishment of a new medium-term, conditional credit facility, the Community Loan Mechanism (CLM) in February 1975, in response to the first oil price crisis of October 1973 (Monetary Committee, 1976, pp. 34–37) (see also Chapter 12). Under the CLM, the EC can raise funds directly from third countries and financial institutions or on capital markets and on-lend the proceeds to the member state(s) in difficulties. Although the servicing and repayment of the loans obtained from third parties is the obligation of the debtor country, it is guaranteed by other member states, subject to specified ceilings. For obvious reasons, this option was preferred by potential creditor countries within the EC.

CLM loans were arranged for Italy (in 1976 and 1977), for Ireland (in 1976), for France (in 1983), and for Greece (in 1985). In June 1988, the MTFA and the CLM were merged into a single medium-term financial assistance facility, allowing for the use of both financing methods, that is, taking recourse to outside sources or, if necessary, directly to member states.[6] Under this facility, Greece obtained a credit in 1991. In January 1993, the EC agreed to grant Italy a loan in the amount of ECU 8 billion, part of which was used in March and November of the same year.[7]

THE DEBATE ABOUT THE NARROWING OF FLUCTUATION MARGINS

Another aspect of monetary integration, the narrowing and eventual elimination of fluctuation margins between EC currencies, was a subject of debate for quite some time during the 1960s. In February 1968, the Commission suggested that the Committee of Central Bank Governors and the Monetary Committee examine the possibility of eliminating margins between EC currencies and of introducing common margins against currencies of third countries. Such a measure also would help to prepare a common EC position should nonmember countries adopt floating exchange rates, an option that was part of the discussions about a reform of the international monetary system. In its work program of March 1969, the Commission counted the elimination of the fluctuation margins among the most urgent actions (1969b, p. 9). Among EC countries, it was in particular Belgium and Luxembourg that were in favor of such action.

The narrowing and elimination of exchange rate margins posed a number of problems of a technical as well as an economic nature. In the Bretton Woods system, exchange rates were kept stable, that is, within relatively narrow margins, by means of intervention against the U.S. dollar, the key currency of the system. Arbitrage stabilized exchange rates between third currencies. Under the IMF Articles of Agreement, the market rate of a currency had to be kept within margins of 1 percent around the declared par value in terms of the dollar. The member countries of the European Monetary Agreement (including all EC countries) had adopted the commitment of maintaining margins of ±0.75 percent against the dollar. This implied that their market rates could diverge from their cross parities by ±1.5 percent and move against each other *in extremis* by as much as 3 percent. The narrowing of margins would establish for the currencies involved a preferential zone against the dollar and other third currencies.

Technically, it could be achieved in three ways:

1. The participating central banks would intervene not only in dollars but also in each others' currencies. This would be complicated but feasible; it would require mutual credit lines, the use of which would need to be settled in regular intervals in accepted international reserves, that is, gold or dollars.

2. The participating central banks would coordinate their interventions against the dollar on a daily basis, with the result that their currencies would move together against the dollar. This implied that a central bank could be obliged to intervene in the opposite direction of what the balance of payments situation would require — a policy problem that could provide ample food for conflict.

3. Only one central bank, acting as an agent, would intervene in dollars; all other central banks would intervene against that particular currency, making it into the "key" or "anchor" currency of the zone. Again, there could be a potential conflict of interests.

The debate about the narrowing of margins pitted the arguments of the monetarists on how to promote monetary integration against those of the economists. The monetarists stressed that the narrowing of margins and, even more, their elimination would facilitate intra-EC payments and promote trade and financial integration. Also, distortions in agricultural trade under the Common Agricultural Policy could be avoided. The idea was that such a higher degree of "market integration" would serve as a motor to further "policy integration." Narrower margins, by amplifying the negative effects of differing monetary policies on integration, would induce better policy coordination so as to avoid balance of payments problems that could endanger the common market. The economists argued that narrowing and eliminating the margins would increase balance of payments difficulties because the cushioning effect of the margins would be lost. The loss of flexibility of monetary policy would trigger a demand for more extensive credit facilities. The lessening of monetary policy autonomy would make it more difficult to respond to country-specific economic problems, for example, inflationary versus recessionary tendencies.

The discussion about the narrowing of margins exerted a great influence on the direction of action toward more monetary integration in the EC. The next concrete move, intended as a first step toward economic and monetary union as a follow-up to the Werner Report, was an exchange rate system that entailed narrower margins between EC currencies and common margins against the dollar. The method chosen was the first one described above. As we shall see in Chapter 11, the decision at the Smithsonian conference of December 1971 to widen fluctuations margins in the IMF from ±1 percent to ±2.25 percent gave the EC efforts to narrow margins a high degree of urgency. The collapse of the Bretton Woods system in March 1973 provided for those efforts an altogether different motivation.

NOTES

Literature of general interest for this chapter: Ansiáux and Dessart (1975); Bloomfield (1973); Kruse (1980); Gehrmann and Harmsen (1972).

1. According to Peter Kenen (1995, p. 98), full-fledged coordination "is usually defined as a process involving mutual modifications in the participants' national policies." Jean Monnet once observed: "All too often I have come up against the limits of mere coordination: it makes for discussion, but not decision" (quoted in Padoa-Schioppa, 1994, p. 26).

2. For a detailed discussion of the two strategies, see Kruse (1980, pp. 63–70). For a maximalist statement of the "economist" viewpoint, see Deutsche Bundesbank, Annual Report 1962, pp. 37–38.

3. Legally, this was not a decision of the Council but a "declaration" of the representatives of governments, indicating the delicate nature of exchange rate matters and the desire of member countries to treat parity changes not as an EC matter, which would have been subject to EC procedures, but as an intergovernmental issue. Furthermore, the protocol of the meeting contained the statement that the declaration could not prejudge any interpretation of Art. 145 of the EEC Treaty, which deals with the powers of the Council of Ministers regarding "the general economic policies of the Member States" (compare with Chapter 5). The Commission, in turn, was of the opinion that the declaration could have been a council decision, in other words, that exchange rate changes were part of EC competences. See Gehrmann and Harmsen (1972, p. 53).

4. For a chronology of decisions concerning the EC credit facilities and a synopsis, see Rey (1981, pp. 233–65).

5. With the amendment of 1974, the amounts of the STMS were expressed in European Monetary Unit of Account. One unit of account was equivalent to 0.88867088 grams of fine gold, the gold content of U.S. $1 before the devaluation of December 1971. The MTFA used units of account from the beginning. When the ECU was formed in connection with the creation of the EMS, the ECU became the accounting unit for the STMS as well as for the MTFA.

In connection with the accession of Austria, Finland, and Sweden, the total of STMS debtor quotas was set at ECU 9,985 million and the total of creditor quotas at ECU 19,970 million. The total of debtor rallonges, and that of creditor rallonges, may not exceed ECU 8,800 million.

6. *Official Journal of the European Communities*, No. 50 178, Vol. II, July 8, 1988, pp. 1–4. With the accession of Austria, Finland, and Sweden, the total of creditor ceilings for the merged MTFA facility remained unchanged at ECU 13,925 million.

7. For more details, see Papaspyrou (1993, p. 484).

9

The 1969 Conference in The Hague and the Objective of Economic and Monetary Union

The customs union was realized on July 1, 1968, one and one-half years ahead of schedule, and the Common Agricultural Policy was implemented. Thus, the main projects envisaged by the European Economic Community (EEC) Treaty were brought to completion. Yet, at the same time, the European Community (EC) was shaken by the monetary crises of 1968 and 1969. The widespread notion that intra-EC exchange rates could be kept stable by elaborate consultation and coordination procedures proved illusory. The reason was that economic policies and developments in the EC showed significant divergences because the member states were not able and willing to share economic policy sovereignty and to agree on common policy objectives. The crises occurred against a backdrop of increasing fragility of the international monetary system. A weakened pound sterling was relinquishing its international role, and the dollar was less and less able to meet its responsibilities as the key currency of the international monetary system. The Bretton Woods system of stable although adjustable exchange rates was reaching its twilight. There was concern — most urgently expressed by the EC Commission — that, without a strong commitment to economic and monetary policy cooperation, the common market and other achievements of the 1960s could be at risk.

On the political level, France — after the resignation of President Charles de Gaulle and under the leadership of President Georges Pompidou — adopted a more pragmatic policy stance and showed greater willingness to move ahead with European integration. In Germany, Chancellor Willy Brandt was determined to continue with the pro-European policies of his predecessors. The other four member states of the EC — Belgium, Italy, Luxembourg, and Netherlands — remained committed to the European idea. Four more European countries — Denmark, Ireland, Norway, and the United Kingdom — were knocking at the door to join the "Six."

THE SUMMIT CONFERENCE OF DECEMBER 1969 IN THE HAGUE AND THE ESTABLISHMENT OF THE WERNER COMMITTEE

At this juncture, the EC concentrated on two issues: the admission of new members and the underpinning of the degree of "market integration" already achieved by enhanced "policy integration" through the formulation of harmonized, and eventually common, economic and monetary policies — in today's parlance, the focus was on the "enlargement" and the "deepening" of the EC. On December 1 and 2, 1969, the Heads of State or Government of the EC countries met for their first summit conference in The Hague. The final communiqué spoke of the responsibility "to draw up a balance sheet of the work that has been achieved, to manifest their determination to carry it on, and to lay down broad guidelines for the future" (Monetary Committee, 1974, pp. 13–16). The leaders expressed the "desire to affirm their faith in the political objects which give to the Community its whole meaning and significance." The EC — they declared — was "the original nucleus from which European unity has developed and taken wing." They wanted "to carry on more rapidly with the further development necessary to reinforce the Community and its development into an economic union," with the aim of "a Community of stability and growth."

In concrete terms, the conference agreed that "a plan by stages should be drawn up by the Council . . . with a view to the creation of an economic and monetary union" and that "the development of monetary cooperation should be based on the harmonization of economic policies"; the possibility of setting up a European reserve fund should be examined; negotiations with the applicant countries should be opened; and the EC should progressively be given its own revenue base.

The summit did not give any concrete instructions or indications how economic and monetary union (EMU) should be achieved. However, the communiqué contained a clear "economist" element when it requested that the development of monetary cooperation should be *based* on the harmonization of economic policies; the reference to a European reserve fund bowed to "monetarist" ideas. The main inspiration for the initiative regarding EMU was the belief that EMU would promote economic as well as political integration. In the words of the communiqué: "Entering into the final phase of the Common Market . . . is also preparing the way for a united Europe capable of assuming its responsibilities in the world of tomorrow" — an unequivocal reference to the ultimate political objectives of European integration. That EMU also would be in the national interest of EC countries was taken for granted.

The economics and finance ministers of the EC countries met on January 16, 1970, and — together with the central bank governors — again on February 23 and 24. The discussions revealed wide differences in approach and indicated the reluctance of some member states to give up national sovereignty. Various plans for the establishment of EMU were presented. The German plan, following a clear economist strategy, was supported by the Netherlands and Italy. The plans of Belgium and of Luxembourg were based on the monetarist approach. France did not present a plan of its own but declared its broad agreement with the proposals of Belgium and Luxembourg and the position of the Commission, which issued its plan on March 4.[1]

In a meeting on March 6, 1970, the Council formed a working group to draft a report analyzing the different suggestions and identifying the basic issues for a realization of EMU. Chairman of the committee was the prime minister and finance minister of Luxembourg, Pierre Werner, an ardent advocate of European monetary unification. The Werner Committee (as it was called) submitted its reports in May and October 1970.

In this chapter, we shall discuss the national plans and the plan of the Commission. The plan of the Werner Committee is discussed in Chapter 10.

THE GERMAN PLAN (SCHILLER PLAN)

The German plan, issued on February 12, 1970, proclaimed that EMU was a precondition for the full utilization of the economic resources of Europe, for the realization of political integration, and for the strengthening of the economic and political position of Europe. Recent years had demonstrated that economic imbalances led to distortions and restrictions in the movement of goods, services, and capital in the EC. To bar such risks, decisive progress in the harmonization and coordination of economic, monetary, and tax policies was needed.

A plan for EMU had to be realistic. Overcoming existing economic divergences and structural differences would require a longer time, approximately a decade; the final stage could be entered around the year 1978. Once the risk of serious economic imbalances was decisively reduced, the time would be ripe for the move to fixed and guaranteed exchange rates. The transition from one stage to the next should be contingent on the achievement of the essential elements of the prior stage. The movement toward EMU would have to be associated with a further shift of substantial national competences to the EC, and appropriate responsibilities would have to be granted to the European Parliament.

The German plan consisted of four stages. The first stage would create the basis for the harmonization of economic and monetary policies. It would comprise the harmonization of medium-term economic policies, strengthened consultation on short-term policies, better coordination of structural policies, the improvement of short-term economic and fiscal policy instruments, and the activation of the Short-Term Monetary Support (STMS) and setting up of the Medium-Term Financial Assistance (MTFA). There would be a strengthened coordination of external monetary policies, based on close cooperation between the central bank governors and the Council, aiming at a concerted position in international monetary institutions and prior consultation on recourse to international medium-term credits. The consultation on national interest rate and credit policies in the Monetary Committee and the Committee of Central Bank Governors should be strengthened. Money and capital markets in the EC should be gradually liberalized.

In the second stage, the objectives defined in the first stage would actually be realized by increased and more far-reaching short-term economic policy decisions of the Council under Art. 103, recommendations on the economic orientation of national budgets, consultations on the medium-term budgetary plans, intensified coordination of the national interest and credit policies, and the application of the MTFA.

The German plan envisaged for the first two stages a period up to 1974–75. On the basis of progress in those two stages, the gradual transition to EMU could take place in the third and fourth stages. This would require political decisions of great significance and appropriate changes of the EEC Treaty.

The third stage would entail the transition to EMU and the introduction of EC elements into economic and fiscal policy cooperation: the coordination of medium-term objectives to achieve a further convergence of national policy priorities; measures to improve the economic structure and, thus, the efficiency of the EC; the creation of the EC competences; and the move to majority decisions in important areas of economic, fiscal, and monetary policies. Furthermore, a gradual transition to a Federal Reserve–type European central bank system and a narrowing of fluctuation margins could take place; parity changes would require the approval of EC partners, possibly by qualified majority. The MTFA could become a reserve fund, and a part of national reserves could be gradually transferred to the fund.

In the fourth, and final, stage EMU could be completed, together with the extension of EC institutions. Hereby, the principle of subsidiarity should apply.[2] The final stage would, in particular, include the transfer of the necessary competences in the areas of short-term economic, fiscal, and monetary policies to EC institutions, the transformation of the Committee of Central Bank Governors into a European central bank council that would decide by majority vote, the move to irreversibly fixed and guaranteed exchange rates between member states, and the introduction of a European monetary unit.

The German proposals had two distinct features. First, in line with the economist strategy, the move to "fixed and guaranteed" exchange rates only would follow a high degree of actual convergence in economic performance; consequently, the move from one stage to the next should depend on the achievements of the earlier one. Second, in line with progress toward EMU, EC decisions and institutions should be introduced. As in other plans, the features of the final stage were only outlined, and not much detail was provided with regard to the institutional aspects and responsibilities of a European central bank system. For the preparatory stages as well as for the final stage, the dividing lines between general economic policies and monetary policies; between the respective institutions such as the Council, the Monetary Committee (which includes government as well as central bank representatives), and the central banks; and, in the final stage, between various EC institutions remained undefined. Foreshadowing the debates of the 1990s was the emphasis on the political aspects of integration and the insistence on the principle of subsidiarity and the involvement of the European Parliament.

THE BELGIAN PLAN

The Belgian plan, issued on January 23, 1970, started with a general analysis of the state of economic and monetary policy integration in the EC. The EEC Treaty did not establish a monetary community, and each member state followed the monetary and budgetary policies judged indispensable for the maintenance of its internal and external equilibrium. The possibilities of the EC to intervene were limited, and the coordination procedures did not result in common action or effectively coordinated policies. As a consequence, since 1968, economic problems had emerged more frequently in the EC and hampered its development, and actual monetary and financial integration took place on the international, not the EC, level.

Monetary and fiscal policy strategies could be harmonized only if the objectives were harmonized. The coexistence of a common monetary strategy and autonomous economic policies would lead to difficulties and, in case of conflict, could cause member states to return to monetary sovereignty. After monetary unification, economic developments in member countries should be sufficiently coherent, starting with the coordination of budgetary and fiscal policies because of their importance in the overall framework of economic policies.

The Belgian plan envisaged three stages, from 1971 to 1977. In the first stage, economic policy cooperation would remain voluntary, but the Council could issue recommendations to national governments, in particular on budgetary policies. Income policies gradually would be harmonized. Monetary policy decisions could be made only after consultation in the Committee of Central Bank Governors, which, in turn, could receive from the Council recommendations on the general orientation of monetary and exchange rate policies. Fluctuation margins between EC currencies would be reduced gradually, and parity changes would require a common decision. Member states would take a common position in international monetary institutions.

In the second stage, Council recommendations on economic policy would be replaced by directives. The Committee of Central Bank Governors would approve in advance the main monetary policy decisions within the framework of guidelines by the Council. Techniques of central bank intervention in foreign exchange markets would be harmonized, and regulations on credit institutions and money markets would be unified. The fluctuation margins would be eliminated, and there would be one exchange rate for the dollar. A common currency unit would be established, although prices, incomes, assets, and contracts could be expressed in national currency as well as the common currency unit.

In the third stage, EC institutions would be set up and would pursue a single economic policy. They would define common objectives and take the necessary measures. They would prepare and implement the EC budget and determine the framework for the national budgets. A common monetary system, similar to the Federal Reserve system, consisting of national central banks and a European executive body, would be created. The executive body would approve the operation of national monetary instruments, would carry out a common reserve and foreign exchange policy, and could grant credits to member states. National currencies would be freely convertible, and parities could not be changed anymore. At a later date, national currencies would be replaced by a single currency. The EC would become an autonomous entity vis-à-vis third countries, and foreign exchange reserves would be under common administration.

In a supplementary study, Baron H. Ansiaux, at the time governor of the National Bank of Belgium, presented the rationale and proposals for the establishment of a European reserve fund and the narrowing and elimination of fluctuation margins.

Although the Belgian plan put quite some emphasis on the need to harmonize economic policies, monetary policy integration measures were to be implemented early on. National monetary autonomy would be significantly reduced already in the first stage and even more in the second stage, with the requirement of approval for monetary policy decisions and the elimination of fluctuation margins. As in other plans, hardly anything was said about the autonomy of the envisaged common central bank system.

THE LUXEMBOURG PLAN

The plan of the Luxembourg government was intended as a sketch. It envisaged seven stages, which could be reduced in number or combined, and a time span of seven to ten years. The need for a coordination of economic policies parallel to the realization of monetary union was acknowledged, but the notion that it had to precede monetary union was rejected. In consequence, the plan, although vaguely referring to the need for consultation, concentrated on monetary integration measures.

Already, in the second stage, the fluctuation margins would be reduced. The third stage would bring the definition of a European unit of account, which would promote the fixity of parities. During the fourth stage, parity changes would become subject to common agreement. In the fifth stage, the STMS and the MTFA would be merged into a European fund for monetary cooperation. In the sixth stage, the activities of this fund would be extended to the granting of short-term credits by the EC to international institutions or third countries. To facilitate such operations, member states would transfer the administration of part of their international reserves to the fund. In the seventh stage, the fund would be transformed into a European reserve fund with significantly enlarged competences. With the use of a European unit of account, one would come close to a final stage in which monetary policy would be centralized and a European currency would substitute for national currencies.

The Luxembourg plan piled, somewhat mechanically, one step of institutionalized integration on the other. Yet, it acknowledged that the final step — the introduction of a common currency — could only be a function of "une integration politique plus poussée" (Werner, 1970). Referring briefly to the negotiations with the four countries applying for membership, the paper concluded with the personal view of Prime Minister Werner that the accession of the United Kingdom would strengthen the monetary vocation of the EC ("Personellement, j'attends de l'adhésion britannique une vocation monétaire plus accentuée de la Communauté") — in retrospect, a remarkable misjudgment of British aspirations.

THE PLAN OF THE COMMISSION

It was the last plan to be issued, after member states had presented their plans and stated their positions in the ministerial meeting in February 1970. The Commission submitted a coherent and quite comprehensive set of proposals that included important elements of the national plans. It favored a parallel strategy in which progress in the convergence of economic policies would go hand in hand with the setting up of institutional arrangements.[3]

At the outset, the Commission identified two objectives: the creation internally of an economic area without frontiers and externally of an organized economic and monetary area with its own identity. As economic interpenetration weakened the effectiveness of national instruments, the creation of common instruments was necessary. Whereas a monetary union needed to be based solidly on compatible economic developments and convergent economic policies, closer "monetary solidarity" (with this, the Commission was referring to institutional arrangements) enhanced the prospects for compatibility and convergence.

Stable exchange rates were one of the most important aspects of any plan for the establishment of economic and monetary union. A system of stable rates involved constraints that had to be accompanied by the development of joint policies. Because the achievement of compatibility would take time, short- and medium-term monetary cooperation mechanisms should be set up to deal with any balance of payments difficulties of member states. (Here, the Commission referred to corresponding proposals of the Barre Memorandum of February 1969. It should be noted that, when the Commission prepared its plan, the STMS was just being set up and the MTFA was still under discussion; see Chapter 8.) Although parity changes could not be altogether barred, they should be regarded as permissible only in the last resort and by common agreement. In case of an international agreement on a widening of fluctuation margins, it would be of the greatest importance not to widen the present margins between EC currencies.

The Commission identified four fields of EC activity as being of strategic importance: short-term and medium-term economic policy, monetary policy, and budgetary policy; the progressive establishment of an EC capital market; the harmonization of taxation; and the strengthening of monetary solidarity to make the EC a unit of its own within the international monetary system.

The Commission organized its proposals for three stages around these four fields of activity. The year 1978 could serve as a rough guide for the time horizon, although the timetable should be kept flexible.

The first stage (1970–71) would include a more effective coordination of short-term economic policies; the annual comparison of national budget estimates; the preparation of medium-term guidelines on budgetary policy; the introduction of a value-added tax throughout the EC; and the adoption of a program for the harmonization of excise duties. In the monetary field, the first stage would include renewed efforts to unify money and capital markets; the establishment of the MTFA involving the use of International Monetary Fund Special Drawing Rights; the concertation of credit policies in the Committee of Central Bank Governors; adoption of a common position in international monetary organizations; in case of changes in the international exchange rate system, the establishment of uniform rules for the EC as a whole; and the retention of the present fluctuation margins between EC currencies.

The second stage (1972–75), in transition to EMU, would be devoted to ensuring economic convergence and making a start on the creation of a single monetary area. It would include the common establishment of the main lines of overall economic policy, of short-term economic policy guidelines, of budgetary policy guidelines with respect to main revenue and expenditure categories and to procedures for financing deficits, and the use of harmonized budgetary policy instruments for a better control of cyclical fluctuations. There would be further measures to unify financial markets and to harmonize taxes. From the beginning of 1972, fluctuation margins would be limited to ±1 percent, and concerted central bank intervention policies would be introduced. The Committee of Central Bank Governors would prepare credit policy guidelines, related to the general economic policy guidelines at the EC level.

Upon the completion of the second stage, the Council would examine the overall EC situation and decide whether to move to the final realization of EMU. On the proposal of the Commission, the Council could defer the transition to the third stage by, at most, two years.

For the third stage (starting 1976 or 1978), during which EMU would be realized, the Commission provided only a sketchy outline. The powers necessary for the smooth functioning of EMU would be allocated to the EC institutions. A Council of Central Bank Governors would be established as a step toward an EC system of central banks. A European reserve fund would be established, to be supervised by the Council of Governors, to which member states would divert a progressively larger proportion of their reserves. Fluctuation margins would be eliminated in two stages, and parities would be irrevocably fixed. The free movement of capital would be established, and fiscal borders would be eliminated. The conditions for the introduction of a single currency then would be fulfilled.

Although the Commission plan espoused a parallel strategy, the proposed efforts on policy coordination in the first two stages were more of a programmatic nature, and the introduction of institutional arrangements such as the narrowing of margins was not made contingent on the successful coordination of policies and the actual convergence of economic developments. However, the transition to the final stage could be delayed. Finally, the outline for the third stage did not give any indication about the structure and the degree of autonomy of the EC institutions. This applies in particular to the common central bank system, whose policy objectives, scope of responsibilities, and degree of independence remained undefined.

COMPARISON OF THE PLANS

The various plans had a similar timeframe of about eight to ten years. The German plan and, although to a much lesser degree, the Commission plan would make transition from one stage to the next contingent on the achievements of the prior stages. All plans recognized the need to harmonize economic policies and to achieve convergence of economic performance as important for implementing measures of monetary integration. However, emphasis on this point differed significantly, with the German plan following most pronouncedly an economist strategy. Although some plans envisaged introduction of monetary institutional arrangements (narrowing of margins, pooling of reserves, mutual financial support systems) in the early stages and effectively harmonized economic policies only later or, at best, in parallel, the German plan turned this time sequence around, starting with the harmonization and communalization of policies.

All plans stressed the need to develop common positions in international monetary organizations. There were virtually no discussions of the institutional structures of the EC institutions for the final stage and no reference to the issue of independence for a European central bank system, a characteristic that was carried over to the Werner Report and its follow-up. Undoubtedly, it would have been very difficult at this early stage of discussions about monetary integration to reach agreement on such issues. Later, in particular in the Delors Report and during the discussions leading to the Maastricht Treaty, such issues played a very central role.

One interesting aspect of this phase of the debate about the creation of EMU was that a country as important as France did not present its own plan. One could speculate that, in not doing so, the French government did not want to commit itself already in the planning stage to the surrender of national sovereignty that inevitably would be associated with setting up common decision-making procedures and institutions.

NOTES

1. Commission plan: Commission (1970); German plan: Bundesminister für Wirtschaft (1970); Belgian plan: Ministère des Finances (1970); Luxembourg plan: Werner (1970). For excerpts of the plans of Germany, Belgium, and Luxembourg (in German), see Gehrmann and Harmsen (1972); for a synopsis, see Willgerodt et al. (1972). Both publications also include nonofficial plans by various groups and individuals.

2. "Subsidiarity," a term that gained special prominence in connection with the Maastricht Treaty of 1991, is the notion that the lowest level of government that can efficiently carry out a function should do so.

3. In the following paragraphs, I am relying in part on my own translation of the French and German texts.

10

The Werner Report

In addition to Prime Minster Pierre Werner, the committee that was charged with drawing up a plan for an economic and monetary union (EMU) for the European Community (EC) consisted of high officials of the five other EC countries who were chairmen of the various economic committees and a senior official of the Commission. The composition of the Werner Committee indicated that what was expected was not so much a study by an impartial group of experts (although the committee members served in a personal capacity) but a politically viable and acceptable merging of different national positions. Only two of the seven committee members came from central banks, a striking difference to the composition of the Delors Committee of 1988 (see Chapter 17). The Werner Committee presented an interim report on May 20, 1970, and its final report on October 8, 1970.[1]

The Werner Committee met for the first time on March 20, 1970. It soon was able to agree on a number of issues such as a characterization of the existing state of monetary integration as the point of departure for the creation of EMU and the definition of EMU. However, significant differences of opinion emerged on two points: The first one was the subject of the familiar debate between the "monetarist" camp — France, Luxembourg, Belgium, increasingly also Italy as well as the Commission — and the proponents of the "economist" strategy — Germany and the Netherlands (see Chapter 8). What should be the time sequence for measures in the economic policy field and in the monetary field, respectively; in other words, what should come first? The second one related to the issue of institutional arrangements for the final stage of EMU.[2]

THE INTERIM REPORT

The Interim Report of the committee addressed the first of these unresolved issues. The monetarists already favored for the first stage an "independent exchange system . . . to assert the Community's personality in its dealings with the rest of the world." An initial narrowing of fluctuation margins would reduce "the preferential treatment now accorded to the dollar . . . [and] constitute a first step along the road to a common external monetary policy" (pp. 13–14). The establishment of an exchange stabilization fund would "strengthen the cohesion of the member countries in the conduct of their monetary relations and . . . facilitate progress through the various stages of unification. . . . It will help to harmonize their intervention policies on the exchange markets and their policies towards their reserves" (p. 14).

The economists felt "that neither an institutional reduction of the [fluctuation] bands nor the creation of an exchange stabilization fund are desirable in the first stage. . . . Important measures of Community monetary policy can only be contemplated when, as a result of effective progress in the harmonization of economic policy, certain conditions are fulfilled so that the equilibrium of the economy as a whole throughout the Community can be ensured." The economists concluded: "The convergence of economic policies will in itself curb exchange rate variations between the European currencies" (p. 15).

On the institutional issue, Germany and Netherlands argued for a central economic policy institution with political responsibility (such as a Council for short-term economic policy, or the Commission provided with political responsibility) and an autonomous European central bank. Other countries, in particular France and Luxembourg but also the Commission, felt that it was too early to discuss political and institutional issues of the final stage — an indication of the prevailing apprehension about the issue of national sovereignty. The Interim Report did not enter in a discussion of the institutional questions.

During a conference of the economics and finance ministers and the central bank governors of the EC countries on May 29 and 30, 1970, in Venice and at a Council meeting on June 9, the differences of opinion reflected in the Interim Report were discussed openly. When presenting the report, Committee Chairman Werner tried to prepare the ground for a compromise and emphasized the need to advance simultaneously in the economic as well as the monetary policy field.

THE FINAL REPORT

The Werner Committee continued working toward agreement on the unresolved issues and presented its Final Report in October 1970. A special central bank expert group, chaired by Baron H. Ansiaux, governor of the National Bank of Belgium, prepared as an annex a detailed analysis of the monetary policy and technical aspects of the narrowing of fluctuation margins and the establishment of an exchange stabilization fund.

The main points of the Werner Report were an analysis of the achievements and the shortcomings of the EC so far; a precise definition of EMU; the working out of a parallel strategy for its realization; the design of three stages over a period of ten years, although with particular emphasis on the first stage; and proposals for central decision-making institutions for economic as well as monetary policy for the final stage.

Definition of Economic and Monetary Union

At the outset, the report stated that "economic and monetary union will make it possible to realize an area within which goods, services, people and capital will circulate freely and without competitive distortions. . . . [Its] implementation will effect a lasting improvement in welfare . . . and will reinforce the contribution of the Community to economic and monetary equilibrium in the world. . . . The Community policy should tend to reduce the regional and social disparities and ensure the protection of the environment" (p. 9).

In the definition of the report, a monetary union implied the total and irreversible convertibility of currencies, the elimination of margins of fluctuation in exchange rates, the irrevocable fixing of parity rates, and the complete liberalization of movements of capital. EMU might be accompanied by the maintenance of national monetary symbols or the establishment of a single EC currency. Although, from a technical point of view, the choice between the two solutions might seem immaterial, psychological and political considerations militated in favor of the adoption of a single currency to confirm the irreversibility of the process. To ensure the cohesion of EMU, transfers of responsibility from the national to the EC level would be essential (p. 10).

In the final stage, quantitative medium-term objectives and broad outlines for short-term economic policy would be decided at the EC level. Monetary policy would be centralized. The framework for the main budget aggregates for annual budgets and multiyear projections would be decided at the EC level, but it was necessary to guard against excessive centralization. A true common market for capital should be arrived at. There should be cooperation between EC members on structural and regional policies. The social partners should be consulted prior to the formulation and implementation of EC policy (pp. 10–11).

Institutional Issues

Institutional reforms would necessitate a modification of the EEC Treaty. They would include "the creation or the transformation of a certain number of Community organs to which powers until then exercised by the national authorities will have to be transferred." Although the Committee did not formulate detailed proposals for the final stage, it called for two organs for the control of economic and monetary policy. A "centre of decision for economic policy" would exercise independently a decisive influence over the general economic policy of the EC. It should be able to influence the national budgets, in particular "the level and direction of the balances and the methods for financing the deficits or utilizing the surpluses." In addition, parity changes for the single currency or the whole of national currencies would be within its competence. This transfer of powers to the EC should "go hand-in-hand with the transfer of a corresponding Parliamentary responsibility from the national plane to that of the Community. The centre of decision of economic policy will be politically responsible to a European Parliament" (pp. 12–13).

The "Community system for the central banks" could be similar to the U.S. Federal Reserve System. It would be empowered to make decisions on liquidity, rates of interest, and the granting of loans to the public and private sectors. Externally, it would be empowered to intervene in the foreign exchange market and manage the monetary reserves of the EC. As already mentioned, the power to change the parity of the single currency vis-à-vis third countries was to rest with the "centre of decision for economic policy," and no formal role for the system of central banks was envisaged (p. 13).

The Committee acknowledged that the transfer of powers raised political problems, in particular, the relationship between the center of decision for economic policy and the EC system of central banks as well as that between the EC organs and the national authorities. However, the Committee felt that a deeper study of the institutional problems was outside the framework of its mission (p. 13).

The Stages

The Committee proposed three stages over a period of ten years. The report concentrated very much on the first stage, which was to begin on January 1, 1970, and last three years. To lay down a precise and rigid timetable for the whole period did not seem feasible, because a certain flexibility should be maintained. The decisions on the timetable and the details of the final stages should be made at the end of the first stage.

During the first stage (pp. 15–24), the emphasis would be on the reinforcement of the coordination of economic policies and the common determination of the fundamental guidelines for economic and monetary policy, based on at least three annual surveys of the economic situation in the EC. The Council would be the central organ of decision for general economic policy.

Specifically, the first stage would include in the field of budget and fiscal policy

the harmonization of budget policies with quantitative guidelines on the principal elements of the budgets, notably global receipts and expenditure, the distribution of the latter between investment and consumption, the direction and amount of balances, and the method of financing deficits or utilizing surpluses;

the harmonization of timetables for the presentation and adoption of the budget proposals;

the gradual elimination of fiscal frontiers;

the introduction of a general system of value-added taxes; and

adoption of programs for the alignment of value-added tax rates and excise duties.

With regard to financial markets, the report contained the following recommendations:

abolition of obstacles to capital movements, in particular, residual exchange control regulations and

coordination of policies in relation to financial markets.

Regarding domestic monetary and credit policy, the recommendations were:

definition of common orientations for monetary and credit policy;

prior obligatory consultations within the Committee of Governors;

measures should correspond to guidelines of the Committee and be subject to mutual information before application; and

harmonization of monetary policy instruments.

For external monetary policy, consultations would be strengthened on the utilization and granting of credits (e.g., International Monetary Fund [IMF] drawings, swap credits) and the creation of new international liquidity (IMF quotas, Special Drawing Rights). First steps would be taken to establish a common EC representation at the IMF and other international financial organizations and the adoption of common positions on monetary relations with third countries and international organizations. In particular, the EC should not avail itself of any provisions for greater exchange rate flexibility.

From the start of the first stage, the central banks would experimentally limit de facto the fluctuations between their currencies to narrower margins than those resulting from the application of the margins against the dollar. This could be achieved by concerted action in relation to the dollar. After this experimental period, the narrowing of margins could be formally announced. Concerted action vis-à-vis the dollar could be implemented by interventions in EC currencies, subject to credit limits not larger than those of the Short-Term Monetary Support (STMS). A further reduction in margins could be decided. Finally, a study on the creation and operation of a "European Fund for monetary cooperation" should be undertaken.

During the first stage, an intergovernmental conference should be called to prepare for the necessary adaptation of the EEC Treaty, in accordance with Art. 236 (which deals with amendments).

The report described the second stage and the transition to the final stage only in more general terms (pp. 24–25). In this phase,

the coordination of short-term economic policies would be further strengthened;

strategies would be developed for the realization of an EC optimum that would not necessarily be a simple juxtaposition of national optimums (the German text uses "not necessarily only the sum of national optimums"[3]);

medium-term policies would be geared to EC objectives;

in the field of budgetary policy, the norms for budget volumes and for the direction and size of balances would become increasingly restrictive (the German text uses, more plausibly, "increasingly more binding");

a true common capital market would be established;

with progress in the convergence of policies, member states would no longer need to take recourse to autonomous parity adjustments, but they would not be totally excluded; and

fluctuation margins would be progressively eliminated (p. 28).

The European Fund for monetary cooperation, under the control of the central bank governors, should be established as soon as possible, as a forerunner of the EC system of central banks. The fund would absorb the Short-Term Monetary Support and the Medium-Term Financial Assistance (MTFA) and gradually take over the management of the reserves at the EC level. At the final stage, it would be integrated in the EC system of central banks.

Evaluation

The strategy developed in the Werner Report was one of parallelism in which increasing convergence of economic developments would be concomitant with the setting up of institutional arrangements.[4] Of particular significance was the emphasis the report placed on the importance and the required scope of coordination efforts with regard to budget policy. For the final stage, the "centre of decision for economic policy," acting independently, was to be endowed with important powers, including the responsibility for setting exchange rates in relation to third countries. The relationship between the center and the system of central banks was not discussed. Moreover, the important issues of the degree of independence of the central bank system from political instructions and its primary task — maintenance of monetary and price stability or support for the whole range of economic policy objectives — were not addressed. In general, the report did not deal with the institutional issues of the final stage and concentrated more on procedural questions. Nevertheless, it was made clear that EMU would require the transfer of important responsibilities from the national to the EC level and that this should go hand in hand with a shift of parliamentary responsibility to the EC level.

THE ANSIAUX REPORT

The report of the group of central bank experts, chaired by Baron Ansiaux (Annex 5 to the Werner Report) set out the technical conditions of a narrowing of fluctuation margins and its monetary policy consequences. The group favored a gradual narrowing of margins over the immediate elimination because the latter would entail too severe a reduction in the monetary policy autonomy of member states. The report identified three methods for the narrowing of margins:

concerted action by the central banks to limit de facto the fluctuation margins between their currencies on an experimental basis;

formal (de jure) narrowing as a declared policy following the experimental stage; and

maintenance of the present intracommunity margins and widening of the margins vis-à-vis the dollar; the latter would be subject to IMF authorization if it would go beyond ±1 percent.

All three methods would require agreement on a "Community level" for the dollar that would determine the band of narrower margins (the report used as an example 1.2 percent on either side of parity between EC currencies instead of the prevailing 1.5 percent) and the points of intervention. The same intervention techniques — exclusively in dollars at concerted rates or in dollars and EC currencies — would apply to all three methods of narrowing the margins. An "agent," for example, the Bank for International Settlements, could be entrusted with administering the system.

Some of the experts observed that, because balance of payments trends could still diverge, member states would have conflicting interests regarding an EC level for the dollar. If, however, agreement were reached, the agreed intervention rates might oblige member states to intervene against the "natural trend of the market, which would be contrary to a sound logical policy." These experts also were not convinced "that a reduced autonomy on the monetary plane would necessarily lead to a greater degree of coordination of economic and budgetary policies in general, and they point[ed] out that a similar consequence was expected from the common agricultural market. . . . Certainly the narrowing of the margins would necessitate a reinforcement of cooperation between the central banks of the Community" (p. 44).[5]

DECISIONS IN RESPONSE TO THE WERNER REPORT

In a memorandum, submitted to the Council on October 30, 1970, the Commission generally agreed with the conclusions of the Werner Committee (Commission, 1970b, pp. 3–16). However, the Commission took a distinctly monetarist position by endorsing in particular the views of the Committee on the gradual reduction of fluctuation margins and suggesting a closer examination of the functions and organization of a European Fund for monetary cooperation. The Commission also expressed the view that the important questions concerning both the ultimate goals and the transition to economic and monetary union still should be studied in depth. In obvious deference to the French reluctance to discuss institutional arrangements for the final stage and the transfer of responsibility to the EC level (reflecting French concerns over the potential loss of national sovereignty), the Commission hardly referred to these issues.

The Council discussed the Werner Report and the memorandum of the Commission on November 23 and on December 14 and 15, 1970, without reaching agreement. Germany and Netherlands requested more consideration of the supranational aspects of the Werner Report, and France rejected an early commitment to the concept of common policymaking. In a meeting on February 8 and 9, 1971, a tentative accord was reached, and on March 22, the Council agreed on a set of measures.

The "Resolution of March 22, 1971 on the attainment by stages of economic and monetary union" was full of general intentions and short on concrete measures.[6] It referred to the creation of an area with free movement for persons, goods, services, and capital; the formation of a single currency area within the international system; an EC organization of central banks; and the distribution of powers and responsibilities between EC institutions and member states. However, it shied away from any clear references to the "centre of decision for economic policy," proposed in the Werner Report, other institutional arrangements for the final stage, or the convening of an intergovernmental conference for the recommended amendment of the EEC Treaty.

The resolution contained a number of procedural measures for the coordination of short-term economic policies, for laying down broad outlines of economic policy and quantitative guidelines for budget policy, for the harmonization of taxes, for the liberalization of capital movements, and with regard to regional and structural policies. The Monetary Committee and the Committee of Central Bank Governors were asked to conduct prior consultations and to coordinate monetary policies. The Council agreed further on the progressive adoption of common positions in monetary relations with third countries and international organizations. Also, it was stated that the EC "should not avail itself in matters of exchange rates between Member States of any arrangements which might lead to a weakening of the international monetary system" (p. 20) — a reference to the possibility of world-wide floating exchange rates. Measures for closer policy cooperation were formalized in decisions on the strengthening of coordination of short-term economic policies and on cooperation between the central banks (Monetary Committee, 1974, pp. 101–3).

The most important substantive agreement was to "invite" the central banks of member states to narrow exchange rate fluctuations on an experimental basis from the beginning of the first stage. As a subsequent step, the resolution suggested to move from a de facto to a de jure system of narrower margins, to intervene in EC currencies, and to successively reduce the fluctuation margins. Also, the Council requested a report on the organization, functions, and statutes of a European Monetary Cooperation Fund (paragraphs III.7 and 8 of the resolution).

At the same meeting, the Council adopted the Third Medium-Term Economic Policy Program for 1971–75 and agreed to set up the MTFA as of January 1, 1972 (see Chapter 8).

Although the resolution confirmed a broad consensus to move ahead with the step-by-step realization of EMU, it represented, nevertheless, a step back from the compromises worked out by the Werner Committee.[7] The resolution as well as the MTFA decision dealt specifically only with certain, in essence institutional, monetary measures for the first stage, lacked any clear declaration how and to what end the harmonization of economic policies should be achieved, and gave no indication as to the institutional arrangements for the final stage. It was, therefore, not surprising that the German government was not ready to accept unconditionally this approach and made its approval contingent on the insertion of a precautionary clause (Deutsche Bundesbank, Annual Report 1970,

p. 42). Accordingly, the monetary provisions and the activation of the MTFA would be limited to a period of five years after the beginning of the first stage in order "to ensure that economic measures keep sufficiently in step with monetary measures" (paragraph III.9 of the resolution). Only after agreement to proceed to the second stage had been reached would these provisions remain in force.

Despite the minimalist character of the resolution, a first step on the long road toward the realization of EMU was about to be taken. The objective of EMU as defined in the Werner Report and its acceptance in principle by member states determined for the next 25 years the efforts for monetary integration in the EC.

On the basis of the March resolution, the central bank governors agreed in April 1971 to narrow the fluctuation margins between EC currencies. As of June 15, 1971, currencies were to fluctuate against each other by not more than ±1.2 percent, instead of ±1.5 percent. This would limit maximum shifts between EC currencies to 2.4 percent, compared with 3 percent before.[8]

All was set for the first concrete step toward EMU. However, other events intervened.

NOTES

Literature of general interest for this chapter: Kruse (1980).

1.   Werner Committee, Interim Report, in *Bulletin*, No. 7, 1970, Supplement. Final text in *Bulletin*, No. 11, 1970, Supplement. For the mandate of the committee, see Annex 2; for its composition, see Annex 3 of the final report. Page numbers refer to the reports as published in the *Bulletin*.

2.   For a recollection of the negotiations, see Werner (1991).

3.   The Werner Report was written and published before English-speaking countries joined the EC and English became an official EC language. I, therefore, consulted also other language versions.

4.   Kruse (1980, p. 73) maintained that "parallelism" was not a synthesis of the monetarist and economist approaches and that the two strategies "remained totally incompatible. . . . Yet the acceptance of 'parallelism' did enable the Six to start on the path to EMU."

5.   It is not difficult to recognize the mentioned experts as representatives of the economist school.

6.   Monetary Committee (1974, pp. 20–23). In some publications, the date of the resolution is given as February 9, 1971. The resolution was formally adopted on March 22, 1971.

7.   For evaluations of the resolution see also Kruse (1980, pp. 75–79); Bloomfield (1973, pp. 14–15); Deutsche Bundesbank, Annual Report 1970 (pp. 40–43).

8.   Parities were still expressed in U.S. dollars, around which fluctuation margins of ±0.75 percent were observed, implying margins of ±1.5 percent around the cross-parities of EC currencies. Let us assume that, at a given time, one

currency would be at the upper end of the band formed by the margins and another currency at the lower end; if, then, both currencies would switch positions, a maximum shift of 3 percent would occur.

11

The Breakdown of the Bretton Woods System and the "Snake"

The early 1970s were the years of the great dollar crisis that revealed the frailty of the international monetary system. The crisis had a strong influence on how the European Community (EC) saw its own monetary identity and went about the task of monetary integration. The international agreement (commonly referred to as the Smithsonian Agreement) on a world-wide realignment of exchange rates in December 1971, concluded at a meeting of the Group of Ten in the Smithsonian Institution's neo-Romanesque "castle" on the Mall in Washington, did not lastingly restore the postwar system of fixed exchange rates. For the EC, this posed a tremendous challenge to design and implement an exchange rate system that would safeguard the common market. Yet, adverse international developments and, more importantly, a lack of determination to proceed in earnest with a common strategy in economic and monetary policies made the 1970s a period of trial and instability for the EC.

THE CRISES OF 1971 AND THE SMITHSONIAN AGREEMENT

Throughout the late 1960s and in 1970, the U.S. balance of payments was in a precarious state that in 1971 was aggravated by large outflows of short-term capital. Starting in April 1971, the U.S. trade balance turned into a deficit, generating for 1971 as a whole the first annual trade deficit since the war and, indeed, in this century. In 1950, U.S. gold reserves were nearly three times as high as official liabilities and in 1959 were still at par with liabilities. However, the ratio of official liabilities to gold reserves rose continuously and reached 4.24 in 1970 and 6.21 in 1971 (Crockett, 1977, p. 119). For this reason and because of the inflation differentials between the United States and most European countries and Japan, the dollar was considered more and more overvalued.

The prime destination of capital movements was the German currency, and in April 1971 alone, the Bundesbank had to absorb $3 billion. At an EC finance minister meeting on April 26 in Hamburg, German Finance Minister Karl Schiller reportedly proposed that the EC currencies should float or revalue together against the dollar, while French Finance Minister Valéry Giscard d'Estaing suggested a devaluation of the dollar. Leakages about the discussions to the press further fueled speculation. On May 3, the leading German economic research institutes published a report claiming that the Deutsche mark was undervalued and proposing a floating or revaluation of the German currency.

Following additional large intakes of dollars, the German authorities closed the exchange markets on May 5, followed by the Netherlands, Belgium, and Switzerland. At another EC meeting on May 8 and 9, Germany, supported by the Netherlands, again proposed a joint float for the EC currencies, but France and Italy rejected the idea. The Commission argued strongly against a revaluation of the EC currencies and proposed, instead, several interventionist measures, including the introduction of dual exchange markets (*Bulletin*, No. 6, 1971, p. 15). The Council declared that the present situation and foreseeable developments of the balance of payments of the EC countries did not justify a change in parities but expressed understanding for a temporary widening of fluctuation margins, "despite the incompatibility under normal conditions of a system of internal floating exchange rates with the smooth functioning of the Community" (*Bulletin*, No. 6, 1971, p. 26). Subsequently, as of May 10, Germany let its currency float freely, and the Netherlands followed suit. The mark and the guilder started to appreciate. Belgium strengthened its dual exchange market provisions; France and Italy relied on low interest rates and on existing capital controls. Austria and Switzerland, both not members of the EC but with economies closely linked to the German economy, revalued by 5 percent and 7.1 percent, respectively. The EC central bank governors suspended their agreement to narrow the fluctuation margins by June 15. The crisis passed but left in its wake an EC with a variety of exchange regimes. Progress toward closer monetary integration had come to an abrupt halt.

The calm on the foreign exchange markets did not last very long. The monthly U.S. trade deficits spurred doubts about the sustainability of the dollar exchange rate, and July saw large outflows of dollars. On August 7, 1971, the Subcommittee on International Exchange and Payments of the Congressional Joint Economic Committee issued a report (the so-called

Reuss Report) recommending a devaluation of the dollar. Not surprisingly, the outflow of dollars "reached enormous proportions" (Solomon, 1982, p. 185). Among EC countries, France and Belgium were now the principal destination of dollar funds. On August 13, U.S. President Richard Nixon and his top economic aides convened at the presidential retreat, Camp David. On August 15, he announced a package of measures that included as its centerpieces the "temporary" suspension of the gold convertibility of the dollar, a 10 percent surtax on imports, and a 90-day wage and price freeze.[1] "Thus began a period of turmoil that was to last four months, until December. And, more significant, thus ended the old monetary system of par values and convertibility of the dollar," wrote Robert Solomon (1982, p. 187). It left other countries, particularly in Europe, with the alternatives of observing unilaterally their parities against the dollar, continuing to transfer real resources and accumulating unwanted dollars, or letting their currencies float against the dollar and against each other, with the likelihood of a significant appreciation against the dollar.

At a meeting of the EC Council on August 19, ministers again could not agree on proposals for a joint float. France still rejected a joint float, which would have resulted in an appreciation of the franc, and Germany and the Netherlands remained opposed to the Commission's proposal to introduce an EC-wide two-tier exchange system. Instead, the EC countries adopted differing exchange regimes. Germany continued with the independent float of its currency. Italy let the lira float but influenced the market rate by intervention and strengthened its defenses against capital inflows. Belgium and Luxembourg agreed with the Netherlands to operate a common float by limiting fluctuations between their currencies to ±1.5 percent, an arrangement that later became known as "the worm within the snake." France maintained its official exchange rate on the old dollar basis for commercial transactions but established a two-tier exchange market with a floating rate for capital transactions. As D. C. Kruse observed (1980, p. 94), this meant that "when the foreign exchange markets re-opened on 23 August, there were no fixed exchange rates within the Community except for the Benelux arrangement."

Other important currencies outside the EC also started to float, although many developing countries preferred to maintain for their currencies the peg to the dollar.

Dissatisfaction with the exchange rate situation soon emerged on both sides of the Atlantic. Efforts to come to a viable compromise were undertaken in a flurry of international meetings, which we shall not trace in detail. The most important one took place in the Azores on December 13–14, 1971, between President Nixon and French President Georges Pompidou, who, following an earlier agreement between France and Germany on the future exchange rate relationship between their two currencies, spoke for the EC countries. The two presidents agreed to work, together with other countries, toward a realignment of exchange rates entailing a devaluation of the dollar and revaluations of some currencies as well as the introduction of wider fluctuation margins. This prepared the ground for the Smithsonian Agreement of December 18, 1971, on the reestablishment of fixed exchange rates and a realignment of the most important currencies.

The agreement included:

a devaluation of the dollar by 7.89 percent, representing an increase in the price of gold by 8.57 percent from $35 to $38 per ounce;

a revaluation of the Deutsche mark by 4.61 percent, implying a revaluation against the dollar by 13.58 percent;

a revaluation of the Japanese yen by 7.66 percent (against the dollar by 16.88 percent);

revaluations of the Belgian-Luxembourg franc and the Dutch guilder by 2.76 percent (against the dollar by 11.57 percent); and

a devaluation of the Italian lira by 1 percent, implying a revaluation against the dollar by 7.48 percent.

The British pound and the French franc stayed put, implying a revaluation against the dollar by 8.57 percent.

The fluctuation margins were widened from ±1 percent, as prescribed by the International Monetary Fund (IMF) Articles of Agreement (and ±0.75 percent for most European currencies) to ±2.25 percent. The new exchange rates were not called "par values" but "central rates."[2]

The United States abolished the import surcharge, but the gold convertibility of the dollar was not restored. On a weighted basis, the dollar devaluation against all countries was estimated to be between 6.5 and 7.75 percent and against the Group of Ten countries, about 10 percent (Solomon, 1982, p. 209).

At the end of the conference, President Nixon addressed the participants and then announced on television "the conclusion of the most significant monetary agreement in the history of the world" (Solomon, 1982, p. 208). It turned out to be a very short-term vision of history.

Concerning the events of 1971, Solomon (1982, p. 212) came to the following conclusion:

Under the Bretton Woods system the world experienced an unprecedented expansion of production and trade, and it worked reasonably well until the second half of the 1960's. . . . Had it not been for the Vietnam-caused inflation after 1965, the old system might have gone on for quite a while. . . . What brought the system down was the failure of the adjustment process. . . . What actually happened was that the growing economic and political strength of Europe and Japan made the Bretton Woods system obsolete. A more symmetrical system, in which the role of the United States was more equal to that of the other countries, was called for.

THE "SNAKE IN THE TUNNEL"

The breakdown of the Bretton Woods system in August 1971 was, at the time, seen as a temporary delay for the start of the economic and monetary union (EMU) project. Yet, the Smithsonian Agreement, while reestablishing a system of fixed exchanges rates, posed another challenge for the EC. The widening of margins meant that, while EC currencies could fluctuate against the dollar, the intervention currency, by ±2.25 percent, they could fluctuate against each other by ±4.5 percent; in case of a reversal of positions of two EC currencies at the opposite ends of the band over time, exchange rates could shift by as much as 9 percent.

This was seen as posing great risks for the common market. In February 1972, the Commission presented proposals that revived the concept of narrower margins between EC currencies and the idea of a European Monetary Cooperation Fund (EMCF). Shortly before the Smithsonian Agreement, the central bank governors had asked a group of experts under the chairmanship of Marcel Théron, a high official of the Bank of France, to reexamine, on the basis of the 1970 report of the Ansiaux group (see Chapter 10), the operational problems of a regime of narrower margins.[3] The group considered a narrowing of margins justified by the need to safeguard intra-EC trade, to contribute to a smooth functioning of the Common Agricultural Policy, and to reestablish the basis for progress toward EMU. The choice of intervention currencies, the techniques and financing of intervention, and the settlement of intervention debts were identified as important issues.

The Council met on March 21, 1972, to decide on appropriate measures. In a resolution, the EC central banks were requested, "as a first step towards the creation of [the EC's] own monetary zone within the framework of the international system," to reduce the fluctuation margins among EC currencies to ±2.25 percent (i.e., half the maximum possible under the Smithsonian Agreement) and to intervene at the outer limits of these margins in EC currencies. Intervention in dollars was to take place at the outer limits against this currency. Intervention within the margins would be allowed only after a joint decision of the participating central banks. According to the resolution, the longer-term objective remained the complete elimination of fluctuation margins between EC currencies (Monetary Committee, 1974, pp. 33–34). Although the exchange system as agreed in April 1971 (see Chapter 10) would have narrowed the margins among EC currencies, they still would have been wider than those against the dollar. The newly proposed regime was intended to put relations among EC currencies on the same footing as those between EC currencies and the dollar. In terms of intervention technique, the problem was the same: obligatory intervention to keep EC currencies within their margins would have to take place before intervention to keep the dollar within its margins.

Subsequently, on April 10, 1972, the EC central banks agreed on additional operational aspects of the new system (Basle Agreement) (Monetary Committee, 1974, pp. 60–62). Operations started on April 24. Generally, the central banks whose currencies reached the intervention points intervened simultaneously, with the strong currency central bank buying the weak currency and the weak currency central bank selling the strong currency. For the financing of interventions, mutual short-term credit facilities were established, without any limit as to amount ("very short-term financing"). Financing operations took the form of swaps or outright forward sales. Remuneration on outstanding balances was based on the arithmetical mean of the official discount rates of the participating central banks. Financing operations terminated on the last working day of the month following the month in which intervention took place but could be renewed for three months by mutual agreement. Settlement of intervention debts was effected by using gold and gold-related assets (Special Drawing Rights, reserve positions in the IMF) and dollars or any acceptable currency in proportion to the reserve structure of the debtor country. However, by mutual agreement between creditor and debtor central banks, settlement could take place on different terms and conditions, including settlement in the currency of the creditor central bank. This provision indicated a degree of flexibility that, in a number of respects, became an important feature not only of the snake but also of the snake's successor, the European Monetary System (EMS). The agreement also determined the conversion rates for the use of various reserve elements in settlement.

As mentioned earlier, the Basle Agreement put exchange rate relations among EC currencies on the same footing as relations with the dollar, with a maximal shift of exchange rates over time of 4.5 percent. The system became known as the "snake in the tunnel." The movements of the EC band, the "snake," which, at most, could be 2.25 percent wide, were limited by the selling and buying limits for the dollar, which formed the "tunnel" of 4.5 percent. The "wiggling" of the snake within the tunnel was determined by market forces: a balance of payments surplus for the EC as a whole against third countries (or, in other words, an excess supply of dollars in the markets) would pull up the snake (implying an appreciation) until it reached the ceiling of the tunnel, at which point intervention in dollars would have to take place, and vice versa. A surplus or deficit of a major snake currency against third currencies could exert a strong pull or drag on the snake as a whole. (The former occurrence, in particular the relative strength of the Deutsche mark, was to create major problems for future developments in the snake as well as later in the EMS.) The payments positions of individual partner countries vis-à-vis each other determined the width of the snake and the need to intervene in partner currencies. The special arrangement of August 1971 between the National Bank of Belgium and the Netherlands Bank, to limit fluctuations between the Benelux currencies to ±1.5 percent (the worm), was maintained; it was discontinued in March 1976.[4]

An important aspect of the arrangement was the so-called concertation, that is, the effort to harmonize exchange operations of the participating central banks. This was done, first, by standardizing the dealing hours of the various markets and the earliest and latest time of the day at which intervention might be undertaken so that no central bank would have to bear alone the burden of intervention and, second, by operating a special telephone network among participating central banks for mutual information and consultation on market developments, strategies, and tactics. Later on, the Swiss National Bank, although not a participant in the arrangement, was linked to the network. At an even later stage, the network included also the Federal Reserve Bank of New York and the Bank of Japan. It continued to play an important role in the management of the EMS.

The EC membership candidates United Kingdom (UK) and Denmark joined the arrangement on May 1, 1972, eight months before their accession. Norway, whose bid for EC membership was blocked by a negative referendum, became an associate member on May 23, 1972. Ireland became part of the arrangement by virtue of the link of its currency to the pound sterling. Sweden became associated with the arrangement in March 1973, when the Bretton Woods system collapsed. Austria unilaterally and without formal obligations aligned its currency with the currencies in the arrangement. Switzerland explored, without results, a possible association with the snake in 1975. However, the weak currency countries in the EC were not interested in another strong currency participating in the arrangement.

Neither the Council resolution nor the central bank agreement contained any obligation for a closer coordination of monetary, fiscal, and other economic policies or explicit commitments to strive for more convergence of economic developments beyond those included in the Council resolution of March 1971 or otherwise in existence.

THE FIRST SNAKE CRISIS, THE FINAL BREAKDOWN OF THE BRETTON WOODS SYSTEM, AND THE SNAKE WITHOUT THE TUNNEL

Not long after the Smithsonian Agreement of December 1971, doubts arose concerning the durability of the new set of exchange rates. They concentrated on the dollar and the pound sterling.

In early 1972, the large current account surplus of the UK of 1970 and 1971 melted away. It was, however, not until June 1972 that mistrust in the pound's exchange rate intensified and market pressure built up. Things were not helped by a statement in March of the Chancellor of the Exchequer, Anthony Barber, emphasizing the priority of domestic economic concerns over exchange rate considerations, or by a statement in June by the shadow Chancellor, Denis Healey, that sterling might have to be devalued (Solomon, 1982, p. 221). The threat of a dock strike did the rest. A speculative attack erupted, and within one week, European continental central banks purchased about £1 billion, of which more than 60 percent was absorbed by the Bundesbank. On June 23, 1972, the Bank of England ceased to intervene; the pound left the snake and started to float.

Ireland also departed from the snake because of its close economic ties to the UK and the link between their two currencies. Foreign exchange markets were closed until June 27, and a meeting of EC finance ministers took place on June 26. Denmark announced its withdrawal from the snake as of June 27 but continued to keep its currency within the margins and formally rejoined the snake on October 10, 1972. Italy also contemplated leaving the snake but remained after obtaining agreement for intervening not only in partner currencies but also in dollars and settling intervention debts only in dollars.

In the wake of the crisis, participation in the snake had dwindled from ten to seven countries with one — Italy — just limping along. At a meeting of the finance ministers of present and future members of the EC[5] on September 12, 1972, and a summit conference on October 19–21 in Paris, the EC decided to charge ahead. The conference of Heads of State or Government "reaffirmed the resolve of the Member States of the enlarged Community to move irrevocably" toward EMU. It decided to set up the EMCF before April 1, 1973, and requested reports concerning changes in the Short-Term Monetary Support (STMS) and on the progressive pooling of reserves. The need for closer coordination of economic policies was stressed, and the Council was directed to take specific measures to this end (Monetary Committee, 1974, pp. 24–32). The EMCF was set up nearly in time and the STMS was revised in early January 1973 to take account of the new members, but efforts for a better coordination did not lead to any concrete results. Thus, monetarist considerations prevailed over those of an economist nature. Some observers spoke of a "limping standard of parallelism." The future attrition of the snake appeared preprogrammed.

During the second half of 1972, in hindsight, eerie calm prevailed in international exchange markets. "At the beginning of 1973," wrote Kruse (1980, p. 126), "a flight from the dollar had not yet developed but all the ingredients were already present." What triggered the attack on the dollar was the Italian decision to introduce on January 22, 1973, a two-tier exchange market as protection against reserve losses. The following day, Switzerland, which was the target of massive speculative capital inflows, in particular from Italy, set the franc free to float. The fear that other countries might follow led to a massive flight from the dollar. Some $8.5 billion left the United States in the three weeks to February 9, and Germany — again, the main destination — had to absorb about $6 billion in the first two weeks of February despite controls on capital inflows.

The United States and the EC countries realized the need to act. Although both the United States and Germany had a preference for floating, Germany was not willing to let its currency float independently. After intense consultations with the major countries, the U.S. authorities announced on February 12, 1973, a 10 percent devaluation of the dollar, the second within a little more than one year, raising the official price of gold to $42.22 per ounce. The exchange rate relationships among the snake currencies remained unchanged except for the Italian lira, which, because of continued reserve losses, was allowed to float also in the market for commercial transactions on February 13. The snake had lost another one of its members.

Yet, markets did not come to rest. Within a few weeks, speculation against the dollar resumed, and official exchange markets were closed on March 1. EC finance ministers met on March 4 and again on March 8. In a meeting on the following day, the United States declined to agree to a package of proposals by the EC that included U.S. market intervention financed by IMF and bilateral credits as well as the use of its own reserve assets. In an additional EC meeting on March 11 and 12, French Finance Minister Giscard d'Estaing finally accepted a joint floating of the snake currencies after Germany agreed to revalue, at the same time, the Deutsche mark against its partner currencies by 3 percent. When exchange markets reopened on March 19, snake participants ceased to observe the intervention limits against the dollar (and, implicitly, all other currencies still tied to the dollar). They remained committed to keep the exchange rates of their currencies within 2.25 percent of each other; the Benelux countries continued to observe their 1.5 percent margins. Both France and Belgium-Luxembourg retained their two-tier exchange markets (Monetary Committee, 1974, p. 63).

This was the final breakdown of the Bretton Woods system. The tunnel around the snake disappeared, and the snake was free to move. Whether it was the dollar or the other currencies that were now floating was the subject of some lively discussion.

The decision of the EC countries still participating in the snake (Belgium and Luxembourg, Denmark, France, Germany, Netherlands) to float jointly and to keep the door open for the "lost brothers" had great political significance. It came at a time when the general trend was toward more flexibility in exchange rates. There was a turning away from the doctrine of fixed exchange rates as the indispensable prerequisite for international economic relations, and there existed a heightened awareness of greater economic diversity among countries and of increasingly mobile international capital. For the EC, however, a common exchange rate system was considered essential for maintaining the common market in industrial and agricultural goods. From a political point of view, it was seen as a precondition for further progress in European integration. The fact that non-EC members — Norway and Sweden, and, in an informal way, also Austria — were partners in the common exchange rate system underlined its economic importance without diminishing its political significance.[6] Another question was whether, outside a circle of central bank and financial experts, it was sufficiently recognized that sustaining a system of fixed though alterable exchange rates required more than declarations, good intentions, and recourse to intervention and financing mechanisms, namely, efficient policy coordination resulting in a high degree of economic convergence. The vision of an economic and monetary union, however, had, for the time being, receded into a more distant future.

THE EVOLUTION OF THE SNAKE

The snake had an eventful history. During its lifetime of less than seven years, membership (including associated countries) dropped from 11 to 6 countries, and there was a total of nine realignments, several of them involving more than one currency (see Table 11.1; Thygesen, 1979, pp. 87–125).

The withdrawal of the UK in June 1972 and of Italy in February 1973 as well as the temporary suspension of membership by Denmark from June to October 1972 have already been mentioned. In 1973 alone, there were, in addition to the revaluation of the Deutsche mark at the start of the joint floating, another revaluation of the German currency by 5.5 percent on June 29 and revaluations of the Netherlands guilder by 5 percent on September 17 and the Norwegian krone by 5 percent on November 26.

A momentous event that had a tremendous impact on the world economy was the first oil crisis, which broke out in October 1973. The main Middle Eastern oil producers progressively limited crude oil production, imposed an embargo on exports to a number of countries, including the United States, and raised oil prices in several steps from $3 to nearly $12 per barrel. These measures created severe problems for the domestic economies and the external balances of many countries.[7]

Economic policy response to the oil crisis differed markedly from country to country. Some countries felt that the related shift in terms of trade should be met with restrictive policies so as to facilitate the required transfer of resources to the oil producers. Other countries were more

TABLE 11.1
Chronicle of the Snake

April 24, 1972	Agreement on narrower margins enters into force
May 1, 1972	Accession of the UK, Ireland, and Denmark
May 23, 1972	Association of Norway
June 23, 1972	Withdrawal of the UK and Ireland
June 27, 1972	Withdrawal of Denmark
October 10, 1972	Return of Denmark
February 13, 1973	Withdrawal of Italy
March 19, 1973	Start of joint float; tunnel disappears
	Revaluation of Deutsche mark by 3 percent
	Association of Sweden
June 29, 1973	Revaluation of Deutsche mark by 5.5 percent
September 17, 1973	Revaluation of Netherlands guilder by 5 percent
November 16, 1973	Revaluation of Norwegian krone by 5 percent
January 19, 1974	Withdrawal of France
July 10, 1975	Return of France
March 15, 1976	Second withdrawal of France
March 16, 1976	Narrow margins of ±1.5 percent between Benelux currencies (worm) discontinued
October 17, 1976	Revaluation of Deutsche mark by 2 percent
	Devaluation of Danish krone by 4 percent
	Devaluation of Norwegian krone by 1 percent
	Devaluation of Swedish krone by 1 percent
April 1, 1977	Devaluation of Swedish krone by 6 percent
	Devaluation of Danish krone by 3 percent
	Devaluation of Norwegian krone by 3 percent
August 28, 1977	Withdrawal of Sweden
	Devaluation of Danish krone by 5 percent
	Devaluation of Norwegian krone by 5 percent
February 13, 1978	Devaluation of Norwegian krone by 8 percent
October 17, 1978	Revaluation of Deutsche mark by 4 percent
	Revaluation of Netherlands guilder by 2 percent
	Revaluation of Belgian-Luxembourg franc by 2 percent
December 12, 1978	Withdrawal of Norway
March 13, 1979	The EMS enters into force

Sources: Deutsche Bundesbank (1976a, p. 25); Commission (1979, pp. 81–83); Gros and Thygesen (1992, p. 17).

concerned about a possible recessionary impact and pursued only moderately restrictive or even expansionary policies. As a result, inflationary pressures and balance of payments difficulties varied from country to country. Also, within the EC, there was no consensus on the policies to be followed, reflecting different economic circumstances and policy philosophies. As a consequence, the rise of consumer prices during 1974 and 1975 ranged from an average of 6.5 percent in Germany to 12.7 percent in France and 18 percent in Italy (for comparison: United States, 10 percent, and total Organization for Economic Cooperation and Development, 12.3 percent).

The pronounced divergence in economic policies and developments created tensions within the snake. In particular, France experienced during 1973 a substantial loss of reserves. Because it was not prepared to devalue its currency within the snake for political as well as economic reasons, it decided to withdraw from the snake on January 19, 1974. After stringent monetary and fiscal policies were successful in reducing inflation and improving the balance of payments, France returned to the snake on July 10, 1975, at unchanged intervention rates.

In connection with the return of the French franc to the snake, the Basle Agreement was amended on July 8, 1975. Gold was excluded from the calculation of the reserve structure for settlement purposes and from settlement itself. (Until then, gold had been used only once in a special transaction between the Netherlands Bank and the National Bank of Belgium.) Another important modification of the snake agreement was the possibility for a debtor central bank to request an automatic extension of settlement by a maximum of three months. This provision was subject to some conditions; in particular, total indebtedness was not allowed to exceed the amount of a debtor central bank's quota in the STMS (Monetary Committee, 1976, pp. 19–21).

The renewed pursuit of expansionary policies by France in 1975 produced, in the second half of the year, a reversal in the current account, undermining confidence in the reestablished central rate of the franc. Efforts to come to a multilateral realignment in the snake failed, and on March 15, 1976, the French government was forced to withdraw again. This decision left only one major EC currency, the Deutsche mark, in the snake, around which the currencies of a number of smaller countries with close economic ties to Germany were grouped: Belgium-Luxembourg, Denmark, and Netherlands; as associated members, Norway and Sweden; and, informally, Austria.[8] However, even within this small group of currencies, economic developments required five realignments from October 1976 until the snake was succeeded by the EMS (Table 11.1).[9]

Outside the snake, the Italian lira and the pound sterling suffered a pronounced decline in their exchange rates. Italy took recourse to EC credits as well as IMF credits. The UK relied on IMF drawings in 1976 and 1977. An agreement to allow an orderly reduction in sterling balances has been discussed in Chapter 7.

The attempt to create for the EC as a whole a unifying exchange rate system ultimately ended up in a "mini-snake," frequently characterized as a "Deutschmark zone." It hardly could be called an EC arrangement anymore. The failure to agree on a common policy response to a major external shock, the oil crisis (even if it was, in some part, asymmetrical) and — more generally — to achieve a consensus on economic policy priorities was glaringly obvious. Any illusion that the snake could serve as a first step toward EMU had to be abandoned. For all those reasons, the snake had a generally bad press. Nevertheless, it afforded the remaining participants a certain degree of policy coherence and exchange rate stability. As the first truly multilateral exchange rate and intervention system, it provided the participating central banks with important operational experience that formed the basis for the management of the EMS. The snake owed its survival and its relative success in part to the political motivation of a number of countries to keep established EC arrangements alive but also in part to a remarkable degree of operational flexibility. This allowed countries to leave and join again or to adjust exchange rates and left enough room for regular appraisals and, if necessary, changes of rules.

Yet, if one looks at the overall state of economic and monetary integration in the EC, one has to agree with the blunt conclusions drawn in March 1975 by a study group, appointed by the Commission and chaired by Robert Marjolin, formerly a secretary general of the Organization for European Economic Cooperation and a vice-president of the EC Commission (1975, p. 1):

Europe is no nearer to EMU than in 1969. In fact if there has been any movement it has been backward. The Europe of the Sixties represented a relatively harmonious economic and monetary entity which was undone in the course of recent years; national economic and monetary policies have never in 25 years been more discordant, more divergent, than they are today.

The only thing to be said is that each national policy is seeking to solve problems and to overcome difficulties which arise in each individual country, without reference to Europe as an entity. The diagnosis is at national level; efforts are made at national level. The coordination of national policies is a pious wish which is hardly ever achieved in practice.

NOTES

Literature of general interest for this chapter: Jennemann (1977); Kruse (1980); Solomon (1982); de Vries (1976, Vol. I; 1985, Vol. I); Deutsche Bundesbank, Annual Reports.

1. U.S. Secretary of the Treasury John Connolly provided a colorful summary of the crisis: "Foreigners are out to screw us. Our job is to screw them first." Quoted in James (1996, p. 210).

2.   In the view of the IMF, the central rates and the wider margins constituted a "temporary regime"; the Articles of Agreement did not use the term "central rate," and the Fund lacked the authority to substitute wider margins for those of ±1 percent. See de Vries (1976, Vol. I, pp. 557–59).

3.   This group of experts continued under several chairmen to examine issues of EC exchange rate policy throughout the existence of the Committee of Central Bank Governors. With the establishment of the European Monetary Institute on January 1, 1994, the group became its Foreign Exchange Policy Subcommittee.

4.   For a detailed description of the agreement, see Wittich and Shiratori (1973); see also Banque Nationale de Belgique (1972); Deutsche Bundesbank (1976a); Lambert and de Fontenay (1971).

5.   Formally, Denmark, Ireland, and the UK joined the EC on January 1, 1973.

6.   It was now called the "European *common* margins arrangements" because it was no longer about a *narrowing* of margins and comprised by way of association participants that were not subject to all provisions of the EC agreement of April 1972. See Deutsche Bundesbank (1976a, p. 28).

7.   Solomon (1982, p. 316) commented: "The quadrupling of oil prices at the end of 1973 was probably the most severe shock to the international monetary system — and, more broadly, to the world economy — since World War II."

8.   Sweden eventually left on August 28, 1977.

9.   C. J. Oort, at the time treasurer-general in the finance ministry of the Netherlands, observed (1979, p. 195): "Every time the cross-rates of the smaller countries' currencies vis-à-vis the deutsche mark were considered out of line, they did adjust their central rates. Every time the relation between the major currencies of the Community had to be adjusted, the weaker partner dropped out."

12

The Quest for More Policy Cooperation and a Unified Exchange Rate System in the 1970s

The snake was an ambitious undertaking: it was to be the steppingstone toward economic and monetary union. The main problem was that there was too much emphasis on monetary arrangements and not enough on the policies needed to sustain them. In particular, some European Community (EC) member states were not prepared to accept the policy and institutional consequences of monetary unification and to merge part of their sovereignty in economic policy matters. This needs to be seen, however, in the light of disparities in national interests. Whether these were real or perceived did not matter; what mattered was the existence of differences in the ranking of economic policy objectives.

As a result, the snake as an EC system could not withstand the tensions emanating from world-wide monetary developments and the sharp rise in oil prices in 1973.[1] Although the snake shielded participating countries from excessive exchange rate fluctuations, for the EC as a whole, the situation was very unsatisfactory. It was a blow to the political objective of unification, made progress in economic integration much more difficult, and carried the risk of stagnation if not regression.

The efforts of the EC subsequently were directed toward strengthening the institutional aspects of economic policy cooperation, in the hope that a tighter institutional structure would aid in achieving actual policy coordination. Furthermore, several initiatives were taken, on an official as well as a nonofficial level, aimed at designing a viable exchange rate system that would encompass all EC countries and at devising a European parallel currency, that is, a common but not, at least not initially, single currency.

INSTITUTIONAL DEVELOPMENTS IN ECONOMIC AND MONETARY POLICY COOPERATION

The European Monetary Cooperation Fund

On April 3, 1973 (i.e., shortly after the start of the common float of the EC currencies), the Council set up the European Monetary Cooperation Fund (EMCF), also known as FECOM after its French acronym (Monetary Committee, 1974, pp. 81–88). It started functioning on June 1. The Fund had legal personality and was directed by a Board of Governors consisting of the members of the Committee of Central Bank Governors and — in a limited role — a member of the monetary authority of Luxembourg (which does not have a central bank of its own). A significant point, with ramifications for the future (see note 3), was that, according to the final communiqué of the EC summit conference of October 1972 in Paris, the Fund was to be run "within the overall guidelines of economic policy adopted by the Council of Ministers" (Monetary Committee, 1974, p. 26; see also p. 83).

The Fund was to contribute to the progressive establishment of economic and monetary union (EMU). Its tasks included the promotion of the narrowing of fluctuation margins between EC currencies, of interventions in EC currencies in exchange markets, and of settlements between central banks, leading to a concerted policy on reserves.[2] In a first stage, the EMCF was to be responsible for concerted action necessary for the functioning of the snake agreement, the multilateralization of creditor and debtor positions and of settlements in the snake, and the administration of the very short-term financing facility and the Short-Term Monetary Support (STMS). Proposals concerning the pooling of member states' reserves and the merger of the very short-term financing facility and the STMS mechanism were not accepted.

The tasks of the EMCF as enumerated in the Council regulation sounded quite ambitious, but in view of the protracted discussions about its status and functions, it was no surprise that the EMCF never got really off the ground. It did not acquire any policy role and was, in effect, limited to an accounting function.[3] Its most important task turned out to be the multilateralization of snake transactions. Prior to the EMCF, snake interventions resulted in bilateral creditor and debtor positions. Since then, liabilities and claims resulting from intervention were cleared through the EMCF after conversion into European Monetary Units of Account.[4] In principle, the settlement rules remained the same. However, under the new multilateralization scheme, creditors no longer received assets according to the reserve structure of individual debtors but according to the average reserve structure of all debtors. The Bank for International Settlements acted as an agent for the Fund, carrying out its transactions in an arrangement similar to those with the European Payments Union and the European Monetary Agreement. When the European Monetary Institute was set up on January 1, 1994, it took over the functions of the EMCF.

Procedures for Policy Cooperation

After the snake had survived the turmoil created by the collapse of the Bretton Woods system in March 1973 and following the agreement on establishing the EMCF with a fairly ambitious mandate, monetary integration seemed to make progress. The EC Commission tried to take advantage of the more optimistic climate and on April 30, 1973, presented to the Council a communication on the second stage of realization of EMU that was to run from January 1, 1974, to December 31, 1976 (Commission, 1973). Regarding the first stage of EMU, it was a blunt assessment of the lack of progress in monetary and financial integration. The Commission's proposals for the second stage were based on the principle of parallelism. Five-year moving forecasts should guide the coordination of short-term policies. Budget policies were to be monitored regularly. Norms for internal liquidity, the allocation of credits, and the level of interest rates were to be set. The snake should be extended to all EC currencies, and fluctuation margins should be progressively reduced as the convergence of policies permitted. Recourse to exchange rate changes should be avoided as far as possible, and any adjustments should be made under EC control. The functions of the EMCF should permit coordinated intervention on the exchange markets and foreshadow essential functions of an EC central bank organization. The EMCF should be given resources in EC currencies and reserve currencies. However, the Commission proposals remained fairly vague, and the important issue of transferring policymaking authority from member states to the EC (a particular concern of Germany and the Netherlands) was not addressed in concrete terms.

Based on its communication, the Commission, in November 1973, submitted five draft texts to the Council for action. It emphasized the constraints placed by an emerging economic and monetary union on the policies of member states. The first draft dealt generally with the requirements of the move to the second stage and included a reference to the elimination of fluctuation margins and the attainment of fixed parities by 1980. Another draft consisted of an amendment to the regulation of April 1973 setting up the EMCF. Its aim was to upgrade the Fund's functions, most importantly by pooling 10 percent of member states' international reserves, by giving the Fund a certain role with regard to member states' intervention vis-à-vis third currencies, and by enlarging the amounts of the STMS eightfold and channeling credits under this facility through the Fund instead of bilaterally from one central bank to another. This draft had no chance of being adopted, because some countries saw in its proposals a threat to their stability-oriented monetary policies.

The remaining three drafts were, in essence, of a procedural nature. They were endorsed by the Council on December 17, 1973, and formally approved on February 18, 1974, but not before being significantly weakened.[5] The decision "on the attainment of a high degree of convergence of the economic policies" of EC member states (frequently referred to as the "convergence decision") called for the Council to examine regularly the economic situation of the EC, resulting every five years in a medium-term economic policy program. Special attention was to be given to the public finances. The next text — a directive "concerning stability, growth and full employment in the Community" — provided mainly procedural guidance to the implementation of the convergence decision. Finally, the Council set up an Economic Policy Committee to merge the functions of the Short-term Economic Policy Committee, the Budgetary Policy Committee, and the Medium-Term Economic Policy Committee, established in 1960 and 1964 (see Chapter 8).

The Council actions (and nonactions) illustrated quite clearly the insistence of member states on setting their own policy priorities and their difficulties with establishing efficient coordination procedures, let alone transferring policy responsibilities to EC institutions. D. C. Kruse tried to give a positive spin to the failure of the EC to make substantive progress toward EMU by writing (1980, pp. 164–65):

If the Nine could not agree on advancing to *the* second stage envisaged in the Werner Report, they were nevertheless in accord on proceeding to *a* second stage. . . . Even if no progress in economic and monetary integration occurred during this second stage, the decision to maintain the status quo was nevertheless extremely important . . . because it preserved the achievements of the past three years as a base for any future advance. . . . However, the problems in securing formal approval of even the weakened texts about the second stage brought home the reality that the resumption of movement towards EMU was not on the cards for the time being.

The Community Loan Mechanism

An important institutional innovation was the creation of the Community Loan Mechanism (CLM) on February 17, 1975 (already discussed in Chapter 8). This medium-term credit facility was to deal with balance of payments difficulties of member states in the aftermath of the 1973 oil crisis. Credits were subject to conditionality. The setting up of the CLM was part of the world-wide effort to "recycle" balance of payments surpluses of oil-producing countries to countries that, as a result of the oil price increases, suffered balance of payments deficits and followed the establishment of an "oil facility" (the so-called Witteveen Facility) by the International Monetary Fund in June 1974 (de Vries, 1985, Vol. I, pp. 305–32).

The European Unit of Account

Another innovation was the introduction of the European Unit of Account (EUA) on April 21, 1975. The EUA was defined by a basket of fixed (and unadjustable) amounts of EC currencies that took account, among other things, of the size of each EC country's economy (Monetary Committee, 1976, p. 59; *Official Journal of the European Communities* No. C 21, January 1, 1976; Dixon, 1977). It initially was used for financial assistance from the EC Development Fund to the African, Caribbean, and Pacific countries covered by the Lomé Convention of February 1975 and earlier similar arrangements. Subsequently, the EUA was phased into use in all other areas of EC activity (except the Common Agricultural Policy) and the operations of EMCF, replacing various gold-based units of accounts.[6] Such a unit of account had been under discussion for some time. It was proposed, for example, in the Fourcade Plan of September 1974 (see next section). In December 1978, in connection with the creation of the European Monetary System (EMS), the EUA was replaced by the ECU (European Currency Unit), which initially had the same composition as the EUA.

PROPOSALS FOR A UNIFIED
EXCHANGE RATE SYSTEM

EC countries were rather unhappy about the gradual disintegration of the snake and the lack of a common exchange rate system. In particular, France, traditionally an advocate of stable exchange rates, wanted to be part of a system that, after all, was still community based, despite its limited membership and the association of two non-EC countries. It hoped that participation in such a system would foster exchange rate stability and internal policy discipline, provided the system would impose less policy constraints than the snake and entail some form of a common dollar policy. The Netherlands also looked for a way to tie the floating EC currencies to the snake. The fear was that the lack of a common exchange rate system could distort competition and threaten economic cohesion of the EC and the integration process.

The Fourcade Plan

On September 16, 1974 — several months after France had withdrawn from the snake and as it was contemplating rejoining — French Finance Minister Jean-Pierre Fourcade presented a set of proposals for a revision of the operational rules of the snake (*Bulletin*, No. 9, 1974, pp. 21–23). The snake had displayed "a certain inflexibility, which eliminated any prospect of its being observed . . . by all Member States." EC currencies outside the snake should be linked to the snake by means of "reference rates," which could be changed and temporarily suspended. Wider fluctuation margins that could be reviewed frequently would form "a kind of 'boa'" around the snake (van Ypersele and Koeune, 1985, p. 44). They would not be defined bilaterally in relation to other currencies but by reference to a new unit of account that would be derived from a basket of various European currencies. The plan also proposed to "diversify" the methods of intervention (e.g., by the use of intramarginal intervention) and settlement and a "Community level" for the dollar.

The proposals for a remodeled exchange rate system aimed at making exchange rates more flexible in order to accommodate more easily divergent economic policies and developments, and the proposal for an adjustable "Community level" of the dollar was directed at stabilizing exchange rates against third currencies. Experience had shown (and continued to do so up to the present) that any weakening of the U.S. dollar resulted in tensions within the EC exchange rate system, because the Deutsche mark was considered virtually the only European alternative to the dollar for the "parking" of available or speculative funds. The Fourcade Plan also suggested that, in the longer term, the EMCF could be provided with its own means of intervention.

Moreover, the Fourcade Plan advocated the enlargement of the EC credit facilities. It proposed (referring to a Council agreement to issue an EC loan for the financing of oil price related balance of payments deficits) to issue a loan for at least 2 billion units of account (then about U.S. $2.4 billion) and to place it directly with oil-producing countries. This contributed to the establishment of the CLM. The plan also proposed to enlarge substantially the Short-Term Monetary Support and Medium-Term Financial Assistance facilities.

The Fourcade Plan was met "with a generally unfavorable response" (Gros and Thygesen, 1992, p. 39). However, the issue of "asymmetry" in the operation of an exchange rate system and the idea to use a basket-based unit of account as a reference point for intervention obligations played an important role in the discussions leading to the EMS, and the wider fluctuation margins actually became a feature of the EMS exchange rate mechanism (see Chapters 13 and 14).

The Duisenberg Plan

On July 6, 1976, Dutch Finance Minister Wim Duisenberg presented his proposals in a letter to his EC colleagues, in which he expressed concern about the exchange rate developments in the EC: "There is at present no effective Community framework for the coordination of policies in this area among all members. . . . The large movements of exchange rates [a reference to the sharp depreciations of the lira and sterling in the first half of 1976] have affected our relative competitive positions. . . . Moreover, there is a danger of a growing divergence between the countries that participate in the European snake arrangement and the other countries" (Oort, 1979, p. 210).

The main idea of the Duisenberg Plan was the introduction of declared and adjustable "target zones" for the nonsnake currencies.[7] Because exchange rate movements implied changes in relative competitive positions, target zones were not to be defined in terms of bilateral exchange rates against other currencies but in terms of effective rates, that is, trade-weighted averages of exchange rates. Target zones would not oblige countries to exchange market interventions or other policy measures but could entail the commitment to refrain from policy measures that would push the exchange rate outside the target zone. Breaching the outer limits of the zones would trigger consultations on a country's economic policies and the management of its exchange rate. "Policy obligations, if any, should be deliberately asymmetrical to compensate for the inflationary bias in the world of today" (Oort, 1979, p. 210). The snake would be maintained and would participate as an entity in the system of target zones.[8]

The nonbinding nature of the proposed target zones reflected the view that a return of all currencies to the snake, however modified, would be a realistic option only when differences in economic developments, in particular with regard to inflation and balance of payments positions, would be reduced. Therefore, a start should be made with a sufficiently flexible and initially not too ambitious scheme that would induce a maximum of consultation and coordination of policies that underlie exchange rate developments (Oort, 1979, pp. 201, 207).

After inconclusive discussions in the Committee of Central Bank Governors and the Monetary Committee, the plan was shelved in March 1977. There was agreement, however, "that the main point of this initiative [was] to initiate more consultations in order not only to reduce the danger of divergent developments in exchange rates between members of the European exchange arrangement and other members of the EC, but also to foster convergence in economic policies and exchange rates" (Monetary Committee, 1976, Oral statement to the Council by the chairman).

The van Ypersele Proposal

Some of the ideas of the Duisenberg Plan were taken up in early 1978 in a modified form by Jacques van Ypersele, at the time advisor to the Belgian prime minister and chairman of the EC Monetary Committee (see van Ypersele, 1978; van Ypersele and Koeune, 1985, pp. 44–45). The snake was to be maintained while nonparticipating currencies would adopt a single target zone, to be defined by the weighted average of the movements of the snake and the dollar, with equal weights at the outset. As the weight of the snake would be gradually increased, the target zone would approach the snake. The target zone would serve as a threshold to trigger consultations. The system would include a commitment to avoid policy measures that would bring an exchange rate outside the target zone. Although market intervention would not be obligatory for nonsnake countries, they would be included in the very short-term financing facility of the snake arrangement so as to facilitate intervention in snake currencies as a means of keeping their currencies within the target zone. For the settlement of intervention debts, a "European currency" could, at least in part, be used. It would be defined in terms of the basket-based European Unit of Account and would be issued by the EMCF, partly against deposits of countries' gold holdings, thus, mobilizing a part of gold reserves. (It should be recalled that, since 1975, gold was excluded from the settlement provisions of the snake arrangement.) This idea became later a part of the EMS.

The Tindemans Report

In another indication of unhappiness about the state of affairs in the EC in general and monetary integration in particular, the European Council at its meeting on December 10–11, 1974, asked the Belgian Prime Minister Leo Tindemans to define what was meant by the term "European Union" and how to advance European integration. In his report (1976), Tindemans adopted a pragmatic approach and avoided any far-reaching recommendations. It dealt not only with economic and social policies but also with foreign and security policies.

Tindemans stressed the need for a common economic and monetary policy and recommended that the snake be the starting point. Countries that were able to progress had a duty to forge ahead while the other countries should receive aid and assistance to enable them to catch up. EC countries not participating in the snake should be brought into the discussions to avoid increasing divergence and to enable any opportunities for alignment to be seized. To the external policy obligations under the snake, obligations should be added for domestic monetary policy (control of money supply), for budgetary policy (extent and financing of deficits), and for key aspects of short-term economic policy. There should be joint decisions on changes of snake central rates. Countries in the snake would undertake to withdraw only in cases of "manifest crisis." To underpin these obligations, the machinery for short-term and medium-term credits between snake members should be made automatic and strengthened. The effectiveness of the EMCF should be increased, and it should become the embryo for a European central bank, in particular, by some pooling of reserves.

The Tindemans Report "was rapidly and only half decently buried" (Ludlow, 1982, p. 22), which was perhaps not surprising, given the vacillation of its recommendations between monetarist and economist ideas.

PROPOSALS FOR A EUROPEAN PARALLEL CURRENCY

Concern about the lack of progress in monetary integration was not confined to official institutions. Academics of reputation, either on their own or by invitation, came up with ideas that were not timidly limited to building on existing arrangements but were bold and imaginative instead.

The All Saints' Day Manifesto

On November 1, 1975, nine economists from eight EC countries, "concerned at the lack of progress towards the goal of European monetary union . . . and at the harmful consequences of the inflation we are experiencing," published a manifesto in which they recommended that the EC central banks issue a European parallel currency with a constant purchasing power, called the "Europa," that would circulate along with existing national currencies (Basevi et al., 1975).

The authors felt that the Werner Report had suffered from "an excess of idealism" and concluded that, in view of differing priorities with respect to employment and inflation, a common policy of EC countries was not feasible. A major weakness of the approach based on coordinated decision making was its nonautomatic nature and reliance on political discretion. Instead of relying on the locking of exchange rates, it aimed at monetary unification through monetary reform based on the free interplay of market forces. This would combine gradualism and automaticity. The manifesto rejected the argument that monetary union would result in an unwanted combination of unemployment and inflation. Recent studies (i.e., in the early 1970s) had indicated that, in the long run, employment was independent of the rate of inflation. Because the "natural" rate of employment was determined by labor market conditions, taxation policy, and structural and institutional factors, any attempt to drive unemployment below the natural rate by means of expansionary monetary policies was self-defeating. Therefore, a monetary union could not be regarded as a cause of unemployment.

In order to maintain a stable Europa, the price level of a representative basket of commodities should be kept stable in terms of the Europa. The exchange rates between national currencies and the Europa would be adjusted according to a crawling peg formula based on a weighted average of inflation rates of consumer prices expressed in national currencies. Initially, the central banks would issue Europas only against national currencies. Their quantity would be determined solely by the desires of those who wanted to hold them. Only at a later stage would Europas be issued through the rediscounting of bills, open market operations, and so on. When the Europa finally had replaced national currencies, its supply should be controlled according to a monetary rule that would guarantee its purchasing power stability. To this end, the institutions that eventually would replace the national authorities should have "the same independence from political power and the same responsibilities to the rule of law we have accorded the judicial system." As we shall see in Chapter 17, some of the ideas of the manifesto resurfaced in the British proposal for a "hard ECU" of June 1990.

The Optica Reports

In January 1976, a small group of independent experts set up by the EC Commission put forward ideas that were similar to those in the All Saints' Day memorandum.[9] Although they agreed that the All Saints' Day proposals were perfectly sound from a purely economic point of view, economic *and* political considerations required a less radical solution. Therefore, instead of a parallel currency with a constant purchasing power, the group suggested a currency with the same standard as the currency of the country with the lowest inflation rate. They rejected the use of the most stable national currency (presumably the Deutsche mark) because of psychological difficulties, and a basket-based currency would be unattractive in low inflation countries. As in the All Saints' Day proposal, the new European parallel currency initially would be issued against national currencies on a voluntary basis. Later, a European central bank, which would need to have "a degree of independence at least similar to that of the Bundesbank," would issue the parallel currency by means of traditional monetary instruments.

The same group issued a follow-up report in early 1977.[10]

The Times Group Proposal

Another high-powered group of academics, under the chairmanship of the Earl of Cromer, a former governor of the Bank of England, pulled together several ideas discussed earlier.[11] Target zones for exchange rates would be defined in terms of the EUA and could be modified subject to changes in underlying economic conditions. A country would not be obliged to maintain its exchange rate in its target zone, but it should refrain from policies that would move its exchange rate outside the zone. A parallel currency (also called "Europa") would be based on the EUA because it would best approximate "some average of the performance of the individual European currencies."

CONCLUDING REMARKS

Why were the various initiatives with respect to a unified exchange rate system and a parallel currency unsuccessful? The exchange rate proposals were, after all, not particularly ambitious when compared with the recommendations of the Werner Report and the obligations under the snake arrangement. The main idea common to all proposals was to build on the existing institutions, in particular, the snake in its reduced form, and to gradually bring the floating currencies closer to the snake. This was to be achieved by flexible arrangements, such as "reference rates" or "target zones," and by intensified policy consultation and coordination. Existing credit mechanisms and the scope of the EMCF would be enlarged to provide encouragement and support to countries with weaker currencies.

The countries outside the snake might have shied away from entering commitments, no matter how flexible, that they feared they could not meet and that would impose certain constraints on their policies. On the other hand, the strong-currency snake countries were worried that the obligations under the snake — considered "a stimulus to economic and monetary discipline" (Oort, 1979, p. 215) — would be weakened and that easier access to credit would undermine such discipline and create for them an undue financial burden. Yet, several ideas entered the official discussions and some became part of the EMS.

The proposals for a European parallel currency did not find much of an echo, not only because of their boldness but also because they appeared unrealistic. Apart from the novelty of the ideas, which were in conflict with official thinking that favored an institutional approach, the proposals did not sufficiently address a number of important questions, such as the time path toward a *single* currency, institutional issues of a European central bank and its relation to the political authorities, the interdependence between monetary and budgetary policies, and any resistance on a national level to a gradual phasing out of national currencies.

On a more general plane, the answer to our question may well be what the Tindemans Report (Tindemans, 1976, pp. 11, 20) characterized as a loss of the EC's "air of adventure," a "resurgence of purely national preoccupations," and "the absence of adequate mutual trust." By 1977, the sense of crisis was widespread, and it became evident that, in the prevailing atmosphere of caution and doubt, only a major political initiative could succeed in overcoming the stagnation in the integration process.

NOTES

Literature of general interest for this chapter: Kruse (1980); Ludlow (1982).

1.   For an analysis of the main causes for the failure to advance in monetary integration, see Peter Ludlow (1982, pp. 2–12).

2.   It should be noted that a strict application of the settlement rules of the snake agreement would have led over time toward a harmonization of reserves in the EC.

3.   Daniel Gros and Niels Thygesen (1992, p. 21) observed: "The main reason why the fund developed only a shadowy existence was its formal subordination to the ECOFIN Council. . . . Since this was unacceptable to several [central bank] governors, substantive work remained firmly with 'their committee.'"

4.   One European Monetary Unit of Account had a value of 0.88867088 grams of fine gold, equivalent to the gold content of the pre-Smithsonian dollar and the Special Drawing Right.

5.   For a discussion of the Commission proposals and the Council actions, see Kruse (1980, pp. 135–41, 158–65); for the texts adopted by the Council, see Monetary Committee (1974, pp. 104–10).

6.   For a description of various units of accounts, see *Official Journal of the European Communities*, No. C 158, July 12, 1975. Following the breakdown of the Bretton Woods system and the introduction of floating exchange rates, the use of gold-based units of account led increasingly to distortions. Technically, there is an important difference between a unit of account with a fixed base, such as gold, and a basket-based unit of account. In the first case, the value of a currency expressed in terms of the unit of account changes only with a move of its own exchange rate; in the second case, the move of the exchange rate of one currency in the basket results also in changes of the values in terms of the unit of account of all other basket currencies.

7.   This summary is based on C. J. Oort (1979, pp. 207–18), who was the main author of the plan. The plan was in part inspired by the International Monetary Fund's "Guidelines for the Management of Floating Exchange Rates" of June 1974 (International Monetary Fund, Annual Report 1974, pp. 112–16).

8.   Gros and Thygesen (1992, p. 40) mention that it was gradually clarified that the system of target zones would apply only to floaters.

9.   Optica Report '75. The title is in reference to the theory of optimum currency areas as developed in the 1960s by Robert A. Mundell, Ronald A. McKinnon, and Peter Kenen (see Chapter 21).

10.   Optica Report 1976. Three of the four members of the two Optica groups (Giorgio Basevi, Pascal Salin, and Niels Thygesen) were also members of the All Saints' Day group.

11.   Statement simultaneously published on July 26, 1976, in *The Times*, *Le Monde*, *La Stampa*, and *Die Welt*. Members included Alexandre Lamfalussy, C. J. Oort, Robert Triffin, and Jacques van Ypersele.

13

The Creation of the European Monetary System

On October 27, 1977, Roy Jenkins, then president of the European Community (EC) Commission, delivered the first Jean Monnet lecture at the European University Institute in Florence. The subject was "Europe's Present Challenge and Future Opportunity."[1] His intention was "to re-launch a major public debate on what monetary union has to offer." He called the oil crisis the "sharp confirmation of the end of the old international monetary order" and continued: "The relocation of monetary policy to the European level would be as big a political step for the present generation of European leaders as for the last generation in setting up the present Community. But we must face the fundamental question. Do we intend to create a European union or do we not?"

There was no immediate positive response from EC countries, but it is known that some leading politicians discussed matters informally with Jenkins, and at its meeting on December 5 and 6, 1977, the European Council "reaffirmed its attachment to the objective to EMU [economic and monetary union]" (Monetary Committee, 1986, p. 38).

The Commission's communication to the Council of November 1977 was somewhat more fainthearted than Jenkins' speech and did not contain any specific proposals (*Bulletin*, No. 10, 1977, pp. 15–22). Nevertheless, after the Belgian president of the ECOFIN Council had identified in July 1977 the reduction of economic divergences between EC countries as the EC's fundamental aim, the Commission went one step further by declaring that the prime objective for a proposed five-year action program should be "the establishment of lasting convergence" and that member countries should "in particular give first priority to countering inflation."

THE BACKGROUND

The global economic situation in the 1970s was characterized by high inflation and widespread economic stagnation. In the EC, the seriousness of the situation was exacerbated by large divergences from country to country. In the four years from 1974 to 1977, inflation in the nine member countries ranged from 15 percent to nearly 100 percent, while growth varied from less than 1 percent to more than 10 percent.

The exchange rates of the EC currencies fluctuated widely and unevenly against the U.S. dollar, inserting a worrisome element of uncertainty into international trade relations. There was great concern about the ability of the U.S. government to cope with the consequences of the oil crisis and its attitude of "benign neglect" (or, as some called it, "malign neglect") with regard to the balance of payments and the position of the dollar.

However, concern over U.S. policies, in particular after President Jimmy Carter took office in January 1977, was not limited to economic and exchange rate policies. It extended into other fields, such as East-West relations and nuclear energy. The leaders of France and Germany, President Valéry Giscard d'Estaing and Chancellor Helmut Schmidt, took exception to important aspects of the new U.S. administration's policies. Their uneasiness over what was seen as the fallibility of the Carter administration, thus, added to the concern over the impact on the EC of global economic difficulties and the lack of progress in European integration.[2]

Chancellor Schmidt was unhappy particularly about U.S. pressure on Germany to reflate its economy in order to help pull the world economy out of recession ("locomotive theory"). This, in his view, greatly overestimated the economic strength of Germany. Furthermore, he was worried about the disproportionally large appreciation of the Deutsche mark against the dollar — a result of its status as a "refuge currency" — following the sharp deterioration of the U.S. balance of payments in 1976 and 1977 and the impact this had on the exchange rate structure within Europe and the cohesion of the snake. (There were four exchange rate realignments in the snake from October 1976 to February 1978.)

Beneath all this, there was the deep concern of many EC leaders over the stagnating integration process and the risk that the achievements of the past could unravel.

THE NEGOTIATIONS

The strengthening of their domestic political positions gave the leaders of Germany and France the final impulse needed for a major initiative on

European integration: to design a common exchange rate system for the EC as a whole. In this, they were helped by their good personal relations, which went back to their having been the finance ministers of their countries at the same time. The chance of success of their initiative had increased since the three large member countries outside the snake that recently had suffered balance of payments and exchange rate problems — France, Italy, and the United Kingdom (UK) — had embarked by 1977 on stabilization programs in which the struggle against inflation took priority. In France, it was the stabilization program of Prime Minister Raymond Barre that gave President Giscard d'Estaing the confidence to move ahead with a new effort to stabilize exchange rates in the formal framework of a common system.

Although the Schmidt–Giscard d'Estaing initiative was more limited in ambition than the proposals of the Werner Report, their motivation was primarily political. Among the main objectives were to restore momentum to the integration process and to resume the efforts toward economic and monetary union. They decided to work outside the established channels of the Council of Ministers and the specialized monetary affairs committees in order to avoid their initiative being bogged down from the beginning in detailed technical discussions.[3] Instead, they relied on trusted advisors, Bernard Clappier, the governor of the Banque de France, an old hand in European monetary affairs, who had been a member of the Werner Committee, and Horst Schulmann from the chancellor's office.[4]

Following informal high-level meetings, Giscard d'Estaing and Schmidt presented their ideas to their fellow summiteers at the meeting of the European Council in Copenhagen on April 7 and 8, 1978.[5] Although British Prime Minister James Callaghan expressed serious misgivings, he agreed to the formation of a small discussion group, consisting of Clappier, Schulmann, and Ken Couzens, second permanent secretary at the British treasury. In parallel, although initially not fully in the picture, the EC finance ministers and the Monetary Committee returned to the issue of monetary unification and eventually arrived at a set of principles for a common exchange rate system, which provided a good basis for an agreement (Ludlow, 1982, pp. 103–4). In the meantime, the group of three went to work. After a while, Couzens dropped out (p. 105), and it was up to Clappier and Schulmann to prepare a paper.

At the next meeting of the European Council in Bremen on July 6 and 7, a proposal for a "scheme for the creation of a closer monetary cooperation (European Monetary System) leading to a zone of monetary stability in Europe" was presented. It outlined the main features of the envisaged system and became known as the "Bremen Annex."[6] It was, for all purposes, a French-German venture that, on the one hand, had the features of a precise, albeit not detailed, blueprint for an agreement and, on the other hand, hid behind its finely chiseled language a number of ambiguities. It remained, for instance, unclear what the phrase "The European Currency Unit (ECU) will be at the centre of the system" really implied. The Bremen Annex stated that the European Monetary System (EMS) would be "at least as strict" as the snake and called for policies that should be "conducive to greater stability at home and abroad" and were to apply to "deficit and surplus countries" alike. Yet, if surplus countries (presumably those who aimed at "stability at home") directed their policies at the avoidance of exchange rate tensions ("stability abroad"), there would be a potential conflict with their domestic policy objectives, which could put into question the "strictness" of the new system. Significant in this context was that the choice of intervention system was left open. An intervention system based on the future ECU (like the European Unit of Account, a basket of currencies), as favored by France, would oblige the central bank of any country, whether in surplus or deficit, to intervene when its market exchange rate expressed in ECU deviated from its ECU-based central rate, that is, from the (weighted) average of all currencies included in the ECU basket. If the ECU market rate for the currency of a country with a high degree of domestic monetary stability diverged from the average, an obligation to intervene unilaterally could jeopardize the stability orientation of its policy. A system based on a grid of bilateral central rates (as in the snake) would oblige the central banks of deficit as well as surplus (i.e., more and less inflationary) countries to assume the burden of intervention together, regardless of the market in which intervention took place, leaving the impact on the "stability at home" in the balance. This issue was at the center of the question of whether the new system was meant to be "symmetric" or "asymmetric." We shall return to this question at a later stage.

The European Council discussed the document at its Bremen meeting at some length. Although all other participants were sympathetic to the idea of an EMS, Prime Minister Callaghan, mindful of the British experience with the snake, was very reluctant to commit himself in any way. Nevertheless, it was agreed to take the document as a starting point for more detailed discussions and to aim for reaching a decision at the next meeting of the European Council in early December. In order to forestall any misinterpretations by the public, it was explicitly stated that the snake in its present form would remain fully intact. At the insistence of some countries, it further was agreed to conduct "concurrent studies on the action needed to be taken to strengthen the economies of the less prosperous member countries in the context of such a scheme" (conclusions of the presidency, Commission, 1979, p. 93).

The following months were full of hectic activity on the diplomatic front as well as on the expert level.[7] Of special interest were discussions within Germany, in which the concerns of the Bundesbank over the risk of losing control over its money supply played a prominent role.[8] More generally, serious doubts existed about the viability of the new system, especially in view of the short and troubled history of the snake. The conservative line of Germany was broadly supported by the Netherlands and Denmark; in Belgium and Luxembourg, any reasonable initiative that would benefit European integration was welcomed.

In France, on the other hand, but also in the UK and Italy, criticism concentrated on the concern that Germany would continue with its policies, which were seen as overly restrictive, giving a snakelike system, based on a grid of parities, a possible deflationary bias. In Italy, the debate whether or not to join the system concentrated on the weakness of domestic economic policies, particularly in the fiscal and wage fields, and whether, on this basis, Italy could survive within the system. However, in contrast to the British, the Italians "began with the presumption that participation in any new Community initiative was the proper objective" (Ludlow, 1982, p. 148). In the UK, there was widespread hostility toward joining the system, although some leading politicians seemed to lean in this direction. The formula used was that the UK still might join "if the terms were right." Pro-EMS observers, however, felt that "by remaining aloof, the British government would ensure the consolidation of the Franco-German axis . . . and *de facto* relegation [of the UK] to the second division of a two-tier or two-speed Europe" (Ludlow, 1982, p. 224). Ireland, whose currency was linked to the pound sterling and whose economy was heavily dependent on the British, would have to face negative economic consequences if the UK would not join the system. Yet, the Irish were determined to play the European card as a way of strengthening their ties to continental Europe and to establish more clearly their European identity. As Peter Ludlow (1982, p. 153) noted, "a break with sterling had long been on the agenda of Irish politics."

On a technical level, a number of issues remained to be settled. Most importantly, the questions of whether and how the ECU could form the basis for the intervention system were still open. After further debate, which made the technical problems of an ECU-based system more apparent and the general opposition of Germany, in particular of the Bundesbank, to an ECU-based system more articulate, agreement on the adoption of a grid of bilateral parities as the basis for intervention obligations was reached at a meeting between Schmidt and Giscard d'Estaing in Aachen on September 14 and 15. Part of the Aachen agreement was the so-called Belgian compromise, which specified that the parity grid be supplemented by a "divergence indicator," based on the ECU. It was to signal a need for action in case a currency's position in the system diverged significantly from the average presented by the ECU (for a discussion of the divergence indicator, see Chapter 14). Ludlow wrote (1982, p. 184) that the Aachen agreement "provided an indication of the determination of both leaders that, whatever the technical problems, the timetable agreed at Bremen should . . . be adhered to."

THE AGREEMENT

Nearly all of the remaining obstacles were removed in a flurry of high level meetings. The most important issues were the scope of action required if the divergence indicator signaled a currency's position as being significantly out of line, the width of fluctuation margins, and the extent to which the existing credit facilities — the Short-Term Monetary Support and the Medium-Term Financial Assistance — would be enlarged.

When the European Council gathered on December 4, 1978, in Brussels, it appeared that final agreement on the creation of the EMS was at hand. However, not totally unexpected, difficulties arose over two issues: the elimination of the monetary compensatory amounts (MCAs) in the Common Agricultural Policy and the transfer of resources to the less prosperous countries. Regarding the MCAs, it was agreed that the creation of permanent MCAs was, henceforth, to be avoided and that existing MCAs would be progressively reduced. On the issue of a transfer of resources, no acceptable compromise could be found. The Brussels summit ended on December 5 with the adoption of the resolution on the establishment of the EMS, but with only six member states signing up.[9] The UK considered the new system as insufficiently different from the snake; it had made it clear some time ago that it would not join. In view of the unsatisfactory response to their request for financial assistance, Italy and Ireland asked for more time to reflect. Efforts to bring the two countries into the system continued. A special aid package for Ireland was put together by Germany, Denmark, the Benelux countries, and France (which insisted, however, that its share should be spent exclusively on purchases in France). On this basis, Ireland announced on December 15 that it would join the EMS. Italy already had decided on December 12 to join, without having asked for or received any concessions. Why then the delay? As Ludlow suggested (1982, pp. 271–73), the reasons most probably rested with the complicated domestic political situation in Italy.

All appeared set for the inauguration of the EMS on January 1, 1979. The big surprise came when French Finance Minister R. Monory told his colleagues, at a meeting on December 18 and 19, that France put a reserve on the activation of the EMS agreements until the component of the summit resolution of December 5 regarding the avoidance and reduction of MCAs was implemented. At a meeting on March 5 and 6, 1979, the EC agricultural ministers' countries reached a compromise, and the French reserve was lifted. The EMS went into operation on March 13, 1979. At the same time, the snake ceased to exist.

THE REACTION OF THE OUTSIDE WORLD

The Council resolution contained a section that stated that "European countries with particularly close economic and financial ties with the European Communities may participate in the exchange rate and intervention mechanism." It was directed at the countries formerly associated with the snake, Norway and Sweden, as well as Austria and Switzerland. Austria, in particular, had shadowed the snake by unilaterally maintaining a close link to the Deutsche mark. In any event, no formal relations with any of the four countries were established, but procedures for central bank cooperation were set up. Austria joined the EMS after becoming a member of the EC in January 1995.

The same section of the resolution included the somewhat apodictic declaration that "the EMS *is and will* remain fully compatible with the relevant articles of the IMF [International Monetary Fund] Agreement" (emphasis added). At IMF headquarters in Washington, one was not prepared to accept this statement without further discussion. When in mid-December 1978 Commission President Jenkins was in Washington, he was invited to meet with IMF Managing Director Jacques de Larosière and a few of his closest aides. The questions raised by the IMF team concentrated on three issues, all closely related to the main responsibilities of the IMF: first, on the impact that the operation of the EMS exchange rate mechanism and decisions on central rates might have on IMF surveillance of exchange rate policies of its members; second, on the enlarged scope of financial assistance within the EC and the risk of inconsistent standards of conditionality; third, on the possibility of creating ECUs against national currencies or *ex nihilo*, that is, not in exchange for national reserves, and the consequences for international liquidity.[10] These questions, which were entirely legitimate, because the operations of the EMS fell clearly within the global mandate of the IMF, were also discussed by the IMF's Executive Board.[11] Developments in European monetary integration became a regular subject of Board discussions in the Fund.

After initial doubts, the U.S. attitude on the new European initiative was supportive. This was particularly the case for the State Department; the Treasury had some concerns that the EMS could give gold a new lease on life as an important element of the international monetary system and that the role of the IMF would be affected. In the end, Anthony Solomon, under secretary of the Treasury, summarized the U.S. position as follows: "We have always supported . . . the concept of fuller European economic integration, and I think it's a decision for the Europeans themselves. It's perfectly compatible with the broad international monetary system as we know it today, . . . and therefore we would have no problem with it" (quoted in Ludlow, 1982, p. 120).

NOTES

Literature of general interest for the chapter: Ludlow (1982).

1. Published by the European University Institute and reprinted in *Bulletin*, No. 10, 1977, pp. 6–14.

2. Regarding the extent of Chancellor Schmidt's irritations about the policies of President Carter, see Schmidt's memoirs (1990, pp. 222–80).

3. On this point, see Schmidt (1992, pp. 251–54).

4. Horst Schulmann (1992) noted later that the creation of the EMS "was a very political act and certainly not a matter of translating a textbook of monetary economics."

5. See Ludlow (1982, pp. 88–94). There was always some discussion whether the new initiative was a brainchild of Schmidt or Giscard d'Estaing. When, during the Copenhagen meeting, Giscard d'Estaing was asked about the "father" of the plan, he is said to have replied with a quotation from Napoleon: "En matière de paternité, Monsieur, il n'y a que des hypothèses" (p. 98). Schmidt (1992, p. 249) wrote that the idea originated in talks between them; "vielleicht," he added, "lag [der Gedanke] in der Luft."

6. Annex to the conclusions of the presidency (Commission, 1979, p. 93).

7. For a detailed account, see Ludlow (1982), in particular Chapters 5 and 6.

8. In many places in his book, Ludlow (1982) made reference to the skepticism of the Bundesbank and its president, Otmar Emminger, toward the EMS initiative, to the point of giving his narrative an overly "obstructionist" spin. Although the memoirs of Emminger (1986, pp. 356–71) largely corroborate Ludlow's story, Emminger also emphasized the positive aspects of the relations between the Bundesbank and him and Chancellor Schmidt. The Bundesbank was insistent, however, on one important point: that excessive intervention obligations could endanger the Bundesbank's mandate to secure price stability. In his memoirs (1986, p. 361), Emminger mentioned a letter, addressed by him to the German government in November 1978 (so-called Emminger letter), in which he referred to assurances from the chancellor and the finance minister "that in such a case the Federal Government will safeguard the Bundesbank from such a dilemma either by an exchange rate correction in the EMS or, if necessary, also by a temporary release from its intervention obligation" (my translation). Barry Eichengreen and Charles Wyplosz (1993, p. 109) inexplicably omit the word "temporary" in their translation. In a March 1979 article, Emminger stated (pp. 3–4; my translation): "In the most extreme emergency, [the Bundesbank] can also temporarily suspend interventions in the foreign exchange market until a decision on the exchange rate has been made."

9. For the text of the resolution, see Commission (1979, pp. 94–97) and Monetary Committee (1986, pp. 42–46).

10. The latter question was related to the somewhat opaque reference to an *initial* supply of ECUs in paragraph 2 of the Bremen Annex and in paragraph A.3.8 of the December 1978 resolution (emphasis added). The Jenkins visit at the IMF had a minor sequel: When, during one of my regular visits to EC countries to discuss European monetary developments, I called on the EC Commission in

Brussels, I was "summoned" to the office of one of President Jenkins' advisors. To my surprise, he complained in fairly strong terms about the "questioning" to which Jenkins had been subjected during his visit at the IMF.

11.   In an Occasional Paper, published in May 1983, a team of IMF economists addressed these issues (Ungerer, Evans, and Nyberg, 1983, pp. 19–21). See also Baquiast (1979, pp. 53–56) and McMahon (1979, pp. 90–92).

14

The Objectives and Main Features of the European Monetary System

THE OBJECTIVES

The objectives of the European Monetary System (EMS) were clearly stated in the conclusions of the presidency of the European Council meeting on December 4 and 5, 1978, in Brussels (Commission, 1979, p. 94): "The purpose of the European Monetary System is to establish a greater measure of monetary stability in the Community. It should be seen as a fundamental component of a more comprehensive strategy aimed at lasting growth with stability, a progressive return to full employment, the harmonization of living standards and the lessening of regional disparities in the Community. The European Monetary System will facilitate the convergence of economic development and give fresh impetus to the process of European Union."

The European Council also stressed "that, within the context of a broadly based strategy aimed at improving the prospects of economic development and based on symmetrical rights and obligations of all participants, the most important concern should be to enhance the convergence of economic policies towards greater stability. We request the Council (Economics and Finance Ministers) to strengthen its procedures for cooperation in order to improve that convergence" (Resolution of December 5, 1978, paragraph B.1, Commission, 1979, p. 97).

THE FEATURES

The EMS as launched on March 13, 1979, was based on a number of documents. The main document was the European Council resolution of December 5, 1978. Because the European Council was formally not an organ of the European Community (EC), the resolution was not a legal document but, by its very nature, represented a strong political commitment. The features and operational rules of the EMS were set out in an Agreement Between the Central Banks of the Member States of the European Economic Community Laying Down the Operating Procedures for the European Monetary System. Additional aspects of the EMS were dealt with in several decisions of the European Monetary Cooperation Fund (EMCF) and regulations of the Council of Ministers concerning the creation of the ECU (European Currency Unit), the Short-Term Monetary Support (STMS), and the Medium-Term Financial Assistance (Commission, 1979, pp. 98–108; Committee of Governors of the Central Banks, 1979, 1985).[1]

In essence, the EMS consists of fixed but adjustable exchange rates that are kept within agreed fluctuation margins by "obligatory intervention." Such intervention is financed by mutual very short-term credit facilities of participating central banks, administered by the EMCF. The settlement of intervention debts can take place in a variety of ways. The EMS took over several of the operational features of the snake.[2]

The ECU and Its Functions

The ECU was to play an important role in the EMS, even though the phrase in the resolution that the ECU would be "at the centre of the EMS" does not reflect its actual role but, rather, the idea, referred to earlier, to have it serve as the basis for the intervention mechanism.[3] The ECU as a unit of account is used as the denominator for the exchange rate mechanism, for operations in both the intervention and credit mechanisms, and for transactions of the EMCF and as the basis for the divergence indicator. As a reserve asset, it is a means of settlement among the monetary authorities of EC countries.

At the outset, the value and composition of the ECU was equal to that of the European Unit of Account, which was introduced in April 1975. Accordingly, the ECU was made up of a basket of fixed amounts of the nine EC currencies.[4] Market exchange rates determine the (external) value of the ECU in terms of individual currencies. No automatic revision of the composition of the basket was envisaged. However, in contrast to the European Unit of Account, the basket composition was to be reexamined and, if necessary, revised within six months of entry into force of the EMS (no revision took place) and thereafter every five years or on request if the relative weight of any currency had changed by 25 percent or more (revisions took place in 1984 and 1989). Revisions were to be made in line with underlying economic criteria, had to be mutually accepted, and were not to modify the external value of the ECU at the time of the shift. The Maastricht Treaty stipulated that the basket composition will not be changed any more (Art. 109g).

The Exchange Rate and Intervention Mechanism

For each currency participating in the exchange rate and intervention mechanism (ERM), a central rate in terms of the ECU was fixed by mutual consent.[5] These central rates formed the basis for a grid of bilateral central rates, around which fluctuation margins of 2.25 percent in both directions are normally to be established. Currencies that had been floating could opt temporarily for wider margins of up to ±6 percent. (Italy made use of this provision.) Changes in central rates are subject to "mutual agreement" by a common procedure involving the countries participating in the ERM and the Commission.

In principle, exchange market interventions were to be made by buying or selling partner currencies and were obligatory at the agreed intervention limits (defined in terms of partner currencies). As a consequence, interventions at these limits were to be unlimited as to amount. Intervention within the margins ("intramarginal intervention") was not expressly provided for but was not excluded. If it was carried out in participating currencies, it was subject to permission by the issuing central bank. Moreover, intervention policies of participating central banks were the subject of close concertation on a daily basis and would be discussed at the monthly meetings of the Committee of Central Bank Governors in Basle. Intramarginal intervention also could take place in third currencies (for all practical purposes, in U.S. dollars).

The Divergence Indicator

In addition to the grid of central rates, a "divergence indicator" was established that links the market exchange rates of the currencies in the ERM to the ECU. The indicator was intended to serve as an early warning device to signal whether the market exchange rate of a currency diverged in its movements from the weighted average of the others. It was to flash when a "threshold of divergence" was crossed.[6] (It was promptly dubbed the "rattlesnake.")

When a currency crossed its divergence threshold, this was to result in a "presumption" that the authorities concerned will correct this situation by adequate measures. The European Council resolution lists diversified intervention (which can be assumed to include intervention in more than one currency at the opposite end of the divergent currency and in third currencies), measures of domestic monetary policy (in particular, interest rate measures that would have an immediate impact on exchange rates), changes in central rates, and other measures of economic policy. A country was not obligated to take immediate action, but failure to do so would trigger consultations.

The Very Short-Term Financing Facility and Settlement

Under a "very short-term financing facility" (VSTF), mutual credit lines were opened by participating central banks in unlimited amounts for the financing of obligatory intervention at the intervention limits. The claims and obligations resulting from intervention were to be converted into ECUs and entered into the books of the EMCF. The interest on outstanding claims was set as the average of the official discount rates of all EC central banks weighted by their shares in the ECU basket.

Settlement of intervention debts originally was to take place 45 days after the end of the month in which intervention occurred. Obligations not exceeding ceilings equal to the quotas in the STMS could be automatically extended by three months. Settlement could be deferred by another three months subject to agreement of the creditors. At the request of the debtor central bank, advance settlement was permitted. For settlement, a debtor central bank was to use first any holdings in the creditor's currency. Of the remaining debt, 50 percent was to be settled in ECUs; a further use of ECUs required the consent of the creditor. Otherwise, the remaining debt was to be settled according to the composition of the reserves of the debtor in Special Drawing Rights–denominated assets and third currencies. Gold also could be used in settlement if the parties agreed on the valuation. If a debtor central bank ran out of ECUs, it could acquire further ECUs in the first instance from central banks whose holdings exceeded 20 percent of their gold and dollar reserves or possibly from the EMCF. (For interest payments in connection with the use of ECUs, see next section.)

The Creation of ECUs

The central banks participating in the ERM were obliged to deposit 20 percent of their gold holdings and dollar reserves with the EMCF against the issue of ECUs. These transactions were to take the form of revolving three-month swaps, although each central bank continued to manage the gold and dollar reserves it deposited with the EMCF. Gold deposits were to be valued at the average market price of the previous six months or at the average market price of the penultimate working day, whichever was lower, to avoid valuation above the prevailing market price. The deposits with the EMCF were to be adjusted according to changes in total holdings of gold and dollars and changes in their valuation.

Interest was to be paid by central banks whose holdings of ECUs were below the amounts received from the EMCF against their deposits of reserves, that is, on the amount of ECUs that had been used. Interest was to be earned on ECUs in excess of the amounts received from the EMCF, that is, that had been received from partner central banks in settlement. The interest rate is the same as for the VSTF.

Countries not participating in the ERM have the option of also depositing 20 percent of their reserves against ECUs with the EMCF.

Credit Facilities

Already in 1970 and 1971, the EC had established credit facilities, the STMS, and the Medium-Term Financial Assistance to aid member countries in balance of payments difficulties (see Chapter 8). Both facilities were extended when Denmark, Ireland, and the United Kingdom (UK) joined the EC in 1973 and were substantially enlarged in later years. In connection with the creation of the EMS, both facilities again were substantially enlarged. Both facilities remained available to all EC countries whether they participated in the ERM or not, but the enlarged creditor and debtor quotas of the UK in the STMS were to be used only after the UK had become a participant in the ERM.

Measures to Strengthen the Economies of the Less Prosperous Member States

In Chapter 13, reference was made to the "concurrent studies" on the transfer of resources to the less prosperous EC countries. Section B of the resolution contained the measures agreed to after difficult negotiations. They were intended to strengthen the economic potential of the less prosperous countries with the aim of facilitating the convergence of economic policies and performance. They were limited to countries participating in the ERM (i.e., Ireland and Italy) and concentrated on the financing of selected infrastructure projects by the European Investment Bank and under a more recent facility for the financing of investments, the so-called New Community Instrument (or Ortoli Facility) of 1978 and on interest subsidies for such loans.

INTENDED FUTURE DEVELOPMENTS

The resolution of December 5 dealt primarily with what was called the "initial phase" of the EMS. Not later than two years after its start, the EMS as outlined was to be "consolidated" into a final system. This was to entail the creation of a European Monetary Fund to replace the EMCF and the consolidation of the existing credit facilities into a single fund. The ECU was to be fully utilized as a reserve asset and a means of settlement. The phrase that the issue of ECUs against 20 percent of countries' international reserves would constitute an "initial supply" of ECUs left three possibilities of interpretation. First, that, in the future, more than 20 percent of national reserves could be deposited against ECUs; second, that ECUs could be issued against national currencies (as indicated in the Bremen Annex); and third, that ECUs could be created *ex nihilo*, that is, without any deposits of international reserves or counterparts in national currencies.

THE IMPLEMENTATION OF THE AGREEMENT

Flexibility in Operations

The EMS provisions established a number of unequivocal obligations, such as the setting of central rates, the width of the fluctuation margins, and the requirement for obligatory intervention at the intervention limits. However, they also left room for flexibility, for example, the choice of the intervention currency, except for obligatory intervention at the margins; the options with regard to the settlement of intervention debts in terms of timing and the choice of assets to be used; or the possibility for different courses of action in case of a flashing of the divergence indicator. Operational questions were discussed regularly in the Committee of Central Bank Governors, ensuring that special problems of individual central banks or issues relating to the operation of the system in general were taken into account. An important tool in central bank cooperation was also the daily telephone concertation between the EC and a few other important central banks, which already had been organized at the time of the snake (see Chapter 11).

One particular example of the system's flexibility relates to intramarginal intervention. Certain central banks soon developed the practice of intervening long before their exchange rate had reached its obligatory intervention point. For this, they used partner currencies (in particular, the Deutsche mark), acquired in the markets at times of strength, or dollars, as appropriate. This technique helped to avoid the buildup of market pressures as the exchange rate would move closer to the obligatory intervention point. In such cases, no recourse had to be taken to the VSTF, avoiding the need for settlement under the agreed procedures. For transactions involving partner currencies, the consent of the respective central banks had to be sought and usually was granted (Ungerer, Evans, and Nyberg, 1983, pp. 14–15).

The Working of the Divergence Indicator

As discussed in Chapter 13, the divergence indicator was established as a supplementary system to the grid of bilateral parities to provide more "symmetry" in the distribution of burden resulting from intervention. At the time of its invention, it attracted considerable interest as a tool to aid the international adjustment process (Triffin, 1979, p. 67).

The idea to base the intervention system on the ECU had been abandoned during the EMS negotiations. There were two important concerns. Although an ECU-based system conceivably might lead to more convergence, this convergence would have been based on an *average* of economic performance, which very well could have been in conflict with the intention of realizing "a greater measure of stability" (European Council, December 1978, conclusions of the presidency [Commission, 1979, p. 94]). Another problem was the determination of the currency in which the diverging country would have to intervene. The emergence of "involuntary" debtors or creditors as a consequence would have raised technical as well as policy problems.

Similar problems arose in connection with the divergence indicator. Taking the underlying idea of "symmetry" to its logical conclusion would mean that monetary policy measures would not necessarily be directed at (or result in) monetary stability. Rather, they would lead to some average of monetary and price developments. Furthermore, the implicit assumption of the divergence indicator proposal was that, normally, one of the larger currencies would be close to one end of its maximum divergence spread (to be more precise, it was expected that the Deutsche mark would breach its upper divergence threshold) while the other currencies would be clustered somewhere in the middle. The emerging reality was different. Ironically, the one currency that, early on (in May 1979), diverged most from the other currencies, but with a negative sign, was the Belgian franc. Also, more often than not, the bilateral intervention limits were reached before the indicator would flash, rendering the indicator ineffective. It was, therefore, not surprising that the divergence indicator never played the role for which its proponents had hoped and that, after some time, it was virtually abandoned as a tool of policy and analysis.[7]

The ECU

The other important innovation incorporated in the EMS, the ECU, fared not much better. As already mentioned, it did not function as "the centre of the EMS" except in a purely formal sense. Although it served a number of accounting purposes within the EMS as well as in the EC at large, its role as a means of settlement was limited by the tendency of central banks to opt, in part, for other forms of settlement and to engage in intramarginal intervention. Moreover, its reserve role was confined to the EC and within the EMS by the 50-percent limit on its use for settlement purposes, until the limit was eliminated in 1987. By contrast, the ECU developed a life of its own in the financial markets (see Chapter 15).

The attitude of the EC countries toward the ECU has been, from the beginning, somewhat ambiguous, as exemplified by the fact that ECUs were issued on the basis of revolving three-month swaps. A further element that stood in the way was that the total volume of ECUs created was essentially a result of developments that largely were outside the control of the EC central banks, such as the fluctuations in the free market price of gold and the exchange rate for the dollar.

At the beginning of the EMS, ECU 23 billion were created. In July 1979, the UK decided to voluntarily deposit 20 percent of its gold and dollar reserves, raising the amount of ECUs issued by the EMCF to 27 billion.[8]

COMPARISONS WITH THE BRETTON WOODS SYSTEM AND THE SNAKE

It often has been said that the EMS was not much more than an enlarged snake and a regional Bretton Woods system (BWS). Both views, although understandable, are not correct. What the three systems have in common is that they are based on fixed but adjustable exchange rates where market exchange rates are allowed to fluctuate around their parities or central rates only within certain margins.

The BWS from the start has been operated as an asymmetric system. The obligations of the key currency country differed in a number of respects from those of the other countries. The fluctuation margins between two currencies other than the dollar were twice as large as those between the dollar and any other currency. Intervention took place almost exclusively in dollars. There were no provisions for the automatic financing of intervention or for the time-delayed settlement of intervention debts. In the BWS, in the case of a deficit country, intervention and settlement took place simultaneously, except for the United States, for which "intervention debts" (i.e., the accumulation of dollar holdings by other countries) were settled at the discretion of the creditor country as and when it decided to convert dollar holdings into gold, thus, greatly reducing the pressure for adjustment on the United States.

In contrast, the EMS was, by design, a symmetric multicurrency system, in which the same rules and obligations applied to all participants. The alleged asymmetry of the EMS did not derive from those rules and obligations but from their consequences, depending on whether a country had a strong or a weak currency. However, theoretically at least, any country had the potential of switching positions and being a strong or weak currency country. The later evolution of the EMS and the emergence of the Deutsche mark as the "anchor currency" of the system was not a matter of design but a result of policy preferences and operational developments on the part of its member countries, in particular, the deficit countries. That this evolution over time gave rise to economic as well as political questions was another matter (see Chapter 16).

Consistent with the general objectives of the EC, the EMS with its provisions for credit and settlement was a cooperative system. Debtor countries were allowed some time to settle intervention debts and could obtain agreement with creditor countries on a further easing of settlement obligations. Also, the existence of common decision-making procedures for exchange rate changes underlined this cooperative element. In the BWS, exchange rate decisions were made solely by the country concerned and required only the "concurrence" of the International Monetary Fund. (To my knowledge, in all cases but one, such a concurrence has been granted; the exception was France in 1948 [Horsefield, 1969, Vol. I, pp. 200–204].) Although the BWS was, for all purposes, a system with strictly economic objectives, namely, to provide for stable exchange rates and to aid in observing common rules for payments, the objectives of the EMS went further. Economic convergence and exchange rate stability were to go hand in hand, and both were to advance economic integration and serve as a basis for increased political cooperation.

The obvious difference between the snake and the EMS is that the EMS at its start comprised a larger number of EC countries, including three of the four largest countries. More importantly, the EMS arrangements entailed a commitment not just to stable exchange rates but also to the convergence of policies toward greater *internal* monetary stability. At the time of the snake, the somewhat naive belief that establishing an exchange rate constraint would, more or less automatically, lead to more convergence was still very much in evidence. When the EMS was established, and even more after the first years of operation, it was widely recognized that convergence in performance required, first and foremost, convergence and compatibility in policies. This was an important reason why, during the negotiations, some countries raised the issue of symmetry in the new system: they were concerned that what they perceived as asymmetric features in the snake would stand in the EMS in the way of achieving convergence in performance (albeit not necessarily toward a high degree of monetary stability), thus, jeopardizing the sustainability of the system. The divergence indicator was an interesting although flawed attempt to foster convergence.

Furthermore, although, in the snake, consultations did precede exchange rate adjustments, exchange rate changes in the EMS were explicitly subject to common decisions that, over time, gained increasingly in importance. I have characterized the interplay between exchange rate action and internal adjustment measures in the EMS as follows:

"There is strong emphasis and peer pressure to rely in case of imbalances not only on 'corrective' central rate changes but also on internal adjustment policies. This implies a preference for not only correcting *past* policy actions and their consequences but for providing a disciplinary constraint for *future* policy actions" (Ungerer, 1990, p. 333).

In a nutshell, the snake was a common exchange rate system, whereas the EMS also was intended as, and became over time, a monetary policy system. The big questions at the start of the EMS were how the large existing divergences between participating countries could be reduced, what role exchange rate adjustments would have to play in that process, and whether striving for convergence toward internal monetary stability could be made compatible with the objective of external stability, that is, with a high degree of stability in exchange rates.

THE EUROPEAN MONETARY SYSTEM: MONETARIST OR ECONOMIST STRATEGY?

Was the EMS more an outgrowth of a "monetarist" or of an "economist" strategy to monetary integration? By the time of the creation of the EMS, the two positions had somewhat lost their apodictic character. Neither was it anymore believed that elaborate institutional arrangements would quasi-automatically result in policy coordination, nor was it considered indisputable that a high degree of convergence would have to precede any institutional steps. Rather, it was increasingly accepted that there existed an interlinkage between institution building and convergence achievements in the sense that institutions could indeed provide policymakers with effective constraints and that effective convergence would pave the way for institutional arrangements. All this was reflected in the design of the EMS, with its emphasis on mutual obligations and commitments on the one side and clear references to stability-oriented policies on the other side that went beyond the somewhat mechanical concept of parallelism of earlier times.

The principal challenges for the operation of the system were, thus, to find out exactly how far convergence toward internal monetary stability would have to go and where the balance between institutional encouragement to and actual achievement of convergence would lie. As we shall see, for an extended period, the EMS was highly successful. Difficulties arose when the challenges became too great or when, in the early 1990s, in an atmosphere of premature euphoria with regard to the realization of monetary union under the Maastricht Treaty, the real nature of these challenges was not sufficiently recognized.

NOTES

Literature of general interest for this chapter: Banque de France (1979); Banque Nationale de Belgique (1979); Bank of England (1979); Central Bank of Ireland (1979); Commission (1979); Deutsche Bundesbank (1979); de Vries (1980); Hellmann (1979); Thygesen (1979); Ungerer (1979); U.S. Congress (1979); van Ypersele and Keoune (1985).

1.   Rainer Hellmann commented (1979, pp. 24–25): "The EMS of the initial phase does not rest on a solid legal basis. . . . A government resolution is not more than a declaration of intent which does not bind member states. . . . The agreement between the central banks . . . is in practice an arrangement which can be revoked anytime" (my translation).

2.   The following description is, in part, based on my commentary of March 1979. It applies to the original form of the EMS and generally does not take into account subsequent changes, which will be discussed in later chapters. For valuable suggestions on this and other chapters on the EMS, I am particularly grateful to Wolfgang Rieke, former head of the International Department of the Deutsche Bundesbank. For other descriptions, see the general note to this chapter.

3.   On the one hand, ECU is the abbreviation of European Currency Unit; on the other, it is a proper name, derived from the name of a French gold coin (écu) that was minted under French King Louis IX in the thirteenth century. At the time, its inventors were quite proud to cover in one term meanings in two important languages of the EC. However, the fact that it did not have any evident meaning in German and other EC languages undermined its chances of becoming the name for the envisaged single currency. After a long debate, in 1995, this currency-to-be was christened "euro" (see Chapter 23). The main advantages of this name are that it does not seem to favor or offend anyone because it is not related to any one country, currency, or language; has some meaning; and is similarly pronounced in all EC languages. Yet, at the same time, it is void of any historical significance.

4.   For the initial composition and weights of the ECU basket and later revisions, see Louw (1991, pp. 121–23).

5.   A distinction can be made between EMS members, that is, all countries that signed the EMS agreement (that included from the beginning the UK), and ERM participants, that is, those countries that participate in the ERM. I normally use the term "EMS member" but the term "ERM participant" when this distinction is of importance.

6.   For a detailed description of how the indicator works, see Ungerer (1979, p. 98); Commission (1979, pp. 85–91); also Ludlow (1982, pp. 163–64, 230–37).

7.   For some of the analytical issues of the divergence indicator, see also Rieke (1979, pp. 130–31); U.S. Congress (1979, pp. 65–78); Rey (1982); Ungerer, Evans, and Nyberg (1983, p. 15).

8.   For the amounts of ECUs issued through 1989 and their counterparts in gold and dollars, see Ungerer, Hauvonen, Lopez-Claros, and Mayer (1990, p. 63).

15

Developments in the European Monetary System, 1979–90

At the start of the European Monetary System (EMS), views on the prospects of the new system differed widely. On the one hand, there were concerns that the constraints of the system would exert a strong deflationary influence on policies and developments, because countries with relatively high rates of inflation increasingly would have to resort to restrictive policies in order to guard against reserve losses.[1] On the other hand, a number of critics, particularly in low inflation countries, were worried that the intervention obligations and credit facilities of the system would enable high inflation countries to continue with expansionary policies, thus, undermining the ability of low inflation countries to control domestic monetary developments.

A third group of commentators predicted an early demise of the system because it could not survive the contradiction between the orientation toward exchange rate stability and the continued pursuit of divergent autonomous monetary policies. It was a view widely held by academic economists who, in their analysis, were mindful of past experiences with the Bretton Woods system and the snake. They adopted an "extrapolationist" approach with built-in *ceteris paribus* assumptions regarding the policies the participating countries would follow.[2] For a while, it looked as if these critics were right, because, in its early phase, the EMS lacked a sense of direction and was characterized by instability.

In the event, however, the EMS showed remarkable resilience and up to 1990 delivered generally increasing convergence, in particular, a narrowing of inflation differentials, and a high degree of exchange rate stability, with exchange rate developments essentially in line with relative costs and prices (Figures 15.1 and 15.2).

The following is a description and analysis of developments and policies in the EMS during its first decade. It may be useful to divide this period into three phases: the first up to March 1983; the second up to January 1987; and the third up to 1989–90, when the increase in the number of countries participating in the EMS exchange rate mechanism (ERM) and the prospect of an economic and monetary union resulted in a qualitative change in attitude regarding exchange rate policy.[3]

THE FIRST PHASE, 1979–83

The start of the EMS was surprisingly smooth. Several factors played a role in this. Most importantly, perhaps, the weakness of the dollar that had stimulated the formation of the EMS was dramatically reversed in autumn 1978. The Carter administration responded with various measures to the dollar crisis during which the U.S. currency fell, from the beginning of August 1978 to the end of October, by 18 percent against the Deutsche mark and by 10 percent against the French franc. As the measures proved to be insufficient, the U.S. authorities announced on November 1 a comprehensive program that included several monetary policy measures, a large drawing on the International Monetary Fund, the sale of 2 billion Special Drawing Rights, and an increase in gold sales. The impact of these measures was striking: by the end of November, the dollar had risen sharply against major currencies.[4]

Furthermore, in a last realignment of central rates within the snake on October 15, 1978, the Deutsche mark was revalued by 2 percent against the Belgian franc and the Dutch guilder and by 4 percent against the Danish and the Norwegian currencies. Both developments tended to deflect potential future upward pressure on the mark. Also, the exchange rate at which the French franc entered the EMS was considered undervalued by many observers, thus, providing some breathing space. Finally, the German balance of payments registered substantial deficits in 1979 and particularly in 1980.

The first phase of the EMS, which ended in 1983, can best be described as a period of trial and orientation, during which the system, indeed, resembled the snake in a number of respects. Economic developments in European Community (EC) countries continued to diverge strongly as the national authorities responded differently to the challenges of the second large oil price shock of late 1979, triggered by the revolution in Iran, and to the generally inflationary world economic climate that coexisted with low growth and high unemployment. From 1974 to 1978 (i.e., the period following the first oil price shock), the consumer price index for the ERM

FIGURE 15.1

Rates of Inflation, ERM Countries, 1979–90

(Consumer Price Indexes — Quarterly Averages)

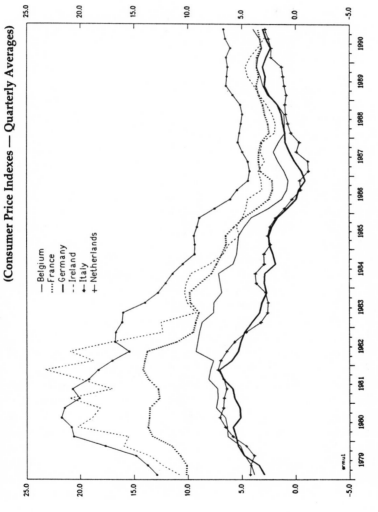

Source: International Monetary Fund, *International Financial Statistics.*

FIGURE 15.2
Movements of Exchange Rates against the ECU, ERM Countries, 1979–90

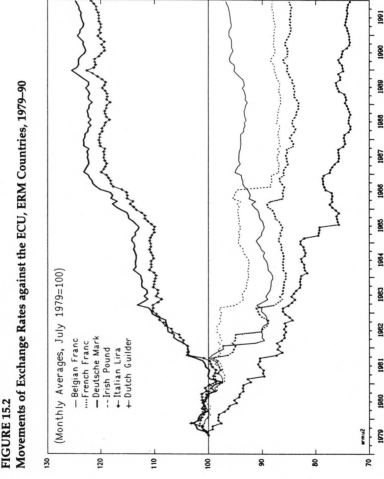

Source: International Monetary Fund, *International Financial Statistics.*

countries as a whole rose by an annual average of 8.9 percent. In Germany, the increase was only 4.7 percent, and in the Netherlands, 7.9 percent, while in France, the increase amounted to 10.7 percent, and in Italy, 16.4 percent. In the years 1979–81 (i.e., following the inception of the EMS), the average annual rise of the consumer price index in Germany was 5.2 percent, and in the Netherlands, 5.8 percent; in France, it was 12.5 percent, and in Italy, 17.9 percent. Yet, short-term interest rates in Germany nearly tripled from 1978 to 1981, while in France, they increased for the same period less than twofold, and in Italy, even less. A similar picture emerges if one compares the rates of growth of domestic credit. These differences show that inflation in France and Italy was significantly worse than in Germany but also that, in France and Italy, less of an effort was made to correct the situation. One important factor for developments in France was the shift to expansionary policies after François Mitterand was elected president in May 1981.

The consequence of that divergence was a total of seven realignments of central rates in the ERM from 1979 to March 1983, involving a downward shift of all currencies except the Netherlands guilder against the Deutsche mark, in particular of the French franc and the Italian lira (Table 15.1). In addition, the Deutsche mark suffered bouts of downward pressure in October 1980 and February 1981 that, however, did not result in exchange rate action.[5]

A turnaround in the history of the EMS was reached with the realignments in February 1982 and March 1983. They clearly established that EMS central rate changes were no longer a matter of unilateral decisions, with which partner countries would concur, but the outcome of common decision making. Not surprisingly, the discussions of finance ministers and central bank governors on realignments became more and more politically charged. Proposals that aimed at avoiding such difficulties, for example, by using many small exchange rate adjustments or a crawling peg, were not taken up, largely because they failed to recognize the dynamics of a common decision-making process that placed strong emphasis on domestic adjustment policies to accompany exchange rate changes. As economic convergence improved, realignments became smaller and fewer.[6]

The significance of the February 1982 realignment was that Belgium and Denmark accepted noticeably lower devaluations than they had initially sought and seemed justified by the commonly used indicators of competitiveness. This established in the EMS the "hard currency" strategy, which avoided compensating fully for past losses in competitiveness and took a dynamic, forward-looking approach with emphasis on domestic adjustment. With the size of the exchange rate adjustments agreed, a clear stand was taken also against even a presumption of preemptive and competitive devaluations, reflecting concerns of other EC countries.

TABLE 15.1
European Monetary System Realignments: Percentage Changes in Bilateral Central Rates

Effective Dates	BF/LF	DK	DM	FF	IRP	ITL	NLF	STG	PES	ESC
September 24, 1979		-3.0	2.0							
November 30, 1979		-4.8								
March 23, 1981						-6.0				
October 5, 1981		-3.0	5.5	-3.0		-3.0	5.5			
February 22, 1982	-8.5									
June 14, 1982			4.25	-5.75		-2.75	4.25			
March 21, 1983	1.5	2.5	5.5	-2.5	-3.5	-2.5	3.5			
July 22, 1985	2.0	2.0	2.0	2.0	2.0	-6.0	2.0			
April 7, 1986	1.0	1.0	3.0	-3.0			3.0			
August 4, 1986					-8.0					
January 12, 1987	2.0		3.0				3.0			
January 8, 1990						-3.7				
September 14, 1992	3.5	3.5	3.5	3.5	3.5	-3.5	3.5	3.5	3.5	3.5
September 17, 1992									-5.0	
November 21, 1992									-6.0	-6.0
January 30, 1993					-10.0					
May 14, 1993									-8.0	-6.5
March 6, 1995									-7.0	-3.5

Notes:

Changes against the reference currencies in the realignments. The realignments of March 13, 1983, July 22, 1985, and September 14, 1992, are against a hypothetical zero line.

BF/LF = Belgian/Luxembourg francs; DK = Danish krone; DM = Deutsche mark; FF = French franc; IRP = Irish pound; ITL = Italian lira; NLF = Netherlands guilder; STG = pound sterling; PES = Spanish peseta; ESC = Portuguese escudo.

Source: Official Communiqués.

The realignment of March 1983 was significant in a number of respects. First, it was the most comprehensive realignment so far, with devaluations or revaluations of all participating currencies against a hypothetical zero line (Table 15.1). From a purely economic standpoint, it may not matter whether exchange rate changes are expressed as a devaluation of one currency against all others or as revaluations of all other currencies against one currency; it is the relative shift in central rates that is relevant. Psychologically, things are somewhat different. Market perceptions of policy credibility and, hence, expectations of future policies may be influenced by whether a shift in central rates is formally called a devaluation or not. Politically, the word "devaluation" still carries a notion of defeat, which may adversely affect the standing of a government.

Second, and most importantly, the March realignment signaled a reordering of economic policy priorities in those countries that previously had assumed that stable exchange rates were compatible with expansionary policies. France, in particular, decided to abandon its expansionary fiscal and social policies and to give top priority to domestic cost and price stability.[7] To this end, the French authorities under the leadership of Finance Minister Jacques Delors adopted a comprehensive stabilization program, making the commitment to stay in the ERM and to aim at stable exchange rates credible by the introduction of a series of domestic adjustment measures. The French program was supported by a medium-term credit of ECU 4 billion under the Community Loan Mechanism. The stabilization program was successful in restoring external competitiveness and reducing inflation, with favorable effects on exchange rate expectations.

The French decision, as well as the support for it by partner countries, reconfirmed a joint commitment to the EMS and to continued economic and political cooperation within the EC. Moreover, France realized that, by not changing course decisively, it most probably would have had to leave the ERM temporarily or permanently. This most probably would have resulted in a significantly larger depreciation of the French franc than undertaken in the realignment, fueling inflation and seriously undermining the credibility of French economic policy for a long time to come. It also would have meant a serious setback for European integration more generally, not just in the monetary field. Nevertheless, another devaluation of the French franc became necessary in April 1986.

Very shortly after the EMS started to operate, the parity between the Irish pound and the pound sterling was broken on March 30, 1979, as sterling, which was not constrained by participation in the ERM, appreciated and the Irish pound reached its upper intervention limit.[8] This experience encouraged Ireland to orient its economy more toward EC member states other than the United Kingdom (UK). Nevertheless, the economic ties of Ireland to the UK remained close, and the nonparticipation of the UK in the ERM and later, after the UK had joined the ERM in October 1990, its departure in September 1992, caused serious problems for Ireland.

It also was during this first phase of the EMS development that, in December 1980, the initial plans to consolidate the EMS "not later than two years after the start . . . into a final system" (December 1978 resolution) were postponed indefinitely. This final system was to entail the creation of the European Monetary Fund and the full utilization of the ECU as a reserve asset and a means of settlement. Important reasons for the failure to reach agreement on what was called the "institutional phase" of the EMS were that a consolidation of the various credit facilities in a single fund would have blurred the lines of responsibility between central banks and governments and concerns about the risk of an excessive creation of liquidity.[9]

Already, before the creation of the EMS, there had been calls for a common dollar policy of the EC, which, in view of the different interests of EC countries, remained without results. In January 1981, the EC Commission presented a proposal to "multilateralize," under the umbrella of the European Monetary Cooperation Fund, the bilateral swap lines of EMS central banks with the U.S. Federal Reserve System (so-called "fecomisation," based on the French acronym FECOM, for the EMCF). Accordingly, the Federal Reserve would consult with its European partners about the currencies to be used in activating and unwinding swap credits, to avoid the triggering of tensions within the ERM. Although the proposal found some support, it also was criticized for its potential to undermine national control over money supply and subsequently was abandoned.

THE SECOND PHASE, 1983–87

The second phase of the development of the EMS, which followed the realignments of 1982 and 1983, was a period of consolidation. It was characterized by a general consensus to follow stability-oriented policies; increasing convergence in the development of costs, prices, and monetary aggregates; and long periods without realignments of central rates.[10]

During this time, the Deutsche mark evolved as the anchor currency of the system, and the anti-inflationary policies of the Bundesbank became the reference point for partner countries. Already, during the time of the snake, the Netherlands had conducted policies that moved more or less in tandem with Germany. Now, after the economic turmoil of the 1970s and the early 1980s, other countries also recognized the importance of anti-inflationary policies for their own economies. In terms of exchange rate policy, this meant that countries increasingly sought to stabilize the exchange rates of their currencies against the Deutsche mark by intervention in that currency within the margins and to support such a link by appropriate interest rate differentials vis-à-vis Germany. In linking their currencies to the mark, other countries were able "to import stability," to exert adjustment pressure on their own economies, and to gain credibility in their stabilization efforts by being associated with the successful policy strategy of the German authorities.

Already in the early phase of the EMS, intramarginal intervention had gained preference over intervention at the margins. It then was mainly seen as a tool to counter exchange rate movements from the start, before they could develop a momentum of their own. Because of the institutional constraints on the use of partner currencies for intramarginal intervention and the more ready availability of dollar reserves, the dollar initially was preferred as intervention currency. Only in periods of strong market pressure, which, at times, led to a realignment, were exchange rates allowed to move to the outer limits of the margins where obligatory intervention took place, with the consequent activation of the very short-term financing facility (VSTF) and the settlement rules.

With the reorientation of policy priorities, the Deutsche mark became the preferred currency for intramarginal intervention. Central banks would buy marks in the market at times of strength of their own currencies (or acquire them through borrowing in international markets) and use them at times of weakness of their own currencies. Although the Bundesbank had misgivings on some aspects of this emerging practice, the practice was accepted not only because it saw the advantages of intramarginal intervention for the stability of the EMS but also for reasons of its own monetary policy. Any intervention at the margins that required the provision of Deutsche marks under the VSTF led to an increase in bank liquidity, with the potential of upsetting the Bundesbank's monetary targets. By contrast, intramarginal intervention, involving the use of central banks' holdings of marks in the markets, did not result in additional liquidity creation in the German banking system. This consideration also explains why the Bundesbank initially took such a strong line against allowing the automatic financing of intramarginal intervention through the VSTF.

Although, in most situations, intramarginal intervention worked well, there were complaints. First, to obtain approval for such intervention in suddenly changing market conditions could prove to be too time-consuming. Second, there was the more political aspect of central banks having to seek approval from a partner central bank to carry out such transactions. Another concern was that, because of the important position of the Deutsche mark in international exchange markets and its role as an alternate reserve currency, the exchange rate relationships between the U.S. dollar and the EMS currencies were determined increasingly by the dollar policy and transactions of the Bundesbank. Because the dollar exchange rate exerts a powerful influence on trade and inflation in EC countries, there were calls for a common dollar policy for the EMS. In view of the exposed position of the Deutsche mark as an international reserve currency, the Bundesbank, however, was concerned that a common dollar policy would not be consistent with its domestic monetary targets (see also Ungerer, 1989, pp. 242–47).

Various proposals on how to modify the EMS were put forward. The EC Commission presented, in 1985, a package of measures. Some countries felt that their adoption would strengthen the EMS and contribute to exchange rate stability; others emphasized that any mechanism that would weaken the resolve to adjust in good time would actually weaken the EMS. No agreement on the Commission proposals could be reached. The only result was that, beginning July 1, 1985, the existing mechanisms of the EMS were supplemented so as to improve the usability and attractiveness of the ECU (so-called Palermo package) (Commission, 1989, Annex 1). The new rules set up a mobilization mechanism that allowed central banks in need of currency for intramarginal intervention to obtain dollars from other central banks in exchange for ECUs, linked the interest rate on net positions of ECUs more closely to market rates, and provided for the possibility of "other holders" (i.e., holders other than EMS members) of official ECUs. The mobilization scheme was used twice by Italy. The Bank for International Settlements, the Swiss National Bank, and the Austrian National Bank became other holders. In general, however, the agreement was of limited importance.

THE PRIVATE ECU

In contrast to its official use, the ECU became quite popular as a financial instrument in private markets. In essence, the private ECU is an asset that consists of the same basket of EC currencies as the official ECU but is being made available by commercial banks for transactions between private market participants. It served as a hedge against exchange rate risks of individual currencies and allowed investors to benefit from the higher interest rates for assets denominated in weaker currencies. The market for private ECUs grew quite rapidly in its first years, although it was limited largely to interbank transactions.[11] A controversy developed between a number of EC countries and the EC Commission, which treated the private ECU as a foreign currency and permitted private transactions in ECUs (subject, however, to existing restrictions on capital movements), and Germany, which, in a strict interpretation of paragraph 3 of its Currency Law, considered the ECU as a technical device akin to an indexation clause and not as a currency. German residents were not allowed to accept ECU liabilities but were permitted to hold ECU assets without any restriction. The German position was modified in June 1987, and private transactions in ECUs were, henceforth, treated like transactions in foreign currencies (Deutsche Bundesbank, 1987, p. 37). Proposals to establish a link between official and private ECUs did not lead to any results.[12] Nevertheless, on a limited scale, a number of EC central banks used private ECUs, which previously had been acquired in the market, for exchange market intervention in support of their currencies (Moss, 1988).

THE THIRD PHASE, 1987–90

During the third phase in the development of the EMS, doubts concerning the future of the EMS and of monetary integration in the EC became more pronounced. In the second phase, lowering inflation had become the main monetary policy priority, and the Deutsche mark had emerged as the anchor currency for the system. A substantial degree of convergence toward low inflation was achieved, and exchange rates within the EMS were stabilized. However, several policy and operational features of the EMS started to be questioned, particularly in France and Italy. There were perceptions that the system was "asymmetric" because of the dominant role of the Deutsche mark and that the management of the system (which favored intramarginal intervention, thus, precluding the financing of intervention through the VSTF) put too much of a burden on countries with weaker currencies. Also, in the context of efforts to complete the common market by the Single Market Program, it was asked whether the EMS in its present form could adequately meet the challenges of the future. We shall return to these issues in Chapter 16.

The realignment of January 12, 1987, was small in scale: the Deutsche mark and the Netherlands guilder were revalued by 3 percent and the Belgian and Luxembourg francs by 2 percent against the other ERM currencies. However, two aspects were the subject of critical observations. First, there was wide agreement that the realignment had not been caused by the loss of competitiveness of some countries but by disturbances in international markets. The drastic fall in the U.S. dollar in the second half of 1986 and at the beginning of 1987 affected various ERM currencies differently. In combination with social unrest in France, particular pressure was put on the French franc, while Germany experienced large speculative inflows of funds. Second, it was felt that the realignment could have been avoided by a better coordination of monetary policies and if the system had the provisions that allowed a more timely and adequate response to the emerging crisis.

THE BASLE-NYBORG AGREEMENT

During the realignment meeting in January 1987, the finance ministers and the central bank governors requested the Committee of Central Bank Governors and the Monetary Committee to examine ways to strengthen the EMS. The result was a package of measures that was adopted by the

Governors Committee in Basle and endorsed by the finance ministers at their meeting in Nyborg on September 12, 1987, the so-called Basle-Nyborg agreement. Its main elements were:

First, a liberalization of the existing rules on the financing of intervention; the financing of intramarginal intervention under the VSTF, subject to specified conditions and quantitative limits; and the increase in the acceptance limit for ECUs in the settlement of intervention debts from 50 to 100 percent for a trial period of two years. (Later, this was made permanent.)

Second, intensified surveillance of monetary developments by the Committee of Governors and the Monetary Committee, in particular to highlight any policy inconsistencies within the EMS and incompatible approaches to third currencies; more emphasis on the use of interest rate differentials to defend the parity grid; the flexible use of the fluctuation margins to deter speculation and avoid prolonged bouts of intramarginal intervention; and infrequent and smaller realignments.

Finally, the communiqués of the meetings underlined the significance of "sufficient convergence towards internal stability" and of "maintaining the primary objective of establishing a greater degree of internal (prices) and external (exchange rates) stability" (Ungerer et al., 1990, pp. 87–89).

The Basle-Nyborg agreement had a mixed reception. Official central bank circles considered it a balanced package, but, in some countries, it was regarded as insufficient. Public opinion in other countries, in particular in Germany, saw in the liberalization and extension of intervention financing an excessive concession to the request for more symmetry. This view, however, overlooked that the alternative to the newly agreed VSTF financing of intramarginal intervention, which was subject to consent and conditions, was intervention at the margins where financing was unlimited in amount, unless tensions in the ERM would be resolved by changes in central rates.

The Basle-Nyborg agreement was soon severely tested. In the wake of the Wall Street crash of October 1987, the dollar dropped against European currencies by more than 10 percent within a few weeks. As international funds sought refuge in the Deutsche mark, strong tensions developed within the ERM, and some currencies, in particular the French franc, came under heavy pressure. The affected central banks managed the situation successfully by a series of measures. The Banque de France increased its interest rates significantly, and the Bundesbank reduced its interest rates to near record lows. The French franc was allowed to depreciate within the band by about 2 percent. At the same time, massive intramarginal intervention, financed to the newly agreed maximum limits through the VSTF and additionally by a bilateral agreement between the Bundesbank and the Banque de France, kept the market rate of the franc above its lower intervention point, thus, convincing the markets of the determination of the authorities to stick to existing central rates.

The coordinated action had proven the viability of the EMS and enhanced the credibility of the participating monetary authorities. Periods of lesser tension in 1988 were similarly overcome. In general, the EMS functioned smoothly, and the stability of the ERM was buttressed by appropriate interest rate differentials.

OTHER DEVELOPMENTS

Central Rate Adjustment for the Lira in January 1990

In the first EMS exchange rate action in three years, the bilateral central rate for the Italian lira was lowered by 3.7 percent on January 8, 1990, and the lira was placed in the narrow fluctuation band of ±2.25 percent. Although formally a devaluation, the Italian move was a consequence of the adoption of the narrower margins. It did not increase the room for any depreciation of the lira, because the lower intervention point remained unchanged.

Liberalization of Capital Movements in the European Community

In February 1986, the EC Council of Ministers signed the Single European Act. The most important objective was to establish for the EC by the end of 1992 a single market without internal frontiers. In the financial field, progress in the liberalization of capital movements since 1961 had been very slow. On June 24, 1988, the Council of Ministers adopted a new directive. It stipulated for most EC members complete liberalization by July 1, 1990, but granted certain derogations to Greece, Ireland, Portugal, and Spain (Ungerer et al., 1990, pp. 34–35). This was a crucial step in the internationalization of financial markets.

Subsequently, Denmark abolished virtually all remaining restrictions on capital movements on October 1, 1988. France removed its remaining restrictions effective January 1, 1990. Italy lifted its capital controls still in existence as of May 14, 1990. Contrary to widespread expectations, the removal of capital controls, particularly in France and Italy, did not trigger capital outflows but contributed to capital inflows because it added to the attractiveness of the respective currencies to investors. This was testimony to an enhanced credibility of the EMS as a system of stable exchange rates and of the policies of the respective countries. That this credibility rested, however, on the expectation of a continuation of stability-oriented policies and to that extent was a blank check on the future, was not fully realized at the time.

Under the capital liberalization directive of June 1988, Belgium and Luxembourg were obliged to terminate the dual market arrangements for their currency area and complied on March 12, 1990. In June 1990, the Belgian authorities affirmed in an official announcement the policy of linking their currency closely to the Deutsche mark and keeping it well within the maximum fluctuation margins of ±2.25 percent. A key objective was to bring domestic interest rates closer to the level of rates prevailing in Germany and the Netherlands (by removing the need for maintaining a premium vis-à-vis those countries), an important consideration for a country with high public sector debt. In this, the authorities succeeded.

The Dollar, the Plaza Agreement, and the Louvre Accord

Other events of significance for the functioning of the EMS took place on a global plane. As mentioned earlier, already in late 1978, the downward exchange rate trend of the dollar was reversed after the Carter administration abandoned its policy of "benign neglect" by adopting a strict stabilization program. In response to a continued restrictive monetary policy of the Federal Reserve System and following the implementation of a conservative fiscal policy by President Ronald Reagan, who assumed office in January 1981, the dollar continued its upward movement from about DM 1.75 per dollar to a peak of DM 3.47 per dollar on February 21, 1985. Such an extreme appreciation of the world's leading currency against the Deutsche mark and other European currencies as well as the Japanese yen clearly had no basis in fundamental economic developments. It was one of the most obvious examples of exchange rate "overshooting" and created great concern inside and outside the United States.

In a meeting at the Plaza Hotel in New York on September 22, 1985, the finance ministers and central bank governors of the five largest industrial countries (the so-called Group of Five) agreed to work toward a lower and eventually more stable exchange rate for the dollar (the key words in the official communiqué were "some further orderly appreciation of the main non-dollar currencies against the dollar"). The dollar had by then already lost some of its value against other currencies, and this trend continued for the rest of 1985, throughout 1986 and, on average, also in 1987. By the end of 1987, the dollar had dropped more or less to its level (against the Deutsche mark) of 1979–80, on the way triggering (or at least contributing to) the EMS crisis of January 1987 and the tensions within the EMS in the wake of the Wall Street crash of October 1987.

The concern about the rapid and sustained fall of the dollar led to another meeting, this time of six leading countries, in Paris on February 21–22, 1987. It resulted in the Louvre Accord, which aimed at cooperation "to foster stability of exchange rates around current levels" (official communiqué of the meeting). There are somewhat conflicting reports about what actually had been agreed in the two meetings in New York and Paris, and assessments as to their effectiveness differ.[13] The fact, however, is that the fluctuations of the dollar against other important currencies, although still significant, were more limited in the late 1980s and the early 1990s compared with the period from 1980 to 1987.

NEW PARTICIPANTS IN THE EXCHANGE
RATE MECHANISM AND FOLLOWERS

In January 1986, Spain and Portugal joined the EC. The accession of Spain to the ERM on June 19, 1989 (applying the wider margins of ±6 percent), did not pose any immediate problems, but within a short time, high interest rates caused the peseta to soar within the ERM. In October 1990, the UK decided to join the ERM, also taking advantage of the wider margins, after the political authorities had apparently come to the conclusion that "the time was right." At the time, there were some misgivings that the British authorities had announced a bilateral central rate (of DM 2.95 to the pound) before an official decision by the EC finance ministers and central bank governors had been made, and there were concerns that the chosen central rate might be too high. The British move followed a period during which, at the initiative of then-Chancellor of the Exchequer Nigel Lawson, the pound "shadowed" the movements of the Deutsche mark, a strategy that later earned the scorn of then-Prime Minister Margaret Thatcher.[14] Portugal entered the ERM on April 6, 1992, also applying the wider margins. By now, all EC countries but Greece (which had signed the EMS agreement in June 1985 but did not join the ERM) participated in all aspects of the EMS.

The stability of the EMS also proved attractive to other European countries. In October 1990, Norway pegged its currency to the ECU, with a fluctuation band of ±2.25 percent. Sweden, in May 1991, and Finland, in June 1991, followed suit with similar arrangements; Sweden adopted fluctuation margins of ±1.5 percent, and Finland of ±3 percent. The decisions by the three Nordic countries were part of their strategy to move their economies closer to the EC. This was in the context of the formation of the European Economic Area, which aimed at the free movement of goods, services, labor, and capital between the EC and the remaining European Free Trade Association member countries.[15]

THE EUROPEAN MONETARY SYSTEM — MODEL FOR A REFORM OF THE INTERNATIONAL MONETARY SYSTEM?

As the EMS showed signs of success, an international debate ensued whether the EMS could not serve as a model for a reform of the international monetary system. If the European countries were able to cooperate effectively in monetary affairs, why should this not be possible for the main players on a global scale? I addressed this issue in a seminar held by the International Monetary Fund and the Austrian National Bank in October 1983 and came to the conclusion that the political commitment implicit in the EMS agreement, in particular, the common interest of EC countries to advance economic integration, did not exist on a world-wide scale. Political and economic preconditions in the EC and in the world were too different to make a return to a global system of stable exchange rates feasible.[16]

The EMS seemed set for smooth sailing, and it appeared as if realignments were a thing of the past. The EMS came to be called the "New EMS": a system characterized by stable exchange rates and seen by many as a precursor to a monetary union. However, there were warnings regarding relapses in economic convergence and the persistence of high budget deficits in some countries, and a number of observers, among them the Bundesbank, pointed out that future realignments could not be ruled out. We shall discuss developments in the EMS after 1990 in Chapter 22.

NOTES

Literature of general interest for this chapter: Commission (1982, 1989); Deutsche Bundesbank (1989); Gros and Thygesen (1992); Guitián (1988); Russo and Tullio (1988); Scholl (1981); Economic and Social Review (1989); Taylor and Artis (1988); Ungerer (1990); Ungerer et al. (1983, 1986, 1990); Zis (1984). For surveys of literature: Deville (1986); Bank of England (1991).

1. For example, Chancellor of the Exchequer (1978, p. 5); Commission (1979, p. 71). Of interest in this debate is the use of the word "deflationary" when perhaps "disinflationary" would have been more appropriate.
2. For example, Cohen (1979). Roland Vaubel (1978, p. 418) commented: "The new system will not only be suboptimal, but a step back from the present situation. For these reasons, it is not likely to survive for long."
3. The following sections draw extensively on Ungerer (1990), courtesy of Duncker & Humblot GmbH, Carl-Heinrich-Becker-Weg 9, D-12165 Berlin.
4. For details, see Solomon (1982, pp. 344–50); Ludlow (1982, pp. 246–48).
5. Daniel Gros and Niels Thygesen (1992, pp. 72–85) provide a discussion of the realignments. Exchange rate developments in the EMS and of the U.S.

dollar in 1979–90 are summarized in Ungerer et al. (1983, pp. 5–7; 1986, pp. 11–16; 1990, pp. 12–20). For an account of periods of strain in the EMS, excerpts from the official announcements of the realignments, and summaries of major measures taken in connection with realignments up to January 1990, see Ungerer et al. (1990, Tables 1 and 2).

6.   One aspect of central rate changes smaller than 4.5 percent is that market rates generally do not need to change, thus, avoiding disturbances in the markets. This is because, following a realignment, the strongest and the weakest currencies normally swap places in the fluctuation band.

7.   For a characterization of the French policies after 1981 and their consequences, see James (1996, pp. 476–77).

8.   For most of the nineteenth century and up to 1928, there was no Irish currency. Following the creation of an independent Irish state, an Irish currency was created and the policy of exchange rate parity with the pound sterling instituted (McCarthy, 1980, p. 31).

9.   See also Gros and Thygesen (1992, pp. 54–56). For proposals of the further development of the EMS, see Commission (1982, pp. 39–128).

10.   Economic convergence and exchange rate variability for EMS currencies are discussed in Ungerer et al. (1990, pp. 20–31).

11.   See Banque Nationale de Belgique (1986); Deutsche Bundesbank (1987, 1992b); International Monetary Fund (1987); Louw (1991, pp. 126–35). Also, private banks such as Banque Bruxelles Lambert; Kredietbank, Brussels; and Istituto Bancario San Paolo di Torino have discussed developments relating to the private ECU in their publications.

12.   For example, Rainer Masera (1987) proposed that the ECU should be developed into a full-fledged international reserve asset and acquire the status of a true European currency, functioning in parallel with national currencies. For this, the ECU should be made fully convertible, which could be achieved by making the official and the private sectors interchangeable.

13.   Yoichi Funabashi (1989) gives a detailed account of the Plaza and Louvre meetings and related events. For a more skeptical view, see James (1996, pp. 433–53).

14.   Thatcher (1995, p. 478). She called the ERM a "combination of rigidity and fragility" (p. 493).

15.   For more on the European Economic Area (initially called "European Economic Space") see Abrams et al. (1990).

16.   Ungerer (1984, pp. 106–7). For an updated version in English, see Ungerer (1989, pp. 240–42); see also Padoa-Schioppa (1988a, pp. 23–24).

16

The Political Debate about the European Monetary System

By the end of the 1980s, the European Monetary System (EMS) had worked effectively for a decade and come close to meeting its objective of achieving "greater stability at home and abroad." Its "constitution" — the European Council resolution of December 1978 and the central bank agreement of March 1979 — provided the flexibility necessary for adjustments of the system to changing circumstances and policies. A number of formal changes in the rules that governed the system, incorporated in the Palermo package of March 1985 and, more importantly, the Basle-Nyborg agreement of September 1987, addressed problems that arose from the evolution of the system, in particular, the emergence of the Deutsche mark as the anchor currency and the related changes in the operation of the system.

Yet, differences of view persisted as to the equity and the long-term viability of the system. Although some countries, in particular Germany and the Netherlands, felt that the system would continue to function well as long as efforts to strive for convergence toward monetary and price stability were maintained, other countries, most prominently France and Italy, questioned whether the EMS met the needs of all member countries in a balanced fashion and whether it could deal satisfactorily with the challenges of the future. It was especially in two areas that doubts were aired. First, there remained the concern of some countries about what they saw as asymmetry in the way the EMS worked. This, in their view, put more of an adjustment burden on countries with weaker currencies. Second, as the European Community (EC) embarked on the implementation of the

Single Market Program, laid down in the Single European Act of 1986, the question was asked whether a single market did not require for its realization a single European currency. These issues were raised first within the committees and expert groups responsible for the management of the EMS and by academics. Later, they were taken up by members of government in a number of countries, according the discussion about future monetary integration in the EC a new dynamic and pronounced political dimension.

An issue that found particular interest among academics was whether the working of the EMS caused or contributed to disinflation in countries participating in the exchange rate mechanism (ERM).

At the same time, the United Kingdom (UK) — never an enthusiastic participant in European integration — felt increasingly uncomfortable about the direction of monetary integration in the EC. It had joined the ERM only in October 1990, and doubts lingered whether the EMS was not indeed "half-baked," as Alan Walters, a former monetary advisor to Prime Minister Margaret Thatcher, had claimed (1990, p. 15).

ASYMMETRY IN THE EUROPEAN MONETARY SYSTEM

Complaints about asymmetry in international exchange rate systems have a long history. In the 1960s, France found fault with the "privileged" position of the U.S. dollar in the Bretton Woods system, which, it was suggested, allowed the United States to pursue its own policies without regard to the impact on other countries. On the other hand, a number of countries called for a more balanced international adjustment process that would provide for "burden sharing" by having surplus countries shoulder more of the adjustment burden. In the EC, nearly as soon as the snake started to operate in March 1972, it was criticized for a "deflationary" bias as, in short sequence, the UK and Italy left the arrangement. France raised similar objections after it left the snake in January 1974.

The negotiations about the establishment of the EMS were marked by attempts to make it "at least as strict as the snake" while providing similar treatment for all members, whether in surplus or deficit — a circle that could not be squared. The final design of the EMS was based on a grid of bilateral parities and not on a mechanism in which the obligation to intervene would be tied to divergences from ECU central rates, a concept that was faintly maintained with the invention of the divergence indicator. That a system could not aim at monetary stability and, at the same time, require each "diverging" country to adjust, regardless of the direction in which it deviated, became obvious. The changes in EMS rules in 1985 and 1987 were in part a response to the asymmetry allegation and aimed at enabling the EMS to cope with problems experienced by weak currency countries without sacrificing the stability orientation of the system.

We can subdivide the asymmetry issue into a number of interrelated questions: Was the EMS asymmetric by design? Did it become asymmetric in its operations as a result of its evolution? Were the consequences of its functioning asymmetric in their impact on different countries? An additional concern was that the strict stability orientation of monetary policy in Germany would fuel stagnation and add to existing unemployment in other countries.

The EMS (or, more precisely, the ERM) was in its design symmetrical: all participants have the same rights and obligations with regard to intervention, the provision and the use of the very short-term credit lines, and the settlement of intervention debts. In the grid system, both sides — deficit as well as surplus countries — are obliged to share the burden of intervention. (It is the central bank that is offered a currency for purchase that actually intervenes.) By nature, the consequences are different: a surplus country gains reserves, a deficit country loses reserves; as a counterpart, the surplus country loses real resources (assuming no change in the capital account of the balance of payments), while the deficit country gains real resources. The surplus country may be subject to an expansion of its money supply; the deficit country, to a shrinkage.[1] What happens in the surplus country is the mirror image of what happens in the deficit country. In reality, much depends on whether a country succeeds in sterilizing the impact of reserve changes on its money supply. Sterilization, that is, avoiding the automatic effects on bank liquidity or money supply, is easier for a deficit country than a surplus country, at least in the short run. (Obviously, for a deficit country, the size of its reserves is the ultimate limit, while — at least in theory — a surplus country can go on accumulating reserves; that is an element of asymmetry.)

An important aspect of symmetry in the EMS is that the role of a country — surplus or deficit — is not predetermined and may change; it depends mainly on its own policies and developments, very much like in the gold standard. An ECU-based intervention mechanism would, in fact, have been less symmetrical than a grid system, because only the country with the divergence (whether positive or negative) would have been obliged for sure to intervene and bear the burden, while its counterpart would not have been predetermined (the "involuntary debtor-creditor" problem). The perceived asymmetry in the grid system, therefore, did not result from the way the system worked but from the fact that countries followed different policies. To that extent, it was a matter of choice. One way to avoid the consequences of being a deficit (or surplus) country would have been to change the central rate, an option that, in the first decade of the EMS, had been taken quite frequently. (The question remains, though, whether, in the longer run, that would have been a solution.) However, deficit countries have been reluctant to choose this option, because they believed that it undermined their policy credibility. (In fact, it was the *need* to devalue that affected their credibility.) This was why elaborate efforts were undertaken to present in EMS realignments a balanced picture of devaluations and revaluations (as in March 1983 and April 1986) or to avoid devaluations in a formal sense at all (as in January 1987), although the relative shifts in exchange rates were not affected by such cosmetic exercises (see Table 15.1).

As noted earlier, the EMS evolved over time. There was no deliberate attempt to change the *system* and to convey to one currency the role of an anchor currency. Rather, it was a result of a change in *policies* on the part of the more inflationary countries. After the first years of the EMS, which were very much "business as usual," the more inflationary countries decided to pursue stability-oriented economic policies as the view gained ground that expansionary policies per se would not, certainly not in the longer run, secure high employment. If such policies of stabilization and of linkage to the Deutsche mark would have been followed under the original working principles of the EMS, intervention — if and when needed — would have taken place mainly at the outer limits of the fluctuation margins. However, the weak currency countries chose to secure the linkage of their currencies to the Deutsche mark by intervening in this currency before the intervention points were reached. This is how the mark became the anchor currency of the system.

Initially, the German authorities were not enthusiastic about this development. They saw in the full use of the margins an element of needed flexibility. More generally, they were adverse to their currency being assigned the role of a reserve currency.[2] The countries who opted for intramarginal intervention, on the other hand, hoped to gain more leverage in the exchange markets and to avoid being placed with their backs against the wall in case of a weakening of their currencies. At the same time, they hoped to secure more credibility in their stabilization efforts by being closely linked, technically as well as psychologically, with the strongest currency in the system. The timing and the amount of intramarginal intervention were determined by the country that opted for a strategy of intramarginal intervention, not by the country whose currency was being used. Here, too, asymmetry was a matter of choice (see also Rieke, 1988, p. 290).

Some attention, mainly by academic observers, was devoted to the consequences of the way the system operated on various countries. Daniel Gros and Niels Thygesen (1992, pp. 136–57) examined different indicators for the degree of asymmetry, namely, the sensitivity to fluctuations in the dollar–Deutsche mark rate, the distribution of intervention activity, efforts to sterilize the effects of intervention on domestic money supply, patterns in money supply correlations, and interest rate linkages. They discussed the findings of a number of authors. According to their summary, "the empirical evidence on asymmetry . . . presents a mixed picture. . . . The overall picture that emerges is therefore that Germany has a strong influence on the other countries, but there is also some weak influence the other way around" (pp. 149–50). Not surprisingly, this finding is in line with the deliberate option of other EMS countries to orient their policies toward those of Germany, with the aim of providing their own disinflationary efforts with a stability anchor. It is, therefore, logical that "formal tests of asymmetry fare best in the 1983–6 period when the EMS might indeed have functioned primarily as a disciplinary device" (p. 150).

THE BALLADUR AND AMATO MEMORANDA

In many ways, the central issues of the asymmetry debate were the role of the central bank issuing the anchor currency, the Bundesbank, in the management of the system and the relative weight of financing and adjustment in addressing imbalances. Both issues had important political implications, relating to the issues of economic policy autonomy and national sovereignty. The asymmetry question became a highly political issue. This was already the case in the debate leading to the Basle-Nyborg agreement. It was even more so when the asymmetry question was reopened in early 1988 by France and Italy.

On January 6, 1988, French Finance Minister Edouard Balladur, in an interview with the TV channel Antenne 2, expressed the view that the functioning of the EMS "n'est pas très égalitaire et très complet" (1988a). On January 8, he submitted to his EC colleagues a "Mémorandum sur la construction monétaire européenne" (Balladur, 1988b). He acknowledged the progress achieved with the Basle-Nyborg agreement but also asserted that the ERM still presented several important defects that, if not dealt with, could carry serious risks for monetary Europe and for Europe in general. Therefore, "the rapid pursuit of the monetary construction of Europe [was] the only possible solution" (my translation). Balladur emphasized the asymmetry of the system. Although the discipline imposed by the ERM might have good effects when it served as a constraint on insufficiently rigorous policies, it produced an abnormal situation if it exempted countries whose policies were too restrictive from the necessary adjustment. Balladur called also for full participation of the UK and Italy in the ERM and for common action vis-à-vis the main third currencies, the dollar and the yen. Most importantly, he proposed that all participants in the ERM should, together, determine the main objectives of economic and monetary policies and coordinate closely their policies for the implementation of these objectives. Because one national currency (i.e., the Deutsche mark) should not serve as intervention and reserve currency for the whole system, a diversification of reserves would be desirable, meaning that the Bundesbank should hold other EMS currencies in its reserves.

On February 23, Italian Treasury Minister Giuliano Amato transmitted to his EC colleagues a memorandum of his own (Amato, 1988). He put even more stress on what he considered the deflationary bias of the EMS, attributable to the absence of a "motore della crescita," an engine of growth. Like Balladur, he favored a common identification of economic policy goals that should include price stability as well as growth. Amato called for a reform of the financing mechanism of the EMS and a strengthening of the European Monetary Cooperation Fund and he proposed the creation of a recycling mechanism to counter tensions resulting from short-term capital movements not justified by fundamentals. Procedures for the coordination of economic policies should include mechanisms for identifying divergent countries, irrespective of the direction of the imbalance, from which a greater adjustment effort would be required — a sort of reinforced divergence indicator.

Both Balladur and Amato referred to the creation of a single currency and a common central bank system in a not too distant future.

The proposals of Balladur and Amato were directed at a wholesale overhaul of the EMS. By contrast, some other EMS countries, in particular Germany, were satisfied with the working of the EMS. They could see no merit in a mutual holding of reserves, which would have amounted to credits to weak currency countries, and they were against a softening of the EMS rules, such as the introduction of a reinforced divergence indicator. They insisted that an exchange rate system such as the EMS required an anchor currency, which had to be the one with the best record of stability.[3] The only way to replace the anchor would be the introduction of a common monetary policy, which, however, was still some time off. Yet, it was evident that the concerns of two important member countries like France and Italy could not be dealt with by a defensive strategy carried out in technical committees. They required a political response. We shall return to this in the final section of this chapter.

THE DISCIPLINARY EFFECT OF THE
EUROPEAN MONETARY SYSTEM

Another question that found quite some interest, especially among academics, was whether the EMS exerted a disciplinary influence on ERM participants by forcing or encouraging them to follow disinflationary policies.[4]

The notion that the EMS as such would have a built-in disciplinary effect was, of course, somewhat simplistic. An exchange rate system could have such an effect only if some of its members followed stricter policies than others, and the latter would be unequivocally committed to not using exchange rate adjustments as an escape and, consequently, would have to fall in line. At the same time, it could be imagined that all members of an exchange rate system would conduct equally unrestrained monetary policies, without resulting in any exchange rate tensions within the system.

The more pertinent question was, therefore, whether ERM participation offered a policy and operational framework for a credible disinflation strategy and, thus, encouraged countries to adopt a stability-oriented policy stance. For most politicians and monetary policy managers, this was not a question at all.[5] Indeed, an important reason for countries to join or to stay in the EMS was the belief that participation in a system with fixed exchange rates, in which some countries adhered strictly to a stabilization strategy, would make it easier to achieve domestic stability for themselves by enhancing policy credibility. A tactical consideration was that stabilization policies could, at times, be more easily defended in the political marketplace if somebody else (the EMS or partner countries) could be blamed for unpopular measures or if arguments of political prestige and of general integration policy could be used for staying the course. (However, arguments that did not rely on the merit of stabilization as such had the drawback that they could be turned around: to call for a departure from the EMS or to abandon a stabilization policy in order to shed the "dictate" of others.)

One argument of those who doubted the disciplinary effect of the EMS was that, in the early and mid-1980s, there was a general trend toward monetary stability: the Reagan administration (in combination with the Federal Reserve Board led by Paul Volcker) in the United States and the Thatcher government in the UK were successfully pursuing price stability, as were countries like Japan and Switzerland. There was, however, a significant difference. In the case of the United States and the UK, new governments had come to power with an explicit commitment to stability, and Japan and Switzerland had a record of stability. In those EC countries that changed course, it was the same government, as in France, or similarly structured governments, as in Italy, that had followed inflationary policies and now saw virtue in stabilization and were ready to embark on disinflationary policies, using the EMS framework as the vehicle for their policies. Similar observations apply to Ireland. Furthermore, although inflation fell also in other countries, the deceleration in several ERM countries was more pronounced than in other countries.[6]

ONE MARKET, ONE MONEY?

The European Economic Community (EEC) Treaty of 1957 proclaimed as its main task the progressive establishment of a "common market." By the end of the 1960s, major elements of the common market were in place, in particular, the customs union and the Common Agricultural Policy. In other areas, however, progress was less spectacular. This applied in particular to financial market integration but also to the harmonization of legal provisions in a number of areas and the elimination of nontariff trade barriers.

On the initiative of Jacques Delors, president of the European Commission since January 1985, the Commission in June 1985 presented a White Paper on the completion by the end of 1992 of the common market and the creation of a "single market" (Commission, 1985). The European Council convened an intergovernmental conference that worked out a general legal framework, the Single European Act (*Bulletin*, 1986, Supplement No. 2). It was adopted in February 1986 and ratified by all EC member countries in 1987. The Single European Act, which took the form of amendments to the treaties establishing the European Communities, called for an internal market that "shall comprise an area without internal frontiers in which the free movement of goods, persons, services and capital is ensured" (p. 11). It also broadened the scope for majority decisions by the Council of Ministers and the competences of the European Parliament.

In the financial area, it was on the basis of the Single European Act that the Council adopted in June 1988 a directive on the complete liberalization of capital movements by EC countries (see Chapter 14), a directive that governed the authorization of credit institutions and the provision of financial services throughout the EC, and a supplementary directive aiming at harmonizing and strengthening solvency rules for financial institutions (Ungerer et al., 1990, pp. 32–37; *IMF Survey*, 1988, pp. 283–84; *IMF Survey*, 1990, pp. 68–69).

In the monetary field, a general consensus developed in the 1980s that any deepening of monetary integration within the EC and a transformation of the EMS into a more far-reaching and tightly organized system of monetary policy cooperation would call for a major political initiative. It could not be realized on the basis of the existing EEC Treaty and agreements but would require a new legal framework, that is, an amendment of the EEC Treaty. The Single European Act included the insertion in Title II of the treaty of a new chapter, entitled "Cooperation in Economic and Monetary Policy (Economic and Monetary Union)," consisting of Art. 102A. The article referred to the "experience acquired in the framework of the European Monetary System (EMS) and in developing the ECU." It went on: "In so far as further development in the field of economic and monetary policy necessitates institutional changes, the provisions of Article 236 shall be applicable." Art. 236 of the EEC Treaty deals with the amendment of the treaty.

The prospect of a single market without frontiers and especially with unrestricted capital movements not only within the EC but virtually also vis-à-vis most other industrialized countries gave rise to some important questions: Was a single market feasible without a common monetary policy and a single currency, or was a single currency needed for the optimal realization of the single market? In other words, Did one market require one money?[7] What would be the best way to implement a common monetary policy and to create a single currency?

It was, in particular, the potential for large and rapid capital movements across borders, triggered by differences in economic and monetary developments (in particular, changes in interest rates), and by expectations about future economic and political developments that led many to believe that a very high degree of monetary policy cooperation, if not a common monetary policy, was needed. It was argued that, in the past, the continued existence of capital controls had contributed to the success of the EMS, although this view seemed to neglect the occurrence of serious exchange market crises even under regimes of strict capital controls throughout the 1960s, 1970s, and 1980s.

Tommaso Padoa-Schioppa encapsulated the issue in the memorable phrase of an "inconsistent quartet." He wrote: "Economic theory and historical experience have repeatedly shown that these four elements [free trade, full capital mobility, fixed (or managed) exchange rates, and monetary policy autonomy] cannot coexist, and that at least one has to give way (1986b, p. 373).[8] Padoa-Schioppa came to the conclusion, as did many others, that, in the longer run, the only solution to the inconsistency was to complement the internal market with a monetary union.

In response to this line of thinking, it was pointed out that monetary policy was not conducted in full independence as long as monetary authorities in various countries, in their quest for convergence toward stability, followed the German lead. Moreover, the fluctuation margins in the ERM provided some flexibility, and the possibility of central rate changes allowed the decoupling of a currency from the anchor currency.

What is actually needed for the optimal functioning of a single market is not so much stability in *nominal* exchange rates (a monetary union being the ultimate form of stable nominal exchange rates) but stability in *real* exchange rates or appropriate adjustments as needed to safeguard competitiveness. Because real exchange rates are nothing else but nominal rates adjusted for relative indicators of competitiveness, such as costs and prices, they can be influenced by changes of nominal rates and by domestic adjustment. A high degree of convergence of the factors determining competitiveness at stable nominal rates would ensure stable real exchange rates. An important aspect is, however, that business transactions are carried out on the basis of nominal rates. If those are distorted, for example, by the failure to adjust them as needed in a system like the EMS, or by misalignments under a regime of floating currencies, a single market cannot function optimally. Similarly, if in a monetary union (i.e., a regime of irreversibly fixed nominal rates), disparities in competitiveness would emerge, the single market would suffer from contortions.

It has, therefore, been argued that a single market could function satisfactorily without a formal monetary union provided there is a high degree of convergence. It was along these lines that the Board of Academic Advisers to the German Federal Ministry of Economics (Wissenschaftlicher Beirat, 1989a) advocated a "hardening" of the EMS. More convergence toward stability would, however, by necessity be asymmetrical, whereas more symmetry in adjustment meant a "softening" of the EMS. The problem of the dominance of the Deutsche mark could be solved by other currencies gradually becoming as strong as the mark. A hardening of the EMS also would reduce the need for central rate adjustments.

However, a number of questions remained. Would it always be possible to engineer sufficiently large and timely central rate changes to keep real exchange rates in line? Could central rate changes break speculative attacks, considering that market tensions, especially in the short to medium term, are not so much driven by changes in fundamentals as by interest rate developments and — very significantly — by expectations on a whole range of economic and political developments? Was it not true that large speculative attacks could cause the EMS to collapse, leading to floating rates with the likelihood of misalignments? How would the prospect of frequent changes in nominal rates affect marketing strategies and investment decisions of enterprises in a single market? The EMS crises in 1992 and 1993 provided some answers to these questions. Finally, even if the EMS would continue to function satisfactorily, could other EC countries in the longer run be expected to accept the hegemonial role of Germany in determining monetary policy within the EC as well as vis-à-vis third countries? Would they not want to have a part in deciding the course of monetary policy in Europe, "to have a chair at the table," as it were?[9]

Such political concerns had been forcefully expressed by Balladur and Amato in their memoranda of early 1988. In her memoirs, Thatcher made it clear that the British reluctance to join the ERM was, in large part, motivated by political concerns about national sovereignty, although her and many conservative politicians' conclusions were totally different from those of politicians in other European countries. The UK wanted less monetary integration; countries like France and Italy wanted more.

THE GENSCHER AND STOLTENBERG MEMORANDA

On January 20, 1988, German Foreign Minister Hans-Dietrich Genscher, in an address to the European parliament in Strasburg in his capacity as president of the General Affairs Council (Foreign Ministers), termed the concepts of a monetary union and of a European central bank "essential" and "logical" for the creation of a single market. In a memorandum in February (Genscher, 1988), he called the creation of a European monetary area and a European central bank "the economically necessary complement to the internal market and a catalyst for the necessary convergence of economic policies of member states." However, a single monetary area required agreement on basic economic policy principles ("ordnungspolitische Grundauffassungen"). This included the degree of autonomy for a European central bank that, in its policy, had to give priority to price stability and should not be obliged to finance national or EC budget deficits. Genscher proposed the convening of a group of "wise men" by the European Council at its meeting in Hanover on June 27–28, 1988. The group should work out the principles for a European monetary area and the statute of a European central bank.

On March 15, German Finance Minister Gerhard Stoltenberg followed with a markedly more reserved statement that had been coordinated with the Bundesbank (Stoltenberg, 1988). It called for more convergence regarding inflation, budget deficits, and current account balances. It termed the creation of an economic and monetary union the long-term goal that "must be founded above all on a far-reaching political and institutional reorganisation of the Community towards a more comprehensive union."

Additionally, nonofficial groups, academics, and senior central bank officials, acting in a personal capacity, presented detailed proposals for a common monetary policy and a European central bank.[10]

With these various initiatives, the stage was set for the next chapter in the history of European monetary integration.

NOTES

Literature of general interest for this chapter: de Cecco and Giovannini (1989); Fratianni and von Hagen (1992); Giavazzi, Micossi, and Miller (1988); Gros and Thygesen (1992).

1. For a similar view, see also U.S. Congress (1979, pp. 78–84).
2. On the role of the Deutsche mark as a reserve currency, see Tavlas (1991).
3. Wolfgang Rieke, from the Bundesbank, stressed the view "that a system of fixed but adjustable exchange rates needs a firm 'anchor'" (1990, p. 30).
4. For some of the literature, see Ungerer et al. (1990, pp. 24–25); Giavazzi and Pagano (1988).
5. Jean-Jacques Rey, from the Banque Nationale de Belgique, observed (1988, p. 138): "This change in policy [toward stabilization since 1982] did not occur because of the EMS, but for other reasons. . . . However it did restore the credibility of the EMS as an arrangement for exchange-rate stabilisation and it did engineer a shift in expectations." See also Rieke (1988, p. 289).

6.   See Ungerer et al. (1990 p. 25). For studies on disinflation in individual countries, see Kremers (1990); Gressani, Guiso, and Visco (1988); Artus and Bourginat (1994). See also Woolley (1992); Tavlas (1994).

7.   A study of the Commission (1990c) on the benefits and costs of EMU had the title "One Market, One Money."

8.   In 1972, Henry Wallich had drawn attention to what he called the "inconsistent trinity" when he wrote that "fixed exchange rates, free capital movements, and independent monetary policies are inconsistent" (pp. 6–7).

9.   It had, indeed, been suggested that other central banks should literally get a seat in the Central Bank Council of the Bundesbank; see, for example, Goodhart (1989, p. 30).

10.   For example, Committee for the Monetary Union of Europe (founded by Helmut Schmidt and Valéry Giscard d'Estaing, 1988); Gros and Thygesen (1988); Kloten (1988).

17

The Delors Report

The European Council at its meeting in Hanover on June 27 and 28, 1988, took an important step to advance European monetary integration when it entrusted to a committee, chaired by the president of the European Community (EC) Commission, Jacques Delors, "the task of studying and proposing concrete stages leading towards [economic and monetary] union." Instead of following Minister Hans-Dietrich Genscher's suggestion of forming a group of "wise men," it invited the central bank governors of the EC countries, another member of the EC Commission, and three independent experts to join President Delors.[1]

Two aspects of the decision of the European Council are of particular interest. First, the Council did not ask *whether* but *how* an economic and monetary union (EMU) should be established. Second, by having the heads of central banks form the core of the committee, it signaled its expectation of obtaining technically viable *and* politically acceptable proposals. Because central bankers have a "natural" inclination toward a cautious monetary policy stance, the composition of the committee virtually also guaranteed conservative financial policy advice. Yet, although the committee members participated in a personal capacity, their opinions were likely to reflect the political thinking in their respective countries, which they helped to shape and implement. A suggestion to have the Monetary Committee associated with the preparation of a report was not taken up.[2]

THE WORK OF THE DELORS COMMITTEE

In its deliberations, the Delors Committee soon reached a consensus on important basic aspects of the report. Other issues, however, could not be resolved easily. One of the latter was the speed with which EMU should be realized. Although the French, Italian, and Spanish members, in particular, were in favor of an early move toward EMU, their German, British, and Luxembourg counterparts took a much more cautious line, insisting on significant progress in the liberalization of capital movements and policy convergence as preconditions. Highly controversial was the proposal by the governor of the Banque de France, Jacques de Larosière, for the establishment of a European Reserve Fund during the first stage on the way to EMU. This fund was to foreshadow a future common monetary authority. Its resources would be provided by a limited pooling of reserves, and it could intervene in exchange markets. Although supported by some other committee members, the proposal was not accepted (Paras. 53, 54).

Strong support was expressed for a high degree of coordination of national budgetary policies. This did not come as a big surprise, considering that central banks have to carry the main burden of an unbalanced mix of budgetary and monetary policies. The request of Bundesbank President Karl Otto Pöhl that a future European central bank should be committed unequivocally to price stability, be politically autonomous, and be federally organized was generally accepted and formed the basis of the provisions for the structure and status of the future European central bank not only in the Delors Report itself but also in the Maastricht Treaty.

In April 1989, it looked as if the committee would not be able to finish its work in time for the June meeting of the European Council in Madrid. There was quite some dissatisfaction with an early draft of the report, and extensive revisions were requested. However, the committee felt that it should make a special effort to come to an agreement. In a final spurt — the Italian newspaper La Repubblica of April 13 spoke of a "two-day-non-stop debate" — the report was completed on April 12, signed by all committee members (including Governor Robert Leigh-Pemberton of the Bank of England), and submitted to the European Council. President Delors presented the report in a press conference on April 17.

In July 1989, a collection of papers was published, together with the report itself. The papers had been submitted by committee members and provide some insight into the discussions of the committee and the views of its members.

SUMMARY OF THE DELORS REPORT

The report was organized in three sections.[3] The first reviewed the state of economic integration in the EC. The second provided a definition of monetary and economic union and a characterization of the final stage. The third section described the stages toward EMU.

The assessment of the achievements of the European Monetary System (EMS) in the first section merits extensive quotation (Para. 5):

The EMS has served as the focal point for improved monetary policy coordination and has provided a basis for multilateral surveillance within the Community. In part, its success can be attributed to the participants' willingness to opt for a strong currency stance. Also important has been the flexible and pragmatic way in which the System has been managed, with increasingly close cooperation among central banks. Moreover, the System has benefited from the role played by the Deutschmark as an "anchor" for participants' monetary and intervention policies. The EMS has evolved in response to changes in the economic and financial environment, and on two occasions (Palermo 1985 and Basle/Nyborg 1987) its mechanisms have been extended and strengthened.

At the same time, the EMS has not fulfilled its full potential. Firstly, a number of Community countries have not yet joined the exchange rate mechanism and one country participates with wider fluctuation margins. Secondly, the lack of sufficient convergence of fiscal policies as reflected in large and persistent budget deficits in certain countries has remained a source of tensions and has put a disproportionate burden on monetary policy. Thirdly, the transition to the second stage of the EMS and the establishment of the European Monetary Fund, as foreseen by the Resolution of the European Council adopted in 1978, have not been accomplished.

The report laid stress on the need for greater convergence of economic performance and emphasized that "the integration process . . . requires more intense and effective policy coordination, even within the framework of the present exchange rate arrangements. . . . While voluntary cooperation should be relied upon as much as possible . . . , there is also likely to be a need for more binding procedures" (Paras. 11, 12, 13).

The Final Stage of Economic and Monetary Union

At the outset, the report stated that "economic and monetary union form two integral parts of a single whole and would therefore have to be implemented in parallel." The "principle of subsidiarity," according to which "the functions of higher levels of government should be as limited as possible and should be subsidiary to those of lower levels," was an essential element in defining the appropriate balance of power within the EC (Paras. 20, 21).

Monetary union was defined as the total and irreversible convertibility of currencies, the complete liberalization of capital movements and the full integration of financial markets, and the elimination of fluctuation margins and the irrevocable locking of exchange rates (Para. 22). Economic union was described as a single market in which persons, goods, services, and capital could move freely, with common competition, structural and regional policies, and macroeconomic policy coordination, including binding rules for budgetary policies (Para. 25).

At the heart of the Delors Report was the proposal to create a single currency in three stages and to set up a European System of Central Banks (ESCB). The adoption of a single currency, although not strictly necessary for a monetary union, would clearly demonstrate the irreversibility of the move to monetary union (Para. 23). The ESCB would be committed to the objective of price stability and, subject to the foregoing, should support the general economic policy set at the EC level. The ESCB would be responsible for formulating and implementing monetary policy as well as managing the EC's exchange rate policy vis-à-vis third currencies (Para. 32).

The ESCB would have a federative structure that would correspond best to the political diversity of the EC. It would consist of a central institution (later named the European Central Bank) and the national central banks. A council, the highest decision-making body of the ESCB, would be composed of the governors of the national central banks and the members of the board of the central institution. The ESCB Council should be independent of instructions from national governments and EC authorities, and the ESCB would not lend to public sector authorities. It would submit annual reports to the European Parliament and European Council, and the chairman of the ESCB could be invited to report to these institutions (Para. 32).

The Delors Report did not recommend the creation of a new central institution for economic policy, because an institutional framework already was established under the European Economic Community Treaty. However, the new treaty would have to provide for additional or changed roles for the existing bodies, such as the Council of Ministers, the Commission, and the Monetary Committee (Para. 33).

The Stages

For the three stages envisaged for the realization of EMU, the Delors Committee did not suggest any deadlines, except that the first stage should start no later than July 1, 1990, to coincide with the full liberalization of capital movements. The transition from one stage to another should not be automatic but depend on the progress achieved in the prior stage.

Stage one would aim at greater convergence of economic performance through the strengthening of economic and monetary policy coordination within the existing institutional framework. In the economic field, stage one would center on the completion of the single market and the reduction of regional disparities. The convergence decision of 1974 should be reinforced, in particular by setting up a new procedure for budgetary policy coordination with precise quantitative guidelines and medium-term orientations (Para. 51). In the monetary field, all obstacles to financial integration and all impediments to the private use of the ECU would be removed. All EC currencies should participate in the exchange rate mechanism (ERM). The mandate of the Committee of Central Bank Governors would be expanded, and the Committee could formulate opinions on the overall orientation of monetary and exchange rate policy and express opinions to individual governments and the Council of Ministers. It would set up three subcommittees for various policy areas and provide them with a permanent research staff (Para. 52).

In stage two, the ESCB would be set up and absorb existing institutions such as the European Monetary Cooperation Fund and the Committee of Central Bank Governors. The key task for the ESCB would be to begin the transition from the coordination of independent monetary policies to a common monetary policy in the final stage. The Committee did not consider it possible to propose a detailed blueprint for this transition, because this, among other things, would depend on the effectiveness of policy coordination and would have to take account of the impact of financial innovation and the degree of financial integration. A certain amount of reserves could be pooled and used to conduct exchange market interventions in accordance with ESCB guidelines. As circumstances and progress in convergence permitted, the fluctuation margins would be narrowed (Para. 57). The main feature in the economic field would be the setting of precise, although not yet binding, rules for the size and financing of budget deficits.

The final stage would commence with the irrevocable locking of exchange rates. Common structural and regional policies would be further strengthened. Rules in the macroeconomic and budgetary field would become binding, and the Council of Ministers, in cooperation with the European Parliament, would have the authority to make directly enforceable decisions on national budgets, on structural policies, and relating to countries' adjustment efforts. The EC would take its full role in international policy cooperation. The transition to a single monetary policy would be made, and the ESCB would assume all its responsibilities. Decisions on exchange market interventions in third currencies would become the sole responsibility of the ESCB, and official reserves would be pooled and managed by the ESCB. The changeover to a single currency would take place during this stage (Paras. 58–60).

Because the European Economic Community Treaty, as amended by the Single European Act, would be insufficient for the full realization of the EMU, a new political and legal basis would be needed. Two options existed, namely, to conclude a new treaty for each stage or to conclude a single comprehensive treaty. The Committee indicated a preference for the second option (Paras. 61–63). In order to lend credibility to the whole process toward EMU, the Delors Committee called for "a clear political commitment to the final stage" (Para. 39).

COMPARISON WITH THE WERNER REPORT

In the nearly two decades between the Werner Report and the Delors Report, the EC had grown from the 6 founding members to 12 countries. Although the "Six" had broadly similar economic structures, this was no longer the case for the Community of 12. During the same period, the EC lived through the monetary turmoil caused by the breakdown of the Bretton Woods system and the oil price shocks of the 1970s. The snake and the EMS provided the EC with valuable experience in the operation of a multilateral exchange rate system and insights into the relationship between economic convergence and exchange rate stability. The naive view that setting up institutional arrangements would ensure compatible economic developments (the "monetarist" approach) and also the belief that monetary integration could advance only after a sufficient degree of convergence had been achieved (the "economist" approach) had given room to the recognition of the interdependence between institution building and convergence.[4] At the same time, a consensus on stability-oriented policies had emerged, and experience had shown that an independent central bank was an important, if not the crucial, factor for success in the quest for monetary stability. All this was reflected in the Delors Report and helps to explain the significant differences between the two reports (see also Baer and Padoa-Schioppa, 1989). The different composition of the two committees also played an important role, as discussed earlier.

The Werner Report was in its proposals more process and procedure oriented, whereas the Delors Report concentrated on the objectives of a common monetary policy and the institutional framework for such a policy, as shown by the detailed recommendations for the structure, status, and tasks of the ESCB.

The Delors Committee did not see a need for a decision center for economic policy and referred, instead, to already-existing institutions. This may have reflected consideration for the desire of countries to safeguard their sovereignty but was also in line with the Delors Committee's support for the principle of subsidiarity. Nevertheless, the Delors Committee felt very strongly about the need for binding rules on the size and financing of national budget deficits (note that there is no longer reference to surpluses!). However, it did not go as far as the Werner Committee, which also wanted a more general harmonization of budgetary policies, including their main elements such as revenue and expenditures, and the distribution between investment and consumption expenditures.

Both reports envisaged a process in three stages. The Werner Report recommended for the first stage a duration of two years and for the whole process, ten years. In contrast, the Delors Committee, conscious of the negative experiences with the Werner Plan and the second stage of the EMS, did not propose any deadlines and preferred instead to make the transition from one stage to the next contingent on progress in the prior stage.

THE RESPONSE TO THE DELORS REPORT

After a discussion in the Monetary Committee, the EC finance ministers endorsed the Delors Report at their meeting in S'Agora, Spain, on May 19 and 20, 1989. The European Council, convening in Madrid on June 26 and 27, "considered that the report by the Committee . . . fulfilled the mandate given in Hanover. The European Council felt that its realization would have to take account of the parallelism between economic and monetary aspects, respect the principle of subsidiarity and allow for the diversity of specific situations (*Bulletin*, 1989, No. 6, p. 11).

The response of the general public in EC countries was somewhat varying, ranging from clear support in countries like France and Italy to some skepticism in other countries. In Germany, the reaction from business leaders and politicians was broadly positive, but among academic economists, doubts were quite pronounced. The Board of Economic Advisors to the Federal Ministry of Economics (Wissenschaftlicher Beirat, 1989b), for instance, expressed serious concerns about the proposals of the Delors Report. Already earlier the Wissenschaftlicher Beirat (1989a) had advocated a "hardening" of the EMS to further monetary integration.

In the United Kingdom (UK), public opinion in journals and newspapers was partly positive, while reaction at the highest level of government was clearly negative. Nigel Lawson, at the time Chancellor of the Exchequer, declared on June 12, 1989: "We would entirely agree with the idea of improving economic and, in particular, monetary cooperation within the Community, within the framework of the existing Treaty. But the idea that we should sign up now to a new Treaty, as is called for, and sign up now to full economic and monetary union is not something which we accept." Lawson added that the irrevocable surrender of control of monetary policy to another authority would have to be accompanied by the creation of a proper democratically elected and accountable government and European Parliament, which was not something he wished to see. "Certainly this was not the prospectus on which the British people and the British House of Commons . . . agreed to membership of the European Community."[5]

Prime Minister Margaret Thatcher, appearing before the House of Commons immediately after the Madrid meeting, pointed out that, although the objective of progressive realization of EMU was reaffirmed, stages two and three of the Delors Report were not endorsed. These stages "would involve a massive transfer of sovereignty which I do not believe would be acceptable to this House." She went on to say that "the Delors Report will not be the only document taken into account in considering how to come to closer economic and monetary union. We shall be able to put up alternative schemes. . . . We look for a way forward by voluntary agreement and co-operation to which we can gladly give our support." She emphasized that "one of the most worrying features of . . . stages 2 and 3 of the Delors Report would be that the Council of Twelve, or the central bank governors, would have the deciding say in the guidelines to which the rest of us would have to agree. Those central bank governors would not be democratically accountable in any way" (House of Commons, 1989, pp. 1107, 1110, 1112).

The proposal of the Delors Committee for binding rules on the size and financing of budget deficits proved to be very controversial. The criticism had a political and an economic component. It was argued that such far-reaching rules would be in conflict with national sovereignty and the prerogatives of national parliaments. At the same time, such rules were considered economically unnecessary. With an effective "no bailout" rule and without monetary financing of deficits, markets would exert the discipline needed to keep profligate governments in line (Bishop, 1991, p. 5).

THE UNITED KINGDOM PROPOSALS

In November 1989, the UK (H. M. Treasury, 1989) presented a proposal on how to proceed with monetary integration in Europe. Instead of the institutional approach of the Delors Report, involving a single monetary policy and a single currency, the paper advocated an "evolutionary approach," which would be built on the twin pillars of the creation of the single market and the fuller development of the EMS. National monetary policies would be maintained within the context of a strengthening ERM, and national currencies would compete to provide the noninflationary anchor in the EMS. This approach would center on national monetary authorities and, thus, minimize problems of political accountability. In this way, a multicurrency system would be achieved with increasingly interchangeable currencies constituting a "practical monetary union."

The British proposal found a reception in which widespread interest was mixed with pronounced criticism. A true monetary union, it was argued, was characterized by irrevocably fixed exchange rates, and only a common monetary policy could lead to monetary union. The coexistence of free capital movements with greater competition of currencies would increase rather than decrease instability in the EMS. Also, one could not expect from the continued existence of national currencies the same benefits for the functioning of the single market as from a single currency.

It was rather curious that the British authorities, with their emphasis on national sovereignty, would present a concept under which one national currency (which most probably would not be the pound) would become the standard for the EC as a whole. Also, the concept was based on the ERM, in which the UK did not even participate at the time.[6]

It was, therefore, not surprising that the UK followed soon with a new plan, presented by then-Chancellor of the Exchequer John Major (Major, 1990; see also Grice, 1990). He criticized as "Big-Bangism" the approach of the Delors Report and proposed the creation of a new "hard ECU," which would be issued by a European Monetary Fund (EMF). The hard ECU would become a genuine currency in its own right — the thirteenth EC currency, as it were — and be a participant in the narrow band of the ERM. It would never devalue against other EC currencies. ECU-denominated deposits and notes would be issued, on demand, in exchange for national currencies. In this way, the hard ECU would not add to inflationary pressure in the EC, because an increase in ECUs would be matched by a reduction in national currency. There would be a repurchase requirement for national currencies from the EMF against hard ECU or some other strong currency if preset limits on the amounts of currency holdings by the EMF were exceeded. "In time the ECU would be more widely used: it would become a common currency for Europe. In the very long term, if peoples and governments so choose, it could develop into a single currency" (Major, 1990).

The new proposal did not fare much better than the first one and, as the *Financial Times* of June 22 put it, "drew a lukewarm to hostile response from the UK's European partners and the City of London." Main criticisms were that the institutional features of the EMF and its relation to other institutions remained undefined and that the plan did not provide any guidance on when the conditions were right for moving to the final stage of EMU. Behind all this was a widespread suspicion that the main intention behind the UK proposals was to derail the efforts toward the creation of a single currency.

In general, there was not much sympathy for the idea of a parallel currency. The Delors Committee in its report had two main arguments (Para. 47): "An additional source of money creation without a precise linkage to economic activity could jeopardize price stability . . . [and] the addition of a new currency . . . would further complicate the already difficult endeavour of coordinating different national monetary policies." Although the UK proposal addressed the first concern, it did not address the second.[7]

The Delors Report turned out to be a very influential document and the trailblazer for important provisions of the Maastricht Treaty for the creation of EMU. The authors were politically prominent and technically highly competent, independence-minded people. On the other hand, the recommendations of the report, in particular on the status and responsibilities of the future ESCB and on the need to support a single monetary policy by effectively coordinated budgetary policies, while respecting national sovereignty as far as possible, were in harmony with what over the years has become the common wisdom among policymakers and scholars alike.

NOTES

Literature of general interest for this chapter: Hasse et al. (1990); Louis (1989); Rieke (1990); Thygesen (1989).

1.   For the committee members, see Delors Committee (1989, p. 235). References to the report are to the numbered paragraphs.
2.   This would have meant that not only central bankers but also government representatives would have participated.
3.   This summary is in part based on Ungerer (1990, pp. 351–53).
4.   The German Ministry of Economics (Bundesminister für Wirtschaft, 1989, Para. 5) put it this way: "In moving toward EMU, a far-reaching parallelism between measures of economic and monetary policy without rigid rules is required. . . . This does not imply absolute parallelism at any point in time. . . . Such a principle of a 'competition between forward-thrusting and consecutive moves' which avoids a rigid ranking of decisions on the path to EMU is an essential element of a dynamic integration process" (my translation).
5.   Lawson (1989, pp. 14, 18). On the same occasion, in response to a question why, at the Hanover conference in June 1988, the UK government went along with the progressive realization of EMU, Lawson replied: "I suppose it was felt at the time that the terms of economic and monetary union were rather vague. . . . I assume we went along with it because it was felt that what was meant was closer co-operation on both the economic and monetary fronts and that is something we are certainly in favour of" (p. 5).
6.   Charles Goodhart (1990) commented that the plan rested on a very favorable interpretation of the ERM, "which is, to say the least, odd coming from the UK."
7.   For a general discussion of the parallel currency approach, see Pöhl (1989). For a critique of the hard ECU plan, see Hasse and Koch (1991).

18

Stage One of Economic and Monetary Union and Preparations for the Intergovernmental Conference on Economic and Monetary Union

In addition to accepting the Delors Report as a basis for further work on economic and monetary union (EMU), the European Council at its meeting in Madrid in June 1989 decided that stage one of the realization of EMU would begin on July 1, 1990. The European Council asked the Council of Ministers, the Committee of Central Bank Governors, and the Monetary Committee "to adopt the necessary provisions for the launch of the first stage . . . , [and] to carry out preparatory work for the organization of an Intergovernmental Conference [IGC] to lay down the subsequent stages" (*Bulletin*, 1989, No. 6, p. 11).

The Madrid meeting was followed by a string of meetings. The next meeting of the European Council took place in Strasbourg on December 8 and 9, 1989. At the end of the meeting, the president of the European Council "noted that the necessary majority existed for convening [the IGC] . . . before the end of 1990" (*Bulletin*, 1989, No. 12, p. 11). Prime Minister Margaret Thatcher had not agreed.

The finance ministers and central bank governors met in Ashford Castle (Ireland) on March 31 and April 1, 1990, and concluded that there was "a need for a single monetary policy geared to price stability." Broad agreement was reached on "an independent and federally structured central banking institution that was democratically accountable" and on "close cooperation on macroeconomic and budgetary policies (including rules proscribing the monetary or compulsory financing of budget deficits and the automatic bailing-out by the Community of any Member State in difficulties)" (*Bulletin*, 1990, No. 4, p. 14). Meeting in Dublin on

April 28, 1990, the European Council stated that the IGC would open in December 1990 and should "conclude its work rapidly with the objective of ratification [of the new treaty] by member states before the end of 1992" (*Bulletin*, 1990, No. 4, p. 10).

An important item on the agenda of the meeting was the progress toward German unification and the integration of East Germany into the European Community (EC). In this context, President François Mitterand and Chancellor Helmut Kohl proposed the formation of political union with the aim of anchoring a united Germany firmly in the EC and to provide a political basis and complement to EMU. At its next meeting on June 25 and 26, again in Dublin, the European Council agreed to convene a separate IGC on political union, with its own agenda. Both conferences were to open in mid-December in Rome.

STAGE ONE OF ECONOMIC AND MONETARY UNION

The main aims for stage one were the completion of the single market, including the removal of all obstacles to financial integration, and greater convergence of economic performance. It was, therefore, deliberate that the start of stage one was set on the date by which capital movements were to be fully liberalized for most EC countries.

In discussing the first stage, the Deutsche Bundesbank (1990a) noted that the stability cohesion between some EC countries was tending to decrease again. Although convergence had made headway, particularly in those countries that had opted for the discipline imposed by the exchange rate mechanism (ERM), inflation rates and fiscal deficits were rising, especially in countries with the largest need for correction. Also, in other areas, imbalances persisted or new ones emerged. This applied to external imbalances that were substantial in a number of countries and whose reduction might be additionally impeded "if the persistent divergences in price performance are not offset by a realignment of nominal exchange rates" (p. 30).

Furthermore, the Bundesbank drew attention to what it called an "unnatural" situation. Some ERM countries with high budget deficits and inflation rates required particularly high interest rates to attract capital. However, because of their ERM participation, markets did not perceive the interest rate advantage to be accompanied by any medium-term devaluation risk. This triggered a persistent real appreciation[1] of the currencies concerned, which counteracted the desirable decline in the trade and current account deficits.

The circumstances described by the Bundesbank applied in particular to the Spanish peseta, which, soon after joining the ERM in June 1989, had moved to the upper limit of its fluctuation band of ±6 percent. Later on, the peseta weakened within the ERM and eventually had to be devalued three times during the EMS crises of 1992–93, after the notion of the European Monetary System as a de facto monetary union proved illusory.

Concerning the legal framework for stage one, the Council of Ministers on March 12, 1990, adopted two important decisions (*Official Journal of the European Communities*, March 24, 1990, No. L 78, pp. 23–26). The amendment of the February 1974 decision on economic convergence required the Council to undertake multilateral surveillance geared to compatible policies based on the principles of price stability, sound public finances and monetary conditions, sound balances of payments, and open, competitive markets. Budgetary policies would be reviewed "possibly ahead of national budgetary planning" with particular focus on the size and financing of budget deficits and the medium-term orientation of budgetary policy, so as to reduce excessively high deficits and avoid monetary financing.

The second decision amended the 1964 decision that had set up the Committee of Central Bank Governors. The Committee was to promote monetary policy coordination with the aim of achieving price stability as a necessary condition for the proper functioning of the European Monetary System and the realization of monetary stability; to formulate opinions on the orientation of monetary and exchange rate policy; and to express opinions on policies to individual governments and the Council of Ministers. The Committee was to prepare annual reports to the European Parliament, the Council of Ministers, and the European Council, and its president might be invited to appear before the European Parliament.

The Committee itself reorganized its structure and working procedures in June 1990. It extended the duration of the chairmanship from one to three years. President Karl Otto Pöhl was elected chairman with the extended term of office. A Committee of Alternates was established, with Jean-Jacques Rey from the Banque Nationale de Belgique as chairman. Three subcommittees, for monetary policy, for foreign exchange policy, and for banking supervision, were set up, and an economic unit was added to the secretariat of the Committee.

DRAFT STATUTE FOR THE EUROPEAN SYSTEM OF CENTRAL BANKS AND EUROPEAN CENTRAL BANK

The Committee of Governors of the Central Banks did not lose any time and went to work on a statute for the European System of Central Banks (ESCB) and the European Central Bank (ECB). The Committee (1990) submitted a draft to EC finance ministers on November 27, 1990, accompanied by an introductory report and a commentary. The governor of the Bank of England recorded that the United Kingdom (UK) authorities did not accept the case for a single currency and monetary policy but had participated fully in the deliberations of the Committee.

The draft encompassed a detailed and comprehensive set of institutional and organizational provisions. However, it did not deal with transitional arrangements, and a number of questions remained under consideration. The statute reaffirmed that the ESCB should consist of a new central institution — the ECB, endowed with legal personality — and the national central banks. The report pointed out that this structure met several requirements. It respected the federative structure of the EC, allowed monetary policy decisions to be placed firmly in the hands of the central decision-making bodies, and offered the possibility of operating through both the ECB and the national central banks.

The primary objective of the ESCB was to maintain price stability, although this did not mean that monetary policy would be carried out in isolation and without due regard to other economic policy objectives.[2] The single most important characteristic of monetary policy was that it was indivisible and that responsibility for monetary policy could not be shared among autonomously acting bodies.[3] The council of the ECB, consisting of the president, vice president, the other members of the executive board, and the governors of the national central banks, would be the supreme decision-making body. The daily management of monetary policy would be in the hands of the executive board. The ECB, the national central banks, and their decision-making bodies should act independently of instructions from political authorities. The Committee stressed that the favorable experience with independent monetary authorities made by a number of countries was particularly relevant for a plural EC "where competing interests may tend to give greater thought to short-term considerations and thus lead to pressure in favour of a monetary policy stance which would not always be compatible with price stability in the longer run" (Committee of Central Bank Governors, 1990, Introductory Report, section "The Basic Principles," subsection d).

An important question for the Committee was whether voting in the council should be weighted according to the relative economic size of EC countries or whether the rule "one member, one vote" should apply. The report mentioned that the decision in favor of the principle of one vote per member (except in some internal financial matters) was conditioned by the need to direct monetary policy decisions to the requirements of the EC as a whole rather than to regional considerations.

The most important unresolved issue concerned the responsibility for the exchange rate policy of the EC. There was a consensus that the responsibility for decisions concerning the exchange rate *regime* rested with the political authorities, while the ECB would have the task of conducting foreign exchange *operations*. However, what about the responsibility for exchange rate and intervention *policy* vis-à-vis third countries in the absence of an international exchange rate system?

Exchange rate policy is a powerful policy instrument that exerts great influence on trade, international investment, and domestic growth and employment. Yet, monetary policy cannot be divided into domestic and external components, and exchange rate policy can undermine monetary policy and severely impair the ability of the ECB to attain its primary objective of price stability. According to the report, a majority on the Committee were of the view that decisions on exchange rate policy should be made in the same way as decisions on the adoption, abandonment, and changes in central rates vis-à-vis third currencies (i.e., they should rest with the political authorities, subject only to a *consensus* consistent with the objective of price stability). Significantly, in this first draft, the subject was dealt with under the heading of "advisory functions." Some Committee members were, however, of the view that such decisions should be subject to the *consent* of the ECB.

One commentator (Lomax, 1991, p. 2) called the provisions of the draft on exchange rate policy and their purely advisory nature "a devastating attack on the independence of the Central Bank." In his view, shared by many others (e.g., Begg et al., p. 14), it was not possible for a central bank to do two things at the same time. It might have either an internal policy objective, of combating inflation, or an external policy objective, such as maintaining a particular exchange rate level or a particular exchange rate policy.

In a later draft of the Committee, the provisions for exchange rate policy were modified so as to give the ECB a stronger say. However, the issue remained controversial throughout the negotiations of the IGC and was resolved only very late (see Chapter 19). With the draft statute, the Governors influenced greatly the thinking about the structure and tasks of the ESCB and the ECB, providing an important follow-up to the Delors Report and, in a way, writing their own brief. Their draft became the basis for the relevant provisions of the Maastricht Treaty.

EXCHANGE RATE POLICY AND THE COORDINATION OF BUDGETARY POLICIES

Other EC institutions participated in the preparatory work for the IGC and made important conceptual contributions.

Report of the Monetary Committee

The Monetary Committee (1990) covered in part the same ground as the Committee of Central Bank Governors in its work on the statute and arrived at the same conclusions regarding the objectives of monetary policy and the status and tasks of ESCB and ECB. On exchange rate policy, there was a similar split of opinions as in the Governors' Committee.

Some members considered that "all decisions on intervention should be assigned to the [ECB]" because this was "a necessary condition for the conduct . . . of a stability-oriented monetary policy." Others emphasized that exchange rates and intervention "have implications for general economic policy, as well as for the . . . balance of payments, responsibility for which falls on the political authorities." Moreover, the EC's exchange rate policy would have consequences for other countries and could not be separated from broader political issues. Therefore, the main decisions on intervention should rest with the political authority.

On the issue of national budgetary policies, the Monetary Committee took the same hard line as the Delors Committee. Monetary and compulsory financing of public deficits should be excluded, there should be no bailout of individual member countries, and excessive deficits must be corrected. Markets would exert a certain disciplinary force on governments pursuing unsound budgetary policies, but they could not be relied upon by themselves to induce corrections in due time. Although it was not possible to lay down an upper limit for acceptable deficits (e.g., in terms of gross domestic product) that would be universally valid, objective criteria would have to be developed, such as levels of public debt, the sustainability of deficits, inflation performance, and the functions attributed to the public sector. Another criterion could be whether a deficit exceeded public investment expenditure (the so-called golden rule of public finance). The Council of Ministers should be in a position to press for compliance and to enforce any legally binding positions it might take by sanctions. Furthermore, it should be considered whether the Council should define an appropriate budgetary stance for the EC as a whole.

Reports of the Commission

The Commission issued in March and August 1990 papers that presented its views on the benefits and costs of EMU, on different conceptions of EMU, and on the main points to be covered by the new treaty (Commission, 1990a, 1990b).[4] We shall return to the question of benefits and costs of EMU in Chapter 21. Here, we concentrate on the Commission's main points on the coordination of budgetary policies and exchange rate policy.

With regard to the coordination of economic and, in particular, budgetary policies, the Commission argued that, even if potential tensions could be controlled by market forces, the lack of an economic policy complement to monetary union could lead to an excessive burdening of monetary policy. However, the centralization of economic policy through a new EC institution did not reflect the political preferences of the EC and would be at odds with the principle of subsidiarity, because it did not take sufficient account of the diversity of member states. Concerning constraints on national budget deficits and public debt, the Commission expressed the opinion that even specific binding rules to constrain national budget deficits and public debt were difficult to justify, because they might not be equally applicable to the circumstances of all member states. Instead, the Commission favored binding *procedures*, under which member states would have rules or guidelines incorporated into national law. The adequacy of such rules, adapted to national structures, should be discussed and agreed at the EC level. For monitoring, adjustment, and enforcement, there should be peer group pressure and, in the event of noncompliance, instruments of graduated EC response.

In the later paper, the Commission held that the judgment of whether a deficit was excessive should be related to the sustainability of the fiscal position, which could not be evaluated in isolation from an overall assessment of the economic situation. With regard to the kind of objective criteria that could be used, the Commission somewhat changed its position. Despite shortcomings, the "golden rule" of public finance appeared most satisfactory from an analytical point of view. Other objective criteria, such as the deficit and debt to gross domestic product ratios, might be helpful.

On exchange rate policy, the Commission attempted to satisfy both sides in the dispute. It argued that exchange rate policy had a double aspect, monetary (in a narrow sense) and economic. This required the participation of two actors, the monetary authority and the body responsible for economic policy. Exchange rate policy should be defined in a framework of close cooperation but should not be in contradiction with the principle of monetary policy, that is, price stability. However, the Commission's formula left open the questions of how such cooperation should be organized and who would have the final say — the key question when it comes to safeguarding a monetary policy directed at stability.

The Commission proposed January 1, 1993, as the date for the start of the second stage. The transition to the third stage should be short, and the second stage should be a phase of intensive preparation.

THE RATIONALE FOR STAGE TWO

The Delors Committee had given short shrift to the content of the second stage and the issues of transition to the third and final stage and had considered it impossible to propose a detailed blueprint for the transition. The Committee of Central Bank Governors also excluded the issues of transitional arrangements from its conclusions on the statute.

A number of commentators, in particular those in favor of a speedy realization of EMU, questioned the need for a second stage or argued for a relatively short duration. In a way, they were not wrong, because, in certain respects, stage two was to be a continuation of the first stage with emphasis on progress in policy coordination and economic convergence, although the ultimate responsibility for monetary policy would remain with national authorities. However, the position of the Delors Committee had been somewhat ambiguous when it recommended that the ESCB should be set up during the second stage and that its monetary policy functions would gradually evolve as experience was gained. Also, the Committee thought that, in the second stage, general monetary orientations for the EC as a whole should be set and a certain amount of reserves could be pooled and used to conduct exchange market interventions — ideas that were difficult to reconcile with the principle of the indivisibility of monetary policy.

It was this recommendation of setting up the ESCB during the second stage that provided the advocates of a short second stage with the argument that the ESCB should not remain an empty shell and that it was, therefore, preferable to move speedily to the final stage. Of course, the obvious answer would have been to wait with the establishment of the ESCB until a common monetary policy was required, that is, until the third stage. In hindsight, it became evident that a relatively short duration of the second stage — say, two years — would not have been enough to solve the complex problems of preparing for the final stage, which will be discussed in Chapter 23.

AN AGENDA FOR THE INTERGOVERNMENTAL CONFERENCE

The Bundesbank Statement of September 1990

On September 19, 1990, the Deutsche Bundesbank published a statement (1990b) in which it reiterated its views with regard to the realization of EMU. It stressed that, in the final analysis, a monetary union was "eine nicht mehr kündbare Solidargemeinschaft," an irrevocable community bound together in solidarity.[5] If it was to prove durable, it required, judging from past experience, even closer links in the form of a comprehensive political union. Economic and economic policy trends still were marked by great differences among member states. These divergences were particularly pronounced in the case of the non-ERM countries — the UK, Portugal, and Greece — but also in the case of Italy and Spain. An early irrevocable fixing of exchange rates would involve considerable risks to monetary stability. Therefore, a contractual safeguarding of a number of points was indispensable to the design of the final stage, among them an efficient, market-oriented competitive system and budgetary policies geared to a lasting anti-inflationary stance.

With regard to the ESCB, the statement restated the well-known demands for price stability as the primary objective of monetary policy, the independence of the ESCB, and a federal structure of the ESCB. The indivisibility of monetary policy required that national central banks should, to a large extent, become integral parts of the ESCB and, thus, no longer be able to pursue policies of their own; they should be granted beforehand the same degree of independence as the ESCB. The ESCB should be given sole responsibility for exchange market intervention. It should be involved in all other decisions on external monetary policy on the basis of "coresponsibility," especially in the case of exchange rate policy decisions. The Bundesbank also suggested that the statute of the ESCB and the rules on budgetary policy should be laid down in the treaty.

Regarding the transitional period, inflation should very largely be eliminated, budget deficits should be reduced to a sustainable level, and the durability of convergence should be reflected in the judgment of the markets by a far-reaching approximation of capital market interest rates. A particularly important point was "that the transition to another stage (no matter whether a transitional stage or the final one) must be made dependent solely on the fulfillment of previously defined economic and economic policy conditions, rather than on any particular timetable" (Deutsche Bundesbank, 1990b, p. 44).

The European Council Meetings of October and December 1990

At a meeting of the EC finance ministers and central bank governors on September 8 and 9, 1990, in Rome, the Commission proposal to start with stage two in January 1993 was supported by Belgium, Denmark, France, and Italy; Germany, Luxembourg, the Netherlands, Greece, Ireland, Portugal, and Spain favored a more measured pace.

At the special European Council meeting of October 27 and 28 in Rome, the EC countries (with the exception of the UK) agreed on January 1, 1994, as the start of the second stage. This was made contingent on the following (*Bulletin*, 1990, No. 10, pp. 7–13):

the single market had been achieved;

the Treaty had been ratified, and by its provisions, a process had been set in train to ensure the independence of the members of a new monetary institution, and the monetary financing of budget deficits had been prohibited and any bailout had been precluded;

the greatest possible number of countries had adhered to the ERM;

further satisfactory and lasting progress toward real and monetary convergence had been achieved, especially as regards price stability and the restoration of sound public finances.

A new monetary institution, comprising national central banks and a central organ, would be established at the start of the second stage.

The nature of that institution was not spelled out, and the fact that the conclusions of the presidency referred ambiguously at various places to *a* as well as *the* new institution led later to differing interpretations.[6]

The UK was unable to accept this approach to the second stage. It felt that decisions on the substance of the move to stage two should precede decisions on its timing.

The European Council met again in Rome on December 14 and 15, 1990, and the IGCs on EMU and political union opened on December 15. The European Council confirmed "that the work of the two Conferences will proceed in parallel and should be concluded rapidly and at the same time. The results will be submitted for ratification simultaneously with the objective of ratification before the end of 1992." The path toward Maastricht had been entered upon.

NOTES

Literature of general interest for this chapter: Schönfelder and Thiel (1994; available only in German).

1. The English language version of the report (p. 30) erroneously refers to "*de*preciation" instead of "*ap*preciation" (compare p. 31 of the report in the original German).

2. In an interim report on the work of the committee at a meeting of EC finance ministers on September 8, 1990, the chairman of the committee emphasized that, in the event of a conflict between price stability and other economic objectives, the governing bodies of the ESCB would have no choice but to give priority to its primary objective.

3. What is meant by "indivisibility of monetary policy"? It refers to the fact that, in a unified currency area, monetary conditions are essentially the same and monetary policy decisions have virtually the same impact throughout the area. Therefore, the consequences of discriminatory monetary policy decisions, whether made by central or other authorities (e.g., preferential credit conditions for certain regions or economic sectors) will rapidly and evenly spread throughout the area and may counteract the single policy.

4. In these and in other documents, the Commission used consistently the term "EuroFed" when referring to the ESCB. This term was favored by President Jacques Delors but, for obvious reasons, was less appreciated by European central bankers. Later on, only "ESCB" was used.

5. The translation of the statement as issued in September used for "nicht mehr kündbare Solidargemeinschaft" the phrase "an irrevocable sworn confraternity — 'all for one and one for all'" — more of an explanation than a translation. The October Monthly Report used, instead, "an irrevocable joint and several community."

6. Wilhelm Schönfelder and Elke Thiel (1994, p. 107) report that this lack of precision was deliberate.

19

Proposals for a Treaty on Economic and Monetary Union and the Negotiations of the Intergovernmental Conference

Already, before the Intergovernmental Conference (IGC) on economic and monetary union (EMU) convened in mid-December 1990, the European Community (EC) Commission presented on December 10 its proposals for amendments to the European Economic Community (EEC) Treaty (*Bulletin*, 1991, Suppl. No. 2). The French government submitted a complete set of amendments on January 26, 1991,[1] and the German government followed suit on February 26.[2] The proposals of the Commission and Germany were drafted as changes and amendments to the existing text of the EEC Treaty. The French proposal was a set of sequentially numbered articles to be incorporated in the EEC Treaty at the appropriate places. In early January, the United Kingdom (UK) submitted a document that put its proposals of June 1990 for a "hard ECU" and a European Monetary Fund (EMF) in legal language (H. M. Treasury, 1991). On January 24, the Spanish government presented a paper limited to issues of the ECU and the second stage as an addition to the Commission and British proposals (Spain 1991). The other countries did not table any comprehensive proposals but, in the course of the IGC, presented drafts for individual articles.

The following sections summarize and compare the proposed amendments with regard to the main issues. References to the articles of the respective amendment proposals are provided in parentheses.

MONETARY POLICY

European System of Central Banks and European Central Bank

The drafts of France, Germany, and the Commission contained detailed provisions for the creation of the European System of Central Banks (ESCB) (respectively, Art. 2-1 to 2-6; Art. 4a, 109a and b; Art. 4.2, 105–7). The ESCB was to consist of the European Central Bank (ECB) as a separate legal entity and the central banks of member states. There would be a council consisting of the central bank governors of the 12 member states and six members of the executive board, to be appointed by the European Council or the Council of Ministers for eight years (Commission, Art. 107.3; draft statute for ESCB and ECB of the Committee of Central Bank Governors, Art. 11.3) or five years (France, Art. 2-5). The statute of the ESCB and the ECB would be attached to the treaty as a protocol. Although the French and the Commission proposals provided for later modifications of some of the articles of the statute by the Council of Ministers, the German draft did not contain such a provision.

According to all three drafts, the ECB was to have price stability as its primary objective and would be independent of instructions from national and EC authorities. Implicitly, the term "independence" seemed to have been interpreted somewhat differently. Of particular interest in this connection were the French ideas of an "economic government," discussed below, which subordinated the ECB to a certain degree to policy guidelines by the European Council and the Council of Ministers and the proposals on exchange rate policy.

Single Currency and "Hard ECU"

All but the UK amendments were broadly in line with the recommendations of the Delors Committee. Accordingly, in the third stage, there would be a single monetary policy and a single currency. The UK envisaged, as in its proposal of June 1990, the creation of the hard ECU as a currency in its own right, to be issued by the EMF. In contrast to the single currency, the hard ECU already would be launched in the second stage, and there would be no explicit final stage. At the end of an evolutionary process, it could become the single currency.

The EMF would be organized along similar lines as the ECB, with a governing board, consisting of the central bank governors of member states and six members of an executive board, to be appointed for eight years. The overriding objective of the EMF would be price stability. The functions of the EMF, however, would be limited to the issue and management of the hard ECU, but the Council of Ministers could entrust the

EMF with additional tasks. With respect to independence, the British draft offered two alternatives: the first stipulated independence of any instructions; the other stated that the provisions of the treaty would be without prejudice to the existing relationships between national central banks and the governments of member states.

The Spanish proposal envisaged for the second stage a hard ECU not as a separate currency, issued in parallel to existing EC currencies, but as a "hard-basket" ECU. At each realignment, the currency components of the ECU would be adjusted so as to preserve the central rates between the ECU and nondevaluing currencies. Thus, the ECU's performance would always match but never outperform that of the best performing EC currencies. The ECB would issue ECU notes and coins but only in exchange for national currencies: it would act as a "currency board" or "substitution account," and no additional liquidity would be created. The ECU would be legal tender in the countries that so decide. In the third stage, it would become the single currency.

France wanted the ECU to become a "strong and stable currency" and to develop its role and use during the transitional stage (Art. 5–6). Germany proposed that the ECU would not be devalued anymore on a central rate basis (Art. 8e.3). The Commission called for the "development" of the ECU during the second stage (Art. 109d.1).

Exchange Rate Policy

In the runup to the IGC, the Committee of Central Bank Governors and the Monetary Committee could not agree on who should be responsible for the various aspects of exchange rate policy. This debate was reflected in the proposed amendments. The drafts of the Commission (Art. 108) and France (Art. 3-1) proposed that the Council of Ministers, acting by qualified majority and after consulting the ECB, should lay down guidelines for exchange rate policy. Within these guidelines, the ECB would conduct interventions in third currencies and manage foreign exchange reserves.

Germany took a different approach (Art. 109c). The Council of Ministers would decide unanimously on the exchange rate regime and, within such a regime, on the central rates vis-à-vis third currencies, after having consulted the ECB, aiming at a consensus consistent with price stability. The ECB would be authorized to conduct exchange market interventions while safeguarding its primary task.

ECONOMIC POLICIES

Budgetary Policies

Before the start of the IGC, a clear consensus had emerged that there should be no monetary financing of budget deficits, only limited recourse to borrowing in non-EC currencies, and neither the EC nor the member states would be liable for the debts of individual member states ("no bailout" rule). The draft amendments of France, Germany, and the Commission contained provisions to this effect.

However, there were different views on whether (and, if so, how) upper limits on budget deficits of individual member states should be imposed. The draft amendments of France, Germany, and the Commission reflected these different viewpoints only to a limited degree. High deficit countries such as Italy, Spain, and Greece, who were more apprehensive about strict budgetary rules, had not submitted formal proposals. The British opposition was based on concerns that such rules would lead to infringements on national sovereignty. The amendments of France, Germany, and the Commission stipulated that "excessive" deficits should be avoided. However, only Germany offered a definition of "excessive" (Art. 105b) and called for strict expenditure discipline and deficit limitation. The public sector deficit should not exceed investment expenditure ("golden rule"). There would be a "presumption" of an excessive deficit if the deficit–gross national product ratio (alternatively, the deficit–national savings ratio) exceeded yet unspecified magnitudes. In case of noncompliance, the Council of Ministers could set a binding upper limit for the deficit. Should this limit be breached, the Council could, by qualified majority, suspend certain EC payments or take other appropriate action. The French draft (Art. 1-4) contained also the possibility of sanctions, however, of a much less severe nature.

The French Proposal on Economic Government

In a communication of December 5, 1990, the French government argued for the establishment of a "gouvernement économique" (France, 1990). A parallelism should be ensured between the "pôle monétaire" and the "pôle économique" of EMU. The independence of the new monetary institution could be understood only in the interdependence with an "economic government" that had to be democratic and should engage directly the member states, which continued to implement economic policy.[3] France was not aiming at a new and separate institution in charge of economic policy but, rather, had in mind existing institutions representing member states, such as the Council of Ministers and the European Council. In a document dated January 29, 1991, the French ideas were made more explicit, and a reinforced Council of Ministers was identified as the center of the "economic government" (France, 1991b).

The French draft amendments assigned an important role to the European Council. The European Council would define the broad guidelines of EC economic policy. Within these guidelines, the Council of Ministers would coordinate the economic policies of member states. To member states that did not comply with the guidelines, the Council could direct recommendations, which could be made public (Art. 1-3). The guidelines would serve as a framework for the multilateral surveillance of national economic policies, and the Council of Ministers would decide on appropriate measures (Art. 1-5).

With the intention to establish a link between economic and monetary policy, the French draft, furthermore, envisaged that "on the basis of a report by the Council, the Commission and the ESCB, the European Council shall determine the broad guidelines for Economic and Monetary Union" (Art. 4-1). As mentioned earlier, the French text proposed that the Council of Ministers would lay down guidelines for exchange rate policy (Art. 3-1); it also proposed that the Council could submit motions on monetary policy for discussion by the ECB Council (Art. 4-3). The president of the Council of Ministers as well as a member of the Commission might attend meetings of the ECB Council, without the right to vote, and ask the ECB Council to postpone a decision for up to 15 days, similar to a provision in the law establishing the Deutsche Bundesbank (Art. 4-3).

Other Proposals on Economic Policy

The German amendments put significant emphasis on the general objectives and principles of economic policy such as a competition-based market economy with open domestic and external markets (Art. 102b.1), free consumer choice and free price formation (Art. 102b), and the freedom to negotiate collective wage agreements (Art. 102d). The establishment of a cartel office was proposed (Art. 90a). The Council of Ministers would adopt guidelines for the economic policies of the EC and the member states and carry out multilateral surveillance (Art. 105).

The Commission proposal quite naturally assigned a major initiating role to the Commission. The Commission would submit multiannual guidelines to the European Council, which would discuss them after consulting the European Parliament (Art. 102c.1). These guidelines would range from budget balances of member states, the control of production costs, and the level and promotion of saving and investment to EC policies on economic and social cohesion and structural policies in member states. The Council of Ministers, taking into account the deliberations of the European Council and the opinion of the European Parliament, would then adopt these guidelines by qualified majority (Art. 102c.2). Under similar procedures, the Council of Ministers also could adopt recommendations to individual member states (Art. 102d). The guidelines and recommendations would serve as a framework for multilateral surveillance (Art. 103.1).

In contrast to the French and German proposals, the Commission envisaged the granting of EC financial assistance to member states in difficulties or seriously threatened with difficulties, subject to certain conditions (Art. 104).

To sum up: The French proposals, with their emphasis on "economic government," envisaged economic policy to be defined and implemented by national governments and their representatives on various levels and made interdependent with the common monetary policy. The emphasis on the European Council and the Council of Ministers, at the cost of the Commission, gave the French proposals a pronounced flavor of intergovernmental cooperation, which was underlined by the lack of any proposal for an explicit role of the European Parliament. The Commission proposals involved more strongly the Commission as well as the European Parliament. The German texts concentrated on the Council of Ministers. That the European Parliament played hardly a role in the German proposals appears somewhat odd, considering that Germany was generally in favor of a greater role for the European Parliament in European integration.

ISSUES OF TRANSITION

Stage Two

At its meeting in October 1990, the European Council had agreed to move to stage two on January 1, 1994, subject to a number of preconditions mentioned in Chapter 18. This decision was reflected in the proposed amendments of France, Germany, and the Commission. France made no explicit reference to specific preconditions, although Germany (Art. 8d.2) and the Commission (Art. 109b and c) listed several of them.

Regarding the content of the second stage, the most important differences of opinion related to the nature of the new monetary institution to be established. In line with the Delors Report, France, the Commission, and Spain proposed to establish the ESCB and the ECB. Germany, supported by the Netherlands, wanted to set up a Council of Central Bank Governors. It would be responsible for promoting central bank cooperation and the coordination of monetary policies and would assist national central banks in developing the instruments needed for the future single monetary policy (Art. 8e.1 and 2). France and the Commission also envisaged for the ECB operational tasks, such as the holding and managing of foreign exchange reserves and interventions on the foreign exchange markets — a reactivation of ideas to set up a European Reserve Fund for the first stage, which France had proposed to the Delors Committee. The ECB would perform the tasks of the European Monetary Cooperation Fund and the Committee of Central Bank Governors and ensure the smooth operation of the European Monetary System (Art. 109.e and 5-5).

The French draft was the only one that advocated limiting the fluctuation of exchange rates within the ERM (Art. 5-2).

Move to the Final Stage

The Commission and the French drafts proposed that, within three years after the start of stage two, the European Council would establish — on the basis of reports from the Commission and the ECB and after consulting the European Parliament — that the conditions for moving to the third and final stage were met. Then, the Council of Ministers, acting by a qualified majority, representing at least 8 members out of 12, should immediately make the required decisions. The Council would adopt the fixed exchange rates between EC currencies and the measures necessary for introducing the ECU as the single currency (Art. 109f and g; 5-9, 5-10, and 5-11).

The German draft was somewhat more elaborate and stringent (Art. 8f). The European Council would, in particular, examine whether the preconditions for a move to the final stage had been met. Explicitly mentioned were the achievement of a high degree of price stability, the reduction of public sector deficits to levels that were sustainable and compatible with stability, and the durability of the achieved economic convergence as expressed in a significant approximation of long-term interest rates. (These ideas would later find their way into the convergence criteria of the Maastricht Treaty.) After the European Council had established that these conditions were met for the majority of member states, it would decide unanimously on the date for the move to the final stage and instruct the Council of Ministers and the Council of Central Bank Governors to adopt the necessary institutional and organizational measures for the final stage.

All three proposals contained provisions that would allow member states not yet ready for EMU to join at a later time (Art. 5-10 and 5-11.2; 8f.3; and 109g).

EVALUATION OF THE PROPOSALS

The main drafts of amendments to the EEC Treaty, submitted by France, Germany, and the Commission, were quite comprehensive. They showed a remarkable consensus on most of the important issues. This can be traced back, to a significant extent, to the intensive discussions that had taken place in the Delors Committee, in the Committee of Central Bank Governors, in the Monetary Committee, during the meetings of finance ministers and central bank governors, and at the meetings of the European Council.

A few but nevertheless crucial questions were controversial, and the lack of agreement in these areas was revealed in the draft amendments. To come to agreement on these issues required, in the course of the IGC, a willingness to compromise on the part of the major protagonists. Once France and Germany were able to agree, the other countries (but generally with the exception of the UK) felt able to join as long as their main aspirations and vital interests were respected.

The one issue — in essence, of a deeply political nature — that overshadowed the conference negotiations to the very end was whether and under what conditions the UK would agree to a comprehensive treaty even if it would continue to oppose the creation of the ECB and of a single currency. Earlier considerations in some quarters, if necessary, to move ahead without the UK and to aim at an agreement between the remaining 11 countries outside the formal framework of the EC, had been more or less discarded because of the possible adverse political consequences and the tremendous legal and institutional difficulties.

The building blocks for creating EMU were made available in numerous meetings and in documents of various institutions such as the Committee of Central Bank Governors, the Monetary Committee, and the Commission, as well as governments. It was now up to the IGC to put them together in technically coherent and politically acceptable treaty provisions.

THE INTERGOVERNMENTAL CONFERENCE NEGOTIATIONS

Early on, it became obvious that the two conferences would extend into the second half of 1991. As a consequence, the objective to have the treaty amendments ratified by the end of 1992 appeared increasingly unrealistic.

The meetings of the conference on EMU were chaired by the finance ministers of the countries that occupied the half-yearly rotating presidency of the EC.[4] These were, for the first half of 1991, Luxembourg and, for the second half, the Netherlands. The conference convened monthly at the level of ministers and, between those meetings, twice at the level of the personal representatives of the ministers, who were civil servants in the rank of state secretary, permanent secretary, and so on. Representatives of the central banks attended the meetings on EMU. There were provisions for the necessary coordination between the IGCs on EMU and political union.

The Luxembourg presidency successfully used the device of "nonpapers," that is, documents without formal status, organized by articles, to move the negotiations forward. The nonpapers contained the provisions on which an understanding had been reached, alternative proposals on unresolved questions, and compromise formulas by the presidency for further discussion.[5]

In June, agreement was reached on the procedures that would govern the move to the final stage. With regard to the request of the UK for an "opting-out" clause, a compromise formula, presented by the Dutch finance minister, was accepted. Accordingly, no member state should be obliged to join the final stage, no member state should prevent others from doing so, and no member state should be excluded from the final stage if it met the required conditions.

An important point in the negotiations was reached at a meeting of the finance ministers in Apeldoorn on September 21. A consensus emerged on some important issues, most significantly, on the nature of the new monetary institution and the basic characteristics of the convergence criteria that were to determine a country's qualification for entering the final stage. Following a Belgian proposal, it was agreed to establish a European Monetary Institute as a forerunner to the ESCB. The convergence criteria would refer to inflation performance, the size of budget deficits, the behavior of exchange rates, and the level of interest rates. It also was agreed that the criteria should not be applied mechanically but that sufficient room for a political evaluation should remain.

On October 28, 1991, the Netherlands presidency submitted a complete draft for a new treaty combining the already settled questions and the informal agreements of the Apeldoorn meeting with alternative proposals for the open questions as a basis for the final phase of the conference (Netherlands, 1991). In a last meeting on December 2 and 3 before the European Council conference on December 9 and 10 in Maastricht, the finance ministers succeeded in preparing a draft treaty for the final negotiations of the European Council. The unresolved issues were settled at the Maastricht conference: the precise definition of the convergence criteria, the provisions for external monetary policy, the opting-out clause for the UK, the exclusion of any veto over the realization of EMU, the voting modalities for the move to the final stage, and the timetable for the move to the final stage.

NOTES

1. France (1991), Projet de Traité sur l'Union Economique et Monétaire, reprinted in Revue Financière Internationale (1991, pp. 51–61).

2. Germany (1991), Proposal for an Amendment to the EEC Treaty with a View to Achieving Economic and Monetary Union, reprinted in Revue Financière

Internationale (1991, pp. 63–78). This translation of the German text is not very good. The German text was reprinted in Krägenau and Wetter (1993, pp. 331–34).

3.   The reference to "democratic" in this context presumably related to the role of national governments that emanate from democratic elections. The French proposals regarding the responsibility for economic policy did not contain any specific role for the European Parliament. Similarly, the UK saw democratic legitimacy to rest solely with national governments.

4.   This and the following paragraphs are, in part, based on Schönfelder and Thiel (1994, pp. 119–44); see also Kenen (1995, Chap. 2) and various *Bulletin*s for 1991.

5.   One such "nonpaper," dated May 10, 1991, was reprinted in Krägenau and Wetter (1993, pp. 218–22).

20

The Maastricht Treaty

After more than three years of discussions and negotiations, the European Community (EC) was ready to create an economic and monetary union (EMU) as a crowning achievement to the realization of a single market under the European Economic Community Treaty and the Single European Act. The European Council, at its conference on December 9 and 10, 1991, in the Dutch city of Maastricht, near the borders with Belgium and Germany, settled the last open issues. At the same time, agreement was reached on ways to strengthen political cooperation in a number of areas. The Treaty on European Union — commonly called the "Maastricht Treaty" — combined the amendments of the treaties establishing the three communities (European Economic Community, European Coal and Steel Community, and European Atomic Energy Community), the provisions on foreign and security policy, and justice and home affairs, as well as a number of protocols (Council of the European Communities, 1992). The treaty was signed on February 7, 1992.

In essence, the objective of the Maastricht Treaty in the economic and monetary field is to complete the "market integration," which had been accomplished over the past decades, with the creation of a single currency and to underpin it with "policy integration," comprising both a single monetary policy and strengthened cooperation on economic policies, in particular, budgetary policies. Full parallelism in monetary and economic policies was neither aimed at nor provided for — a reflection of concerns about national sovereignty and of respect for the principle of subsidiarity. Whereas it was recognized that monetary policy was indivisible, a highly centralized economic policy for the EC was not found necessary. The treaty assigns, therefore, economic policy responsibility primarily to member states. What degree of centralization is actually required to ensure the achievement of the objectives of the treaty has been and probably will remain a hotly debated issue.

The treaty provides for the establishment of the European System of Central Banks (ESCB), comprising the national central banks and the European Central Bank (ECB), to conduct the single monetary policy and issue the single currency, the ECU (in December 1995 renamed "euro"). There would be no central decision-making institution for economic policy, but a certain degree of EC control over the budgetary policies of member states was to be exercised. The start of the third and final stage of EMU would be subject to complicated procedures, and participation of member states in EMU would be decided on the basis of several conditions. Special provisions allow the United Kingdom (UK) and Denmark to delay joining EMU or to remain outside.

THE MAIN ISSUES

Instead of summarizing all aspects of the treaty, this chapter will concentrate on the following main issues of EMU:

independence of the ESCB and the ECB,

responsibility for exchange rate policy,

provisions for economic policy,

rules for the coordination of budgetary policies,

content and length of the second stage and start of the final stage,

convergence criteria, and

special provisions for the UK and Denmark.

THE INDEPENDENCE OF THE EUROPEAN SYSTEM OF CENTRAL BANKS AND THE EUROPEAN CENTRAL BANK AND THE OBJECTIVE OF PRICE STABILITY

Early during the EMU discussions, a consensus was established that the ESCB should be independent of any instructions and that price stability should be its primary objective. It was generally accepted that, in the longer run, price stability was the best basis for a policy to maintain economic and social stability and to foster growth and high employment and that no trade-off existed between inflation and employment. Indeed, experience and various studies suggested that an independent central bank provided better prospects for price stability without adverse consequences for growth and employment than central banks subject to political influence (Alesina, 1988; Neumann, 1991; De Long and Summers, 1992; Cukierman, 1992; International Monetary Fund, 1996, pp. 128–29).

There are several aspects to the independence of a central bank. Political or institutional independence should protect a central bank from political interference regarding the definition and implementation of monetary policy. Functional or instrumental independence would be assured by providing a central bank with all the monetary policy instruments necessary for carrying out its tasks. Personal independence relates to the terms of appointments of members of the decision-making bodies.

On some aspects of independence, different views had been presented, for example, with regard to the length of appointments (5 versus 8 years; note that members of the Federal Reserve Board are appointed for 14 years). Of great significance for functional independence were the differences with regard to the responsibility for exchange rate policy. Also, the French ideas about the relation between the ESCB and what was called "economic government" would have limited the political independence of the ESCB.[1]

In the Maastricht Treaty, legally, the independence of the ESCB was clearly established. Art. 107 states that "neither the ECB, nor a national central bank nor any member of their decision-making bodies shall seek or take instructions from Community institutions or bodies, from any government of a Member State or from any other body." Art. 108 obliges member states to grant independence to their central banks at the latest at the date of the establishment of the ESCB. An important aspect of functional independence is that the ECB and the national central banks are prohibited from granting any kind of credit to EC or national public institutions (Art. 104).

The ESCB shall be governed by the Governing Council and the Executive Board of the ECB (Art. 106). The Council shall comprise the governors of the national central banks and the members of the board, consisting of the president and vice-president and four other members. Each Council member has one vote, and the Council shall act normally by a simple majority (Protocol on the Statute of the ESCB and of the ECB, Art. 10). The members of the board shall be appointed by common accord of member governments. Their term of office shall be eight years and not renewable (Art. 109a; Statute Art. 11). The term of office of a governor of a national central bank shall be no less than five years (Statute Art. 14). The president of the Council of Ministers and a member of the Commission may participate, without the right to vote, in meetings of the Governing Council, and the president of the Council of Ministers may submit motions for consideration (Art. 109b.1). No agreement was reached on the seat of the ECB.

According to Art. 105, the primary objective of the ESCB shall be to maintain price stability. Without prejudice to the objective of price stability, the ESCB shall support the general economic policies in the EC (a formulation similar to the one in the 1957 law establishing the Deutsche Bundesbank, Para. 12). The tasks of the ESCB are defined in Art. 105 and 105a and in more detail in various articles of the statute.

It has been noted that the independence of ESCB and ECB will be greater than that of any national central bank, including the Bundesbank. However, Wilhelm Schönfelder and Elke Thiel (1994, p. 148) pointed out that some of the provisions of the treaty belonged in Germany to the "stabilitatspolitischen Selbstverständnis," that is, they were self-evident elements of a stability-oriented policy, something that was not necessarily the case in member states with only limited traditions of central bank independence.

EXCHANGE RATE POLICY

The somewhat tortured formulations governing the responsibility for exchange rate policy reflect the difficult negotiations in the Intergovernmental Conference. According to Art. 109, Para. 1, "the Council [of Ministers] may, acting unanimously on a recommendation from the ECB or from the Commission, and after consulting the ECB in an endeavour to reach a consensus consistent with the objective of price stability, after consulting the European Parliament, . . . conclude formal agreements on an exchange rate system for the ecu [euro] in relation to non-Community currencies." Following the same procedure but acting by a qualified majority, the Council may "adopt, adjust or abandon the central rates of the ecu within the exchange-rate system."

With regard to the "gray area" of exchange rate policy, that is, in the absence of an exchange rate system in relation to non-EC currencies, the Council may, according to Art. 109.2, "acting by a qualified majority either on a recommendation from the Commission and after consulting the ECB or on a recommendation from the ECB . . . formulate general orientations for exchange rate policy in relation to these currencies. These general orientations shall be without prejudice to the primary objective of the ESCB to maintain price stability."

Several elements of these provisions are of importance. First, the need for consistency with price stability is relevant for all aspects of exchange rate policy. Second, in the absence of an international exchange rate system, there may be *general orientations* for exchange rate policy, which would be nonbinding, instead of *guidelines*, which could be seen as more binding.[2] Third, because the ECB will be in charge of actual intervention policy, not to mention interest rate policy, which exerts strong influence on exchange rates, it will be up to the ECB to decide whether its interpretation of such orientations would be consistent with price stability and up to the Council to prove otherwise. The possibility of an agreement with third countries on target zones or rates was not explicitly included in the treaty; Art. 109.1 mentions only central rates. Because target zones or rates would provide less close links to third currencies than central rates, they would appear to belong to the gray area.

GUIDELINES FOR ECONOMIC POLICY

Art. 103, Para. 1 states: "Member states shall regard their economic policies as a matter of common concern and shall coordinate them within the Council." Para. 2 calls on the Council, acting by a qualified majority on a recommendation from the Commission, to formulate a draft for broad guidelines of economic policies of the member states and the EC and to report to the European Council. The European Council, in turn, shall "discuss a conclusion on the broad guidelines." On the basis of this conclusion, the Council shall, "acting by a qualified majority, adopt a recommendation setting out these broad guidelines" and inform the European Parliament.

The Council shall monitor economic developments as well as the consistency of economic policies with the guidelines. In case of inconsistency or if economic policies risked jeopardizing the proper functioning of EMU, the Council, acting by a qualified majority, may make recommendations to the member state concerned and make its recommendations public (Art. 103.3 and 4). The treaty contains no specific provisions for guidelines or orientations on monetary policy.

Art. 103a.2 provides for the possibility of EC financial assistance "where a Member State is in difficulties or is seriously threatened with severe difficulties caused by exceptional occurrences beyond its control." The Council must act unanimously or, in case of natural disasters, by qualified majority.

At the start of the third stage, an Economic and Financial Committee will replace the Monetary Committee. It will have similar tasks as the Monetary Committee (Art. 109c.2 and 3).

RULES FOR THE COORDINATION
OF BUDGETARY POLICIES

The treaty contains no automatically binding rules for national budgetary policies in the final stage. Instead, there are rules on the financing aspects of budgetary policies and procedures that aim at enforcing a responsible fiscal behavior of member states, that is, the avoidance and correction of "excessive" budget deficits.

Art. 104 prohibits any credit by the ECB or national central banks to the EC and national institutions or bodies, and Art. 104a prohibits privileged access by such entities to financial institutions. Art. 104b states that neither the EC nor a member state shall "be liable for or assume the commitments of central governments, regional, local or other public authorities, other bodies governed by public law, or public undertakings of any Member State" (no bailout rule).

Art. 104c.1 obliges member states to "avoid excessive government deficits," "government" being defined in the Protocol on the Excessive Deficit Procedure as "general government, that is central government, regional or local governments and social security funds." For determining whether an excessive deficit exists, two criteria will be applied (Art. 104c.2 and Protocol, Art. 1): the ratio of the planned or actual government deficit to gross domestic product exceeds 3 percent, unless "the ratio has declined substantially and continuously and reached a level that comes close to the reference value, or, alternatively, the excess over the reference value is only exceptional and temporary and the ratio remains close to the reference value;" and the ratio of government debt to gross domestic product exceeds 60 percent, "unless the ratio is sufficiently diminishing and approaching the reference value at a satisfactory pace."

Following a rather elaborate procedure, involving the Commission and the Economic and Financial Committee, the Council of Ministers shall decide whether an excessive deficit exists (Art. 104c.3–11). The Council then shall make recommendations to the member state concerned with a view to rectifying the situation; it may make its recommendations public. The next step is that the Council may give notice to the member state to take the necessary measures within a specified time limit.

If a member state fails to comply, the Council may decide on the following sanctions:

to require the member state to publish additional information before issuing long-term bonds and securities;

to "invite" the European Investment Bank (whose Board of Governors consists of ministers of member states) to reconsider its lending policy toward the member state concerned;

to require the member state concerned to make a noninterest-bearing deposit of an appropriate size with the EC until the excessive deficit has been corrected; or

to impose fines of an appropriate size.

The various decisions are to be made by qualified majority, as defined in Art. 104c.13.

The ban on central bank credit to the public sector, the privileged access and no bailout rules, as well as the excessive deficit procedure are to be applied already during the second stage, except that, in case of excessive deficits, Council action will be limited to making recommendations (Art. 109e.3).

It has been argued that the quantitative criteria, in particular, the debt criterion, did not make much economic sense. They were, indeed, not derived from strict economic analysis but were based on the average of member states. They disregard other important variables such as the national savings ratio and the relation of the government deficit to government investment expenditure ("golden rule"). It is, therefore, only logical that the criteria are not to apply in a mechanical way and that there is room for discretion (see also Schlesinger, 1996, p. 20). The golden rule and other relevant factors, including the medium-term economic and budgetary position of the Member State, are to be taken into account, and decisions by the Council shall be made after an overall assessment (Art. 104c.6). Although the criteria may serve as important points of departure for any judgment on the existence of excessive deficits, there has been widespread criticism and calls for a more effective control of the budgetary behavior of member states, for example, by a "stability pact" among those member states participating in EMU (which would include automatic sanctions, absent in the treaty provisions), as proposed by German Finance Minister Theo Waigel in November 1995 (see Chapter 23). There also have been suggestions to apply the deficit criterion to the "structural" deficit, not the actual deficit, that is, after adjustment for cyclical influences (see Chapter 24).

THE SECOND STAGE

The second stage was scheduled to (and did) begin on January 1, 1994. A number of preconditions for the start of the second stage are listed in Art. 109e. They include progress regarding economic convergence and the implementation of multiannual convergence programs. During the second stage, member states will endeavor to avoid excessive government deficits; any form of central bank credit to public institutions and privileged access to financial institutions will be prohibited; and member states shall start the process leading to independence of their central banks.

The most significant feature of the second stage is the establishment of the European Monetary Institute (EMI) (Art. 109f and Protocol on the Statute of the European Monetary Institute). The EMI is being directed by a Council consisting of a president (appointed by the European Council) and the central bank governors, one of whom serves as vice-president. The EMI took over the tasks of the European Monetary Cooperation Fund and the Committee of Central Bank Governors on January 1, 1994. It will go into liquidation upon the establishment of the ECB (Art. 109l).

The EMI is to strengthen cooperation between EC central banks and the coordination of monetary policies and to monitor the functioning of the European Monetary System. Its most important task is the preparation of the third stage, that is, to prepare the instruments and procedures for the single monetary policy, promote the harmonization of statistics in the monetary field, prepare the rules for operations of national central banks within the framework of the ESCB, promote the efficiency of cross-border payments, and supervise the technical preparation of banknotes. The EMI may formulate opinions or recommendations, without binding force, on monetary and exchange rate policies and may submit opinions or recommendations to governments and to the Council of Ministers. It may decide to publish its opinions and recommendations. The EMI may receive monetary reserves from the central banks and issue ECUs against such assets. It is entitled to hold and manage monetary reserves as an agent and at the request of national central banks, without interfering with the policies of national monetary authorities. There are no provisions for the EMI to intervene on exchange markets.

As noted earlier, it was only after some disagreement that the EC countries agreed on the establishment of the EMI. It was, in a number of ways, a wise decision. It avoided the ambiguities of having the ESCB and ECB in existence already at a time when the responsibility for monetary policy still rested with member states. Yet, the tighter institutional framework of the EMI — with a president from outside the central banks and its own staff — provided a good basis for carrying out the complex and time-consuming task of preparing the final stage of EMU.

THE START OF THE FINAL STAGE

The Delors Committee had not suggested any deadlines for the move from one stage to another. In later discussions, different preferences were expressed concerning the length of the second stage. Some countries wanted to move relatively quickly to the third and final stage in order to maintain the political momentum toward EMU and to reap the benefits of EMU: a single currency as a basis for the single market and a single monetary policy to allow all countries to share monetary decision making. Other countries emphasized the importance of achieving a high degree of economic convergence so as to provide EMU with a solid foundation and to avoid the risk of severe tensions that could endanger the EMU. This created a dilemma: Trying to get all or as many member states as possible on board would result, in all likelihood, in a drawn-out transitional period that could generate economic and political problems. However, a fast move to the final stage inevitably would leave some countries behind if convergence was to reach a level consistent with a monetary union, resulting in a multispeed process. Some countries, such as Spain and Italy, which initially had preferred a speedy transition but later feared being left behind, changed their position over time and argued for a longer transition.

The Maastricht Treaty tried to solve these problems by offering the possibility of an early date for the move to the final stage. It was to be decided not later than December 31, 1996, whether a majority of countries (not counting the UK and Denmark if they would activate their opting-out clauses) met the conditions for entering the final stage (Art. 109j.3). It was envisaged that EMU could have started as early as January 1, 1997. If, by the end of 1997, no date had been set for the beginning of the final stage, it was to start on January 1, 1999. (In December 1995, the European Council determined that January 1, 1999, would be the starting date for EMU.) The same procedures concerning the qualification of individual countries were to be used for both dates, but — very importantly — for the 1999 date, no majority of countries is required. The decision of which countries will form EMU is to be made before July 1, 1998 (Art. 109j.4).

The procedures for the selection of countries are laid down in Art. 109j. The Commission and the EMI shall report to the Council of Ministers on the progress that member states made in fulfilling their obligations regarding the achievement of EMU. These include the required changes in the statutes of national central banks to ensure their independence and, most importantly, the achievement of "a high degree of sustainable convergence," judged by reference to the various convergence criteria. The Council shall then, acting by qualified majority, assess for each member state whether it fulfills these conditions. After consultation of the European Parliament, the Council, meeting in the composition of Heads of State or Government (i.e., the European Council), shall confirm by qualified majority which member states fulfill the conditions.

Immediately after the decision on the beginning of the third stage, the president, the vice-president, and the other members of the Executive Board of the ECB shall be appointed. The ESCB and the ECB shall be established and shall prepare for their full operation (Art. 109l.1). At the beginning of the third stage, the Council, acting with the unanimity of the participating member states, on a proposal from the Commission and after consulting the ECB, shall adopt the conversion rates at which their currencies shall be irrevocably fixed and at which rate the ECU (now euro) shall be substituted for these currencies. This measure by itself shall not modify the external value of the ECU (Art. 109l.4), that is, the "new" euro shall have the same value as the "old" ECU at the moment of transition.

The agreement to advance to the final stage at the start of 1999, regardless of the number of qualifying countries, was reached in the final hours of the Maastricht meeting. It was proposed by France, reportedly on a suggestion by Italy (Kenen, 1995, p. 26). It was accepted in order to avoid a loss of momentum in case an earlier date could not be realized. Although enshrined in the treaty, it seems obvious (and has been widely accepted) that this deadline hardly can be observed if one of the key countries — France or Germany, not to mention both — would not qualify for the final stage. In Germany, this provision was strongly criticized, in particular by those who were skeptical about the merit of EMU in the first place, and it has been suggested that it was a concession on the part of Germany in order to gain the endorsement of German unification by other EC countries, notably France. Be that as it may, the fact remains that Germany perceived a strong economic and political interest in keeping the process toward EMU moving.

QUALIFICATION FOR ECONOMIC AND MONETARY UNION AND THE CONVERGENCE CRITERIA

According to Art. 109j.1 and the Protocol on the Convergence Criteria, whether individual member states have achieved "a high degree of sustainable convergence" is to be examined with reference to four criteria:

1. the average inflation rate over a period of one year before the examination not exceeding by more than 1.5 percentage points that of, at most, the three member states with the best inflation performance (this has been interpreted in different ways: as the average of those three countries and as the one country out of the three with the best performance as long as there were no distorting factors of a special or temporary nature);

2. the sustainability of the government financial position, that is, without an "excessive deficit" as determined by Art. 104c (see section on budgetary policies);

3. the observance of the "normal" fluctuation margins in the exchange rate mechanism for at least two years, without devaluing against the currency of any member state on its own initiative (the widening of the exchange rate mechanism fluctuation margins to ±15 percent in August 1993 has created a problem of interpretation in this respect); and

4. as a measure of the durability of convergence, the average nominal long-term interest rate of a member state, over a period of one year before the examination, not exceeding by more than two percentage points that of, at most, the three member states with the best inflation performance.

In addition to the four criteria, the reports of the Commission and the EMI shall, among other things, take account of "the situation and development of the balances of payments on current account and an examination of the development of unit labor costs and other price indices" (Art. 109j.1, second paragraph).

The situation of the countries that did not qualify will be reexamined at least every two years or at the request of a country concerned (Art. 109k.2). The Council in the composition of the Heads of State or Government shall decide by qualified majority which member states with a derogation (i.e., the countries that cannot or do not want to participate in EMU from the start) fulfill the necessary conditions. The voting rights of member states with a derogation shall be suspended for a number of Council decisions listed in Art. 109k.5, for example, with regard to the excessive deficit procedures, exchange rate policy, and the appointment of the members of the ECB Executive Board.

In order to provide a link between participants and nonparticipants in EMU, there will be a General Council of the ESCB as a third decision-making body of the ECB (Art. 109l.3, and Art. 45–47 of the Statute of ESCB and ECB). It shall consist of the president and vice-president of the ECB and the governors of the national central banks. The other members of the ECB Executive Board may participate, without the right to vote, in meetings of the General Council.

The convergence criteria faced immediate criticism. Some considered them too tough, while others saw them as too soft. It was, for instance, criticized that the inflation criterion was expressed in relative and not in absolute terms, but others defended them on the grounds that, for the cohesion of a newly established monetary union, it was inflation differentials that counted. (Undeniably, however, low initial rates will facilitate the achievement and maintenance of price stability, once EMU is established.) The discretionary nature of the assessment process was deplored as inviting a lax interpretation of the criteria, and a strict *and* narrow interpretation has been demanded. A contrasting view held that the criteria either did not make sense or were unnecessary because EMU would, over time, equalize inflation and interest rates (see, e.g., De Grauwe and Tullio, 1994, p. 196). The latter argument, however, begs the question: over what time and at what level.

SPECIAL PROVISIONS FOR THE
UNITED KINGDOM AND DENMARK

In Maastricht, it was decided that the UK would not be obliged or committed to move to the third stage without a separate decision to do so by its government and parliament. The UK shall notify the Council whether it intends to move to the third stage before the Council makes its assessment on which member states qualify for participation. The UK may change its notification at any time and shall have the right to move to the third stage provided it satisfies the necessary conditions (Protocol on Certain Provisions Relating to the United Kingdom). The UK obtained also an exemption from the agreement on social policy that aims at improving working conditions and the protection of workers (Protocol on Social Policy).

At a late stage of the negotiations, Denmark requested and was granted a similar exemption. It takes into account provisions of the Danish constitution that might imply a referendum prior to participation in the third stage (Protocol on Certain Provisions Relating to Denmark). The mentioned referendum should not be confused with the one regarding ratification of the Maastricht Treaty, which took place in June 1992.

As long as the two countries do not participate in EMU, their voting rights will be limited.

ECONOMIC AND SOCIAL COHESION

According to Art. 130a, "the Community shall develop and pursue its actions leading to the strengthening of its economic and social cohesion . . . [and] aim at reducing disparities between the levels of development of the various regions and the backwardness of the least favoured regions." In addition to the already existing structural funds, the European Investment Bank, and other financial instruments, Art. 103d envisaged the setting up of a "Cohesion Fund" before December 31, 1993, to help finance projects in the fields of environment and transport infrastructure.

THE RATIFICATION OF THE MAASTRICHT TREATY

Ratification of the treaty initially was targeted for the end of 1992 but was completed by all 12 member states only in October 1993, after a number of obstacles were cleared. First, Danish voters rejected the treaty with the slim majority of 50.7 percent in a referendum on June 2, 1992. Only after a number of concessions on the part of Denmark's partners did the Danish electorate approve the treaty in a second referendum on May 18, 1993, with a majority of 56.8 percent.[3] In France, where a referendum was not constitutionally required but was called by President François Mitterand, the treaty was narrowly passed on September 20, 1992, with 50.95 percent. The British House of Commons agonized over ratification for a long time in a process that was tied as much to domestic and intraparty difficulties as to the merits of the treaty itself but approved the treaty on August 2, 1993. In Germany, the parliament (Bundestag) overwhelmingly approved the treaty in December 1992. However, in a resolution, Bundestag and Bundesrat (the upper house representing the German Länder [states]) made a positive vote of the government on the start of EMU subject to the evaluation and consenting vote by the Bundestag and called for a "narrow and strict" interpretation of the convergence criteria. A complaint about the constitutionality of the treaty was lodged with the Federal Constitutional Court but rejected on October 12, 1993.[4] The ratification process was completed the same day, making Germany the last country to ratify the treaty. The treaty finally entered into force on November 1, 1993.[5]

Perhaps the most remarkable feature of the economic and monetary policy provisions of the Maastricht Treaty is how closely they were modeled on the conceptions of the more conservative EC countries, in particular, Germany. This reflects, notwithstanding the initially significant differences of view on a number of issues, the common judgment that an EMU needed to be based on economic and monetary policies that were stability oriented and carried the promise of continuity and credibility. However, it also denotes the recognition that every effort had to be made to win over a skeptical German public and that, without the participation of Germany, EMU would not be meaningful.

The Maastricht Treaty has acquired the reputation of being too complicated and, in places, ambiguous. It also is correct that some issues hardly have been addressed or were inadequately addressed (this applies mainly but not only to political union). However, the critics failed to fully recognize that the treaty deals with complicated and highly political issues on an unprecedented scale, yet, had to satisfy the aspirations and concerns of a large number of countries of various economic and political weight and with differing traditions and histories.

Article N (in Title VII "Final Provisions") of the treaty called for a new Intergovernmental Conference to be convened in 1996 to examine those treaty provisions for which revision is provided. The conference (sometimes called Maastricht II) started on March 29, 1996, in Turin. It is not expected to deal with monetary questions.

NOTES

Literature of general interest for this chapter: Bank of England (1992a); Deutsche Bundesbank (1992a); H. M. Treasury (1992); Habermeier and Ungerer (1992); Kenen (1995); Monar, Ungerer, and Wessels (1993); Seidel (1996).

1. Following the European Council meeting in Dublin in December 1996 (see Chapter 23), high French officials (including President Jacques Chirac) revived the idea of an "economic government" by advocating a "pouvoir politique," an instrument of political power, as a counterweight to the ECB. The proposal was met with strong resistance in other countries, particularly in Germany, because it was seen as a threat to the independence of the ECB and as being incompatible with the Maastricht Treaty.

2. For interpretations that consider "general orientations" as nonbinding, see Bank of England (1992b, p. 203); Deutsche Bundesbank (1992a, p. 48); Pisani-Ferry (1992, p. 61); Kenen (1995, p. 32). Peter Kenen also addressed the question of who would decide whether such orientations conflict with price stability.

3. Most importantly, the European Council, at its meeting in Edinburgh on December 11 and 12, 1992, accepted Denmark's notification that it will not participate in stage three of EMU.

4. With regard to EMU, the Court declared "that the convergence criteria . . . in Art. 109j . . . cannot be changed without the consent of the German

parliament. . . . The Court continued by stating that 'the Treaty provides for long-range prerequisites, with stability as the standard for the currency union, which seek to secure that standard through institutional arrangements and which ultimately — as a means of last resort — do not prohibit breaking away from the Community should the common goal of stability not be reached'" (Ress, 1994, p. 545).

5.   For an overview of the ratification process, see *Bulletin*, 1993, No. 10, pp. 121–22.

21

The Debate about the Maastricht Treaty — Benefits and Costs of Economic and Monetary Union

As soon as the Maastricht Treaty was agreed, an intense debate about its merits and the desirability of economic and monetary union (EMU) developed in several European Community (EC) countries where, hitherto, only a small number of people outside the circle of experts had followed the complicated and seemingly arcane discussions of the Intergovernmental Conference. The exception, in this respect, was the United Kingdom (UK), where, already, after the European Council meeting in Hanover in 1988 and especially after the publication of the Delors Report, a wider debate about future monetary integration and the general direction of European integration had emerged.

In France, strong concerns were expressed by some prominent politicians and in parts of the media that the Maastricht Treaty would serve mainly to consolidate the "hegemonial" position of a united Germany. In Germany, the treaty was seen by many commentators solely as an attempt to neutralize the powers of the Bundesbank and to eliminate its key role in European monetary policies, with the consequence of an erosion of the stability of the Deutsche mark. Slogans such as "Hands off the mark!" were not uncommon, and the *Frankfurter Allgemeine Zeitung*, a respected newspaper with national circulation, published a critical article by a well-known economist with the headline "The End of Price Stability" (Vaubel, 1992). Another criticism was that the treaty did not entail significant progress toward a political union, which many considered a necessary corollary to EMU. In the UK, although Prime Minister John Major had negotiated an opting-out clause for EMU, there was a wave of criticism concerning the loss of sovereignty and widespread suspicion about the ulterior motives of the "continental" countries. Before the Maastricht conference, criticism of the single currency project had been strong and had reached a climax when a prominent member of the Conservative Party called the plans for EMU "a German racket to take over the whole of Europe" (Sir Nicholas Ridley, quoted in Stephens, 1996).

Apart from the skepticism displayed by Danish voters, there has been broad agreement in the other EC countries with the economic and political objectives of the treaty. This was particularly true for the Benelux countries, which, from the very beginning, had been staunch supporters of European integration. Yet, in member states in southern Europe, there were marked anxieties about the risk that the lack of progress in economic convergence might delegate them to a "second league" of EMU latecomers.

This chapter examines the debate about the Maastricht Treaty that has involved primarily German economists but is also representative of the wider debate, the relevance of the optimum currency area theory for the EC, and the question of whether the history of monetary unions in the nineteenth century could provide guidance in today's world. A brief survey of costs and benefits of monetary union concludes the chapter.

A DEBATE AMONG ECONOMISTS

In June 1992, not long after the signing of the Maastricht Treaty, 62 German professors of economics issued a manifesto on the monetary policy provisions of the treaty (German economists, 1992).[1] Although EMU was seen as a worthwhile objective, the group judged the treaty provisions on a number of key points as inappropriate for achieving this goal and warned against a ratification of the treaty. The main arguments ran as follows. A lasting convergence was a prerequisite for the proper functioning of EMU, yet, the convergence criteria of the treaty were too lax. The setting of a final deadline for the implementation of monetary union (January 1, 1999) carried the risk that the criteria would be watered down so as to avoid discriminating against individual countries. The European Central Bank (ECB) would not ensure price stability because the personal independence of the members of its decision-making bodies was not guaranteed, and there were no sanctions should price stability not be achieved. Because the ECB lacked the responsibility for exchange rate policy vis-à-vis third currencies, exchange rates could be subject to political influence and a stability-oriented monetary policy could be undermined. A consensus on price stability, as it existed in Germany, was not evident throughout Europe. Such a consensus among the central bank, the government, and the people was required to pursue a coherent stability-oriented policy. With a single currency, the weaker countries would be exposed to greater competitive pressures and suffer growing unemployment, which would require high transfer payments. The group came to the conclusions that there was "no convincing argument in favor of superimposing from above a monetary union on Europe which is still not united economically, socially and in terms of political interest" and that the single market did not require a European currency. The "overhasty" introduction of monetary union would expose Europe to economic strains, lead to a major test of political wills, and, thereby, jeopardize the goal of integration. A number of these critical views were shared by economists from outside Germany, including the United States (Feldstein, 1992, pp. 19–22; see also De Grauwe et al., 1992).

The manifesto reflected the high priority that price stability enjoys in Germany, but it also revealed misgivings about the general direction of European integration toward a tighter institutional framework. It was a notable example of policy advice that largely ignored the dynamics of the political process (e.g., the incentives for weaker countries to strengthen their economies by appropriate policies). It also disregarded past achievements such as the European Monetary System (EMS) and the Single Market Program, which had been considered unlikely by many of the same professors. It assumed that, in case EMU would not be realized, everything else would remain unchanged (e.g., the functioning of the EMS; the integration of the goods, services, and financial markets) and no negative fallout would occur.

The manifesto was based on a combination of worst-case scenarios. It did not consider other possible, by no means unrealistic, scenarios, nor did it offer alternatives. The group also misrepresented the treaty on several points (e.g., regarding the independence of the ECB, the safeguards concerning exchange rate policy) and implied that clear legal commitments of the treaty (e.g., with regard to price stability as the primary objective of monetary policy) would be disregarded. It overlooked that, for a number of years within the EC, a wide consensus on the desirability of price stability had emerged and, in most countries, had been translated into actual policies.

Soon afterward, the chief economists of the three largest German commercial banks issued jointly a point-by-point rebuttal of the manifesto (Lipp, Ramm, and Walter, 1992, pp. 1–2; see also Classen, 1992). In their view, the manifesto was "breathing the spirit of the seventies," ignored economic policy developments of the 1980s, and played down the risks of a retrogression to national narrow-mindedness in the 1990s. The three economists highlighted the convergence already achieved and the existence of a stability consensus among the "hard currency bloc" of the EMS. They rejected the assertion of an overhasty introduction of monetary union and pointed out that experience had shown that deadlines raised the pressure for convergence in member states. Their final argument stressed that maintaining the status quo would be impossible and that the challenges of history called for a deepening as well as an enlargement of the EC.

Not long afterward, another critical reaction to the manifesto of the 62 was initiated by a small group of German economists (Gros and Steinherr, 1992). The manifesto "In Favour of EMU" was signed by 70 European economists (among them, 10 from Germany), including several well-known experts on European monetary policy matters. Their manifesto reiterated some of the arguments of the three bank economists. Additionally, it emphasized that the ECB would not be created out of the blue. Rather, it would be directed by a Council composed of the governors of the 12 (by then independent) national central banks who had shown their attachment to price stability by the way they had operated the EMS in the past and by six direct appointees (the members of the Executive Board of the ECB) who would be chosen, *inter alia*, for their attachment to price stability. The experience in the EMS and the very fact of signing the Maastricht Treaty suggested "that politicians and union leaders everywhere in Europe have come to understand that 'inflation does not pay.'"[2]

The debate continued, often in the form of letters to leading newspapers, at times in highly emotional tones. As some issues fell to the wayside, the economic debate concentrated more and more on a few key issues, such as the risk of "asymmetric" external shocks that would affect individual EMU participants differently and the impact of national budgetary policies on the single monetary policy.

The severe EMS crisis in September 1992 threw a spotlight on some points of the debate. Opponents of the Maastricht Treaty felt confirmed in their view that the EC was not yet ready for EMU. Others saw it as a sign that the EMS could neither ensure general exchange rate stability nor prevent speculative attacks against countries whose fundamental financial situation was sound. In that view, the need for a monetary union was evident.

IS EUROPE AN OPTIMUM CURRENCY AREA?

The "traditional" theory of optimum currency areas (OCAs) was developed in a series of articles by eminent economists in the 1960s and early 1970s (see Ishiyama, 1975; Bayoumi, in press, Chap. 5). It looked at the costs and benefits of belonging to a single currency area and sought to identify the characteristics of a country (or region) that would allow it to reap optimal results from being part of a single currency area. The theory found renewed interest as efforts to create a single European currency gathered speed, and the question of whether the EC was an OCA was examined (Bofinger, 1994a; Eichengreen, 1991; Masson & Taylor, 1992; Overturf, 1994).

The traditional OCA authors concluded that the costs of a single monetary policy would be limited if a group of regions (or countries) would be exposed to similar economic disturbances, or shocks. Should the regions face dissimilar disturbances, that is, asymmetric or region-specific shocks, the costs would be higher. Certain criteria were discussed that would mitigate such costs and, thus, delimit an OCA. Robert Mundell (1961) concentrated on the mobility of production factors (capital and, in particular, labor) as the criterion for the ability to absorb asymmetric shocks. Ronald McKinnon (1963) viewed a high degree of openness of an economy (i.e., a high share of tradeable goods in domestic production) as the criterion. Peter Kenen (1969) looked at a high degree of product diversification as the decisive element. James Ingram (1969), on the other hand, suggested that one should examine financial, not real, characteristics and proposed the degree of financial integration as the criterion for an OCA.

Ishiyama characterized the traditional OCA literature as "primarily a scholastic discussion" (1975, p. 378). Its shortcomings for "real world" policy issues are indeed apparent: the choice of a single criterion in the framework of a static analysis, explicit or implicit narrow assumptions about the ability of economies to adjust (e.g., about the "stickiness" of wages and prices), and the emphasis on the costs for a region or country of belonging to a currency area without examining the benefits, including those that could flow from dynamically evolving conditions, such as a politically motivated process of economic and monetary integration. Such issues have been addressed in what George Tavlas called the "new" theory of OCAs, which indicated "that there are somewhat fewer costs (in terms of the loss of autonomy of domestic macro policies), and somewhat more benefits (e.g. gains in inflation credibility) associated with monetary integration" (1993, p. 682). Tavlas suggested that, ultimately, "the major determinant underlying the move to monetary integration is the political will to integrate on the part of the prospective members" (1994, p. 225).

Political aspects had been examined early on by authors such as Gottfried Haberler, James Ingram, and Edward Tower and Thomas D. Willet (see Ishiyama, 1975, p. 357). The similarity of policy attitudes — in other words, a consensus on economic policy priorities — was more relevant than the economic characteristics of countries.

The traditional OCA theory does not yield unambiguous answers to the question of whether the EC formed an OCA. Paradoxically, even the Belgium-Luxembourg Economic Union as well as individual EC countries would have difficulties qualifying. Although a high, although differing, degree of openness and product diversification exists in most EC countries, labor mobility across national borders is relatively low. In countries like Germany, Italy, Spain, or the UK, significant structural disparities exist between various regions, in particular between the north and the south, and, in the case of the unified Germany, also between the "old"

Länder (states) and the "new" ones in the eastern part of the country. Even within countries, labor mobility often is relatively low, and demand shocks may have asymmetric effects on different regions within a country. More recently, various empirical studies have tried to shed more light on the relevance of the question of whether the EC is an OCA.[3] However, by nature, such studies are based on existing conditions and correlations, and the results sometimes are contradictory.

All this suggests that the theoretical and empirical work on OCAs, with its emphasis on economic aspects while neglecting the political dimension, can serve only to a limited extent as a guide in the debate about the costs and benefits of European monetary union. Yet, despite its limitations, the OCA analysis may be useful in identifying "soft spots" of the European economies and indicating in what areas future common policies may have to be strengthened if EMU is to succeed.

THE EXPERIENCE WITH MONETARY UNIONS IN THE NINETEENTH CENTURY

Another approach to explore opportunities and risks of a monetary union was to look back to the experience with past monetary unions. In a study undertaken at the time of the Werner Report, Hans Krämer (1970) examined several historical monetary unions. He came to the conclusion that such unions had a better chance of success if economic policies of the participating countries were in harmony. He compared the Scandinavian monetary union, established by Denmark, Norway, and Sweden in 1873, with the Latin currency union, founded in 1865 and consisting of France, Belgium, Switzerland, Italy, and Greece. In the years before World War I, economic conditions and policies in the three Scandinavian countries were practically the same. The union came to an end when this situation changed and differing economic policies were adopted. The only monetary unions that survived were those that were related to political, economic, and monetary unification, as in the case of Switzerland, Italy, and Germany. No historical monetary union had brought about political unification.

These conclusions were backed by a comprehensive study of historical monetary unions by Theresia Theurl (1992). In a summary of her findings (1995), she wrote that each monetary union had its inherent centrifugal forces that always stemmed from the fact that the common monetary systems did not include all matters that could influence its results. The issuing of banknotes (in most cases) and budgetary problems (in all cases) were managed in a decentralized manner, which was burdensome for the union. Each union had its "destabilization trap." In the case of the Maastricht Treaty, Theurl saw such a trap in the decentralization of budgetary and income policies.

It is always an interesting exercise to look at history; yet, drawing conclusions for the present often is fraught with difficulties. The failed monetary unions of the last century in a number of ways did not resemble the type of monetary union envisaged for Europe. Not all means of payment were included (no banknotes and not all circulating coins), opening the door for the debasement of one type of monetary medium in relation to others. There were no central monetary authorities to conduct common monetary policies with the responsibility of ensuring monetary stability throughout the union. Instead, members of those unions adopted differing versions of the gold standard, without following uniformly the "rules of the game" that the gold standard implied. In contrast, the Maastricht Treaty envisages an independent common central bank system with a clearly defined policy objective and safeguards with regard to decentralized (i.e., national) budgetary policies.

The EC also has elements of a political union, in particular, the Council of Ministers, which, in a number of cases, can decide by majority. (However, history shows that the existence of a political union per se is no guarantee for stability-oriented economic policies.) What the history of the monetary unions reminds us of is that, in the longer run, the pursuit of exclusively national interests will be incompatible with common endeavors and that the insistence on national sovereignty in the conduct of national economic policies, in particular in the budgetary field, can result in centrifugal tendencies. Such tendencies can be curbed only by effective policy coordination. Similar views had been expressed in the discussions on the need for a tighter coordination of economic policies in the 1960s and quite distinctly by the authors of the Werner Report and the Delors Report. Whether the provisions of the Maastricht Treaty in this respect are sufficient has been questioned frequently and led to proposals to strengthen the budgetary policy oversight by the EC. A case in point is the German proposal for a "stability pact" (see Chapter 23).

BENEFITS AND COSTS OF MONETARY UNION: A SUMMARY

The debate about the potential benefits and costs of participation in a system of fixed exchange rates (monetary union being its most institutionalized form) has been going on since the 1960s, when it was one of the main issues in the discussions about a reform of the international monetary system. The issue has attracted much attention as the efforts to create a European single currency gained momentum, culminating in the Maastricht Treaty. This section will summarize briefly the main arguments in the debate.[4]

The most obvious benefit of a monetary union is the reduction of transaction costs for business (and for travelers). Within the common currency area, business does not have to protect itself anymore against exchange rate risks by costly forward contracts. There will be no need to conduct business and to keep books in different currencies. Although obviously of significant benefit to large companies, it may be of even more importance for small companies, enabling them to take advantage of a larger market.[5] A large currency area also can be expected to promote economies of scale and higher productivity, although it has been pointed out that, in the short run, this may imply costs in the form of changes in economic structure, greater geographic concentration of industry, and significant reductions in employment (Bayoumi, in press, Chap. 6).

The benefits of monetary union reach, however, beyond the cost aspect. Because a single currency means the elimination of exchange rate variability and uncertainty within the currency area, it will contribute to a stabilization of expectations and, thus, provide business with a sounder basis for planning. This will encourage entrepreneurs to invest and eliminate an important source of wrong investment decisions. In this way, the single market can be expected to yield benefits not only in a static sense — by abolishing barriers and reducing costs for intraunion trade — but also in a dynamic sense — by contributing to confidence, thus, fostering growth and employment in the longer run.

The institutional framework for the single monetary policy — an independent ECB with price stability as its primary objective, exchange rate policy provisions that will shield monetary policy from external influences, rules for responsible budgetary policies if strictly applied — will provide the basis for the achievement of a high degree of price stability throughout the union. The absence of speculative attacks by market operators will allow economic policies to be more clearly directed to financial stability, economic growth, and high employment. In addition to the budgetary policy provisions of the Maastricht Treaty, the pursuit of a stability-oriented monetary policy may further contribute to sound budgetary policies by a "good example factor." Any country not sufficiently adhering to the common code of good fiscal behavior will suffer in terms of missed investment opportunities. It will have to face higher costs for debt service, including — assuming a strict application of the no bailout rule — market-imposed risk premiums on interest rates.

It also has been argued that EMU would provide the EC with a more influential voice in international monetary and economic matters, for example, in such institutions as the Group of Seven, the International Monetary Fund, and the World Trade Organization. Without going into any details, reference is made to the literature mentioned in Chapter 24.

Those who want to move beyond economic integration to political unification see in EMU one more important benefit. The history of the EC has been a sequence of developments in which economic, political, and sociopsychological factors interacted. At times, this has led to regression, as in the 1960s, with Charles de Gaulle's policy of the "empty chair," or in the 1970s, when the failure to find a common policy response to the challenges of the breakdown of the Bretton Woods system and the oil price increases reduced the common exchange rate arrangement, the snake, to a "mini-snake" and plans for EMU had to be abandoned. At other times, and more often than not, there were significant advances in integration; the success of the EMS in the 1980s and the Single Market Program are important examples. It has been argued that the realization of EMU will exert a similar stimulating effect. The requirements of a single monetary policy would exert pressure on member states to follow compatible economic and budgetary policies lest EMU gets into trouble. Successfully coordinated policies beyond the monetary sphere then might extend the readiness to cooperate to other important policy areas. This expectation is, of course, the deeper reason why the UK but also Denmark are very reluctant to join in EMU — they see it as the beginning of a road leading ultimately to the loss of political sovereignty.

The debate about the costs of monetary union concentrated by and large on two issues. Can a single monetary policy safeguard price stability, and will differences in "stability culture" among EC countries and possible economic dislocations in some countries as a consequence of EMU result in political pressure on the ECB to lower its standards? The other issue is whether the loss of autonomy in monetary and exchange rate matters is acceptable in economic terms, in the face of structural disparities among countries and the possibility of asymmetric shocks, and in political terms.[6] The economic aspects of these questions have been the subject of the OCA theory, as surveyed above.

The doubts regarding the stability prospects of the single currency were discussed earlier in this chapter. Also, reference was made to the widely held view that, in the longer run, no trade-off existed between inflation and growth and employment. Nevertheless, there may be a temptation for politicians to press for short-term gains in growth out of concern that high employment may trigger social and political disturbances. In such a situation, the attitude of those members of the governing bodies of the European System of Central Banks (ESCB) who have affinities to countries in trouble may become an issue.[7]

The most important cost of a monetary union is the loss of an independently conducted monetary policy and, in particular, of the nominal exchange rate as a means of adjustment on the national level. This not only has to do with the notion of political sovereignty but also has great relevance in an instrumental sense. Without the exchange rate instrument, any decline in relative competitiveness in one part of the union must be addressed by domestic policy changes, such as a lowering of wages and related costs relative to those in other parts of the union, and a reduction in public expenditure and social benefits, which could lead to political difficulties. However, this argument should not be taken too far. Experience has shown that devaluations will not improve competitiveness on a lasting basis unless accompanied by domestic adjustment measures. Moreover, these measures may have to be even more severe than common indicators would suggest in order to counter the loss in policy credibility associated with devaluations. Otherwise, repeated devaluations may be necessary.

Will EMU result in an equalization of wage rates, regardless of productivity differences, and, thus, create regional unemployment? This is an important point, but there is a fairly widespread view that it is not very likely. The lack of labor mobility among countries would work against such a development. There already are significant differences in wage levels within countries, and the prevalence of general industrywide wage agreements is receding in favor of enterprise-based agreements. Also, high unemployment and global competition are putting a lid on real wage increases, and there is an increasing awareness of the need to make labor markets less rigid. The argument can even be turned around: if the tool of devaluations is not available any longer, there will be direct pressure on cost and wage developments to protect competitiveness and employment. However, a Europe-wide harmonization of social benefits, as advocated by some, would certainly be the wrong prescription.

Although the arguments about the costs of monetary union are, to a degree, an outgrowth of worst-case scenarios, they should not be dismissed altogether. They illustrate, as pointed out by Deputy Governor of the Bank of England Howard Davies (1996, p. 20), "that some flexibility will be required both at national and European level to cope with differential impacts of a single currency on different regions of the Union."

The issue of national sovereignty has additional facets. One of great significance is whether the need to shore up a stability-oriented single monetary policy by sound budgetary policies requires more centralized decision making on the union level, that is, a higher degree of political unity, if not some form of a central government. This issue is being used by those who object to more political unity as an argument against EMU and by those who want more political unity as an argument in favor of EMU. One view is, however, that the absence of a central political institution actually may shield the ESCB-ECB from undue political pressure, because the governments of the individual member states are likely to have differing points of views as well as overlapping election cycles.

It is somewhat risky to summarize the views of member states on EMU. Should it relate to the views of the politicians, leaders in business and banking, a selected public as represented by the media, or the public at large? There is not always a complete congruity of opinions among those different groups. We shall return to the views of the people briefly in Chapter 24. The following is an attempt to characterize the more or less official views of countries on EMU and their attitudes on closer political cooperation.

One view rejects any more substantial EC role in foreign, defense, and social policy matters, and there is strong resistance to a single currency. In this category fall the UK, Denmark, and, perhaps, Sweden.

Another view, particularly in France, shows continued attachment to national sovereignty with regard to foreign and defense policy. EMU, however, is strongly favored, in part because it is hoped to compensate for a loss in monetary policy autonomy by joint responsibility. In short, France is willing to trade sovereignty for influence.[8] Yet, the French position frequently has been somewhat ambiguous. Sweden appears to share some of the reservations on political integration.

In several countries, EMU is considered not only a worthy objective by itself but also an important step toward political union. More political integration is seen as providing some protection against a possible hegemony of any of the larger countries or a coalition of larger countries. To this group belong in particular the Benelux countries, as well as Ireland, Italy, Spain, Portugal, and Greece. Finland also can be counted in this group; its position is greatly influenced by security concerns over its geographical closeness to Russia. The countries in southern Europe and Ireland see integration also as the key to further economic development.

Mainly in Germany and the Netherlands, there are distinct concerns about the stability of a single currency unless supported by strict economic policy rules and closer political cooperation. The question often has been asked what Germany has hoped to gain from more monetary integration through arrangements such as the snake, the EMS, and, in particular, EMU, considering its strong stability orientation and the lesser achievements of some partner countries in this respect. The answer is threefold: First, for an export-oriented country, stable exchange rates are important, even if a common monetary area is initially limited in size. Second, EMU holds out the promise of a "European area of monetary stability," in contrast to an "island of stability"[9] with all its consequences for monetary disturbances and a speculation-induced disproportional appreciation of the German currency. Third, Germany — as a geographically, politically, and historically exposed country — has since the end of World War II consistently placed the greatest importance on economic as well as political integration as a means to be firmly anchored in Europe and the Western world.

At the end of this chapter, we turn to a non-European highly respected expert on international financial matters. In his assessment of the Maastricht Treaty and the prospects for EMU, Kenen (1995) pointed out that EMU should not be compared with the "hard" EMS of the 1980s and the early 1990s but with the wide-band EMS after August 1993 (see

Chapter 22). Then, he writes, "the case for EMU gets stronger" (p. 181). As for the question of whether the Maastricht blueprint makes sense, Kenen's answer is: "It does" (p. 193). In his view, the adolescent ESCB may be quite different from the newborn institution, and the speed of adaptation will depend on the further development of the EC as a political entity. "The move to EMU, however, should not be delayed until that political entity has been developed fully or because the economies of the EC countries have not converged completely." To do so would be "inconsistent with the whole history of the Community, which has been built by taking risks, not by waiting until they have vanished" (pp. 193–94).

NOTES

Literature of general interest for this chapter: Commission (1990c, 1991a); De Grauwe (1992); Gros and Thygesen (1992); Kenen (1995); Taylor (1995).

1. The English translation is not very precise (Steinherr 1994, pp. 72–74). On some points, therefore, I use my own translation.
2. An earlier version of the manifesto had additionally stated that the leading role of Germany in the EMS, although generally appreciated, had also given rise to frictions, and the hard currency countries in the Deutschmark zone expected, with justified impatience, the right to have a say (*Mitspracherecht*) (Krägenau and Wetter, 1993, p. 402).
3. For a survey of empirical studies, see Bayoumi (in press, Chap. 6); Kenen (1995, pp. 81–90).
4. In part, based on Ungerer (1993b). References in this chapter are only to a few selected publications. In addition, the views of monetary policy practitioners, in particular, of high central bank officials, are very informative; see various central bank publications.
5. Estimates for efficiency gains from monetary union are provided in Commission (1990c, pp. 63–86).
6. German unification and its costs for the West German economy often have been mentioned as a warning example. This argument overlooks the fact that German unification was, in many respects, a unique event. The costs were a result of the need to integrate a centrally planned and inefficient economy and its workforce into a highly efficient market economy without allowing, for political reasons, the disparities to be reflected in the conversion rates between the eastern and western currencies, resulting in a huge real appreciation for the economy of the former German Democratic Republic vis-à-vis the West. Even if somewhat different conversion rates would have been applied, the costs in terms of transfer payments and unemployment still would have been tremendous. Realistic conversion rates, on the other hand, would have made unification politically unmanageable. In contrast, the conversion rates of the currencies of EMU participants into the new currency will be based on market exchange rates, reflecting the relative strengths of the economies concerned. For a comparison of German and European monetary union, see Kloten (1995).

7.   More recently, in late 1996 and early 1997, as unemployment in several European countries continued to increase, there has been a renewed debate, particularly in France, on whether monetary policy should not be more eased as a means for fighting unemployment.

8.   This idea has been developed by Dillingham (1995).

9.   These terms were used by Bofinger (1993a).

22

The Crises of the European Monetary System in 1992 and 1993

The events in the international financial markets in September 1992 and afterward put into question a number of assumptions, hopes, and seemingly well-founded views about the achievements and prospects of monetary integration in the European Community (EC). For a number of years, calm had prevailed in the exchange rate mechanism (ERM) of the European Monetary System (EMS), and the integration of the newcomers to the ERM — Spain in June 1989, the United Kingdom (UK) in October 1990, and Portugal in April 1992 — appeared to pose no problems. Exchange rates were stable (Figures 22.1 and 22.2). Only one member state, Greece, remained outside the ERM. There was talk of the "New EMS,"[1] a system characterized by progress toward more convergence and without a need for exchange rate realignments. The EC seemed to be well on the path to economic and monetary union (EMU).

The controversial realignment of January 1987 — although modest in size — had two interrelated consequences. It initiated a period of stable nominal, albeit increasingly diverging real exchange rates. This was particularly the case for countries that had joined the ERM later but also for Italy, which, in January 1990, had managed to move smoothly within the ERM from the wider to the narrow fluctuation margins of ±2.25 percent. Those countries followed policies of "borrowed credibility and monetary stability," shored up by high interest rates and built on overly optimistic convergence expectations in anticipation of monetary union. However, divergences in economic performance persisted.

FIGURE 22.1

Movements of Exchange Rates against the Deutsche Mark, 1990–96 (Belgium, Denmark, France, Ireland, the Netherlands)

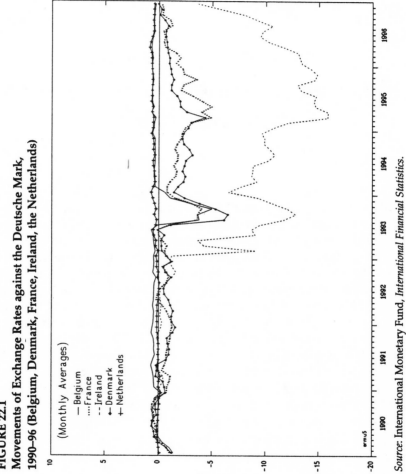

Source: International Monetary Fund, *International Financial Statistics.*

FIGURE 22.2

Movements of Exchange Rates against the Deutsche Mark, 1990–96 (Austria, Italy, Portugal, Spain, Sweden, and the United Kingdom)

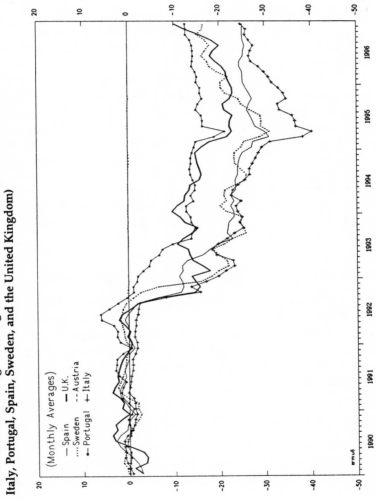

Source: International Monetary Fund, *International Financial Statistics.*

259

The 1987 realignment also had triggered a political debate about asymmetry in the EMS engendering moves toward EMU, which culminated in the Delors Report and the Maastricht Treaty. However, widespread doubts about the desirability of EMU, particularly in the UK and Germany, spawned an undercurrent of skepticism. At the same time, German unification contributed to the underlying imbalances within the EMS, and the collapse of the satellite system of countries in Central and Eastern Europe, dominated by the Soviet Union, the disintegration of the Soviet Union itself, and the war in the former Yugoslavia, changed dramatically the political landscape in Europe.

A particularly important precondition for the volatility of foreign exchange markets was the rapid integration of international financial markets and the innovation in financial instruments. The potential of market operators to move large sums swiftly from country to country had increased tremendously. Daily turnover on foreign exchange markets has been estimated at $1,000 billion and more, of which only a relatively small part is related to nonfinancial transactions. Such sums surpassed by far the possibilities of central banks to manage, in the absence of other policy measures, foreign exchange markets by intervention. All this together formed the backdrop against which the EMS crises of 1992 and 1993 unfolded.[2]

THE CAUSES OF THE CRISIS OF SEPTEMBER 1992

The main causes of the crisis of September 1992 were the weakness of the U.S. dollar in the final phase of the Bush administration; tensions within the ERM because of the insufficient convergence of economic developments and the incompatibility of fiscal and monetary policies of ERM countries; and, finally, the uncertainties surrounding the ratification of the Maastricht Treaty.

The Weakness of the U.S. Dollar

The weakness of the dollar in foreign exchange markets during the summer of 1992 resulted mainly from the low interest rate policy of the United States in response to economic stagnation but also from the lack of economic policy orientation, particularly in the budgetary field, of the Bush administration before the elections in November 1992. The dollar weakness also was related to the high interest rate policy of the Bundesbank in the face of inflationary developments and the strong demand for capital in the wake of German unification. During summer 1992, the dollar lost about 15 to 20 percent of its value against ERM currencies. At the same time, the familiar pattern according to which a substantial weakening of the dollar leads to a disproportional strengthening of the Deutsche mark within the ERM reestablished itself.

Tensions within the Exchange Rate Mechanism

For several years, the countries that participated in the ERM since the start of the EMS in 1979 had pursued prudent monetary policies. Also, countries that joined the ERM later adopted a conservative monetary policy stance in order to fight inflation and to buttress the credibility of their exchange rates. This created the paradoxical situation that the markets pushed up the exchange rates of the Spanish and Portuguese currencies, in particular, in response to high interest rates while ignoring insufficient convergence. As the economic situation in some countries deteriorated, their authorities found it more and more difficult to maintain restrictive monetary policies. Yet, they were not prepared to change their EMS central rates, because they regarded a stable exchange rate as a useful disciplinary device and did not want to endanger their policy credibility.

In the case of Spain and Portugal, the "borrowed stability" became less and less credible in view of high budget and external deficits. The UK had tightened its monetary policy in 1990 and considered ERM participation a part of this strategy. However, as recessionary tendencies became more pronounced, the government was hard-pressed to justify its high interest rate policy. Italy was in a near permanent state of crisis, and the government had neither the strength nor the domestic political support to stop the deterioration of the budgetary situation.

France, on the other hand, experienced in 1992 the lowest inflation rate in 36 years — 2 percent — and a sizable surplus in the current account of the balance of payments. Its budgetary situation was favorable. However, unemployment — at 10 percent — was quite high. Nevertheless, the government was determined to continue its stability-oriented policy that had been pursued since March 1983. However, the eroding authority of President François Mitterrand and the socialist government, as well as calls by some prominent opposition politicians for loosening the link between the franc and the Deutsche mark, led to doubts about the continuity of government policy and to uncertainties about the policy orientation of an increasingly likely future conservative government. As a consequence, France — with a better performance than Germany — had to struggle to maintain its exchange rate against the Deutsche mark. For the markets, which are credited with having the "'memory of an elephant," France evidently had not yet acquired unquestionable credibility.

Germany experienced great difficulties in financing the tremendous costs of German unification but also because of large wage increases. Faced with accelerating inflation — the rate of increase in the consumer price index for the western part of Germany moved from an average of

1.3 percent in 1988 to 4.8 percent in March 1992 — the Bundesbank stepped on the brakes. From the beginning of 1991 to July 1992, the discount rate was raised by 2.75 percentage points to 8.75 percent, compared with 2 percent in December 1987, its lowest level ever. To the extent that inflation in Germany rose significantly faster than in most other ERM countries, however, Germany did not fully meet anymore the requirements of an anchor currency to which a currency link would be of benefit.[3] Yet, the Deutsche mark remained the point of orientation for other ERM currencies because of the long-established credibility of German monetary policy and the recognition of unification as a unique event (or, in economic parlance, a one-time asymmetric shock).

Uncertainties about Ratification of the Maastricht Treaty

In addition to the differences in the economic situation of the major countries of the EC that put in question the continuation of the common anti-inflationary strategy, there were uncertainties about the fate of the Maastricht Treaty. The unenthusiastic attitude of the UK was well-known, but that a number of conservative members of parliament continued to oppose the Maastricht Treaty, despite the significant concessions that Prime Minister John Major had obtained at the Maastricht conference, indicated general British misgivings about European integration. Strong doubts about the merits of EMU existed also in Germany and — although less pronounced and with a different emphasis — in France. Into this volatile situation burst the narrow defeat in the Danish referendum on the Maastricht Treaty on June 2, 1992. One day later, President Mitterand made the risky decision to submit the Maastricht Treaty to a referendum, although this was not constitutionally required, obviously with the hope to boost acceptance of the treaty but also to bolster his own domestic position. Soon, polls indicated that, also in France, the treaty was in danger. Its rejection would have been the end of the EMU process, at least for some time.

The notions of the New EMS as a de facto monetary union and of a seamless transition to formal EMU were shown to be illusions. The "undeserved credibility" (Artus and Bourginat, 1994, p. 148) of the New EMS was revealed. Serious doubts emerged as to whether the moves toward ever more convergence, started in 1982–83, would continue. Even more, it seemed evident that the motivation for reducing existing divergences would be greatly weakened, in particular in those countries where convergence efforts were driven mainly by the desire to qualify for EMU participation from the beginning. Belatedly, the markets recognized the accumulated price and cost differentials, the disparities in fiscal positions, and the deterioration in the current account balances of some countries.

The existing central rates now appeared unsustainable. In late summer of 1992, speculation on a realignment of ERM exchange rates started to unfurl and eventually became an avalanche that threatened to bury the EMS.

THE EVENTS OF SUMMER 1992 AND AFTERWARD

The lowering of the discount rate by the Federal Reserve System by half a percentage point to 3 percent on July 2, 1992, and the increase of the Bundesbank's discount rate on July 16 from 8 to 8.75 percent (the highest rate since the establishment of the new central bank system in Germany in 1948) was followed by a pronounced weakening of the U.S dollar in foreign exchange markets. By the end of August, the British pound came under severe pressure. Soon, the Italian lira also became subject to heavy speculative attacks. On August 28, the Monetary Committee concluded that a change in central rates would not be the appropriate response to the tensions in the EMS. However, the turmoil continued, and the Bundesbank, forced to absorb large inflows of funds, which threatened to upset its policy, asked the German government "to seek a realignment of exchange rates in the European exchange rate mechanism."[4] During the weekend of September 12 and 13, 1992, agreement was reached on a devaluation of the Italian lira by 7 percent, effective as of September 14, and a modest lowering of the German discount and Lombard rates, followed by similar cuts in Belgium and the Netherlands, but the central rate of the British pound was not changed. Heavy speculation against the pound reached a peak on September 16, which became known as "Black Wednesday."[5] Despite massive market intervention and a last-minute increase of the Bank of England's key interest rate in two steps from 10 to 15 percent, on the next day, the authorities felt forced to take the pound out of the ERM. At the same time, they reinstated the earlier interest rate of 10 percent. Following a night meeting of the Monetary Committee, the lira, too, left the ERM, and the Spanish peseta, which also had become a target of heavy speculation, was devalued by 5 percent.

In the following days, the markets unleashed severe speculative attacks against the French franc. A joint German-French declaration on September 23 that the existing bilateral central rates accurately reflected underlying economic conditions and that rate changes were not justified, substantial interest rate increases by the Banque de France, and large scale concerted intramarginal intervention by the Bundesbank and the Banque de France stabilized the situation. The central rate of the franc remained unchanged.

On September 23, Spain, Portugal, and Ireland reintroduced temporarily capital controls, but in October 1992, the peseta and the escudo had to be devalued. The substantial depreciation of sterling (against the mark by more than 10 percent from September to the end of 1992; Figure 22.2) had a strong adverse impact on the Irish pound, which, despite sound economic fundamentals and a last-minute increase in its short-term interest rate to 100 percent, had to be devalued by 10 percent on January 30, 1993.

The currencies of Norway, Sweden, and Finland, which had been pegged unilaterally to the ECU in October 1990 and May and June 1991, respectively, also came under pressure. Finland severed the link to the ECU on September 8, 1992; Sweden followed on November 19; and Norway on December 10.

There had, from time to time, been warnings that the instrument of exchange rate changes should not be discarded prematurely and that realignments within the ERM still might be necessary (Deutsche Bundesbank, Annual Report 1990, p. 66; Masera, 1994, p. 267). In the end, this turned out to be correct. However, although exchange rate movements within the ERM proved to be inevitable, their actual timing and extent as well as the atmosphere of panic that gripped the markets and some policymakers also were influenced by the behavior of the main actors.

In the case of the UK, one early error was to fix the sterling central rate for entering the ERM in October 1990 at too high a level (vis-à-vis the Deutsche mark at 2.95). Later miscalculations included the lowering of the key interest rate by half a percentage point on May 5, 1992 — two days ahead of local elections. Most importantly, although intervening heavily in the market in August and September 1992, the authorities failed to increase their official interest rates. In public declarations, leading members of the government vowed to stay the course — a claim that became increasingly unconvincing. Finally, the UK was not prepared to devalue together with Italy on September 13. Instead, in a last-minute effort, it sharply raised the key interest rate on September 16 but to no avail. After leaving the ERM, the UK engineered a virtual U-turn in its monetary policy by lowering its interest rate in several steps from 10 percent to 6 percent on January 19, 1993, inducing the rapid depreciation of the pound sterling.

In Italy, the main culprit was the general political situation. The new government headed by former Treasury Minister Giuliano Amato was willing to deal with the budget situation but was not able to do so decisively. Finally, the Banca d'Italia convinced the government of the need to devalue. Attempts (undertaken together with Germany over the weekend of September 12–13, 1992) to come to a more comprehensive EMS realignment were unsuccessful and apparently not carried out with sufficient determination. No meeting of the Monetary Committee or the finance ministers and central bank governors was called for that weekend (Muehring, 1992; Norman, 1992; Norman and Barber, 1992; Stephens, 1996a).

France, in turn, had, for some time, steadfastly declined to consider any possibility of an ERM realignment. With regard to its own currency, this was justified in view of a sound financial situation and understandable because of the perceived risk to the credibility of its near decade-long stabilization strategy. Yet, France also was against a devaluation of other countries, shying away from the likely real appreciation of its currency and fearing — with some justification as events showed later — that the franc might be the next currency to be tested by the markets.

The German government failed to respond to the large financing needs of unification with an appropriate fiscal policy, that is, an immediate substantial increase in taxes. A revaluation of the Deutsche mark, apparently suggested by the German authorities, was unacceptable to some EC partners (Masera, 1994, p. 271). It was monetary policy that, in view of rising inflation, had to bear the burden of adjustment. Although recognizing the justification of the restrictive policy stance of the Bundesbank, one can harbor, however, differing views on the timing and scope of certain decisions. For instance, the decision to raise the discount rate on July 16, 1996, shortly after the upset in the Danish referendum, was bound to increase tensions. Later, interest rates should have been lowered earlier and perhaps more decisively. This probably would have defused existing market pressures and lowered the intervention obligations of the Bundesbank. (Intervention in September 1992 alone amounted to DM 92 billion, at the time equivalent to about $64 billion.) However, in view of the existing divergences in the economic performance of ERM countries, the need to realign exchange rates would have remained.

THE CRISIS IN SUMMER 1993

In the first half of 1993, international financial markets calmed down, and it seemed that the EMS had weathered the most severe crisis in its 14-year history. The Bundesbank gradually lowered its key interest rates, and several other European central banks followed. France, Belgium, Denmark, and Ireland pursued this strategy somewhat impatiently, and at the end of June, money market rates were below those in Germany. Nevertheless, bowing to market pressure, another devaluation of the Spanish peseta, by 8 percent, and the Portuguese escudo, by 6.5 percent, took place on May 14, 1993.

In France, there was a strong feeling that holding onto the exchange rate ultimately had been rewarded. The new conservative government of Prime Minister Edouard Balladur, formed on April 2, 1993, continued the policy of the "franc fort." On June 2, the authorities felt encouraged to lower the interest rate for short-term advances to banks to 7 percent, slightly below the Bundesbank discount rate. With the rate of inflation at 2 percent, more than 2 percentage points below the German rate, there was some musing that the French franc was replacing the Deutsche mark as the anchor currency for the EMS. The position of the franc was enhanced further by the presentation of a law on May 11 to grant the Banque de France independence.

However, a few weeks later, doubts resurfaced whether, with the unemployment rate approaching 12 percent, the French government could resist calls for a further relaxation of monetary policy. Speculation against the franc reemerged, and soon, heavy pressure developed. Despite a substantial increase of the short-term interest rate of the Banque de France and heavy intervention in the foreign exchange markets, the franc fell to the bottom of its fluctuation band. On July 29, the Bundesbank lowered its Lombard rate by half a percentage point but not its discount rate. This action was less than the markets had expected. On Friday, July 30, the franc came under severe pressure, and the situation became untenable. In July, the Bundesbank had to purchase foreign exchange, mainly French francs, amounting to DM 107 billion (equivalent to some $62 billion), of which DM 59 billion resulted in an increase in German bank liquidity.[6]

German Finance Minister Theo Waigel requested a meeting on the ministerial level. On Saturday, July 31, the Monetary Committee convened to discuss various proposals but did not come to an agreement. In the night from August 1 to August 2, the finance ministers and central bank governors finally reached the decision "to widen temporarily" the fluctuation margins for the ERM from ±2.25 percent and ±6 percent, respectively, to ±15 percent around unchanged bilateral central rates (*Bulletin*, 1993, No. 7/8, p. 21). The Netherlands and Germany agreed to maintain the narrow margins between their currencies on a bilateral basis.

The decision of August 2 meant that the general framework of the EMS and the existing central rates were maintained but that an essential element of the EMS as originally conceived and implemented was profoundly changed. The intention was to discourage potential speculators from targeting specific currencies by raising the exchange rate risk and to increase the system's flexibility to allow monetary authorities to cope better with market unrest. For countries with strong currencies, the wider margins provided protection against disruptive inflows of funds. Minister Waigel called the decision a "Befreiungsschlag" (stroke of liberation). In their communiqué, the ministers and governors reaffirmed the "determination to put the Treaty on European Union into operation . . . [and] their support for the procedures and criteria laid down in the Treaty with respect to the attainment of a sufficient degree of convergence in order to allow the realization of economic and monetary union" (*Bulletin*, 1993, No. 7/8, p. 21). Many observers, however, spoke of the collapse of the EMS and of a premature end to the Maastricht process.

The Monetary Committee and the ministers and governors had discussed various possibilities to solve the crisis (Barber, 1993a, 1993b; Marsh, 1993). Devaluation of the French franc, combined with lowering the German interest rates, was firmly rejected by France; the Bundesbank was concerned that lowering interest rates under political pressure would affect its credibility. A general temporary suspension of the ERM (which had been proposed by the UK in September 1992) also was unacceptable because it was feared to jeopardize the single market and to undermine the Maastricht process. The French proposal that Germany should unilaterally float the mark had no chance because the smaller countries with a firm stability orientation — Belgium, Denmark, and the Netherlands — made it clear that they would maintain the close link of their currencies to the mark. This would have left France with a few weak currencies in a truncated ERM, which has been described as a solar system without the sun.

The way was open for the widening of the fluctuation margins. Initially, widening to ±6–8 percent was considered, but there was concern that, in the prevailing, highly volatile situation, this might not suffice to restore calm to the markets. In the end, agreement was reached on ±15 percent.[7]

It soon became obvious that there would be no early return to a regime of narrow margins and that Italy, which at the time of its departure from the ERM had declared its intention to rejoin soon, would not do so.

The modified EMS was no longer the one envisaged by the European Council Resolution of December 5, 1978. As Niels Thygesen (1994, p. 216) observed, much of the rule book had become inoperative, and what remained was a largely discretionary system. Whether the EMS in its modified form would be able to secure "a zone of monetary stability at home and abroad" was by no means certain. The consensus on convergence toward stability appeared to have broken down. Indeed, many observers saw the purpose of freeing countries from the commitment to strive for exchange rate stability as a license for relaxing monetary policies in the fight against recession and unemployment. Whether looser monetary policies would succeed in this was hardly seriously analyzed by their advocates.

The authorities of those countries in the "hard core" of the EMS that had been subject to speculative pressures — France, Belgium, Denmark, and Ireland — did not yield to domestic political pressure but maintained their cautious monetary policies. Soon, their exchange rates recovered and approached their old lower intervention points against the Deutsche mark. After some time, they moved generally in a relatively narrow band against the mark, although not necessarily within the previous ±2.25 percent margins (see Figure 22.1).

In the first few months of 1995, new turbulences in the ERM erupted, aggravated by a pronounced weakness of the U.S. dollar in international currency markets. This led on March 6 to another devaluation of the Spanish peseta, by 7 percent, and of the Portuguese escudo, by 3.5 percent.

Heinrich Matthes (1994, p. 77), comparing the policy of shadowing the Deutsche mark without the constraint of the narrow fluctuation band after August 1993 with the previous "one-way bet" system, characterized it as a system in which "the sword of Damocles of severe exchange rate penalties" was hanging over potential speculators. Large speculative upheavals in exchange rates could no longer occur, and exchange rate expectations and pressure on interest rates would ease. The anchor currency was afforded "ideal protection" during the transition to the single currency.

The widening of the margins is of relevance for the interpretation of the criterion of the Maastricht Treaty for admission to the final stage, according to which a member state is to respect the "normal" fluctuation margins of the ERM without severe tensions for at least two years. Should the margins of ±15 percent now be considered normal, as some argued (Thygesen, 1994, pp. 218–19)? Bearing in mind, however, the rationale of this criterion, namely, to serve as proof for sustained convergence, that thought appears unconvincing. What counts is the actual longer-term stability of an exchange rate, which does not necessarily have to be circumscribed by a band of ±2.25 percent but should not be too wide of the mark.

After leaving the ERM in September 1992, the British pound and the Italian lira experienced substantial depreciations, and there were fears of severe inflationary repercussions. Instead, in the UK, the rate of inflation decreased, and Italy managed to limit the acceleration of inflation. Pier Luigi Gilibert, in a study on the performance of the British and Italian economies after their exit from the ERM (1994, p. 136), noted that "in both countries, the price effects of falling exchange rates were kept firmly 'bottled up' at the production stage in the form of higher input costs. They were prevented from filtering through at retail level by a combination of cyclical factors: low domestic demand, ample spare productive capacity, stable international commodity prices and . . . moderate, or even negative, unit labor cost growth."[8] For the UK, however, "the U-turn in economic policy of the post-ERM era might leave a legacy of shattered credibility" (p. 141).

It was not before November 1996 that Italy decided to rejoin the ERM. Effective November 25, the new central rate for the lira was set at L 990 for DM 1, roughly halfway between its old central rate of September 14, 1992, and its lowest level in March 1995 (L 1,275 for DM 1). The reentry of the lira was not only in response to the strengthening of its exchange rate in international markets over more than one-and-one-half years

(Figure 22.2) but was also considered a "fundamental step" toward Italy's participation in EMU from the outset, according to Italian Prime Minister Romano Prodi.

Although the pound sterling also experienced a strong appreciation beginning in late 1995 (Figure 22.2), the UK remained outside the ERM.

REFORM PROPOSALS FOR THE
EUROPEAN MONETARY SYSTEM

Following the 1992 crisis and again after August 1993, a debate ensued whether and how the EMS should be reformed to restore stability. In the discussion in mid-September 1992, the British had complained about "fault lines" in the EMS and called for a reform.

The Monetary Committee (1993) and the Committee of Governors (1993) examined the functioning of the EMS in reports that were presented to a meeting of finance ministers and central bank governors in May 1993. In their view, the main causes of the crisis had been insufficient convergence and the postponement of serious efforts to correct imbalances. The sustainability of central rates depended on the credibility of national policies. The committees did not favor a reform of the EMS but emphasized, instead, that the existing rules needed to be applied consistently. Appropriate interest rate differentials were important, because interventions alone could be of only limited effectiveness in containing tensions. When central rates became unsustainable, there should be timely realignments. Existing procedures left the initiative for an adjustment in the hands of the country whose rate was out of line, but future procedures also should allow other countries to question existing central rates. In hindsight, it appears surprising that the committees either did not recognize the extent to which the credibility of the EMS had been eroded or were not ready to draw appropriate conclusions.

A number of interesting reform proposals were presented by economists in the press and in academia, of which only a few can be highlighted here.

Far-reaching proposals were published by The Economist (May 8, 1993, pp. 17–18), with the obvious objective of depoliticizing exchange rate changes and preventing excessive intervention. They included wider fluctuation margins with "soft buffers" that would let a currency move outside its band under certain circumstances (implying the absence of unconditional intervention obligations) and frequent, possibly automatic, adjustments of central rates (i.e., a sort of "crawling peg") to provide stability in real exchange rates. A crawling peg system had been proposed in the early days of the EMS when recurrent discretionary realignments were feared to destabilize the EMS, but the idea had been rejected because it would have reduced the pressure for domestic adjustment. As discussed above, the concept of wider margins found acceptance in August 1993.

Other proposals went in the opposite direction. Instead of advocating more flexibility, they favored a speedy realization of a de facto monetary union, possibly with a limited number of participants, to avoid the recurrence of self-fulfilling exchange rate crises. Already in 1991, a study published by the Centre for Economic Policy Research (Begg et al., 1991, pp. xiii, 55–57, 65–66) had advocated a fixing of exchange rates two years ahead of formal monetary union. This would result in a "positive shock" that would speed up convergence.

A report prepared by a working party for the French Commissariat Général du Plan (Pisani-Ferry, 1992) argued that, with German unification, the asymmetry of the EMS — previously one of the main virtues of the EMS — had ceased to be beneficial as the economic situation and interests of the anchor country diverged from those of other countries. A de facto monetary union should be established at the beginning of the second stage with formal commitments to EMS central rates, a commitment by all central banks to hold reserves denominated in the currencies of partner countries, and a codification and strengthening of mutual support mechanisms for intramarginal intervention. Germany would have to accept an "internationalization" of its monetary policy (p. 46).

Peter Bofinger (1993b, 1994b) went even further in proposing the establishment of a de facto monetary union between the six countries of the ERM's stability core (Belgium, Denmark, France, Germany, Luxembourg, and the Netherlands) by removing the foreign exchange constraint on these countries. They would purchase each other's currencies at the existing exchange rates without limit and without the obligation to repay intervention balances. This would enable them to defend parities without limit; unwarranted speculative attacks would, thus, be ruled out. National central banks should be made independent, and the duration of the arrangement would be limited until the end of 1996. At that date, member governments would decide unanimously whether to transform the arrangement into a formal monetary union as envisaged by the Maastricht Treaty or to give it up.

Even those short summaries make it obvious why they did not find much favor with policymakers.[9] Other proposals did not fare much better. Suggestions to rein in unjustified speculation against fundamentally solid currencies by returning to floating exchange rates, by reintroducing capital controls, or by levying a tax on foreign exchange market transactions (the "Tobin tax"[10]) were judged to be incompatible with the single market and the drive for further integration. A regime of floating exchange rates also was seen as an invitation to competitive depreciations.

Although the debate about the role of the EMS for advancing monetary integration and the merits of EMU continued, the prediction by some skeptics of an early demise of the Maastricht project proved to be premature. A widely held view was that "the process of monetary integration need not be disrupted by the temporary widening of the margins of fluctuation. . . . The further steps on the road to economic and monetary union will, of course, hinge crucially on whether and how soon the economic and political prerequisites for a common currency can be fulfilled" (Deutsche Bundesbank, 1993, p. 27). Policymakers finally realized — or so it seemed — that "credibility will be achieved only by addressing underlying causes, not merely by attempting to remove their exchange rate symptoms" (Masera, 1994, p. 287). The governments of the EC countries, with the notable exception of the UK, reaffirmed their commitment to the realization of EMU on the basis of the Maastricht Treaty. They undertook — with varying success, to be sure — to strive for convergence in order to qualify as early as possible for the final stage of EMU. The preparations for the final stage, mainly carried out in the framework of the European Monetary Institute, went ahead with full speed.

NOTES

Literature of general interest for this chapter: Cobham (1994); Collignon et al. (1994); Committee of Governors, Annual Reports for 1991 and 1992; Deutsche Bundesbank, Annual Report 1992; Eichengreen and Wyplosz (1993); Goldstein et al. (1993); International Monetary Fund (1993); Padoa-Schioppa (1994); Steinherr (1994).

1. The term "New EMS" was coined by Francesco Giavazzi and Luigi Spaventa (1990).
2. The following analysis is based on Ungerer (1993a, 1994). Both papers contain a chronology of events. See also International Monetary Fund (1993, pp. 42–47).
3. See also Padoa-Schioppa (1994, p. 15); Filc (1994, p. 104). For a characterization of the role of an anchor currency, see Ungerer (1994, pp. 9–10).
4. Deutsche Bundesbank (1992c, p. 15). Thygesen (1994, p. 213) wrote "that the Bundesbank invoked its 1978 understanding with the German government [the 'Emminger letter'] . . . that the presumed mandatory interventions at the margins could be suspended if they began to threaten domestic monetary stability." This interpretation is not complete, because it omits that the "Emminger letter" refers as first possible action to an exchange rate correction; see Chapter 13, note 8. See also Kenen (1995, pp. 162–63).
5. Later, when the exit of the pound from the ERM was followed by a recovery of the British economy, September 16 was labeled "White Wednesday" by some people in the UK.
6. For data on Deutsche mark interventions in the ERM for 1990–93, see Deutsche Bundesbank, Annual Report 1993, p. 89.

7. During a French-German emergency meeting on July 22, 1993, in Munich, the Germans proposed to generalize the wider margins of ±6 percent (Aeschimann and Riché, p. 217). During the meeting on August 1 and 2, Governor of the Banque de France and former International Monetary Fund Managing Director Jacques de Larosière argued for very wide margins; see Marsh (1993) and Aeschimann and Riché (1996, p. 234).

8. In a discussion with me in October 1996, Hari Vittas expressed the view that an important factor was of a structural nature. The ongoing shift in clout from labor to business increased dramatically the effectiveness of devaluations as an instrument of "real" adjustment, implying a simultaneous reduction in the inflationary consequences of devaluations.

9. For a more detailed examination of the proposals, see Ungerer (1994, pp. 15–22).

10. For more on the "Tobin tax," see Eichengreen and Wyplosz (1993, pp. 120–22); Spahn (1996).

23

Stage Two of Economic and Monetary Union, the European Monetary Institute, and the Preparation of Stage Three

The ratification process of the Maastricht Treaty had come to its conclusion on October 12, 1993, and the treaty became effective on November 1, 1993. The European Community (EC) — or European Union (EU), as the EC was now called[1] — embarked on a new phase of its development.

The second stage of economic and monetary union (EMU) started on January 1, 1994, and the European Monetary Institute (EMI) was set up on schedule. The decision of the European Council on October 29, 1993, to determine Frankfurt am Main as the seat of the EMI and of the future European Central Bank (ECB) was not an easy one.[2] Other cities had been proposed as candidates, among them Amsterdam, Luxembourg, and London. The United Kingdom (UK) was particularly concerned that the choice of Frankfurt would unduly strengthen this city's importance as an international financial center at the disadvantage of London. Germany, however, argued forcefully that the choice of Frankfurt was necessary to reassure a skeptical German public about the future loss of their currency, the "symbol of post-war stability," as the *Financial Times* put it (October 30–31, 1993).[3] The decision was part of a package that located various EC agencies in different European cities. Alexander Lamfalussy, from Belgium, general manager of the Bank for International Settlements, was appointed as president of the EMI.[4] Maurice F. Doyle, the governor of the Central Bank of Ireland, was elected as vice-president. He was succeeded in July 1994 by Luis Rojo, governor of the Banco de España. By the end of 1996, the EMI had assembled a staff of 200 people, drawn in large part from the central banks of member states.

The main task for the European Union during the second stage is to lay the foundations for the third and final stage of the realization of EMU. This includes the promotion of economic convergence and the preparations for the establishment of the European System of Central Banks (ESCB) and the ECB, the conduct of a single monetary policy, and the introduction of the single currency. In this, the EMI is assigned major responsibilities.[5]

POLICY COORDINATION AND CONVERGENCE

Already, before the start of the second stage, in July 1991, member states were asked to prepare multiannual convergence programs. Since then, most member states have presented such programs for review by the Council of Ministers.

According to Art. 103 of the Maastricht Treaty, economic policies of member states are a matter of common concern. "Broad guidelines" of economic policies, set out by the Council, are to provide the framework for the policies of member states and their surveillance by the Council. Should policies not be consistent with the guidelines, the Council can address recommendations to the member state concerned. The individual member states, however, remain responsible for their policies.

The first guidelines were adopted by the Council in December 1993 and have been issued since on an annual basis. They have emphasized the need for budgetary discipline and for labor market adjustment to secure the basis for noninflationary growth.[6]

An important and much scrutinized aspect of the second stage has been the progress toward "a high degree of sustainable convergence," as the Maastricht Treaty (Art. 109j) put it. Reviewing developments in November 1995, the Commission saw "further progress towards meeting the convergence criteria" and felt, as an interim assessment, that the situation was largely satisfactory. The EMI was more skeptical when it wrote: "Overall, progress towards convergence in the Community is insufficient."[7] Among the criteria that are to guide the assessment of sustainable convergence as a precondition for the move to the final stage, significant progress has been made with regard to price inflation and long-term interest rates. From 1993 to 1995, inflation declined in most member states (Figures 23.1 and 23.2). In 1995, 4 of the 15 member states — Greece, Italy, Portugal, and Spain — were above the reference value. Projections for 1996 indicate for these countries a better performance, albeit not yet enough to satisfy the criterion (Table 23.1). Regarding long-term interest rates, in August 1996, Greece and Italy did not meet the criterion.

FIGURE 23.1

Rates of Inflation in Belgium, Denmark, France, Germany, Ireland, and the Netherlands, 1990–96 (Consumer Price Indexes — Quarterly Averages)

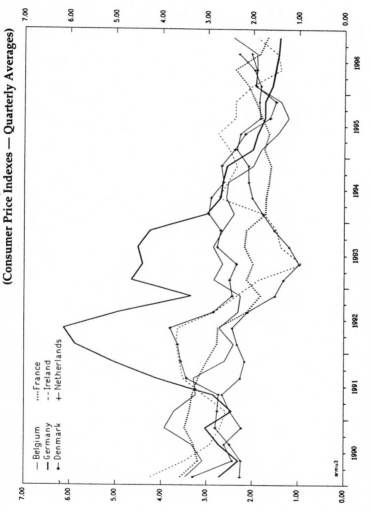

Source: International Monetary Fund, *International Financial Statistics.*

FIGURE 23.2

Rates of Inflation in Austria, Italy, Portugal, Spain, Sweden, and the United Kingdom, 1990–96
(Consumer Price Indexes — Quarterly Averages)

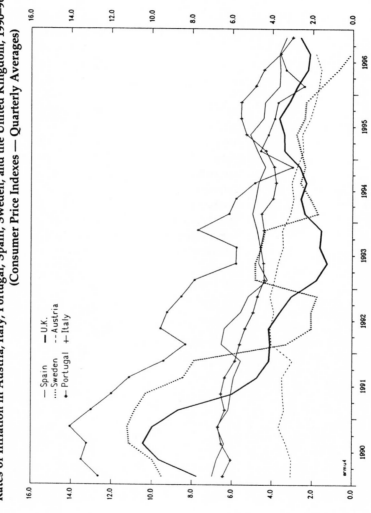

Source: International Monetary Fund, *International Financial Statistics.*

TABLE 23.1
Convergence Indicators for 1995 and 1996
(in percent)

	Inflation[a]		Long-Term Interest Rate[a,b]	General Government Balance/GDP		Gross Government Debt/GDP	
	1995	1996	August 1996	1995	1996	1995	1996
Austria	2.2	2.1	6.4	−6.2	−4.5	69.4	73.8
Belgium	1.5	2.0	6.6	−4.1	−3.2	133.5	129.6
Denmark	2.1	1.6	7.3	−1.6	−1.3	72.0	69.5
Finland	1.0	1.0	7.1	−5.2	−2.9	59.4	61.8
France	1.8	2.1	6.4	−5.0	−4.0	52.9	57.3
Germany	1.8	1.6	6.3	−3.5	−4.0	58.1	61.9
Greece	9.3	8.4	14.2	−9.2	−7.6	111.7	106.2
Ireland	2.5	2.3	7.3	−2.1	−2.4	84.8	76.3
Italy	5.2	3.9	9.5	−7.1	−6.7	124.9	122.8
Luxembourg	1.9	1.8	6.6	0.4	0.0	6.3	6.8
Netherlands	2.0	2.5	6.3	−3.8	−3.1	79.0	77.3
Portugal	4.1	3.3	8.7	−5.2	−4.0	71.7	70.7
Spain	4.7	3.4	8.9	−6.9	−4.6	65.7	67.1
Sweden	2.5	1.6	8.1	−8.1	−5.0	78.7	78.5
United Kingdom	2.8	2.7	7.8	−5.5	−4.4	47.2	50.8
EU-15[c]	2.9	2.6	7.5	−5.2	−4.5	72.2	73.9
Reference value	2.9	2.9	9.2	−3.0	−3.0	60.0	60.0

Notes:
[a]Average for the three lowest inflation countries.
[b]Ten-year government bond yields or nearest maturity.
[c]GDP-weighted average.

Source: International Monetary Fund, World Economic Outlook, October 1996, p. 20. In part, projections.

A much bleaker picture emerged concerning budgetary performance. In 1992, only four member states were below the deficit benchmark of 3 percent of gross domestic product (GDP) and five below the debt benchmark of 60 percent of GDP. By 1995, the situation had not improved; only three countries met the deficit and four the debt criterion. Projections for 1996 indicate some improvement with regard to the budget deficit, but only four countries are expected to remain below the reference value.

In November 1996, the EMI and the Commission presented their most recent convergence reports. The EMI (1996) characterized the current environment of low cost and price pressures as "favourable" but described progress in fiscal consolidation so far as "generally . . . too slow" (p. iii). With an obvious reference to specific measures adopted by France and Italy for their 1997 budgets, the EMI wrote "that the improvement of the deficit by measures with a one-off effect does not ensure sustainable consolidation." In its report, the Commission (1996d) came to the conclusion that "a majority of member states has not yet achieved a sufficiently high degree of sustainable convergence" (p. 5). Nevertheless, the Commission appeared cautiously optimistic when it emphasized the "substantial progress" since the beginning of the second stage (p. 72), and referred to the efforts of member states to further reduce their budget deficits; all but one country (Greece) expected to have a deficit at or below the reference value of 3 percent of GDP in 1997 (p. 43).

The Maastricht Treaty requires for the second stage the surveillance of national budgetary policies on the basis of the procedures outlined in Art. 104c. They were applied for the first time in September 1994, when the Council established the existence of excessive deficits in several member states and addressed, on November 7, recommendations to Belgium, Denmark, France, Germany, Greece, Italy, the Netherlands, Portugal, Spain, and the UK, urging them to correct the situation. A new set of recommendations was adopted in July 1995 concerning 12 member states, including the three newcomers Austria, Finland, and Sweden; only Germany, Ireland, and Luxembourg were not affected.

Because the exercise refers not only to the deficit but also to the debt of the public sector, the question was raised why Ireland, with a public debt ratio of 91 percent of GDP in 1994, was absent from the list of "sinners." However, account was taken of the progress made in the reduction of the debt ratio (European Monetary Institute, 1995b, pp. x, 21). Indeed, putting Ireland on the list would have been difficult to justify, because, from 1987 to 1995, the public debt ratio had been reduced from a peak of 130 percent to about 85 percent, while its public sector deficit ratio was continuously below 3 percent. Projections for 1996 and 1997 indicate further progress.[8]

Another round of budgetary policy surveillance took place in June and July 1996. Germany was taken off the list of achievers and Denmark was added despite a public debt ratio of around 70 percent, which, however, had significantly declined over the past years.

THE STABILITY PACT

Budgetary developments in the first half of the 1990s raised concerns about budgetary discipline once EMU had started. Art. 104c of the Maastricht Treaty stipulates that, after the start of the final stage, the excessive deficit procedures will apply to all member states except the UK, whether EMU participants or not, but the treaty did not make it explicit that the 3 percent deficit should be considered an upper limit, and its procedures for sanctions were considered too time-consuming and not sufficiently automatic.

In November 1995, German Finance Minister Theo Waigel proposed a "stability pact for Europe" under which the rules on budgetary behavior would be tightened for EMU participants and include automatic sanctions (Bundesministerium der Finanzen, 1995; Deutsche Bundesbank, Annual Report 1995, pp. 106–7). The stability pact would be supplementary to the Maastricht Treaty, and EMU participants would commit themselves to certain rules. In particular, the growth rate of public expenditure should, in the medium term, be kept below nominal GDP growth; the public sector deficit should not exceed 3 percent of GDP even during economically unpropitious periods and, in the medium term, should be kept at 1 percent. Exceptions to the 3 percent ceiling would be allowed only in extreme circumstances, subject to a qualified majority in the Council. Countries with a public debt ratio above 50 percent should stay below the deficit ratio of 3 percent; debt positions below the 60 percent ratio should continue to be reduced. The automatic sanctions would consist of non–interest-bearing deposits of 0.25 percent of GDP for each full or partial percentage point transgression of the deficit limit. Should the deficit limit be met in the two subsequent years, the deposit would be repaid; otherwise, it would be converted into a fine. The procedures would be monitored, and, as necessary, additional decisions would be made by a European Stability Council.

The German proposal generally was welcomed, but doubts were raised about the severity of its features, and it was argued that the proposed sanctions would aggravate the budgetary positions of high deficit countries. Another concern was that such an arrangement would be outside the regular institutional framework of the EU. In June 1996, the Council forwarded to the European Council for its meeting in Florence on June 21 and 22, 1996, a progress report on this and other issues of stage three (*Bulletin*, 1996, No. 6, pp. 19–21). The report took up important elements of the German proposal. It mentioned, in particular, that the 3 percent reference value for the government deficit should be seen as an upper limit and that each member state should aim for a budgetary position close to balance or in surplus in the medium term so as to allow automatic stabilizers to work without breeching the 3 percent limit. The report was not specific on other issues but introduced two new elements. First, member states with a derogation should be encouraged to participate in the arrangements for members of the euro area, although on modified terms. Second, the arrangements should be based on the treaty provisions. The procedures with regard to excessive deficits under Art. 104c could be strengthened by expediting their application, notably by setting tight deadlines for the various steps. To this end, recourse could be taken to paragraph 14 of Art. 104c, which empowers the Council to lay down (by qualified majority) detailed rules and definitions for the application of the Protocol on the Excessive Deficit Procedure and to replace that protocol by other provisions (for which unanimity is required).

After extended and tough negotiations, an agreement on a Stability and Growth Pact was reached at the meeting of the European Council on December 13 and 14, 1996, in Dublin (*Bulletin*, 1996, No. 12, conclusions of the presidency). Each member state is to commit itself to aim for a medium-term budgetary position of close to balance or in surplus. Participants in EMU will be required to present stability programs while non-participants are to submit convergence programs that will serve as the basis for early warnings on significant deteriorations in budgetary situations.

The excessive deficit procedure is to be expedited and clarified, and, in case of an excessive deficit, sanctions will be imposed on the basis of Art. 104c. A deficit over 3 percent of GDP "shall be considered exceptional [i.e., not excessive] when resulting from an unusual event outside the control of the relevant member state and which has a major impact on the financial position of general government, or when resulting from a severe economic downturn." As a rule, such a downturn is defined as an annual fall of real GDP of at least 2 percent. If an annual fall in real GDP is less than 2 percent but more than 0.75 percent, a deficit of more than 3 percent can be considered exceptional in light of further evidence, in particular "on the abruptness of the downturn or on the accumulated loss of output relative to past trends." Whether, under such circumstances, a deficit is excessive will be decided by the EMU participants with qualified majority.

Should a member state with an excessive deficit fail to correct the situation within certain deadlines (four months for taking effective action; correction of the deficit in the year following its identification), sanctions can be applied. Sanctions should include a non–interest-bearing deposit, which will be converted into a fine after two years if the deficit continues to be excessive. The amount of the deposit or fine will consist of a fixed component equal to 0.2 percent of GDP, and a variable component equal to one-tenth of the excess of the deficit over 3 percent. There will be an upper limit of 0.5 percent of GDP for the annual amount of deposits. In the whole process, the Commission is assigned an important role.

The debate about the stability pact was, of course, about more than numbers. The underlying issues were, on the one hand, how to shield the common monetary policy from profligate budgetary policies of individual countries, and, on the other hand, how to protect national sovereignty against the prevalence of automatic, technocratic rules. More precisely, the question was whether sanctions should be imposed on the basis of quantitative and automatically applicable criteria without regard to the economic circumstances of a case, and what role the Council of Ministers, the main political body representing member states, should play. The debate also concerned a "moral hazard" problem, namely that governments of potential "sinners" might be more inclined to be lenient in imposing sanctions on a country with unrestrained budgetary policies. In the end, both sides in the debate appeared to be satisfied. The principle of severe sanctions in cases of high deficits, not related to adverse economic circumstances, was confirmed and strengthened. At the same time, the importance of political decisions for less obvious cases was upheld. After the agreement, several commentators felt that most probably financial sanctions would rarely be applied (the imposition of sanctions remains subject to a two-thirds majority, according to Art. 104c.13), but could serve as an effective deterrent.

INSTITUTIONAL CHANGES

The Maastricht Treaty stipulated a number of important institutional changes for stage two, relating in particular to the financing of the public sector and to the legal status of national central banks.

Fiscal Policy Provisions

At the start of stage two, rules prohibiting central bank credit to the public sector and privileged access of the public sector to the financial sector had to be in place, and the no bailout rule, according to which the EC will not be liable for or assume the debts of individual EC countries, went into effect (European Monetary Institute, Annual Report 1994, pp. 107–10; *Official Journal of the European Communities*, December 31, 1993, pp. 1–9).

National Central Bank Independence

During the second stage, member states (except the UK and Denmark) are obliged to grant independence to their central banks as a precondition for participation in the final stage. Art. 108 of the Maastricht Treaty stipulates that national legislation shall be "compatible" with the treaty and the Statute of the ESCB and the ECB. The EMI (1995b, p. 89) pointed out that the term "compatible" indicated "that the Treaty does not require the 'harmonization' of [national central bank] statutes, either inter se or with that of the ECB. National particularities may continue to exist."

At the beginning of the Maastricht process, only the Deutsche Bundesbank was virtually fully independent.[9] The central banks of the Netherlands and of soon-to-be member state Austria had a very high degree of legal independence. Several other central banks enjoyed a relatively high degree of de facto independence in their operations, particularly those of Belgium, Denmark, and (with some qualifications) Italy. Among the least independent central banks — in legal as well as actual terms — were the Banque de France and the Bank of England.[10]

Since 1992, changes of central bank legislation were enacted in several countries (European Monetary Institute, 1995b, Chap. 3, Annexes 1, 2). The most far-reaching adaptations took place in France (January 1994), Spain (June 1994), and Portugal (September 1995). Legislative action also was taken in Italy (February 1992 and November 1993), Belgium (March 1993), and the Netherlands (December 1993). In Luxembourg, a draft law concerning the Luxembourg Monetary Institute and the monetary status of Luxembourg was submitted to parliament in December 1993 but has not yet been enacted. At present, Luxembourg forms a monetary union with Belgium, and the institute does not have all the attributes of a full-fledged central bank. Among the three countries that joined the EU in January 1995, legislative action was taken in Austria and Sweden; in Finland, it is in preparation. In some countries, the issue of whether additional changes in central bank legislation are required is still under examination. Concerning the Bank of England, no changes in legislation have been made or are planned. Should the UK decide to move to the third stage, it will be required to enact the necessary modifications in the legal status of the Bank of England.

THE CHANGEOVER TO THE SINGLE CURRENCY

It became increasingly apparent that the move to the final stage of EMU was not a simple process of replacing national currencies by one single European currency. A number of important and very complicated problems have to be solved, affecting the banking system, financial markets, enterprises, and the public at large. Furthermore, in some countries, skepticism about the merits of a single currency has been widespread, often combined with a lack of understanding of what the changeover to the single currency meant in practice. Uncertainties about the irreversibility of the move toward EMU, in particular after the crises of the European Monetary System (EMS) in 1992 and 1993, and about the technical implications for business, private investors, and consumers made it imperative to prepare for transition in good time.

Various basic models for the changeover to the single currency have been discussed, such as the "big bang," in which the changeover would take place for all sectors in one stroke at the start of the final stage; the "delayed big bang," which would leave more time for preparatory work before a simultaneous changeover; and the "mounting wave," which would allow a gradual introduction of the single currency. Under a "demand-led" or "market-led" approach, the public could choose between using the European currency or national currencies.

A group of independent experts, appointed by the Commission and chaired by Cees Maas, a former treasurer general in the Dutch government, presented in May 1995 a report (Maas Report). The group favored

January 1, 1999, for the start of the final stage. Because the single currency had to be strong and stable, the convergence criteria should be strictly adhered to. The authorities should promote awareness and clarity about the Maastricht Treaty and reduce the uncertainties about the changeover, including the legal and regulatory framework, the timetable, and the technical specifications of notes and coins. Furthermore, the relationship between participating and nonparticipating countries should be addressed.

The "Green Paper" of the Commission

On May 31, 1995, the Commission issued a comprehensive scenario on the changeover to the single currency (1995b). It had as objectives to remove the uncertainties surrounding the changeover; to demonstrate its technical feasibility; and to define possible approaches to encourage public acceptance. A big bang, although most satisfactory, would raise insurmountable difficulties because of the time required for the preparation of technical changes. A delayed big bang, on the other hand, would not be consistent with the Maastricht Treaty's stipulation of a "rapid introduction" of the single currency and would pose problems for public acceptability and familiarization. A purely demand-led scenario was rejected as too complex and costly. The Commission offered, instead, a "specific reference scenario" of three phases with gradualist features. In the terminology used above, the Commission scenario could be described as being of the mounting wave variety with a somewhat delayed partial big bang occurring in its second phase.

At the start of phase A, the participants would be selected. Then, the ESCB and the ECB would be set up and the Executive Board of the ECB appointed. The ESCB-ECB would begin to introduce its operational instruments. The production of notes and coins denominated in the single currency would begin. Phase A should last a maximum of 12 months.

Phase B would mark the entry into force of stage three of EMU and last, at most, three years. At its start, conversion rates of participating countries would be fixed, the ESCB would assume responsibility for the single monetary policy, and the ECU — renamed "euro" in December 1995 — would become a currency in its own right. National currencies, although still legal tender, would, in fact, no longer be distinct currencies but different denominations of the euro. It would be important to create a "critical mass of activities" in euro in order to establish early credibility. In transactions with national central bank commercial banks and in the foreign exchange markets, the ECB would deal exclusively in euro. New issues of public debt would be denominated in euro. Interbank, money, and capital markets should be able to work in euro. National currencies would continue to be used in transactions between banks and most of their customers. Overall, the critical mass would basically concern well-defined and homogeneous market activities. Although private businesses other than banks could conduct some of their operations in euro, consumers would continue to use their national currencies, because of the limited availability of means of payment denominated in the new currency.

In phase C, euro-denominated notes and coins would be introduced and replace national ones. This would last as long as necessary, that is, several weeks. The euro would become the only legal tender. If one assumes January 1, 1999, as the start of the final stage of EMU, phase A would begin in early 1998, phase B on January 1, 1999, and phase C not later than January 1, 2002.

The Scenario of the European Monetary Institute

The EMI issued its scenario for the changeover in November 1995 (1995c). Like the Commission, the EMI suggested three phases (here called "periods") for the introduction of the single currency. Five principles are to ensure transparency and public acceptance of the transition process: a clear legal framework; the changeover should be relatively simple and user-friendly; it should be efficient and aim at avoiding competitive distortions; it should facilitate the implementation of the single monetary policy; and private economic agents, although free to use the European currency, should not be obliged to do so before the deadline for the completion of the changeover.

The first period would begin about one year before the start of the third and final stage of EMU. Participants would be determined, and the ESCB-ECB would be established.

The second period would last from the start of the third stage until the date when euro-denominated notes and coins are put into circulation. At its beginning, the bilateral exchange rates between the currencies of participating member states would be replaced by irrevocably locked conversion rates. Until the introduction of euro banknotes and coins, national ones would, however, remain the only legal tender. The ESCB would start conducting its single monetary policy and execute its operations in euro. As necessary, national central banks would provide national financial institutions with facilities for the conversion from euro into national currencies and vice versa. There would be no more foreign exchange markets between national currencies, only purely arithmetical conversions. In the markets dealing with nonparticipating EU or third currencies, the ECB would carry out its transactions in euro and would encourage other operators to do so. The national central banks would exchange national banknotes of participants at par value. It would be expected that new public debt issues would be denominated in euro and that financial markets would largely change over to the euro at an early stage, although most enterprises and private individuals would continue to operate in national currencies.

At the latest, three years after the start of the final stage of EMU, the third period would begin. Euro-denominated banknotes and coins would be introduced and become legal tender. They would circulate in parallel with the national banknotes and coins. The third period would end when national banknotes ceased to be legal tender. The time frame should be laid down in EU legislation, but some freedom might be left to individual member states. The EMI suggested six months as appropriate. A shorter period could create bottlenecks and would not be sufficient for the required changes in vending and automated teller machines. Also, a six-month period would offer a sufficiently long learning period for the public at large.

At the start of stage three of EMU (i.e., the second period of the changeover), a Trans-European Automated Real-Time Gross Settlement Express Transfer System (TARGET) is to be in place. TARGET will be operated by the ESCB and link the national payments systems of participants. It is to process domestic and cross-border payments and form the technical basis for the money market of the euro area and the conduct of the single monetary policy (European Monetary Institute, 1995c, pp. 18–19; 1995a). Whether non-EMU countries will be able to use TARGET became a controversial issue and is still under debate. The UK and Denmark want the facility to be fully available to all EU member states; other countries, in particular France and Germany, want to limit its use to EMU participants.

Using again the terms introduced at the beginning of this section, the EMI scenario has many elements of a mounting wave with a limited big bang at the end. It has nearly the same general time frame as the Commission's scenario but differs from it mainly by applying a more gradual, pragmatic approach to the all-important period between the start of stage three of EMU and the full use of the single currency. It combines in that period the desirability for a wide use of the euro as the basis for the conduct of monetary policy, including exchange rate policy, with considerations for the differing needs and capabilities of the various sectors of the economy.

This user-friendly approach reflects the concerns of the constituent parts of the EMI, the national central banks, about a possible distortion of competition as well as the results of the EMI's inquiries and other studies. Some central banks were very conscious of the difficulties that smaller banks would face in operating simultaneously in the European and the national currency. This had caused the Bundesbank to initially favor a delayed big bang scenario so as to provide the 9,000 small banks operating in Germany with sufficient time to adapt. Once it was realized that the big banks could not be prevented from using the euro before the final changeover, the scenario proposed by the EMI appeared to be the best solution. The Bank of England had advocated a demand-led or market-led approach, thus, harking back to the earlier UK proposals for a "hard" ECU, to be used in parallel with national currencies (see Chapters 17 and 19).

The Madrid European Council Meeting in December 1995

The finance ministers and central bank governors at a meeting on September 30 in Valencia endorsed the concept prepared by the EMI. On this basis, the European Council, convening in Madrid on December 15 and 16, adopted a changeover scenario (*Bulletin*, 1995, No. 12, pp. 10–11, Annex 1, pp. 26–28). As early as possible in 1998, the Council in the Composition of Heads of State or Government, will confirm which member states fulfill the conditions for EMU participation. (This will allow a decision to be based on actual economic data and not on estimates.) Stage three would begin on January 1, 1999.

Proposals for regulations concerning the legal framework for the introduction of the euro were presented by the Commission on October 10, 1996, and were endorsed by the European Council at its meeting in Dublin on December 13 and 14, 1996 (*Bulletin*, 1996, No. 12, conclusions of the presidency).

Euro — The Name for the Single Currency

At the same meeting, the European Council decided that the single currency should be named "euro," replacing the generic term ECU. It is to be a full name, not a prefix to national currency names. A debate about the name of the new currency had been going on for some time. There was some unhappiness about the name "ECU." Although "écu" appealed to the French for historical reasons (it was President Giscard d'Estaing who had launched it when the EMS was conceived) and "ECU" made sense in English as an abbreviation for European Currency Unit, it did not carry any linguistic or historical meaning in other European languages. (This encouraged a prominent politician in Bavaria to call the future European currency an "Esperanto currency.") Furthermore, the steady loss in value of the basket-ECU against the stronger European currencies had deprived it of credibility. Various names with meaningful historic associations, such as "franc," "guilder-florin," "crown," or "shilling" were discussed and eventually found wanting. (E.g., Spain made it clear that, for obvious reasons, it could not accept "franco" as the name of the European currency.) The German proposal to combine "Euro" with the names of national currencies, such as "Euro-mark" or "Euro-franc," did not find any favor either.

Earlier in 1995, a decision was reached to offer the European currency banknotes in denominations of 5, 10, 20, 50, 100, 200, and 500 units. For the design of the notes, two themes were envisaged: "Ages and styles of Europe," and an abstract-modern design (European Monetary Institute, Annual Report 1995, pp. 64–65). The term "cent" is to be used for euro-denominated coins of small value.

MONETARY POLICY STRATEGY AND INSTRUMENTS OF THE EUROPEAN CENTRAL BANK

Next to the design of a changeover scenario, the most important task for the EMI is to prepare for the monetary policy strategy and the policy instruments of the ECB.

Differences in the structure of banking systems, the size and character-istics of financial markets, and the relationships between governments and central banks in financial matters shaped the history of monetary pol-icy in EC countries. Various monetary policy strategies and instruments have been employed by EC central banks in pursuing their objectives (European Monetary Institute, Annual Report 1994, pp. 123–27; Deane and Pringle, 1994, pp. 127–37; Padoa-Schioppa, 1994, pp. 205–36). Most exchange rate mechanism (ERM) countries are using strategies based on indirect targets. In Germany, monetary policy is based on a monetary aggregate (M3). In other countries, in particular those who want to main-tain a stable link to the Deutsche mark, the exchange rate is used as an intermediate target. France employs simultaneously the exchange rate and a monetary aggregate (M3). Spain targets directly inflation and mon-itors money growth. Italy makes use of a monetary target, and the UK tar-gets inflation directly.

Because the future euro area is to follow an independent exchange rate policy vis-à-vis third currencies, the choice is between using a monetary target to achieve the primary objective of price stability or directly target-ing inflation. The advocates of a monetary target-based strategy empha-size the monetary character of inflation as well as the transparency and, hence, credibility of such a strategy (Deutsche Bundesbank, Annual Report 1994, p. 101; Annual Report 1995, pp. 104–6). Others point to the tenuous relationship between monetary aggregates and inflation, as expe-rienced in the UK and the United States, and, therefore, prefer to directly target inflation. Very much hinges on the question of whether, for the area covered by EMU (which, over time, will change), stable relationships between monetary aggregates and inflation can be demonstrated. A number of studies appear to have succeeded in doing this (Cassard, Lane, and Masson, 1997). Yet, the change in the monetary regime could invalidate preexisting relationships. A combination of the two strategies also could be an option. In the past, a number of central banks have not been following a strict single-target strategy; other factors have also been taken into account. A dual concept that would combine a multiannual inflation target with annual monetary targets has been suggested.

A consensus emerged in the EMI Council about the monetary policy instruments for the ECB. Open market operations, which have been the most important tool of European central banks for quite some time, are to play a central role. Standing facilities (such as a Lombard or discount facility) that can be used by the central bank counterparts at their discretion also could be made available. In accordance with Art. 19 of the Statute of the ESCB and the ECB, minimum reserve requirements are to be at the disposal of the ECB, although opinions about their desirability and effectiveness differ (European Monetary Institute, Annual Report 1995, pp. 51–55; Deutsche Bundesbank, Annual Report 1995, p. 105).

Discussions about the full range of instruments and their particular features are still in progress. A detailed report by the EMI was published in January 1997.[11] Final decisions, however, will be made only once EMU participants have been determined and ESCB and ECB have been established.

THE "INS" AND "OUTS" AND EUROPEAN MONETARY SYSTEM II

The Maastricht Treaty dealt in some detail with the exchange rate policy of the euro area vis-à-vis third, that is, non-EC, countries. The treaty remained silent, however, on the issue of the exchange relationships between the "ins" and the "outs," that is, the countries that participate in EMU and those that do not, although the treaty provided explicitly for the possibility of nonparticipation. The explanation for that omission may be that, at the time of the negotiations, all member states were participating in the ERM with relatively narrow fluctuation margins of ±2.25 percent or ±6 percent, with the exception of Portugal (which joined in April 1992) and Greece; the three soon-to-be members, which maintained close ties to the ERM, were expected to join.[12] The sharp depreciation of the pound sterling and the Italian lira following their departure from the ERM in September 1992, the adoption of fluctuation margins of ±15 percent in August 1993, and the renunciation of ECU ties by Finland and Sweden (as well as Norway) in autumn 1992 raised the specter of extended periods of significantly diverging exchange rates within the EC even after the realization of EMU, because it appeared more and more likely that some countries would not be able or willing to join EMU from the start. There was concern about significant shifts in competitiveness and even competitive devaluations of some currencies that were seen as potential threats to the single market.

The Commission (1995d, p. 2) pointed out that the Maastricht Treaty implied the existence of an exchange rate relationship between nonparticipating countries and the participating group. After the beginning of the third stage, Art. 109m.2 obliged each member state with a derogation to treat its exchange rate policy as a matter of common interest. Moreover, the convergence criterion on exchange rate stability applied, together with the other criteria, also to countries joining EMU later and was defined in terms of ERM participation. This implied the existence of such a mechanism, although not necessarily in its current form, after the start of stage three as long as there were nonparticipants. This interpretation was not shared by the Bank of England, which holds that the ERM had substantially changed since the treaty was agreed to and that it was the substance of exchange rate stability, and not its technical form, that was important (George, 1996).

The debate about the design of an institutional framework for the exchange rate relationships between the ins and the outs (or, more precisely, between the euro area and the currencies of nonparticipating countries, also called "pre-ins") — soon dubbed "EMS II" or "ERM II" — concentrated on a number of issues. There was the question of how to avoid or curb significant exchange rate oscillations not justified by fundamentals. This was, in particular, a concern of France, which worried that the competitiveness of its economy could be adversely affected. In line with its traditional predilection for stable exchange rates, France favored relatively close exchange rate links. Not surprisingly, the UK, which in 1992 had freed itself from what it considered undue constraints of the ERM, was not at all eager to contemplate new constraints. During the negotiations leading to the Maastricht Treaty, the most stability-conscious countries had fought hard to protect the future single monetary policy against destabilizing influences coming from the outside. Now, they were concerned that any tight exchange rate arrangement would lead to intervention obligations for the ECB that, through the back door, could undermine the stability-oriented strategy of the ECB.[13]

The familiar issues of symmetry and asymmetry made a comeback: who should carry the burden of intervention, the group of ins, that is, the euro area, or the outs? A related and important question was the role of the ECB in operating an EMS II. EMI President Lamfalussy had expressed early the view that the ECB should play a key role in running the new system and should have the right to initiate exchange rate changes and the possibility to suspend automatic intervention if price stability within the EMU would be endangered. Another issue was how an EMS II could assist those outsiders who wanted to join EMU as soon as possible to achieve the required degree of convergence.

In its progress report on the preparation of stage three to the European Council meeting in June 1996 (*Bulletin*, 1996, No. 6, pp. 20–21), the Council of Ministers presented an outline of a mechanism for linking the exchange rates between the euro and the currencies outside EMU. The report stressed that the proper functioning of the single market should not be endangered by real exchange rate misalignments or excessive nominal exchange rate fluctuations between the euro and the other currencies and that lasting convergence of economic fundamentals was a prerequisite for sustainable exchange rate stability. All member states should pursue disciplined monetary policies directed toward price stability, and in this, policy coordination in the framework of the General Council of the ESCB (which brings together EMU participants and nonparticipants) had to play a central role. As of January 1, 1999, a new exchange rate mechanism should replace the present ERM. Membership would continue to be voluntary. Exchange rate policies of nonparticipating member states should be assessed at EU level so as to avoid any distortion of the single market.

Further progress regarding the design of the new system was made at the meeting of finance ministers and central bank governors on September 21 and 22, 1996 (Lamfalussy, 1996), and agreement was reached at the European Council meeting on December 13 and 14, 1996, in Dublin (*Bulletin*, 1996, No. 12, conclusions of the presidency).

The new mechanism will be set up by a European Council resolution (like the original EMS), and the operating procedures will be laid down in an agreement between the ECB and the non-euro area central banks. The euro will be the anchor of the mechanism, described as a hub-and-spokes system. For the currencies not included in EMU, central rates will be defined in euro, around which a relatively wide fluctuation band will be established. There will be no formal grid of central rates encompassing all currencies participating in the system, but non-euro area member states can establish, on a bilateral basis, fluctuation bands between their currencies and intervention arrangements, with the aim of limiting excessive bilateral exchange rate oscillations. Central rates and the standard fluctuation band will be set by mutual agreement between the ministers of euro area member states, the ECB, and the ministers and governors of the central banks of the non-euro area member states participating in the new mechanism, following a common procedure, involving the Commission, and after consultation of the Economic and Financial Committee. All parties to the agreement, including the ECB, will have the right to initiate the reconsideration of central rates. The adjustment of central rates should take place in a timely fashion so as to avoid significant misalignments. Closer exchange rate links between the euro and the other currencies in the mechanism will be possible, depending on progress toward convergence. They can take the form of narrower fluctuation margins, which will be made public, or of confidential, informal narrower target ranges.

Intervention at the standard fluctuation margins will, in principle, be automatic and unlimited; it should be used as a supportive instrument in conjunction with other policy measures. The present very short-term financing facility will be continued. Very short-term financing balances will be settled in the creditor's currency, unless otherwise agreed to by the parties concerned. The Short-Term Monetary Support mechanism should be discontinued. The ECB and the central banks of the other participants can suspend intervention if this conflicts with the primary objective of maintaining price stability. The possibility of coordinated intramarginal intervention will be retained.

The most striking feature of the new mechanism, compared with the ERM of 1979, is the high degree of flexibility. Not only will wider margins, probably of a similar magnitude as introduced in August 1993, be retained, but each participant has the right to question existing central rates and is entitled to suspend intervention.

NEW MEMBERS

Negotiations between the EC and four membership applicants — Austria, Finland, Norway, and Sweden — started in early 1993 and were concluded in April 1994, only after a row over voting rights was resolved. The UK and Spain had demanded to retain the blocking minority of 23 votes in the Council of Ministers. The compromise was to accept the new requirement of 27 votes after enlargement but to allow for a reasonable delay on decisions opposed by countries mustering between 23 and 27 votes (now 26, after Norway did not become a member), to permit the search for a consensus (compare Chapter 4, note 10).

Voters in Austria, Finland, and Sweden approved membership in referenda that took place in June, October, and November 1994, respectively, but rejected it in Norway at the end of November in a repeat of a negative vote in 1972. Norway, however, remains linked to the EC — together with Iceland and Liechtenstein — in the framework of the European Economic Area, which was intended as a "halfway house" to membership (Abrams et al., 1990). Switzerland, the only other country that, together with the mentioned six countries, made up the European Free Trade Association, had rejected membership in the European Economic Area in 1992. The European Free Trade Association, formed in 1960, continues to exist, with its membership reduced to four countries.

On January 1, 1995, Austria, Finland, and Sweden became members of the EU and accepted the obligations of the Maastricht Treaty. All three countries joined the EMS, but only Austria decided to participate in the ERM as of January 9, 1995. It continued its policy of unilaterally pegging its currency to the Deutsche mark. Finland joined the ERM on October 14, 1996.

NOTES

Literature of general interest for this chapter: Bank of England (1996); Deutsche Bundesbank (1994, 1996); Enoch and Quintyn (1996); Taylor (1995).

1. Article A of the Maastricht Treaty states "The High Contracting Parties establish among themselves a European Union . . . [which] shall be founded on the European Communities, supplemented by the policies and forms of cooperation established by the Treaty." In this and Chapter 24, we shall use the term European Union (EU) instead of European Community (EC).

2. The EMI moved from its provisional base in Basle to Frankfurt in November 1994.

3. According to a German opinion poll of October 1995, 60 percent of respondents felt that the choice of Frankfurt as seat for the future ECB was important (Köcher, 1995b, Table A26).

4. In May 1996, it was announced that Lamfalussy would step down in June 1997 and that the EMI Council proposed Willem F. Duisenberg as his successor.

5. This chapter, concluded in 1996, can provide only a provisional discussion of the main issues because developments are still in progress.

6. For the full texts, see various *Bulletins*.

7. Commission (1995c, p. i); European Monetary Institute (1995b, p. ix). See also European Monetary Institute (Annual Report 1995, pp. 35–42); Deutsche Bundesbank (Annual Report 1994, pp. 102–6); Deutsche Bundesbank (Annual Report 1995, pp. 98–102); International Monetary Fund (1996a, b). For earlier convergence reports, see Commission (1994, 1995b).

8. I was head of the IMF consultation missions to Ireland in 1986 and 1990 and witnessed firsthand the improvement of not only the budgetary situation but also the economy in general.

9. The 1996 convergence report of the European Monetary Institute (1996, p. 116) mentioned two instances where complete independence was not assured.

10. Assessing the legal preconditions of independence, as done by some authors, is easier than determining the de facto freedom to act. For a comparison of the institutional features of national central banks, see Committee of Governors of the Central Banks (Annual Report 1992, pp. 44–48, 71–89); see also Deane and Pringle (1994, pp. 232–46).

11. European Monetary Institute (1997). The report could not be taken into account anymore.

12. For an examination of various aspects of the issue of ins and outs, see Thygesen (1995).

13. For an analysis of the main issues of the new exchange rate mechanism and the German point of view, see Tietmeyer (1996).

24

Outlook

Since the end of World War II, Europe has embarked on a journey from political disarray and severe economic dislocation to political cooperation and a high degree of economic and monetary integration. Although the path was by no means always smooth, there was rarely a wavering in the determination to move ahead: a continuity of efforts spanning 50 years took Europe to the threshold of an economic and monetary union (EMU). It has been a unique venture in European history: a voluntary merging of important parts of national sovereignty by free and democratic countries.

THE EUROPEAN UNION: PAST AND FUTURE

At the center of this process were the six countries in the heart of Europe that founded the European Communities. They had set their sight — in the words of the Treaty Establishing the European Economic Community (EEC) — on an "ever closer union among the peoples of Europe." The most evident and important aspect of this process has been economic and monetary integration. The success and the inherent logic of integration among the "Six" has not been lost on other countries. Indeed, since the 1960s, successive waves of European countries, including the new democracies in Central and Eastern Europe, have expressed the desire to join the original Six. Yet, this process has by no means been an easy undertaking, given the significant cross-country differences in history and culture as well as political and economic backgrounds that have to be gradually reconciled.

At this writing, at the end of 1996, the European Union (EU) is facing many challenges and uncertainties. When will EMU be realized (some would even add: if it will be realized), and which countries will participate at its start? In this respect, the politicians are confronted with a dilemma: if the new currency is to be based on solid economic foundations, in particular regarding inflation and budgetary performance, so as to gain the trust of the financial markets, the business community, and the citizens, they have to be selective. Yet, if some countries are left out, the objective of a large area without exchange rate risks and with high market transparency will not be fully realized, and political friction may arise. On the other hand, the formation of EMU very well may serve as a catalyst for the "outs" to reinforce their efforts to put their economic houses in order.

A more general question is whether the Intergovernmental Conference that started in March 1996 (often called Maastricht II) will succeed in laying the groundwork for closer political cooperation and in endowing the EU with significant elements of a true political union. Furthermore, when will the applicants for EU membership join the present 15 members, at what speed, and under what conditions? What is the future role of the EU in a world of rapid political, economic, and technological change? These broader questions will, in one way or another, also have a bearing on the future course of European monetary integration and the functioning of EMU.

THE TRANSITION TO ECONOMIC AND MONETARY UNION

It is not my intention to make any predictions as to the start and the initial membership of EMU. In the past, too many have erred in trying to predict future events in European monetary integration: some have been overly and probably too naively optimistic, underrating the inertia of history, and others have been too pessimistic as they internalized "worst case scenarios," thereby underestimating the driving forces behind European integration in the face of adversity. Some politicians and observers, induced in part by tactical considerations, have favored a delay in the start of EMU so as to secure the widest possible participation. Others have insisted on ironclad economic convergence so as to avoid any risk of monetary instability, even if that would mean a significant delay. A few of these may even hope for postponement to "*St. Nimmerleinstag*," that is, for an indeterminate delay, because of serious doubts about the feasibility and desirability of EMU.

Moreover, there are those who, in general, harbor strong misgivings about European unification and, therefore, object to EMU as a matter of principle. They perceive EMU as a threat to national sovereignty (and, from a certain point of view, they are right), no matter how drastically sovereignty already may have been reduced as a result of economic and political globalization.

On the other hand, leading politicians in most EU states are committed to the Maastricht timetable, because they fear that a delay would cause a significant loss of momentum. They see EMU as a worthwhile objective in itself *and* as a crucial step toward political unification. In their view, a postponement of EMU might lead to the abandonment of the whole project and to retrogression in already achieved economic integration and provoke the risk of a gradual dismantling of the single market. This — they fear — would eventually result in a return to policies pursuing narrowly defined national interests without institutionally anchored cooperation and to the discredited "balance of power" strategies of shifting alliances and confrontation among countries — in other words, a future that threatens to turn back to the past.

If EMU will be realized on schedule, initial membership most probably will be confined to those countries that already have come close to meeting the convergence criteria. Much will depend on the success of efforts at fiscal consolidation, which presently are underway in several countries, and on the interpretation by the European Council of the requirement of a "high degree of *sustainable* convergence" (Maastricht Treaty, Art. 109j, emphasis added), in particular with regard to budgetary performance. It has been argued, for instance by former French President Valéry Giscard d'Estaing (Round Table on the Euro, 1996, pp. 88–92), that, for the calculation of the public sector deficit benchmark of 3 percent of gross domestic product, not the actual but the "structural" (i.e., cyclically adjusted) deficit should be used. The economic argument goes like this: the present economic slowdown in several member states was, in large part, responsible for their high budget deficits. To insist on a ratio of 3 percent for the actual deficit would only aggravate recessionary tendencies and unnecessarily limit the number of first round participants or delay the start of EMU. The legal argument refers to the wording in Art. 104c, which allows for a deficit ratio of more than 3 percent if "the excess over the reference value is only exceptional and temporary." However — it should be noted — Art. 104c continues, "and the ratio remains close to the reference value." Others point out that fiscal positions in several countries are unsustainable, Maastricht criteria or not, and, therefore, need to be decisively improved to generate the preconditions for longer-term, noninflationary growth. However, the debate about the interpretation of the convergence criteria is not merely about economic and legal aspects but also about the credibility of EMU beyond its start.

Should EMU indeed be realized in a multispeed process, in application of the principle of "variable geometry" (as an integration process at differential speed has been called), it should be remembered that this principle has been used before, although never in a matter of comparable importance. The snake, virtually from its beginning, did not include all currencies of the European Community, and the European Monetary System was launched without the participation of the pound sterling. The liberalization of capital movements, in the framework of the Single Market Program, allowed temporary derogations for economically weaker member states. The Schengen Agreement on the elimination of border controls was adopted by only a limited number of member states. The crucial issues of the multispeed process in realizing EMU are how much time those that involuntarily stay behind may need to catch up with those who are already in EMU, and whether the countries that stay out on their own may eventually change their minds. Is the argument correct — as I believe it is — that the involuntary latecomers will be induced to reinforce their convergence efforts, or will they rely mainly on political pressure to be admitted? That will depend not least on the "strictness" and credibility of the initial admission decisions. What will be the attitude of the United Kingdom (UK), come 1998?

There is another aspect of the transition to the final stage that may create problems. The decision on EMU membership is to be made in early 1998, and the irrevocable locking of exchange rates is to take place at the beginning of 1999, assuming this to be the start of the final stage. This would leave plenty of time for the foreign exchange markets to test the exchange rates of the currencies that are to form the euro area. It has been suggested that exchange rates should be fixed at the existing central rates (e.g., Kenen, 1995, p. 176). However, if market rates deviate from central rates, this could be in conflict with Art. 1091.4 of the Maastricht Treaty, which stipulates that the adoption of the conversion rates "shall by itself not modify the external value of the ecu," meaning that the external value of the new currency (the euro) on its first day must be the same as the one for the basket-based ECU (which is determined by market exchange rates of its composite currencies) on the day before.

However, a risk to exchange rate stability would also exist if — as was also suggested — already in early 1998 the then-prevailing market rates would be chosen as the basis for the conversion rates. It has been argued that exchange rate stability for this transitional phase could be ensured by very close monetary policy cooperation and unlimited intervention in designated currencies. This would convince the markets that no change in actual exchange rates could be expected. The achievement of "sustainable convergence" in participating countries — the condition for EMU participation — would leave little rational basis for persistent speculative attacks. That expectation presupposes, of course, that the decisions on

EMU participation would, indeed, be based on the achievement of truly sustainable convergence and that no major adverse economic or political events would throw financial markets into turmoil. Even so, there would remain the risk that currencies not slated to join the euro area could experience significant exchange rate fluctuations, with repercussions on the selected currencies (Commission, 1995b, p. 33).

Increasing attention is being given to the future role of the euro in the international monetary system and its place and importance in the triangle of the United States, Japan, and the EU (Alogoskoufis and Portes, 1991; Bekemans and Tsoukalis, 1993, pp. 231–91; Kenen, 1995, pp. 108–23; College of Europe, 1996, IMF Conference, March 17–18, 1997).

THE DEEPENING OF THE EUROPEAN UNION

The Intergovernmental Conference is not expected to deal with monetary matters. It has been charged mainly with devising ways to deepen cooperation within the EU, reforming its institutional framework, and designing a more efficient decision-making process in a union that, by 1995, had grown from 6 to 15 members and is expected to expand further. Among the key issues are the extension of majority voting and whether the principle of variable geometry (more recently also called "flexible integration") should be used more widely to allow a core of willing countries — the "advance guard" — to forge ahead in areas in which they agree, without being blocked by other countries but also without excluding other countries from catching up later on if they are able and willing to do so. How could the institutional problems be solved? Would such an approach still be compatible with the concept of a "union," and how could a "pick-and-choose" Europe be avoided? The term "union" has been seen by a very few countries, most notably the UK, as denoting not much more than an umbrella under which member states would engage in free trade, economic policy coordination (not necessarily of a binding nature), and a relatively loose form of cooperation in other political areas, such as external and internal security, but unequivocally based on the principle of national sovereignty. In contrast, other member states read more into the preamble of the EEC Treaty, which proclaimed the intention "to lay the foundations of an ever closer union among the peoples of Europe," and the preamble of the Maastricht Treaty, which enjoined member states "to continue the process of creating an ever closer union"; in other words, they are aiming at a "political union." How exactly to define "political union" always has been a matter of debate, but extended majority voting, subsidiarity, and more democratic accountability are seen as essential elements.

THE ENLARGEMENT OF THE EUROPEAN UNION

Could an EU, which deserved its name and would be more than a loose association of countries, be envisaged with some 25 members? For quite some time now, the small Mediterranean countries of Cyprus and Malta as well as Turkey have applications for membership pending (in the case of Malta suspended, following a change in government in October 1996). More recent applicants are countries in Central and Eastern Europe (the Czech Republic, Hungary, Poland, Slovakia, Bulgaria, Romania, Slovenia) as well as the Baltic countries of Estonia, Latvia, and Lithuania. Also, sight should not be lost of the remaining European Free Trade Association countries of Iceland, Norway, and Switzerland, which, in the future, may decide that they want to be part of the EU. We have there a wide variety of countries, with very different economic, cultural, and political histories. It seems obvious that, for quite some time, many of these countries may not be able to participate fully in all aspects of EU policies.

This also would be the case for EMU. It is difficult to imagine how, in the foreseeable future, most of the applicant countries could live up to the standards of financial stability envisaged by the Maastricht Treaty.

The question is then, if all countries in Europe are to live in a "common house," as the phrase goes, could they, and do they all need to, live on the "same floor"? The answer to this question in all probability will have to be the principle of variable geometry or (to use a different and widely used term) of "concentric circles," with varying intensity of integration in different areas.

If the magnitude of the problems leaves us with a degree of timidity, one should not underestimate, as often has been done in the past, the political will to advance in European integration. Important questions are, then, to what extent the ambitions of the "political class" will be supported by the people and — returning to monetary integration — whether there will be sufficiently widespread acceptance of the European currency. The inclination to support European unification seemed to have declined after the disappearance of the political and military threat of the Soviet bloc and given way to a certain retreat to national values and interests. Yet, the challenges of the emergence of the "global village" to security and peace, the protection of the environment, and prosperity have not gone unnoticed. The need to meet these challenges by a common European approach appears to be increasingly recognized.

It is instructive to analyze the results of various polls that have been conducted for many years both for the EU as a whole and in individual countries in order to gauge the views of the citizens on issues of European policies. Let us first have a look at prevailing views in Germany, the country that has been playing a key role in the realization of EMU. Polls in late 1995 showed widespread skepticism about the single currency (von Wilamovitz-Moellendorff, 1996; Köcher, 1995a, 1995b). Nevertheless, an impressive majority of respondents favored European integration in general and saw the single currency as part of this process. Consequently, nearly two-thirds expected to have the Deutsche mark replaced by the new European currency in the next few years. More than three-fourths of respondents associated European integration with the notion of "future," and two-thirds with "peace." Köcher (1995a) interpreted these results as showing that "already for quite some time, the [German] population defines the goals and successes of European integration not so much in economic but in political categories" (my translation). These results also help to explain why the German authorities are insisting on a strict interpretation of the convergence criteria and the need for a "stability pact" for budgetary policies while pressing forward with the realization of EMU and toward achieving closer political cooperation.

For the EU as a whole, an interesting pattern emerged from a poll conducted in late 1995 on behalf of the Commission by national institutes (Commission, 1996a, pp. 13–36, 42–44, 49–57). On the single European currency, the EU average indicated an approval rate that was clearly higher than in Germany: more than half were in favor and 35 percent against, and three-fourths expected a single currency to be introduced by the year 2010. However, there were several countries — Austria, Denmark, Finland, Sweden, and the UK — where a majority of respondents were against the single currency. Substantial majorities in all countries (ranging from a high of 86 percent in Italy to lows of around 55 percent in Austria and the UK) were in support of European integration. Similarly, there was widespread support for common foreign and defense policies, although, in both Finland and Sweden — countries with a strong tradition of neutrality — a majority of respondents was against a common defense policy. Support for European integration is strongest among the original six member states plus Ireland and Greece and weakest in Denmark, the UK, and the newcomers of 1995.

The existing skepticism on the single currency can be traced in part to a lack of information and in part to relatively low expectations regarding potential beneficial effects on macroeconomic developments. Interestingly, the highest positive impact appears to be expected in the microeconomic areas of easier travel and shopping, the elimination of conversion costs, and cuts in business costs — matters dear to the heart of consumers and businesses alike.

In January 1996, shortly after the meeting of the European Council in Madrid at which the new European currency was named euro and a changeover scenario was agreed, the European Commission launched an information campaign on EMU at a conference in Brussels. It was attended by some 600 representatives of official institutions, banking, business, trade unions, and consumer organizations of all EU member states. I end this book by quoting from the declaration that was issued by the Committee of Patrons of the conference, consisting of 12 leading European personalities — although not without emphasizing that something as important and at the same time potentially fragile as a new currency needs to be built on a sound economic basis and to earn the trust of the people:

If we create confidence, people will feel that they are not losing anything of fundamental importance with the disappearance of their national currency. Instead, they will come to appreciate that by putting their economies ever more closely together within the Union, they are gaining a strength and a power to influence their future economic affairs that is presently denied to any single Member State. That has been our experience after nearly forty years of building the European Union. (Round Table on the Euro, 1996, p. 95)

Chronology

December 27, 1945	International Monetary Fund established
June 5, 1947	Speech by George Marshall, U.S. Secretary of State, at Harvard University
April 13, 1948	U.S. Congress passes Foreign Assistance Act (Marshall Plan)
April 16, 1948	Organization for European Economic Cooperation (OEEC) established
May 9, 1950	French Foreign Minister Robert Schuman presents plan for a European Coal and Steel Community (ECSC)
September 19, 1950	European Payments Union (EPU) established
July 27, 1952	ECSC established
June 1–2, 1955	Conference of Messina, aiming at the creation of a European Economic Community (EEC) and a European Atomic Energy Community (Euratom)
March 25, 1957	"Treaties of Rome" signed
January 1, 1958	EEC and Euratom established
March 1958	Monetary Committee set up, in accordance with Art. 105 of EEC Treaty
December 27, 1958	Majority of EPU member countries make their currencies convertible; European Monetary Agreement (EMA) enters into force

March 9, 1960	Short-Term Economic Policy Committee set up
May 3, 1960	European Free Trade Association (EFTA) established
May 11, 1960	First EEC directive on the liberalization of capital movements adopted
January 1962	Start of the Common Agricultural Policy (CAP)
October 24, 1962	Action Program of the Commission on coordination of economic and monetary policies
January 1963	Negotiations on accession to EC of Denmark, Ireland, Norway, and the United Kingdom (UK) break down
April 15, 1964	Medium-Term Economic Policy Committee set up
May 8, 1964	Committee of Central Bank Governors and Budgetary Policy Committee set up; Council decisions on coordination of external monetary policies and prior consultations on exchange rate changes
May 1967	Denmark, Ireland, Norway, and the UK reapply to join the EC
July 1967	Merger of institutions of the EC into a single Council of Ministers and a single Commission
July 1, 1968	Customs union completed, 18 months ahead of schedule
February 12, 1969	Commission presents Barre Memorandum on coordination of economic and monetary policies
August 10, 1969	Devaluation of French franc by 11.1 percent
October 24, 1969	Revaluation of the Deutsche mark by 9.3 percent
December 1–2, 1969	First conference of Heads of State or Government of EC countries in The Hague called for establishment of economic and monetary union (EMU)
February 9, 1970	Agreement by EC central banks to set up system of Short-Term Monetary Support
March 6, 1970	Werner Committee formed to work out plan for the creation of EMU
October 8, 1970	Werner Report on the creation of EMU in stages presented
March 22, 1971	Council resolution on creation of EMU; Council decision to set up Medium-Term Financial Assistance mechanism
April 1971	EC central banks agree to narrow fluctuation margins between EC currencies as of June 15

May 10, 1971	Germany and the Netherlands let their currencies float freely; agreement on margins suspended
August 15, 1971	United States suspends gold convertibility of U.S. dollar
December 18, 1971	Smithsonian Agreement on a realignment of exchange rates of most important currencies and introduction of wider fluctuation margins of ±2.5 percent; devaluation of U.S. dollar against gold from $35 to $38 per ounce
April 10, 1972	EC central banks establish system of narrower margins for their currencies ("snake") but wider margins continue to apply against dollar ("tunnel")
June 23, 1972	UK withdraws from snake
January 1, 1973	UK, Ireland, and Denmark join the EC
February 12, 1973	U.S. dollar devalued against gold by raising price of gold to $42.22
February 13, 1973	Italy withdraws from snake
March 19, 1973	Breakdown of the Bretton Woods system of fixed exchange rates as many currencies abandon parities and start floating; EC currencies adopt joint floating and discontinue maintaining fixed margins against the U.S. dollar; "snake without the tunnel"
April 3, 1973	European Monetary Cooperation Fund established
January 19, 1974	France withdraws from snake
February 17, 1975	Community Loan Mechanism (CLM) set up
April 21, 1975	Creation of the European Unit of Account (EUA), based on basket of EC currencies
March 15, 1976	France withdraws from snake for second time after having rejoined in July 1975
October 27, 1977	EC Commission President Roy Jenkins presents Jean Monnet lecture in Florence and calls for renewed debate regarding EMU
April 7–8, 1978	President Valéry Giscard d'Estaing and Chancellor Helmut Schmidt present proposal for the European Monetary System (EMS) at European Council meeting in Copenhagen
July 6–7, 1978	European Council accepts EMS outline (Bremen Annex) as starting point for further discussions
December 4–5, 1978	European Council adopts resolution on the creation of EMS

March 13, 1979	EMS goes into operation; UK does not participate in exchange rate mechanism (ERM); creation of the ECU (European Currency Unit)
January 1, 1981	Greece becomes member of EC
March 21, 1983	Seventh realignment within EMS; French franc devalued against all currencies except Italian lira and Irish pound; France adopts comprehensive stabilization program, supported by financial assistance under the Community Loan Mechanism
July 1, 1985	Minor modifications of EMS agreement concerning the ECU enter into force (Palermo package)
January 1, 1986	Portugal and Spain become members of EC
February 1986	Signing of Single European Act, providing for completion of internal market by 1992
January 12, 1987	Eleventh EMS realignment, mainly related to financial market pressures, triggers widespread debate about future monetary integration
September 1987	Basle-Nyborg agreement introduces changes to EMS operations
June 24, 1988	Council decision on the full liberalization of capital movements by July 1, 1990, with temporary exemptions for Greece, Ireland, Portugal, and Spain
June 27–28, 1988	European Council at its meeting in Hanover sets up Delors Committee, with the task of studying and proposing concrete stages leading toward EMU
April 17, 1989	Delors Committee presents its report
June 19, 1989	Spain joins ERM
June 26–27, 1989	European Council, meeting in Madrid, accepts Delors Report as basis for further work on EMU
December 8–9, 1989	European Council in Strasbourg agrees to convene an Intergovernmental Conference (IGC) on EMU before end of 1990
June 25–26, 1990	European Council in Dublin, acting on a proposal of Chancellor Helmut Kohl and President François Mitterrand, agree on an IGC on political union, to meet in parallel with IGC on EMU
July 1, 1990	Start of the first stage of EMU
October 8, 1990	UK joins ERM
October 27–28, 1990	European Council in Rome sets agenda for IGC on EMU

November 27, 1990	Committee of Central Bank Governors submits to Council draft statute for European System of Central Banks and European Central Bank
December 15, 1990	IGCs on EMU and political union open in Rome
December 9–10, 1991	In Maastricht, European Council agrees on Treaty on European Union (Maastricht Treaty), which contains, as most important features, creation of European Central Bank and single European currency on January 1, 1999, at the latest
April 6, 1992	Portugal joins ERM
June 2, 1992	Danish voters in referendum narrowly reject Maastricht Treaty
September 1992	EMS crisis: on September 14, Italian lira devalued; on September 17, UK and Italy withdraw from ERM, Spanish peseta devalued; further devaluations of Spanish peseta, Portuguese escudo, and Irish pound follow in subsequent months
September 20, 1992	Referendum on Maastricht Treaty in France, with narrow majority in favor
May 18, 1993	Second (positive) referendum in Denmark
August 2, 1993	After renewed unrest in financial markets, ERM fluctuation margins widened to ±15 percent
November 1, 1993	Maastricht Treaty enters into force
January 1, 1994	Start of second stage of EMU; establishment of European Monetary Institute (EMI)
January 1, 1995	Austria, Finland, and Sweden become members of the European Union (EU); Norway, following a negative referendum, does not join
January 9, 1995	Austria joins ERM
May 13, 1995	Green Paper of Commission on changeover to single currency
November 1995	EMI issues changeover scenario German Finance Minister Theo Waigel proposes "stability pact for Europe"
December 15–16, 1995	European Council in Madrid adopts changeover scenario, based on EMI scenario; single European currency to be called "euro"
June 21–22, 1996	European Council agrees on outline for exchange rate system linking the single European currency and the currencies outside the single currency area (EMS II)
October 14, 1996	Finland joins ERM

November 25, 1996   Italy rejoins ERM

December 13–14, 1996   European Council agrees in Dublin on new
                       exchange rate system (EMS II) and on Stability
                       and Growth Pact

Bibliography

Abrams, Richard K., Cornelius, Peter K., Hedfors, Per L., & Tersman, Gunnar. (1990). *The Impact of the European Community's Internal Market on the EFTA*, Occasional Paper No. 74. Washington, DC: International Monetary Fund.

Act Concerning the Conditions of Accession and the Adjustment of the Treaties, Exchange of Letters on Monetary Questions. (1972, March 27). *Official Journal of the European Communities*. Special edition.

Aeschimann, Eric, & Riché, Pascal. (1996). *La guerre de sept ans. Histoire secrète du franc fort 1989–1996*. Paris: Calmann-Lévy.

Alesina, Alberto. (1988). Macroeconomics and Politics. *NBER Macroeconomic Annual*. Cambridge, MA: MIT Press.

Alogoskoufis, George, & Portes, Richard. (1991). International Costs and Benefits from EMU. In Commission (1991a). The Economics of EMU. *European Economy*. Special edition 1.

Amato, Giuliano. (1988). Un motore per lo SME. *Il Sole 24 Ore*, February 25. English translation in Krägenau, Henry, & Wetter, Wolfgang. (1993). *Europäische Wirtschafts- und Währungsunion: Vom Werner-Plan zum Vertrag von Maastricht — Analysen und Dokumente*. Baden-Baden: Nomos Verlagsgesellschaft.

Ansiaux, Baron H., & Dessart, Michel. (1975). *Dossier pour l'histoire de l'Europe monétaire 1958–1973*. Brussels: Vander.

Artus, Patrick, & Bourginat, Henri. (1994). The Stability of the EMS. In Alfred Steinherr (Ed.), *30 Years of European Monetary Integration*. London: Longman.

Baer, Gunter D., & Padoa-Schioppa, Tommaso. (1989). The Werner Report Revisited. Paper annexed to the Delors Report.

Balladur, Edouard. (1988a, January 8). Television interview. *Le Monde*.

____. (1988b). Mémorandum sur la construction monétaire européenne. Reprinted in *ECU*, No. 3.

Bank for International Settlements. Various annual reports.

Bank of England. (1996, February). Changeover to the Single Currency. *Quarterly Bulletin.*

____. (1992a, February). The Maastricht Agreement on Economic and Monetary Union. *Quarterly Bulletin.*

____. (1992b, May). Monetary Aspects of European Integration. *Quarterly Bulletin.*

____. (1991, February). The Exchange Rate Mechanism of the European Monetary System: A Review of the Literature. *Quarterly Bulletin.*

____. (1979, June). Intervention Arrangements in the European Monetary System. *Quarterly Review.*

Banque de France. (1979, March). Le Système Monétaire Européen. *Bulletin Trimestriel.*

Banque Nationale de Belgique. (1986, April). Le developpement de l'Ecu privé et la politique monétaire. *Bulletin.*

____. (1979, July–August). Le Système Monétaire Européen. *Bulletin.*

____. (1972, July–August). Les marges de fluctuation entre monnaies communautaires. *Bulletin.*

Baquiast, Henri. (1979). The European Monetary System and International Monetary Relations. In Philip H. Trezise (Ed.), *The European Monetary System: Its Promise and Prospects.* Washington, DC: Brookings Institution.

Barber, Lionel. (1995, March 11–12). The Men Who Run Europe. *Financial Times.*

____. (1993a, August 2). Politicians Usurp the Technocrats. *Financial Times.*

____. (1993b, August 3). ERM Bands Produce Sort of Harmony. *Financial Times.*

Barre Memorandum. See Commission (1969a).

Barre, Raymond. (1968). Statement before the European Parliament, Strasbourg, November 17. In *Bulletin of the European Communities*, 1969, No. 1, pp. 15–17.

Basevi, Giorgio et al. (1975, November 1). The All Saints' Day Manifesto. *The Economist.*

Bayoumi, Tamim A. (in press). *Financial Integration and Real Activity.* Manchester: Manchester University Press.

Bayoumi, Tamim A., & Eichengreen, Barry. (1993). Is There a Conflict between EC Enlargement and European Monetary Unification? *Greek Economic Review, 15*(1).

Begg, David, Giavazzi, Francesco, Spaventa, Luigi, & Wyplosz, Charles. (1991). European Monetary Union: The Macro Issues. In *Monitoring European Integration: The Making of Monetary Union.* London: Centre for Economic Policy Research.

Bekemans, Leonce, & Tsoukalis, Loukas (Eds.). (1993). *Europe and Global Economic Partnership,* The Bruges Conferences No. 1. Brussels: European Interuniversity Press.

Bergsten, C. Fred. (1988, June 12). The Case for Target Zones. In Bank for International Settlements and Per Jacobsson Foundation, *The International Monetary System: The Next Twenty-Five Years.* Symposium.

Bishop, Graham. (1991). *Valuing Public Debt in the EC: EMU Benefits versus "No-Bail-Out" Risks*. London: Salomon Brothers.

Bloomfield, Arthur I. (1973). The Historical Setting. In Lawrence B. Krause and Walter S. Salant (Eds.), *European Monetary Unification and Its Meaning for the United States*. Washington, DC: Brookings Institution.

———. (1963). *Short-Term Capital Movements under the Pre-1914 Gold Standard*, Princeton Studies in International Finance No. 11. Princeton, NJ: Princeton University Press.

———. (1959). *Monetary Policy under the International Gold Standard: 1880–1914*. New York: Federal Reserve Bank of New York.

Bofinger, Peter. (1994a). Is Europe an Optimum Currency Area? In Alfred Steinherr (Ed.), *30 Years of European Monetary Integration*. London: Longman.

———. (1994b). Creating a "de facto Monetary Union" by Completely Abandoning the Asset Settlement Obligation. In Stefan Collignon, Peter Bofinger, Christopher Johnson, and Bertrand de Maigret. *Europe's Monetary Future* (pp. 216–219). London: Pinter Publishers.

———. (1993a). Stabilitätsinsel Deutschland oder Stabilitätszone Europa. In Rudolf Hrbek, *Der Vertrag von Maastricht in der wissenschaftlichen Diskussion*. Baden-Baden: Nomos Verlagsgesellschaft.

———. (1993b, April). *European Monetary Coordination by the EMS: Faultlines and Reform Proposals*. Mimeographed.

Borchardt, Klaus-Dieter. (1995). *European Integration: The Origins and Growth of the European Union*, 4th ed. Luxembourg: Office for Official Publications of the European Communities.

Bulletin of the European Communities [European Union]. Various issues.

Bundesminister für Wirtschaft. (1989, September). Aufzeichnung zur Wirtschafts- und Währungsunion, Appendix to monthly report. Bonn: Bundesminister für Wirtschaft.

———. (1970, February 27). *Tagesnachrichten*, No. 6122. Bonn: Bundesminister für Wirtschaft.

Bundesministerium der Finanzen. (1995, November). Dokumentation No. 75/95. Bonn: Bundesministerium der Finanzen.

Carli, Guido. (1982). From the European Payments Union to the European Monetary System. In Richard N. Cooper, Peter B. Kenen, Jorge Braga de Macedo, and Jacques van Ypersele (Eds.), *The International Monetary System under Flexible Exchange Rates: Essays in Honor of Robert Triffin*. Cambridge, MA: Ballinger.

Cassard, Marcel, Lane, Timothy D., & Masson, Paul R. (1997). Core-ERM Money Demand and Effects on Inflation. *The Manchester School of Economic and Social Research*, 65(1).

Central Bank of Ireland. (1979, Autumn). A Guide to the Arithmetic of the EMS Exchange Rate Mechanism. *Quarterly Bulletin*.

Chancellor of the Exchequer. (1978, November). *The European Monetary System*, Green paper presented to Parliament. London: Her Majesty's Stationery Office.

Clarke, Stephen V. O. (1977). *Exchange Rate Stabilization in the Mid-1930s: Negotiating the Tripartite Agreement*, Princeton Studies in International

Finance No. 41. Princeton, NJ: Princeton University Press.

_____. (1967). *Central Bank Cooperation, 1924–31.* New York: Federal Reserve Bank of New York.

Classen, Claus Dieter. (1992, June 27). Kein Stabilitäts-Vorbild, Letter to the *Frankfurter Allgemeine Zeitung.*

Cobham, David (Ed.). (1994). *European Monetary Upheavals.* Manchester: Manchester University Press.

Coffey, Peter, & Presley, John R. (1971). *European Monetary Integration.* London: Macmillan.

Cohen, Benjamin J. (1979). Comments. In Philip H. Trezise (Ed.), *The European Monetary System: Its Promise and Prospects.* Washington, DC: Brookings Institution.

_____. (1968). *Reparations in the Postwar Period: A Survey,* Reprints in International Finance No. 9. Princeton, NJ: Princeton University Press.

College of Europe. (1996, March 20–22). Conference on Reshaping Transatlantic Partnership: An Agenda for the Next Years. Bruges.

Collignon, Stefan, Bofinger, Peter, Johnson, Christopher, & de Maigret, Bertrand. *Europe's Monetary Future.* London: Pinter Publishers.

Commission of the European Communities, European Commission. Various annual economic reports and reviews.

_____. (1996a). Eurobarometer, No. 44.

_____. (1996b). Broad Economic Policy Guidelines. *European Economy, 62.*

_____. (1996c, October 10). Proposals for Regulations Concerning the Legal Framework for the Introduction of the Euro. COM(96)499 final.

_____. (1996d, November 11). Report on Convergence in the European Union in 1996. COM(96)560 final.

_____. (1995a). Convergence Report 1994. *European Economy, 59.*

_____. (1995b). One Currency for Europe: Green Paper on the Practical Arrangements for the Introduction of the Single Currency.

_____. (1995c, November). Report on Convergence in the European Union in 1995.

_____. (1995d, November 28). Exchange Rate Relations between Participating and Non-Participating Countries in Stage Three of EMU: Interim Report to the European Council.

_____. (1995e). Broad Economic Policy Guidelines. *European Economy, 60.*

_____. (1994). Broad Economic Policy Guidelines and Convergence Report. *European Economy, 55.*

_____. (1993). *European Economy.* Reports and Studies, 5.

_____. (1991a). The Economics of EMU. *European Economy,* Special edition 1.

_____. (1991b). Draft Treaty Amending the Treaty Establishing the European Economic Community with a View to Achieving Economic and Monetary Union. *Bulletin of the European Communities,* 1991, Supplement 2.

_____. (1990a, March 23 and 24). Economic and Monetary Union: The Economic Rationale and Design of the System. Reprinted in *Europe Documents, 1604/05, 1606.*

_____. (1990b). Communication to the Council: Economic and Monetary Union. *Bulletin of the European Communities,* Supplement 2.

_____. (1990c, October). One Market, One Money. *European Economy, 44.*

_____. (1989, March). The EMS: Ten Years of Progress in European Monetary Co-operation.

_____. (1985). Completing the Internal Market: White Paper from the Commission to the European Council.

_____. (1982, July). Documents Relating to the European Monetary System. *European Economy*, 12.

_____. (1979, July). The European Monetary System. *European Economy*, 3.

_____. (1975). Report of the Study Group "Economic and Monetary Union 1980."

_____. (1973). Communication to the Council on the Progress Achieved in the First Stage of Economic and Monetary Union, and on the Measures to be Taken in the Second Stage. *Bulletin of the European Communities*. Supplement 5.

_____. (1970a). A Plan for the Phased Establishment of an Economic and Monetary Union. *Bulletin of the European Communities* (Supplement) 3.

_____. (1970b). Commission Memorandum and Proposals to the Council on the Establishment by Stages of Economic and Monetary Union. *Bulletin of the European Communities*, 11.

_____. (1969a, February 12). Memorandum to the Council on the Co-ordination on Economic Policies and Monetary Cooperation [Barre Memorandum]. *Bulletin of the European Communities* (Supplement), 3.

_____. (1969b). The Communities' Work Programme. *Bulletin of the European Communities* (Supplement), 4.

_____. (1962, October 24). Memorandum on the Action Programme of the Community for the Second Stage.

Committee for the Monetary Union of Europe. (1988). A Programme for Action. Paris: Committee for the Monetary Union of Europe.

Committee of Governors of the Central Banks of the European Communities. (1993, April 21). The Implications and Lessons to be Drawn from the Recent Exchange Rate Crisis.

_____. (1992). Annual Report.

_____. (1990, December 8). Draft Statute of the European System of Central Banks and of the European Central Bank. *Europe Documents*, 1669/70.

Committee of Governors of the Central Banks of the European Communities, European Monetary Co-operation Fund. (1985). Texts concerning the European Monetary System.

_____. (1979). Texts concerning the European Monetary System.

Coombs, Charles A. (1976). *The Arena of International Finance*. New York: John Wiley & Sons.

Council of the European Communities, Commission of the European Communities. (1992). Treaty on European Union. Luxembourg: Office for Official Publications of the European Communities.

Crockett, Andrew. (1977). *International Money: Issues and Analysis*. New York: Academic Press.

Cukierman, Alex. (1992). *Central Bank Strategy, Credibility and Independence: Theory and Evidence*. Cambridge, MA: MIT Press.

Davies, Howard. (1996, August 2). The Economic Implications of a Single European Currency. *Auszüge aus Presseartikeln* [Deutsche Bundesbank].

Deane, Marjorie, & Pringle, Robert. (1994). *The Central Banks*. London: Hamish Hamilton.

de Cecco, Marcello, & Giovannini, Alberto (Eds.). (1988). *A European Central Bank? Perspectives on Monetary Unification after Ten Years of the EMS*. Cambridge: Cambridge University Press.

De Grauwe, Paul. (1992). *The Economics of Monetary Integration*. Oxford: Oxford University Press.

De Grauwe, Paul, Gros, Daniel, Steinherr, Alfred, & Thygesen, Niels. (1992, July 4). Reply to Feldstein. *The Economist*.

De Grauwe, Paul, & Papademos, Lucas (Eds.). (1990). *The European Monetary System in the 1990s*. London: Longman.

De Grauwe, Paul, & Tullio, Giuseppe. (1994). The Exchange Rate Changes of 1992 and Inflation Convergence in the EMS. In Alfred Steinherr (Ed.), *30 Years of European Monetary Integration*. London: Longman.

De Long, J. Bradford, & Summers, Lawrence H. (1992, 4th quarter). Macroeconomic Policy and Long-Run Growth. *Economic Review* (Federal Reserve Bank of Kansas City).

Delors Committee [Committee for the Study of Economic and Monetary Union]. (1989). *Report on Economic and Monetary Union in the European Community* [Delors Report]. Luxembourg: Office for Publications of the European Communities.

Deutsche Bundesbank. Various annual reports.

_____. (1996, January). Scenario for the Changeover to the Single European Currency. *Monthly Report*.

_____. (1994, January). The Second Stage of European Economic and Monetary Union. *Monthly Report*.

_____. (1993, August). The Recent Monetary Policy Decisions and Developments in the European Monetary System. *Monthly Report*.

_____. (1992a, February). The Maastricht Decisions on the European Economic and Monetary Union. *Monthly Report*.

_____. (1992b, May). The Markets for Private ECUs. *Monthly Report*.

_____. (1992c, October). The Latest Exchange Rate Realignments in the European Monetary System and the Interest Rate Policy Decisions of the Bundesbank. *Monthly Report*.

_____. (1990a, July). The First Stage of European Economic and Monetary Union. *Monthly Report*.

_____. (1990b, October). Statement on the Establishment of an Economic and Monetary Union in Europe. *Monthly Report*.

_____. (1989, November). Exchange Rate Movements within the European Monetary System. *Monthly Report*.

_____. (1987, August). The Markets for Private ECUs. *Monthly Report*.

_____. (1984, May). Monetary Policy Aspects of the Revision of Agricultural Monetary Compensatory Amounts in the European Community. *Monthly Report*.

_____. (1979, March). The European Monetary System: Structure and Operation. *Monthly Report*.

_____. (1976a, January). The European System of Narrower Exchange Rate Margins. *Monthly Report*.

____. (1976b). *Während und Wirtschaft in Deutschland 1876–1975.* Frankfurt: Fritz Knapp.

Deville, Volker. (1986). *The European Monetary System and the European Currency Unit: Bibliography,* EUI Working Paper No. 89/206. Florence: European University Institute.

de Vries, Margaret Garritsen. (1987). *Balance of Payments Adjustment, 1945 to 1986: The IMF Experience.* Washington, DC: International Monetary Fund.

____. (1985). *The International Monetary Fund 1972–1978.* Washington, DC: International Monetary Fund.

____. (1976). *The International Monetary Fund 1966–1971.* Washington, DC: International Monetary Fund.

____. (1969). The Fund and the EPU. In J. Keith Horsefield (Ed.), *The International Monetary Fund, 1945–1965,* vol. 2. Washington, DC: International Monetary Fund.

de Vries, Tom. (1980). *On the Meaning and Future of the European Monetary System,* Essays in International Finance No. 138. Princeton, NJ: Princeton University Press.

Diebold, William. (1952). *Trade and Payments in Western Europe: A Study in Economic Cooperation, 1947–51.* New York: Harper.

Dillingham, Alan J. (1995, May 11–14). The Evolution of France's European Monetary Diplomacy. Paper presented to the Fourth Biennial International Conference, European Community Studies Association, Charleston, SC. Mimeographed.

Dixon, H. Joly. (1977, May). The European Unit of Account. *Common Market Law Review,* 14(2).

Economic and Social Review. (1989, January). European Monetary System: Tenth Anniversary Issue, 20(2).

Economist, The. (1993, May 8). Can Europe Put EMU Together Again? pp. 17–18.

Eichengreen, Barry. (1993). *Reconstructing Europe's Trade and Payments: The European Payments Union.* Ann Arbor: University of Michigan Press.

____. (1991). *Is Europe an Optimum Currency Area?* Working Paper No. 3579. Cambridge, MA: National Bureau of Economic Research.

Eichengreen, Barry (Ed.). (1985). *The Gold Standard in Theory and History.* New York: Methuen.

Eichengreen, Barry, & Wyplosz, Charles. (1993). The Unstable EMS. In *Brookings Papers,* No. 1. Washington, DC: Brookings Institution.

Emerson, Michael, & Huhne, Christopher. (1991). *The ECU Report.* London: Pan Books.

Emminger, Otmar. (1986). *D-Mark, Dollar, Währungskrisen.* Stuttgart: Deutsche Verlagsanstalt.

____. (1979, March 23). Das Europäische Währungssystem und die deutsche Geldpolitik. *Auszüge aus Presseartikeln* [Deutsche Bundesbank].

____. (1977). *The D-Mark in the Conflict between Internal and External Equilibrium, 1948–75,* Essays in International Finance No. 122. Princeton, NJ: Princeton University Press.

Enoch, Charles, & Quintyn, Marc. (1996, September). European Monetary Union: Operating Monetary Policy. *Finance and Development.*

European Communities, European Union. Various bulletins and official journals.

European Monetary Institute. (1997, January). The Single Monetary Policy in Stage Three: Specification of the Operational Framework.

———. (1996, November). Progress towards Convergence 1996.

———. (1995). Annual Report.

———. (1995a, May). The TARGET System.

———. (1995b, November). Progress towards Convergence.

———. (1995c, November). The Changeover to the Single Currency.

———. (1994). Annual Report.

European Parliament. (1966, November 28). Sitzungsdokumente [Documents de Seance] 1966–67, Dok. 138 [Dichgans Report].

———. (1962, April 7). Sitzungsdokumente [Documents de Seance] 1962–63, Dok. 17 [Van Campen Report].

European Payments Union, Managing Board. Annual reports 1951–59. Paris: European Payments Union.

Feldstein, Martin. (1992, June 13). The Case Against EMU. *The Economist*.

Filc, Wolfgang. (1994). Credibility of German Monetary Policy on the Road towards EMU. In Alfred Steinherr (Ed.), *30 Years of European Monetary Integration*. London: Longman.

Ford, A. G. (1985). Notes on the Working of the Gold Standard before 1914. In Barry Eichengreen (Ed.), *The Gold Standard in Theory and History*. New York: Methuen.

France. (1991a, June). Projet de Traité sur l'Union Economique et Monétaire. *Revue Financière Internationale* (International Financial Report) (Numéro spécial).

———. (1991b, January 29). Ministère de l'Economie, des Finances et du Budget, Service de la Communication, Paris.

———. (1990). Conseil des Ministres du 5 décembre, Communication: Les progrès vers l'Union Economique et Monétaire.

Fratianni, Michele, & von Hagen, Jürgen. (1992). *The European Monetary System and European Monetary Union*. Boulder, CO: Westview Press.

Frenkel, Jacob A., & Goldstein, Morris. (1986). A Guide to Target Zones. *IMF Staff Papers*, 33(4).

Friend, Julius W. (1991). *The Linchpin: French-German Relations, 1950–1990*. Westport, CT: Praeger.

Funabashi, Yoichi. (1989). *Managing the Dollar: From the Plaza to the Louvre*, 2d ed. Washington, DC: Institute for International Economics.

Gehrmann, Dieter, & Harmsen, Sabine. (1972). *Monetäre Integration in der EWG: Dokumente und Bibliographie*. Hamburg: Verlag Weltarchiv.

Genscher, Hans-Dietrich. (1988, February 26). Memorandum für die Schaffung eines europäischen Währungsraumes und einer europäischen Zentralbank. Bonn: Ministry of Foreign Affairs.

George, E.A.J. (1996, March 13). Speech at a conference organized by the Royal Institute of International Affairs, London.

German economists. (1992, June 11). Die EG-Währungsunion führt zur Zerreissprobe. *Frankfurter Allgemeine Zeitung*. English translation in Alfred Steinherr (Ed.), *30 Years of European Monetary Integration*. London: Longman.

Germany. (1991, June). Proposal for an Amendment to the EEC Treaty with a View to Achieving Economic and Monetary Union. *Revue Financière*

Internationale (International Financial Report) (Numéro spécial).

Giavazzi, Francesco, & Giovannini, Alberto. (1989). *Exchange Rate Flexibility: The European Monetary System*. Cambridge: Cambridge University Press.

Giavazzi, Francesco, Micossi, Stefano, & Miller, Marcus (Eds.). (1988). *The European Monetary System*. Cambridge: Cambridge University Press.

Giavazzi, Francesco, & Pagano, Marco. (1988). The Advantage of Tying One's Hand. *European Economic Review, 32*.

Giavazzi, Francesco, & Spaventa, Luigi. (1990). The "New" EMS. In Paul De Grauwe and Lucas Papademos (Eds.), *The European Monetary System in the 1990s*. London: Longman.

Gilbert, Milton. (1968). *The Gold-Dollar System: Conditions of Equilibrium and the Price of Gold*, Essays in International Finance No. 70. Princeton, NJ: Princeton University Press.

_____. (1966). *Problems of the International Monetary System*, Essays in International Finance No. 53. Princeton, NJ: Princeton University Press.

Gilibert, Pier Luigi. (1994). Living Dangerously: The Lira and the Pound in a Floating World. In Alfred Steinherr (Ed.), *30 Years of European Monetary Integration*. London: Longman.

Giscard d'Estaing, Valéry. (1996, January 22–24). Address. In Round Table on the Euro. *The Communications Challenge — Conclusions*. Luxembourg: Office for Official Publications of the European Communities.

Goldstein, Morris, et al. (1993). *International Capital Markets* Part I: *Exchange Rate Management and International Capital Flows*. Washington, DC: International Monetary Fund.

Goodhart, Charles. (1990, February 21–22). Economic and Monetary Union (EMU) in Europe. Paper presented at a conference at the Deutsche Bundesbank, Frankfurt.

_____. (1989, May). The Delors Report: Was Lawson's Reaction Justifiable? London: London School of Economics, Financial Markets Group. Mimeographed.

Gressani, Daniela, Guiso, Luigi, & Visco, Ignacio. (1988). Disinflation in Italy: An Analysis with the Econometric Model of the Bank of Italy. *Journal of Policy Modelling, 10*(2).

Grice, Joe. (1990, Autumn). The UK Proposals for a European Monetary Fund and a "Hard ECU": Making Progress towards Economic and Monetary Union in Europe. *Bulletin* (Her Majesty's Treasury).

Gros, Daniel, & Steinherr, Alfred. (1992). In Favour of EMU: A Manifesto of European Economists. In Alfred Steinherr (Ed.), *30 Years of European Monetary Integration* (pp. 74–77). London: Longman.

Gros, Daniel, & Thygesen, Niels. (1992). *European Monetary Integration: From the European Monetary System to European Monetary Union*. New York: St. Martin's Press.

_____. (1988). *The EMS: Achievements, Current Issues and Directions for the Future*, CEPS Paper No. 35. Brussels: Centre for European Policy Studies.

Guitián, Manuel. (1988). The European Monetary System: A Balance between Rules and Discretion. In *Policy Coordination in the European Monetary System*, Occasional Paper No. 61. Washington, DC: International Monetary Fund.

Haberler, Gottfried. (1976). Die Weltwirtschaft und das internationale Währungssystem in der Zeit zwischen den beiden Weltkriegen. In Deutsche Bundesbank, *Währung und Wirtschaft in Deutschland 1876–1975*. Frankfurt: Fritz Knapp.

Habermeier, Karl, & Ungerer, Horst. (1992, September). A Single Currency for the European Community. *Finance and Development*.

Hasse, Rolf H., et al. (1990). *The European Central Bank: Perspectives for a Further Development of the European Monetary System*. Gütersloh: Bertelsmann Foundation.

Hasse, Rolf H., & Koch, Thomas. (1991, July/August). The Hard ECU: A Substitute for the D-Mark or a Trojan Horse? *Intereconomics*.

Hawkins, Robert C. (Ed.). (1965). Compendium of Plans for International Monetary Reform. *Bulletin* (New York University Graduate School of Business Administration), *37–38*.

Hawtrey, R. G. (1947). *The Gold Standard in Theory and Practice*, 5th ed. London: Longman, Green & Co.

Hayes, Alfred. (1959). Foreword. In Arthur I. Bloomfield, *Monetary Policy under the International Gold Standard: 1880–1914*. New York: Federal Reserve Bank of New York.

Hellmann, Rainer. (1979). *Das Europäische Währungssystem*. Baden-Baden: Nomos Verlagsgesellschaft.

Her Majesty's Treasury. (1991–92, Winter). Economic and Monetary Union: The Agreement at Maastricht. *Bulletin, 3*(1).

———. (1991, January). Economic and Monetary Union — Beyond Stage I: Possible Treaty Provisions and Statute for a European Monetary Fund.

———. (1989, November). An Evolutionary Approach to Economic and Monetary Union.

———. (1968). *The Basle Facility and the Sterling Area*. London: Her Majesty's Stationery Office.

Hogan, M. J. (1987). *The Marshall Plan: America, Britain and the Reconstruction of Europe, 1947–52*. Cambridge: Cambridge University Press.

Horsefield, J. Keith (Ed.). (1969). *The International Monetary Fund, 1945–1965*. Washington, DC: International Monetary Fund.

House of Commons. (1989, June 29). Parliamentary debates (Hansard). London: Her Majesty's Stationery Office.

Ingram, James C. (1969). Comment: The Currency Area Problem. In Robert A. Mundell and Alexander K. Swoboda (Eds.), *Monetary Problems of the International Economy*. Chicago, IL: University of Chicago Press.

International Monetary Fund. (1996a, May). *World Economic Outlook*. Washington, DC: International Monetary Fund.

———. (1996b, October). *World Economic Outlook*. Washington, DC: International Monetary Fund.

———. (1993, October). *World Economic Outlook*. Washington, DC: International Monetary Fund.

———. (1990, March 5). *IMF Survey*. Washington, DC: International Monetary Fund.

———. (1988, August 29). *IMF Survey*. Washington, DC: International Monetary Fund.

_____. (1987). *The Role of the SDR in the International Monetary System*, Part II: A Comparative Analysis of the ECU and the SDR, Occasional Paper No. 51. Washington, DC: International Monetary Fund.

_____. (1974). Annual Report.

Ishiyama, Yoshihide. (1975). The Theory of Optimum Currency Areas: A Survey. *IMF Staff Papers*, 22.

James, Harold. (1996). *International Monetary Cooperation since Bretton Woods*. Washington, DC: International Monetary Fund.

Jenkins, Roy. (1977, October 27). Europe's Present Challenge and Future Opportunity. Speech at the European University Institute, Florence. Reprinted in *Bulletin of the European Communities, 10.*

Jennemann, Gerhard. (1977). Der Europäische Wechselkursverbund. In Giovanni Magnifico (Ed.), *Eine Währung in Europa*. Baden-Baden: Nomos Verlagsgesellschaft.

Kaplan, Jacob J., & Schleiminger, Günther. (1989). *The European Payments Union: Financial Diplomacy in the 1950s*. Oxford: Clarendon Press.

Kenen, Peter B. (1995). *Economic and Monetary Union in Europe: Moving beyond Maastricht*. Cambridge: Cambridge University Press.

_____. (1991). Transitional Arrangements for Trade and Payments Among the CMEA. *IMF Staff Papers*, 38(2).

_____. (1969). The Theory of Optimum Currency Areas: An Eclectic View. In Robert A. Mundell and Alexander K. Swoboda (Eds.), *Monetary Problems of the International Economy*. Chicago, IL: University of Chicago Press.

Keynes, John Maynard. (1924). *A Tract on Monetary Reform*. New York: Harcourt Brace.

_____. (1988). *The Economic Consequences of War*. New York: Penguin Books. First published in 1920.

Kindleberger, Charles B. (1993). *A Financial History of Western Europe*, 2d ed. New York: Oxford University Press.

Kindleberger, Charles B. (1984). *A Financial History of Western Europe*. New York: Oxford University Press.

Kloten, Norbert. (1995, July 6). Deutsche und Europäische Währungsunion: Ein Vergleich. *Auszüge aus Presseartikeln* [Deutsche Bundesbank].

_____. (1988). Wege zu einem Europäischen Zentralbanksystem. *Europa-Archiv, 11.*

Köcher, Renate. (1995a, November 15). Kühle Realisten. *Frankfurter Allgemeine Zeitung*.

_____. (1995b). Documentation to 1995a. Allensbach: Institut für Demoskopie.

Krägenau, Henry, & Wetter, Wolfgang. (1993). *Europäische Wirtschafts- und Währungsunion: Vom Werner-Plan zum Vertrag von Maastricht — Analysen und Dokumente*. Baden-Baden: Nomos Verlagsgesellschaft.

Krämer, Hans R. (1970). *Experience with Historical Monetary Unions*. Kiel: Institut für Weltwirtschaft.

Kremers, Jeroen J. M. (1990). Gaining Policy Credibility for a Disinflation: Ireland's Experience in the EMS. *IMF Staff Papers*, 37(1).

Kruse, D. C. (1980). *Monetary Integration in Western Europe: EMU, EMS and Beyond*. London: Butterworths.

Lambert, Marie Henriette, & de Fontenay, Patrick B. (1971). Implications of

Proposals for Narrowing the Margins of Exchange Rate Fluctuation Bands between the EEC Currencies. *IMF Staff Papers, 18*(3).

Lamfalussy, Alexandre. (1996, September 26). A New Exchange Rate Mechanism (ERM II). *Auszüge aus Presseartikeln* [Deutsche Bundesbank].

_____. (1989). Foreword. In Jacob J. Kaplan and Günther Schleiminger, *The European Payments Union: Financial Diplomacy in the 1950s*. Oxford: Clarendon Press.

Lawson, Nigel. (1989). See entry for Treasury and Civil Service Committee.

League of Nations. (1944). *International Currency Experience: Lessons of the Inter-War Period*. Geneva: League of Nations.

Lelart, Michel. (1994). *La construction monétaire européenne*. Paris: Dunod.

Lieberman, Sima. (1992). *The Long Road to a European Monetary Union*. Lanham, MD: University Press of America.

Lipp, Ernst Moritz, Ramm, Ulrich, & Walter, Norbert. (1992, June 16). Stellungnahme zum Manifest der über 60 Professoren über die Maastricht-Beschlüsse zur Europäischen Wirtschafts- und Währungsunion. *Auszüge aus Presseartikeln* [Deutsche Bundesbank]. Reprinted in Krägenau, Henry, & Wetter, Wolfgang. (1993). *Europäische Wirtschafts- und Währungsunion: Vom Werner-Plan zum Vertrag von Maastricht — Analysen und Dokumente*. Baden-Baden: Nomos Verlagsgesellschaft.

Lomax, David. (1991, January 18). The European Central Bank. *International Review*. London: National Westminster Bank.

Louis, Victor. (1989). A Monetary Union for Tomorrow? *Common Market Law Review, 26*.

Louw, André. (1991). The ECU and Its Role in the Process towards Monetary Union. *European Economy, 48*.

Ludlow, Peter. (1982). *The Making of the European Monetary System*. London: Butterworth Scientific.

Maas Report. (1995). Expert Group on the Changeover to the Single Currency. Progress Report on the Preparation of the Changeover to the Single Currency. Submitted to the European Commission on May 10.

Major, John. (1990, June 20). Economic and Monetary Union: Beyond Stage 1. Speech to the German Industry Forum.

Marsh, David. (1993, December 23). Faultlines Show in Franco-German Unity. *Financial Times*.

Masera, Rainer S. (1994). Single Market, Exchange Rates and Monetary Unification. In Alfred Steinherr (Ed.), *30 Years of European Monetary Integration*. London: Longman.

_____. (1987). *An Increasing Role for the ECU: A Character in Search of a Script*, Essays in International Finance No. 167. Princeton, NJ: Princeton University Press.

Masson, Paul R., & Taylor, Mark P. (1992). *Common Currency Areas and Currency Unions: An Analysis of the Issues*, Discussion Paper No. 617. London: Centre for Economic Policy Research.

Matthes, Heinrich. (1994, March–April). "Damocles Shadowing": An Innovation in the Second Phase of EMU. *Intereconomics, 29*.

McCarthy, Colm. (1980). EMS and the End of Ireland's Sterling Link. *Lloyds Bank Review, 53*.

McMahon, Christopher. (1982). The United Kingdom's Experience in Winding Down the Reserve Role of Sterling. In *Reserve Currencies in Transition*. New York: Group of Thirty.

_____. (1979). The Long-Run Implications of the European Monetary System. In Philip H. Trezise (Ed.), *The European Monetary System: Its Promise and Prospects* (pp. 81–92). Washington, DC: Brookings Institution.

Ministère des Finances. (1970, January 27). Un plan de solidarité monétaire européenne en trois étapes. Brussels. Reprinted in *Europe Documents*, March 11, 1970.

Monar, Joerg, Ungerer, Werner, & Wessels, Wolfgang (Eds.). (1993). *The Maastricht Treaty on European Union: Legal Complexity and Political Dynamic*, Bruges Conferences No. 2. Brussels: European Interuniversity Press.

Monetary Committee of the European Communities. (1993, April 13). Lessons to be Drawn from the Disturbances on the Foreign Exchange Markets.

_____. (1990, March 31). Economic and Monetary Union Beyond Stage I. Reprinted in *Europe Documents, 1609*, April 3.

_____. (1986). *Compendium of Community Monetary Texts*, new ed. Luxembourg: Office for Official Publications of the European Communities.

_____. (1976). *Compendium of Community Monetary Texts*, Supplement. Luxembourg: Office for Official Publications of the European Communities.

_____. (1974). *Compendium of Community Monetary Texts*. Luxembourg: Office for Official Publications of the European Communities.

Moss, Frank. (1988, January). EC Central Banks and Private ECU Interventions. *EBA Newsletter* (ECU Banking Association).

Muehring, K. (1992, October 12). Currency Chaos: The Inside Story. *Institutional Investor*.

Netherlands. (1991, November 1). Draft Treaty on Economic and Monetary Union. *Europe Documents, 1740/41*. Also found in Krägenau, Henry, & Wetter, Wolfgang. (1993). *Europäische Wirtschafts- und Währungsunion: Vom Werner-Plan zum Vertrag von Maastricht — Analysen und Dokumente*. Baden-Baden: Nomos Verlagsgesellschaft.

Neumann, Manfred J. M. (1991). Central Bank Independence as a Prerequisite of Price Stability. In Commission, The Economics of EMU. *European Economy*. Special edition 1.

Noël, Emile. (1979). *The European Community: How It Works*. Brussels: Commission of the European Communities, European Perspectives.

Norman, Peter. (1992, December 12–13). The Day Germany Planted a Currency Time Bomb. *Financial Times*.

Norman, Peter, & Barber, Lionel. (1992, December 11). The Monetary Tragedy of Errors that Led to Currency Chaos. *Financial Times*.

Oort, C. J. (1979). Managed Floating in the European Community. In Samuel I. Katz (Ed.), *U.S.-European Monetary Relations*. Washington, DC: American Enterprise Institute for Public Policy Research.

Optica Report '75. (1976, January 16). *Towards Economic Equilibrium and Monetary Unification in Europe*. Commission of the European Communities II/909/75-E final. Brussels.

Optica Report 1976. (1977, February 10). *Inflation and Exchange Rates: Evidence and*

Policy Guidelines for the European Community. Commission of the European Communities, II/855/76-E final. Brussels.

Organisation for Economic Co-operation and Development (OECD). (1978). *From Marshall Plan to Global Interdependence.* Paris: Organisation for Economic Co-operation and Development.

———. (1972). *History — Aims — Structure.* Paris: Organisation for Economic Co-operation and Development.

Organisation for European Economic Co-operation. Annual reports for 1949 through 1961. Paris: Organisation for European Economic Co-operation.

Overturf, Stephen. (in press). *Money and European Union.* New York. St. Martin's Press.

———. (1994). The European Community as an Optimum Currency Area. In Welfens, Paul J. J. (Ed.). (1994). *European Monetary Integration.* Berlin: Springer Verlag.

Padoa-Schioppa, Tommaso. (1994). *The Road to Monetary Union in Europe.* Oxford: Clarendon Press.

———. (1988a, June 12). Towards a New Adjustable Peg? Symposium on The International Monetary System: The Next Twenty-Five Years. Bank for International Settlements and Per Jacobsson Foundation.

———. (1988b). The EMS: A Longterm View. In Francesco Giavazzi, Stefano Micossi, and Marcus Miller (Eds.), *The European Monetary System.* Cambridge: Cambridge University Press.

Panic, M. (1992). *European Monetary Union: Lessons from the Classical Gold Standard.* New York: St. Martin's Press.

Papaspyrou, Theodoros. (1993). Stabilization Policy in Economic and Monetary Union in the Light of the Maastricht Treaty Provisions Concerning Financial Assistance. *European Economy.* Reports and Studies, 5.

Pisani-Ferry, Jean. (1992; English version 1993). *A French Perspective on EMU, Report by a Working Party.* Paris: Commissariat Général du plan.

Pöhl, Karl Otto. (1989). The Further Development of the European Monetary System. Paper annexed to the Delors Report.

Rees, Graham L. (1963). *Britain and the Postwar European Payments System.* Cardiff: University of Wales Press.

Ress, Georg. (1994). Treaty on European Union — Approval of FRG Constitutional Court. *American Journal of International Law, 88.*

Revue Financière Internationale (International Financial Report). (1991, June). Aujourd'hui l'écu — the ecu today. Numéro spécial.

Rey, Jean-Jacques. (1988). Comments. In Francesco Giavazzi, Stefano Micossi, and Marcus Miller (Eds.), *The European Monetary System.* Cambridge: Cambridge University Press.

———. (1982). Some Comments on the Merits and Limits of the Indicator of Divergence of the European Monetary System. *Revue de la Banque, 1.*

———. (1981). Le rôle des autorités monétaires au niveau européen. In Jean-Paul Abraham and Michel Vanden Abeele (Eds.), *European Monetary System and International Monetary Reform.* Brussels: Editions de l'Université de Bruxelles.

Rieke, Wolfgang. (1990). Alternative Views on the EMS in the 1990s. In Paul De Grauwe and Lucas Papademos (Eds.), *The European Monetary System in the*

1990s. London: Longman.

———. (1988). Comments. In Francesco Giavazzi, Stefano Micossi, and Marcus Miller (Eds.), *The European Monetary System*. Cambridge: Cambridge University Press.

———. (1979, April). Comments. *Bulletin* (Banque Nationale de Belgique).

Roll, Eric. (1995). *Where Did We Go Wrong? From The Gold Standard to Europe*. London: Faber and Faber.

Rosenblatt, Julius, Mayer, Thomas, Bartholdy, Kasper, Demekas, Dimitrios, Gupta, Sanjeev, & Lipschitz, Leslie. (1988). *The Common Agricultural Policy of the European Community: Principles and Consequences*, Occasional Paper No. 62. Washington, DC: International Monetary Fund.

Round Table on the Euro. (1996). *The Communications Challenge: Conclusions*. Luxembourg: Office for Official Publications of the European Communities.

Russo, Massimo, & Tullio, Giuseppe. (1988). Monetary Coordination within the European Monetary System: Is There a Rule? In *Policy Coordination in the European Monetary System*, Occasional Paper No. 61. Washington, DC: International Monetary Fund.

Sbragia, Alberta M. (Ed.). (1992). *Euro-Politics*. Washington, DC: Brookings Institution.

Schleiminger, Günther. (1960). Europäischer Wirtschaftsrat (OEEC/OECD). In *Handwörterbuch der Sozialwissenschaften*, 33. Lieferung. Stuttgart–Tübingen–Göttingen: Gustav Fischer–J.C.B. Mohr–Vandenhoeck & Ruprecht.

Schlesinger, Helmut. (1996, September 21). Money Is Just the Start. *The Economist*.

Schmidt, Helmut. (1992). *Die Deutschen und ihre Nachbarn*. Berlin: Goldmann.

———. (1990). *Menschen und Mächte*. Berlin: Goldmann.

Scholl, Franz. (1981). Praktische Erfahrungen mit dem Europäischen Währungssystem. In Werner Ehrlicher and Rudolf Richter (Eds.), *Probleme der Währungspolitik*. Berlin: Duncker & Humblot.

Schönfelder, Wilhelm, & Thiel, Elke. (1994). *Ein Markt — Eine Währung: Die Verhandlungen zur Europäischen Wirtschafts- und Währungsunion*. Baden-Baden: Nomos Verlagsgesellschaft.

Schulmann, Horst. (1992, December 9). *Auszüge aus Presseartikeln* [Deutsche Bundesbank], p. 6.

Schumpeter, Joseph. (1965). *Geschichte der ökonomischen Analyse*, Band II (Göttingen), quoted in Deutsche Bundesbank (1976b), p. 46.

Schwarz, Jürgen. (1980). *Der Aufbau Europas: Pläne und Dokument, 1945–1980*. Bonn: Osang Verlag.

Seidel, Martin. (1996, June 11). The Legal Framework of the Economic and Monetary Union as an Economic Constitution for the Union. *Auszüge aus Presseartikeln* [Deutsche Bundesbank].

Serving the European Union: A Citizen's Guide to the Institutions of the European Union. (1996). Luxembourg: Office for Official Publications of the European Communities.

Solomon, Robert. (1982). *The International Monetary System, 1945–1981*. New York: Harper & Row.

Southard, Frank A., Jr. (1979). *The Evolution of the International Monetary Fund*,

Essays in International Finance No. 135. Princeton, NJ: Princeton University Press.

Spahn, Paul Bernd. (1996, June). The Tobin Tax and Exchange Rate Stability. *Finance and Development*.

Spain. (1991, June). The ECU and the ESCB During Stage Two. Reprinted in *Revue Financière Internationale* (International Financial Report) (Numéro spécial), pp. 41–49.

Steinherr, Alfred (Ed.). (1994). *30 Years of European Monetary Integration*. London: Longman.

Stephens, Philip. (1996a, March 9–10). *Politics and the Pound* (London: Macmillan). Excerpted in *Financial Times*.

_____. (1996b, May 25–26). Britain's Bitter Blast from the Past. *Financial Times*.

Stoltenberg, Gerhard. (1988, March 15). *The Further Development of Monetary Cooperation in Europe*. Bonn: Ministry of Finance.

Tavlas, George S. (1994). The Theory of Monetary Integration. *Open Economics Review, 5*.

_____. (1993). The "New" Theory of Optimum Currency Areas. *The World Economy, 16*(6).

_____. (1991). *On the International Use of Currencies: The Case of the Deutsche Mark*, Essays in International Finance No. 181. Princeton, NJ: Princeton University Press.

Taylor, Christopher. (1995). *EMU 2000? Prospects for European Monetary Union*. London: Chatham House.

Taylor, M. P., & Artis, M. J. (1988). *What Has the European Monetary System Achieved?* Discussion Papers No. 31. London: Bank of England.

Thatcher, Margaret. (1995). *The Path to Power*. New York: HarperCollins.

Theurl, Theresia. (1995, August 12). Sprengsatz war immer das Budget. *Frankfurter Allgemeine Zeitung*.

_____. (1992). *Eine gemeinsame Währung für Europa: 12 Lehren aus der Geschichte*. Innsbruck: Österreichischer Studienverlag.

Thygesen, Niels. (1995). *The Prospects for EMU by 1999 and Reflections on Arrangements for the Outsiders*. Copenhagen: Business School, Economic Policy Research Unit.

_____. (1994). Reinforcing Stage Two in the EMU Process. In Alfred Steinherr (Ed.), *30 Years of European Monetary Integration*. London: Longman.

_____. (1989). The Delors Report and European Economic and Monetary Union. *International Affairs, 65*(4).

_____. (1979, April). The Emerging European Monetary System: Precursors, First Steps and Policy Options. *Bulletin* (Banque Nationale de Belgique).

Tietmeyer, Hans. (1996, May 24). The Forthcoming Monetary Union. *Auszüge aus Presseartikeln* [Deutsche Bundesbank].

Times Group. (1976, July 26). Statement. *The Times*.

Tindemans, Leo. (1976). European Union. Report to the European Council. *Bulletin of the European Communities*. Supplement 1.

Treasury and Civil Service Committee (House of Commons). (1989, June 12). Minutes of Evidence.

Treaty Establishing a Single Council and a Single Commission of the European

Communities. (1967, July 13). *Official Journal of the European Communities*, 152.

Triffin, Robert. (1979). The American Response to the European Monetary System. In Philip H. Trezise (Ed.), *The European Monetary System: Its Promise and Prospects*. Washington, DC: Brookings Institution.

_____. (1960). *Gold and Dollar Crisis*. New Haven, CT: Yale University Press.

_____. (1957). *Europe and the Money Muddle: From Bilateralism to Near-Convertibility, 1947–1956*. New Haven, CT: Yale University Press.

Tsoukalis, Loukas. (1993). *The New European Economy*, 2d ed. Oxford: Oxford University Press.

_____. (1977). *The Politics and Economics of European Monetary Integration*. London: Allen and Unwin.

Ungerer, Horst. (1994). *Die Krise des Europäischen Währungssystems in den Jahren 1992–1993: Ursachen — Lehren — Reformvorschläge*, Forschungsbericht 9406. Saarbrücken: Universität des Saarlandes, Europa-Institut.

_____. (1993a). *Die Krise des Europäischen Währungssystems im Herbst 1992*, Discussion papers in Economic Policy No. 34. Hamburg: Universität der Bundeswehr.

_____. (1993b). European Monetary Union: Chances — Risks — Alternatives. In Joerg Monar, Werner Ungerer, and Wolfgang Wessels (Eds.), *The Maastricht Treaty on European Union: Legal Complexity and Political Dynamic*, Bruges Conferences No. 2. Brussels: European Interuniversity Press.

_____. (1990). The EMS, 1979–1990: Policies — Evolution — Outlook. *Konjunkturpolitik, 36*(6).

_____. (1989). The European Monetary System and the International Monetary System. *Journal of Common Market Studies, 27*(3).

_____. (1984). Das Europäische Währungssystem und das internationale Wechselkurssystem. In Hans Seidel (Ed.), *Geldwertstabilität und Wirtschaftswachstum*. Göttingen: Vandenhoeck & Ruprecht.

_____. (1979, March 19). The European Monetary System. *IMF Survey*.

Ungerer, Horst, Evans, Owen, Mayer, Thomas, & Young, Philip. (1986). *The European Monetary System: Recent Developments*, Occasional Paper No. 48. Washington, DC: International Monetary Fund.

Ungerer, Horst, Evans, Owen, & Nyberg, Peter. (1983). *The European Monetary System: The Experience, 1979–82*, Occasional Paper No. 19. Washington, DC: International Monetary Fund.

Ungerer, Horst, Hauvonen, Jouko J., Lopez-Claros, Augusto, & Mayer, Thomas. (1990). The *European Monetary System: Developments and Prospects*, Occasional Paper No. 73. Washington, DC: International Monetary Fund.

Ungerer, Werner. (1993). On the Way to European Union. In Joerg Monar, Werner Ungerer, and Wolfgang Wessels (Eds.), *The Maastricht Treaty on European Union: Legal Complexity and Political Dynamic*, Bruges Conferences No. 2. Brussels: European Interuniversity Press.

U.S. Congress, Joint Economic Committee and Committee on Banking, Finance and Urban Affairs. (1979). *The European Monetary System: Problems and Prospects*. Washington, DC: U.S. Government Printing Office.

Urwin, Derek W. (1995). *The Community of Europe: A History of European Integration since 1945*, 2d ed. London: Longman.

van Ypersele, Jacques. (1978, April 19). Interview. *L'Echo de la Bourse*.

van Ypersele, Jacques, & Koeune, Jean-Claude. (1985). *The European Monetary System*. Brussels: Commission of the European Communities.

Vaubel, Roland. (1992, March 28). Das Ende der Preisstabilität. *Frankfurter Allgemeine Zeitung*.

_____. (1978). *Strategies for Currency Unification: The Economics of Currency Competition and the Case for a Parallel Currency*. Tübingen: J. C. Mohr.

von Wilamovitz-Moellendorff, Ulrich. (1996, March). Die europäische Währungsunion in der öffentlichen Meinung. Sankt Augustin: Konrad-Adenauer-Stiftung.

Wallich, Henry C. (1972). *The Monetary Crisis of 1971: The Lessons To Be Learned*. Washington, DC: Per Jacobsson Foundation.

Walters, Alan. (1990). *Sterling in Danger*. London: Fontana-Collins.

Weil, Gordon L. (Ed.). (1965). *A Handbook on the European Economic Community*. New York: Frederick A. Praeger.

Werner, Pierre. (1991). *Itinéraires Luxembourgeois et Européens*. Luxembourg: Editions de l'imprimerie Saint Paul.

_____. (1970). *L'Europe en route vers l'Union Monétaire*. Luxembourg: n.p.

Werner Committee. (1970a). Interim Report on the Establishment by Stages of Economic and Monetary Union. *Bulletin of the European Communities* (Supplement), 7.

_____. (1970b). Report to the Council and the Commission on the Realisation by Stages of Economic and Monetary Union in the Community, definitive text [Werner Report]. *Bulletin of the European Communities* (Supplement), 11.

Willgerodt, Hans, Domsch, Alexander, Hasse, Rolf, & Merx, Volker. (1972). *Wege und Irrwege zur europäischen Währungsunion*. Freiburg: Verlag Rombach.

Williamson, John. (1983). *The Exchange Rate System*. Washington, DC: Institute for International Economics.

Wissenschaftlicher Beirat beim Bundesministerium für Wirtschaft (Bonn). (1989a, March 3). Europäische Währungsordnung. *Bundesanzeiger*.

_____. (1989b, July 1). Stellungnahme zum Delors-Bericht. *Bundesanzeiger*.

Wittch, Günter, & Shiratori, Masaki. (1973, June). The Snake in the Tunnel. *Finance and Development*.

Woolley, John T. (1992). Policy Credibility and European Monetary Institutions. In Alberta M. Sbragia (Ed.), *Euro-Politics*. Washington, DC: Brookings Institution.

Working Party No. 3, Economic Policy Committee. (1996). *The Balance of Payments Adjustment Process*. Paris: Organisation for Economic Co-operation and Development.

Zis, George. (1984). The European Monetary System 1979–84: An Assessment. *Journal of Common Market Studies*, 23(1).

Name Index

Subject Index

ABOUT THE AUTHOR

HORST UNGERER is guest lecturer at universities in Europe and the United States. He has had a distinguished career, spanning more than three decades, in central banking and international finance. Ungerer was a senior official in the Deutsche Bundesbank and the International Monetary Fund, from where he retired in 1991 as Assistant Director in the European Department. Ungerer is author and coauthor of many papers on European monetary policy issues published in the United States and Europe.

ISBN 0-89930-981-X

HARDCOVER BAR CODE